STUDIES OF ARIANISM

STUDIES OF ARIANISM

CHIEFLY REFERRING TO THE CHARACTER AND CHRONOLOGY

OF THE REACTION WHICH FOLLOWED

THE COUNCIL OF NICÆA

BY

HENRY MELVILL GWATKIN M.A.

HON. D.D. EDINBURGH,
DIXIE PROFESSOR OF ECCLESIASTICAL HISTORY, CAMBRIDGE.

SECOND EDITION

Wipf & Stock
PUBLISHERS
Eugene, Oregon

Wipf and Stock Publishers
199 W 8th Ave, Suite 3
Eugene, OR 97401

Studies of Arianism
Chiefly Referring to the Character and Chronology
of the Reaction which Followed the Council of Nicea
By Gwatkin, Henry M.
ISBN: 1-59752-196-5
Publication date 5/16/2005
Previously published by Deighton Bell and Co., 1900

TO THE MEMORY OF

MY FATHER

THE FIRST AND BEST OF MY TEACHERS

PREFACE TO THE SECOND EDITION.

THE Second Edition is in the main a reprint of the first, with a few passages inserted (by the courtesy of Messrs Longmans) from my *Arian Controversy*, a few corrections and amendments, and some account taken of more recent work on the subject.

I have not however been in a position to give it the thorough revision I could have wished, so that some things are left unaltered which do not now fully satisfy me. The whole question of Antony in particular urgently needs a comprehensive revision from the Coptic side, which few of us are competent to give. Dom Butler has made a good beginning, though he rightly points out that others may differ greatly from him in their estimate of some conspicuous parts of the evidence. Without entering on particular criticism, it may safely be said that the investigation needs to be much more closely connected with the whole development of Roman Egypt. What for example was the exact relation of Christian asceticism to the old pagan asceticism?

I may add that I cannot follow another of my critics in setting down Athanasius as a genuine ascetic. If indeed all self-denial be called asceticism, there must be a good deal of asceticism in every character that is not contemptible: but if the word be limited as it ought to be to self-denial resting on an idea that the pleasures of sense are of the nature of sin, there are comparatively few traces of it in Athanasius.

PAIGNTON,
July 1900.

PREFACE TO THE FIRST EDITION (1882).

The present work is not so much a formal history of Arianism as a review of the forces at work in the different stages of the controversy, traced out with special regard to the sequence of events and to their connexion with the social characteristics and political history of the Empire. Thus I have felt at liberty in most cases to omit detailed accounts of well-known scenes, and sometimes to leave out subjects of great importance. Anything indeed pretending to the character of a monograph would have been quite beyond my power in the fragments of time which have been at my disposal.

No student is likely to doubt that there is ample room for such a review. Too many of the current church histories pay more attention to the lives of individuals than to the deeper movements of the time, and not unfrequently miss the significance even of these by limiting themselves too strictly to ecclesiastical affairs. Not a few of them also systematically ignore the discoveries of the last forty years. For example, the old date for the council of Sardica is still allowed to stultify history, though it has been untenable since the discovery of the *Festal Letters*. The lives of Antony and Hilarion are not yet recognised to be mere romances and we are still gravely told that the Nicene creed was formally revised at Constantinople. Some are not ashamed even to revive the Athanasian authorship of the *Quicunque*. The Benedictines did a noble work in their generation, but even their oversights are only too faithfully copied.

Far be it from us to undervalue the gigantic labour of

Godefroy or Montfauçon, Valesius or Tillemont; but we do them no honour by slavish copying. What we need is a closer analysis of our original authorities. What is the exact value for example of those parts of Socrates or Sozomen which cannot be traced to Rufinus or Athanasius? What is the relation of the two historians to each other, and of Theodoret to both, and what fragments of original matter can be gleaned from the late Byzantines? It is a mere question of labour to settle these questions, and it has not been done yet. The little of it which has fallen to my share mostly concerns Rufinus and the *Chronicon Paschale*. When once it is completely done, we may hope to be spared the frequent scandal of seeing the *consensus ecclesiæ* resolve itself into some mendacious novel-writer and his tail of copyists.

Now for my obligations to modern writers[1]. These are mostly due to the Germans. The only general history I have used much is Neander's, though Baur is often suggestive. The monographs however are numerous and of the highest value. The chief of them are Zahn's *Marcellus*, Rode's and Mücke's *Julian*, Keim's *Constantin*, Reinkens' *Hilarius*, Ullmann's *Gregorius*, Weingarten's *Ursprung des Mönchtums* with Keim's reply and Israël's extension, and especially the laborious works of Sievers. Doctrine is represented by Dorner, Nitzsch and Caspari's *Quellen*, and on Athanasius we have Kölling, and the complementary works of Voigt and Atzberger. The Roman Catholic view is given by Möhler and Hefele, and the secular side of the history by Preuss, Richter, Hertzberg, Pallmann, von Wietersheim and Kaufmann. Burckhardt's *Constantin* and Dahn's *Könige der Germanen* unfortunately reached my hands too late to be used. Standard works on antiquities and literature hardly need mention, such as Marquardt or Kuhn, Teuffel, Wattenbach, Ebert or Nicolai, or Herzog's *Realencyclopädie*, so far as the new edition is yet published.

English writers are fewer, and too many of them little better than copyists or partizans. By far the most suggestive work is

[1] Full titles are given on p. xii.

PREFACE.

Dr Hort's *Two Dissertations.* Mr Hatch's *Organization of the Early Christian Churches* bears more on an earlier period; but I have learned much from the unrivalled monographs of Bishop Lightfoot and Mr Rendall on Eusebius of Cæsarea and on Julian's attack on Christianity, and from the thoughtful articles of Dr Reynolds and Mr Wordsworth in the *Dictionary of Christian Biography.* For chronology we have Clinton's great *Fasti Romani,* though a new edition of it is much needed; and among secular historians, Gibbon is still beyond comparison. His dislike of Christianity rather limits than distorts his view; but its outbreaks of Roman Jingoism (if the word may be allowed) need to be checked at every step by the juster views of Finlay, Freeman or Professor Seeley. The last original contribution to this part of the subject is Mr Hodgkin's interesting work on *Italy and her Invaders.* In case the reader should notice in the present work coincidences with a review of this last which appeared in the *Church Quarterly,* it may be as well to acknowledge its authorship.

Comparatively little has been done in France since the Revolution. Of recent writers Broglie is lively enough, but too much of a special pleader, while Fialon's works are hardly more than spirited and suggestive sketches. Monographs are scarce, but we may name Chastel's *Destruction du Paganisme* and Couret's *Palestine.* Montaut's *Questions historiques* is also deserving of mention, and the names of some minor works are given below. Still there are few French students of the Nicene age who will bear comparison with the best writers of Germany or England, or with the giant scholars of the Ancien Régime.

My best thanks are due for the sympathy and advice of many friends, especially Mr Graves and Professors Mayor and Bonney of St John's College, and Mr W. E. Barnes of St Peter's College; also for more than one oral hint to Professors Hort and Swainson.

The errors of my predecessors I have usually corrected in respectful silence, and I trust my own will not be found unpardonable. I have at least worked over the originals and endeavoured to make their thoughts my own.

PREFACE. xi

I rise from my subject with an ever-deepening sense of its surpassing grandeur. The Epic of Arianism will task a much abler hand than mine. But let me claim here a student's privilege to record my conviction that the old Eastern controversies on the Person of the Lord were not mere word-battles in their own time. Neither are they obsolete in ours; for they have a direct bearing on our modern scientific difficulties. In a few years the theory of evolution may be as firmly established as that of gravitation. The evidence of genealogy can be applied to other things beside textual criticism. It has already thrown a new light on some of the most difficult problems connected with the history of life, such as those presented by the fauna of New Zealand or Madagascar; and the method is capable of a vast extension as materials accumulate. But whatever evolution may explain, it cannot explain itself. However clearly it may enable us to trace through past ages the working of a power of life, it will never tell us what that power is, or how it came upon the earth. Whatever we may find inside the domain of matter, our cunning must for ever fail us on the mysterious borderland where we come face to face with powers of another order. Yet if our Saviour's resurrection is historic fact, the whole mystery of the Incarnation must have some true kinship to the laws of God in nature, and the Person of the Lord must be a solid link between the world of matter and a world beyond. Now the definition of Chalcedon was not drawn up by men of science, but by bishops; neither was it reached by any zoological investigation, but by the study of Scripture: yet that memorable formula—$\dot{a}\lambda\eta\theta\hat{\omega}s$, $\tau\epsilon\lambda\dot{\epsilon}\omega s$, $\dot{a}\delta\iota\alpha\iota\rho\dot{\epsilon}\tau\omega s$, $\dot{a}\sigma\upsilon\gamma\chi\dot{\upsilon}\tau\omega s$—in which Hooker sums up the council's work, seems to point to a universal law which rules at every meeting-point of earth and heaven, of matter and the spirit world[1]. Adolphe Monod's thought will bear extension. The likeness is not merely of the personal Word of God to his written word. It extends also to at least the Christian conception of prophecy and miracle, to the whole problem of grace and freewill, and even to

[1] Swainson *Authority of the New Testament* 144.

this material frame of ours. The unreasoning confusion of spirit with matter is just as gross a superstition as their arbitrary separation.

Our first impulse may be to dismiss as fanciful the idea that there is a true analogy of the Chalcedonian doctrine to the constitution of nature. Yet the more we ponder it, the more it seems to challenge explanation. Every disbeliever is at least a witness that it is no foregone conclusion from fixed laws of human thought. Little as we know for certain, that little is full of solemn meaning. It points to much, and may hereafter be the clue to more. The eyes of sense survey the realm of matter, the arms of faith stretch outward to the spirit world, and heavenly light will one day fill the intervening gulf of death. That light is even now the light of men; and whenever the scales of sin fall from our darkened eyes, we shall recognize in it the brightness of immortal Love, the effulgence of his glory who liveth and was dead, and is alive for evermore, and hath the keys of death and Hades.

כִּי עִמְּךָ מְקוֹר חַיִּים בְּאוֹרְךָ נִרְאֶה אוֹר׃

Easter 1882.

Ranke, L. *Weltgeschichte.* Bde. III. IV. Leipzig 1883.

Döllinger, J. J. I. *Heidenthum und Judenthum Vorhalle zur Geschichte des Christenthums.* Regensburg 1857.

Hertzberg, G. F. *Griechenland unter den Römern.* Halle 1866—75.

—— —— *Geschichte Griechenlands seit dem Absterben des antiken Lebens bis zur Gegenwart.* Thl. I. Gotha 1876.

Kaufmann, G. *Deutsche Geschichte bis auf Karl den Grossen.* Leipzig 1880.

Pallmann, R. *Geschichte der Völkerwanderung von der Gothenbekehrung bis zum Tode Alarichs.* Gotha 1863.

PREFACE. xiii

Richter, H. *Das Weströmische Reich,* besonders 375–388. Berlin 1865.

Wietersheim, E. von. *Geschichte der Völkerwanderung.* 4 Bde. Leipzig 1859–64.

—— —— ditto Zweite Aufl., besorgt von Felix Dahn. Leipzig Bd. I. 1880. Bd. II. 1881. (Quoted as "Wietersheim-Dahn.")

Dorner, J. A. *History of the development of the Doctrine of the Person of Christ.* transl. W. L. Alexander and others. 5 vols. Edinburgh 1865—68.

Harnack, A. *Lehrbuch der Dogmengeschichte.* Bd. II. 1 Aufl. Freiburg i. B. 1887.

Loofs, F. *Leitfaden zur Dogmengeschichte.* Halle a. S. 2 Aufl. 1890.

—— *Arianismus* in Herzog RE[3].

Nitzsch, Fr. *Grundriss der christlichen Dogmengeschichte.* Thl. 1. Berlin 1870.

Caspari, C. P. *Ungedruckte, unbeachtete und wenig beachtete Quellen zur Geschichte des Taufsymbols und der Glaubensregel.* 3 Bde. Christiania. I. 1866, II. 1869, III. 1875.

—— —— *Alte und neue Quellen zur Geschichte des Taufsymbols und der Glaubensregel.* Christiania 1879.

Atzberger, L. *Die Logoslehre des hl. Athanasius.* München 1880.

Voigt, H. *Die Lehre des Athanasius von Alexandrien.* Bremen 1861.

Hefele, C. J. *History of the Christian Councils,* Vol. I. to 325 transl. W. R. Clark. Edinburgh 1871. Vol. II. 325—429 transl. H. N. Oxenham. Edinburgh 1876.

Dräseke, J. *Apollinarius von Laodicea.* Leipzig 1892.

Lasaulx, E. von. *Der Untergang des Hellenismus und die Einziehung der Tempelgüter durch die christlichen Kaiser.* München 1854.

Schultze, V. *Untergang des griechisch-römischen Heidentums.* 2 Bde. Jena 1887.

Loening, E. *Kirchenrecht in Gallien von Constantin bis Chlodovech.* Strassburg 1878.

Jeep, L. *Quellenuntersuchungen zu den griechischen Kirchenhistorikern.* Leipzig 1884.

Güldenpenning, A. *Die Kirchengeschichte des Theodoret.* Halle 1889.

Preuss, Th. *Kaiser Diocletian und seine Zeit.* Leipzig 1869.

Görres, Fr. *Kritische Untersuchungen über die Licinianische Christenverfolgung.* Jena 1875.

Keim, Dr Theodor. *Der Uebertritt Constantins des Grossen zum Christenthum.* Zürich 1862.

Zahn, Dr Theodor. *Constantin der Grosse und die Kirche.* Hannover 1876.

Möhler, J. A. *Athanasius der Grosse, und die Kirche seiner Zeit.* Zweite Aufl. Mainz 1844.

Zahn, Dr Theodor. *Marcellus von Ancyra.* Gotha 1867 (supersedes older works like Willenborg's; to some extent even Dorner's section on Marcellus).

Krüger, G. *Lucifer B. von Calaris.* Leipzig 1886.

Neander, A. *Ueber den Kaiser Julianus und sein Zeitalter.* Zweite Aufl. Gotha 1867.

Mücke, J. F. A. *Flavius Claudius Julianus, nach den Quellen.* 2 Thle. Gotha 1867—9.

Rode, Fr. *Geschichte der Reaction Kaiser Julians gegen die christliche Kirche.* Jena 1877.

Reinkens, J. H. *Hilarius von Poitiers.* Schaffhausen 1864.

Sievers, G. *Das Leben des Libanius.* Berlin 1868.

—— *Historia Acephala* in *Zeitschr. für die Hist. Theologie* for 1868.

—— *Studien zur Geschichte der Römischen Kaiser.* Berlin 1870.

Ullmann, C. *Gregorius von Nazianz der Theologe.* Zweite Aufl. Gotha 1867.

Weiss, H. *Die grossen Kappadocier Basilius Gregor von Nazianz und Gregor von Nyssa als Exegeten.* Braunsberg 1872.

Klose, C. R. W. *Geschichte und Lehre des Eunomius.* Kiel 1833.

Loofs, F. *Eustathius von Sebaste u. die Chronologie der Basilius-Briefe.* Halle a. S. 1898.

Kaufmann, G. *Der Gothenkrieg* in *Forschungen z. Deutschen Gesch.* XII. 414—438.

Langen, Jos. *Johannes von Damaskus.* Gotha 1879 (for the romance of Artemius).

Weingarten, H.   *Der Ursprung des Mönchtums im nachconstantinischen Zeitalter.*   Gotha 1877.

Keim, Dr Theodor.   *Aus dem Urchristenthum* (VII. *Ursprung des Mönchwesens*).   Zürich 1878.

Lucius, P. E.   *Die Therapeuten.*   Strassburg 1880.

Israël, W.   *De Vita Hilarionis* in *Zeitschrift für wiss. Theologie* for 1880, pp. 129—165.

Eichhorn, A.   *Athanasii de vita ascetica testimonia collecta.*   Halis Saxonum 1886.

English books hardly need enumeration, but good work of varying merit will also be found in Arnold's *Roman Provincial Administration*, Bright's *Athanasius* in *Dict. Chr. Biography*, Historical *Treatises of Athanasius, Canons of the First Four General Councils,* and *Roman See in the Early Church,* Chawner's *Legislation of Constantine,* Kaye's *Council of Nicæa,* Mason's *Persecution of Diocletian,* Stanley's *Eastern Church,* Swainson's *Nicene and Apostles' Creeds,* and Swete's *Doctrine of the Holy Spirit.*

The above will all be found more or less useful to the student. Of Newman's *Arians of the Fourth Century* let it suffice to say that his theories have always been scrupulously examined; so that if they have not often been accepted, it is only because there is usually good reason for rejecting them.

Broglie, Albert de.   *L'église et l'empire romain au IVe siècle.*   Paris (1856) 1867-8.

Chastel, E.   *Histoire de la destruction du Paganisme dans l'Empire d'Orient.*   Paris 1850.

Couret, A.   *La Palestine sous les empereurs grecs 326—636.*   Grenoble 1869.

Fialon, Eug.   *Saint Athanase.*   Paris 1877.

——   *Saint Basile.*   Second Edition.   Paris 1869.

Montaut, L.   *Revue critique de quelques questions historiques se rapportant à Saint Grégoire de Nazianze et à son siècle.*   Paris 1878.

Boissier, G.   *La fin du Paganisme.*   2 vols.   Paris 1891.

The chief later English works are:—

Robertson, A.   *Athanasius.*   [Nicene Library, Vol. IV.]   Oxford 1892.

Dill, S.   *Roman Society in the last century of the Western Empire.*   London 1898.

Allen, A. V. G.   *Christian Institutions.*   Edinburgh 1898.

Butler, E. C. *The Lausiac History of Palladius.* [*Texts and Studies* VI (1).] Cambridge 1898.

The editions I have used are as follows. For Ammianus, Gardthausen with Wagner's notes; for Julian, Hertlein and Neumann with Spanheim's notes; for Eunapius, Wyttenbach; for Libanius, Wolf and Reiske; for the *de mysteriis*, Parthey; for Mamertinus, Arntzen and Jäger; for Themistius, Harduin and afterwards Dindorf; for Suidas, Bernhardy: also the Byzantine *Corpus* for Zosimus and all other writers contained in it, Zonaras excepted. For the *Codex Theodosianus*, Godefroy's notes and Haenel's text, with his *Corpus Legum*.

The Fathers I have mostly used in Migne's *Patrologia*. The chief exceptions are Heinichen and Gaisford for Eusebius, Hussey for Socrates, Sozomen and Theodoret, with Godefroy's notes on Philostorgius; Dindorf's Epiphanius, Garnier's Basil (Gaume), and Schulze's Theodoret.

All the works referred to are quoted from the originals, excepting (*a*) a few German works best known in England by translations, (*b*) the Syriac *Festal Letters* of Athanasius from the translations of Larsow and Burgess, and (*c*) the Armenian Moses of Chorene from an Italian translation (Venice 1850).

CONTENTS.

	PAGE
PREFACES	vii
CONTENTS	xvii
CHRONOLOGICAL TABLE	xxiii

CHAPTER I. INTRODUCTORY SKETCH . . . . . . 1—15

    The Arian Reaction owed its strength neither to Arian doctrine nor to court influence   1

    Doctrine of the Lord's Person; in its traditional stage and as based on Scripture. Two elements, and therefore two elementary errors   4

    Too abstract a conception of deity current among (*a*) later Greeks, (*b*) Orientals, and even (*c*) Jews; confronted by superstition (*de mysteriis*), but influences historic Christianity . . .   9

    The Third Century—subordination theories   14

CHAPTER II. THE COUNCIL OF NICÆA . . . . . 16—55

    Arianism an inevitable reaction of heathen thought, not specially connected with either earlier or later Antiochene school .   16

    Arianism as a doctrine   20

    Athanasius *de Incarnatione*   28

    Outbreak of the controversy. Character and policy of Constantine   32

    Meeting of the Council, and hopes gathered round it. Arian creed torn up   38

    Character and creed of Eusebius of Cæsarea   41

    Persistence of Athanasius   43

    Formation of the Council's creed and objections to it. Conservative hesitation overcome by inability otherwise to exclude Arianism. Letter of Eusebius   44

    Interference of Constantine and end of the Council. Advantages and disadvantages of it to the cause of Athanasius . . .   48

NOTES.

    p. 32.   *Arianism and Supremacy of Alexandria.*

   ,, 34.   *List of early Arians.*

   ,, 35.   *The Legislation of Constantine.*

   ,, 54.   *Athanasius on the Council of Nicæa.*

CONTENTS.

	PAGE
CHAPTER III. THE LATER YEARS OF CONSTANTINE	56—109

Conservatism in East and West. Eastern reaction not Arian but conservative, supported by (*a*) heathen, and (*b*) Jewish influences, and by (*c*) the court 56

Sketch of the Contest to 381 65

Sequel of the Council. Election and character of Athanasius. Return and policy of Eusebius of Nicomedia 68

Formation of Eusebian party. Exile of Eustathius . . . 77

Character and doctrine of Marcellus, and criticism of Eusebius and Athanasius 79

The attack on Athanasius. Suspension during the Gothic war. Councils of Tyre and Jerusalem. Exile of Athanasius to Trier 87

Wavering of Constantine. Arianizing policy of the emperors explained by Asiatic influence 93

NOTES.

 p. 58. *Julian's generals.*
 ,, 62. *The Jewish War in 352.*
 ,, 70. *The Election of Athanasius in 328.*
 ,, 72. *Athanasius and Asceticism.*
 ,, 72. *Athanasius as a man of learning.*
 ,, 76. *Asterius the Sophist.*
 ,, 77. *The Exile of Eustathius.*
 ,, 87. *The Gothic War of Constantine.*
 ,, 89. *The Council of Tyre.*
 ,, 92. *Was Marcellus twice at Rome?*
  A. *The Authority of Rufinus.*
  B. *The Legend of Antony.*
  C. *The Index to the Festal Letters.*

CHAPTER IV. THE COUNCIL OF SARDICA	110—145

Death of Constantine and division of the Empire. Return of Athanasius in 337 110

Character of Constantius. Second exile of Athanasius. Letter of Julius 113

Council of the Dedication. The Lucianic creed. Alarm in the West. The Fourth Creed 118

Councils of Sardica and Philippopolis 125

Scandal of Stephen leads to a reaction. Conciliatory Fifth Creed. Return of Athanasius in 346 128

Interval of suspense till 353. Rise of the Anomœans. Illustration from (*a*) Cyril's *Catecheses*, (*b*) the policy of Leontius at Antioch 132

NOTES.

 p. 111. *The good faith of Eusebius.*
 ,, 112. *Massacre of the House of Theodora.*

CONTENTS.

p. 116. *Expulsion of Athanasius in 339.*
,, 119. *The Bishops at Antioch in 341.*
,, 122. *The Creeds of Antioch.*
,, 124. *Date of the Council of Sardica.*
,, 126. *The spurious Sardican definition.*
,, 130. *Date of the return of Athanasius.*
,, 134. *The rebaptism of heretics.*
,, 136. *Cyril and the Dated Creed.*
,, 138. *Arian hagiology.*
   CC. *The Return of Athanasius in 337.*
   D. *The Legislation of Constantius.*

CHAPTER V. THE HOMŒAN VICTORY . . . . . 146—196

New troubles in the West. Death of Constans. Character and defeat of Magnentius 146
Eusebian intrigues. Council at Sirmium and appeal of Photinus. 149
Constantius and the West. Councils of Arles and Milan. Exile of Lucifer, Hilary, Hosius and Liberius 151
Third exile of Athanasius in 356. His *Apol. ad Ctium, de Fuga* and *Hist. Ar.* Remoter consequences of his flight . . . 155
Break-up of the conservative coalition. Visit of Constantius to Rome. The Sirmian manifesto. Reply of Phœbadius . 160
Alarm in the East. Council of Ancyra. Victory and failure of the Semiarians 164
Formation of a new Homœan party. Leaning of Semiarians to Nicenes 167
Hilary *de Synodis* 168
The Dated Creed. Evasion of Valens and minute of Basil and George 170
Council of Ariminum and Creed of Nicé 174
Council of Seleucia 176
Athanasius *de Synodis* 179
End of the Council of Ariminum. Fraud of Valens. Council of Constantinople and deposition of Semiarians 182
Nature and duration of Homœan Supremacy. Election and exile of Meletius. Divisions among the Homœans 185

NOTES.

   p. 146. *Character of Constans.*
   ,, 149. *The appeal of Photinus.*
   ,, 152. *Language ascribed to Constantius.*
   ,, 153. *Doctrine of Lucifer.*
   ,, 155. *Events at Alexandria, 353—356.*
   ,, 157. *Athanasius and Constantius.*
   ,, 167. *Persecution in the Nicene age.*
   ,, 176. *Isaurian risings.*
   ,, 179. *Eudoxius.*

CONTENTS.

PAGE

p. 182. *End of the Council of Ariminum.*
,, 184. *The Bishops at Constantinople in* 360.
E. *Date of the Council of Gangra.*
F. *The Fall of Liberius.*
G. *The Bishops at Seleucia.*

CHAPTER VI. THE REIGN OF JULIAN . . . . . 197—227

Death of Constantius. Youth and character of Julian. His apostasy 197
Restoration of heathenism and zeal of Julian. Renegades and outrages. Education edict strikes at connexion of Christianity with Hellenic culture. Julian could not lean on the West . 200
Julian's indifference to Christian parties. Recall of the exiles. Policy of Toleration. Universal hatred of Julian . . . 205
Return of Athanasius in 362. Council at Alexandria. Fourth exile of Athanasius 208
Advance of Nicene cause, and operations of Homœans and Semiarians 211
Julian's Persian War. His heathen pride as an element of the military position. His death and character 212

NOTES.

p. 198. *Relations of Constantius to Julian.*
,, 205. *Julian's Christian friends.*
H. *The Legislation of Julian.*
I. *Authorities for Julian's Persecution.*
J. *The return of Athanasius in* 362.
K. *Julian's arrival at Antioch.*

CHAPTER VII. THE RESTORED HOMŒAN SUPREMACY . . 228—278

Results of Julian's reign 228
Election and policy of Jovian. Movements of (*a*) Anomœans and (*b*) Acacius 229
Valentinian and Valens. Strife of church and state. Growth of the ascetic spirit, and its relation to various parties . . 231
Semiarian council of Lampsacus, quashed by Valens. His motives for a Homœan policy. Fresh expulsion of the exiles and Semiarian embassy to Liberius 236
Rising of Procopius. Homœan schemes delayed by the Gothic war. Peace of 369, and return of Valens to the East . . 241
Christianity in Cappadocia. New Nicene party formed of Semiarian and Homœan malcontents 245
Basil of Cæsarea. Overawes Valens. His reunion scheme. Its difficulty, and Basil's own qualifications. Disputes with Anthimus and Eustathius 247
Apollinarianism 250
Deaths of Marcellus and Athanasius 254

CONTENTS.

	PAGE
Confusion in Asia. Affairs in 376	256
The Goths received inside the Empire. War provoked, and battle of Hadrianople. Its results. Theodosius leans on the Goths	257
Empire and Church remain, but Arianism disappears . . .	264
Toleration of Valentinian. Theodosius emperor. End of the Gothic war	265
Baptism and edicts of Theodosius. Ejection of the Arians. Council of Constantinople. Semiarians retire. Fall of Arianism in the Empire	268
Teutonic Arianism. Its weakness	271
Arianism, a failure, doctrinally as well as historically. Badness of its method	273

NOTES.

p. 231. *Election of Valentinian.*
,, 233. *Brigands.*
,, 234. *Rescript of Valens against the monks.*
,, 240. *Valentinian's departure from Italy.*
,, 243. *Exiles of Meletius.*
,, 247. *Doctrine of Basil.*
,, 248. *The new Nicenes.*
,, 249. *The Cyzicene formula.*
,, 262. *Depopulation of the Empire.*
,, 267. *The Gothic war of Theodosius.*
,, 270. *The " Constantinopolitan" creed.*
,, 271. *The second edict of Theodosius.*
    M. *The Chronology of the Council of Lampsacus.*
    N. *The story of the eighty Clerics.*
    O. *Eustathius of Sebastia.*

APPENDIX I. The great Officials of the Empire 337—381 . . .	279
APPENDIX II. Movements of the Eastern emperors 337—381 . .	299
INDEX	304

ERRATA.

p. 22 l. 9, *for* declaration *read* declarations.
p. 147 l. 3 of Note, *for* his guide and *read* and his guide.

CHRONOLOGICAL TABLE.

The following are the dates adopted. References are given in a few cases, but only those marked N are specially discussed in the course of the work. Those marked R are rediscussed by Robertson, *Ath.* lxxx—lxxxvii, but without change.

	269	Defeat of the Goths by Claudius at Naissus.
	297	Capture of Alexandria by Diocletian.
cir.	297 N	Birth of Athanasius (p. 71).
Feb. 23	303	Outbreak of the Great Persecution.
May 1	305	Abdication of Diocletian and Maximian.
July 25	306	Constantine emperor in Britain.
Apr. 30	311	First Edict of Toleration issued by Galerius.
Oct. 26	312	Defeat of Maxentius at Saxa Rubra.
Late in	312	Second Edict of Toleration issued from Milan (Mason, *Persecution of Diocletian* 327 n).
Apr. 30	313	Defeat of Maximin at Heraclea.
Oct. 8	314	Defeat of Licinius at Cibalæ. War not necessarily finished same year, though Licinius was consul in 315.
cir.	318	Athanasius *contra Gentes* and *de Incarnatione Verbi Dei*.
Not before	319	Licinian Persecution (Görres *Christenverfolgung* 5—29).
cir.	321	Arius excommunicated.
June 27 or July 3	323	Battle of Hadrianople against Licinius.
Sept. 18		Final defeat of Licinius at Chrysopolis.

June 16	325	Council of Nicæa. Constantine arrives after anniversary of victory at Hadrianople.
July 25		*Vicennalia* of Constantine (festival perhaps held later).
Summer	326	Constantine at Rome. Executions of Crispus and Fausta.
Apr. 17	328 NR	Death of Alexander at Alexandria, and (June 8) Election of Athanasius (p. 70).
cir.	330	Council at Antioch. Deposition of Eustathius.
Nov. 6	331	Birth of Julian (Rendall *Julian* 285—the day is given by an inaccurate old calendar in Migne *Patrol.* xiii. 686, but cannot be far wrong).
Spring	332	Death of Basilina.
Apr. 20	N	Defeat of the Goths (p. 87).
	334	Council at Cæsarea.
	335	Legendary letter of Constantine to Antony.
Aug.		*Tricennalia* of Constantine. Council at Tyre (Athanasius left Alexandria July 11, and the Egyptian bishops date their protest Sept. 6).
Sept.		Council at Jerusalem. Niceph. *Call.* viii. 30 gives Sept. 17 for the consecration of the Church on Golgotha.
Oct. 30		Athanasius reaches Constantinople, and receives a formal audience Nov. 7.
Feb. 5	336 N	Council at Constantinople. Athanasius exiled to Trier (p. 140). Death of Arius a little later.
May 22	337	Death of Constantine, followed by massacre of the house of Theodora, and proclamation of three *Augusti* Sept. 9. Outbreak of the Persian war, followed by first siege of Nisibis.
Nov. 23	NR	Return of Athanasius to Alexandria (p. 140).
	338 N	Eusebius *Vita Constantini* (p. 111).
July or Aug.		Meeting of the emperors in Pannonia.

CHRONOLOGICAL TABLE.

Winter		Council at Antioch deposing Athanasius. Death of Eusebius of Cæsarea about this time.
Lent	339 NR	Athanasius expelled by Philagrius (p. 108).
	340	Death of Constantine II. after Apr. 9 (*C. Th.* x. 15, 3).
Autumn		Council at Rome. Letter of Julius *ad Danium Flacillum*, &c.
Summer	341	Council of the Dedication (ἡ ἐν τοῖς ἐγκαινίοις) at Antioch, held between May 22 and Sept. 31.
	342 N	Council of Gangra not later than this year (p. 189).
Oct. or Nov.		Death of Eusebius of Nicomedia (Constantinople).
Summer	343 NR	Councils of Sardica and Philippopolis (p. 124).
Summer	344	Council at Antioch to depose Stephen. Issue of the μακρόστιχος.
June 26	345 N	Death of Gregory of Alexandria (p. 109).
Spring	346	Second siege of Nisibis (for three months, ending before the eclipse of June 6).
Oct. 21	NR	Return of Athanasius to Alexandria (p. 109).
	348	Great defeat of Constantius at Singara. Cyril's *Catecheses*.
	344—350	Julian at Macellum (Rendall *Julian* p. 286).
Jan. 18	350	Rising of Magnentius. Death of Constans. Risings of Vetranio (Mar. 1) and Nepotianus (June 3).
		Third siege of Nisibis.
Dec. 25		Deposition of Vetranio.
Mar. 15	351	Elevation of Gallus.
Sept. 28		Battle of Mursa.
Winter	N	Council at Sirmium against Photinus (p. 149).
	352	Jewish revolt.
		Athanasius *de Decretis* (between 346 and 355).

Aug. 13	353		Death of Magnentius.
Oct. (or later)			Council at Arles.
	354		Constantius on the Rhine—winters at Milan.
Winter			Execution of Gallus.
	355		Revolt of Silvanus.
			Julian at Athens.
Spring		N	Appeal of Photinus (p. 149).
			Exile of Hosius and Liberius.
Nov. 6			Julian made Cæsar: leaves Milan Dec. 1.
			Council at Milan.
	356		Legendary date of Antony's death.
Feb. 8		NR	Athanasius expelled by Syrianus (p. 156).
Spring			Council at Biterræ. Hilary exiled.
			Julian's unsuccessful campaign in Gaul.
			Athanasius *Encycl.* (between Feb. 8, 356 and George's arrival, Feb. 24, 357 [1]).
Apr. 28—May 29	357		Constantius at Rome.
August ?		N	Sirmian manifesto issued (p. 161).
August			Julian's victory at Argentoratum.
			Athanasius *Apol. ad Ctium* (between Feb. 24, 357 and Oct. 2, 358) and *de Fuga* later (p. 157).
Lent	358		Council at Ancyra.
			Athanasius *Hist. Arianorum ad Monachos* before Oct. 2[1].
Summer			Renewal of the Persian War.
Aug. 2			Return of Liberius to Rome.
24			Earthquake at Nicomedia.
Oct. 2			Bishop George driven from Alexandria.
Late		N	Hilary *de Synodis* (p. 168).
May 22	359		Conference at Sirmium. The dated creed.
27			Council of Ariminum meets, and (July 21) deposes Ursacius, Valens &c.
cir. July 27—Oct. 6			Siege and capture of Amida by Sapor.
Sept. 27—30			Council of Seleucia.
Oct.			Council at Nicé in Thrace.
Dec. ?			Athanasius *de Synodis.*

[1] Sievers *Einl.* p. 24.

CHRONOLOGICAL TABLE. xxvii

Dec. 31		Acceptance of the Creed of Nicé.
Jan.	360	Julian proclaimed Augustus at Paris.
Before Feb. 15		Council at Constantinople. Semiarian leaders deposed. Homœan supremacy. Capture of Singara and Bezabde by Sapor.
Jan. 6	361	Julian at Vienne.
Early		Elevation and exile of Meletius. Euzoius bishop of Antioch.
Nov. 3		Death of Constantius. Julian enters Constantinople Dec. 11.
Dec. 24	362 } NR	Murder of George, } (p. 224).
Feb. 22		Return of Athanasius,
Before Aug. 27		Council at Alexandria—Athanasius *ad Antiochenos*.
Oct. 22		Temple at Daphne burnt.
July 362—Mar. 5	363 N	Julian at Antioch (p. 226).
June 26		Death of Julian. Election of Jovian next morning.
July 12		Peace with Persia (Ammianus xxv. 6—7 *Kalendis Juliis......tritum est quadriduum......exacto miserabiliter biduo... ...dies quattuor sunt evoluti*).
After Sept.		Council at Antioch.
Feb. 16	364	Death of Jovian. Valentinian elected Feb. 26. Valens associated as *Augustus* March 29.
Autumn	N	Council of Lampsacus (p. 275).
Spring	365 NR	Valens at Antioch (p. 275). Exiles expelled again. Vexation of Massalians by Lupicinus the *magister militum*.
Sept. 28	N	Procopius enters Constantinople (p. 276).
Winter ?	N	Letter of Semiarians to Liberius (p. 241).
Feb. 1	366 N	Final restoration of Athanasius by the notary Brasidas. Return of other exiles (p. 243).
May 21		Procopius defeated at Nacolia.
	367—369	The Gothic War. Valens on the Danube.
Spring	367	Council at Tyana.
cir.	369	Athanasius *ad Afros*.
Summer	370	Basil bishop of Cæsarea.
	371	Death of Marcellus.

Jan. 6	372	Meeting of Basil with Valens, who reaches Antioch in April. Third exile of Meletius (p. 248).
		Basil *Ep.* 92, to the Westerns.
Jan. 1	373 N	Rescript of Valens against the monks (p. 234).
May 2		Death of Athanasius.
	374	Epiphanius *Ancoratus*.
		Ambrose bishop of Milan.
Summer		Exile of Eusebius of Samosata.
	375 N	Eustathius of Sebastia signs at Cyzicus (p. 249).
Nov. 17		Death of Valentinian.
	376	Death of Euzoius.
		Reception of the Goths inside the Danube.
	377	Indecisive battle *ad Radices*.
Aug. 9	378	Battle of Hadrianople. Death of Valens.
Jan. 1	379	Death of Basil. Elevation of Theodosius Jan. 19.
	380	Baptism of Theodosius.
Jan.	381	Reception and death of Athanaric.
May		Council of Constantinople.
		Council at Aquileia against Palladius and Secundianus.
Oct.	382	Pacification of the Goths by Saturninus.
	383	Last overtures of Theodosius to the Arians.

CHAPTER I.

INTRODUCTORY SKETCH.

ECCLESIASTICAL history is the spiritual counterpart of secular, running in the same channel all along its course, pervading it and permeated by it with the subtlest and most various influences. The worshippers of material progress may ignore the one, the ascetics of historic study may despise the other, but the two form one organic and indissoluble whole. History is one in breadth as well as length, claiming for a single record every aspect of human welfare as well as every age of man's existence on the earth. And if we look to their deeper relations, the movements of ecclesiastical history are of much the same sort as those of secular, due to similar causes and often fairly coincident even in date. The wranglings of theologians no more make up the one than the intrigues of politicians constitute the other. In both we see periods of splendour and of deep corruption, of heroic effort and of selfish quarrelling, of creative energy and of ignoble stagnation. In both we find trains of obscure causes silently transforming the face of history, or bursting out in earthquake shocks which seem to break its continuity. These sudden revolutions are the problems of history, and it is in their study that we can best trace the forces which in times of quiet are working underneath.

Such a problem, and one of the most striking in the whole course of ecclesiastical history, is the reaction which followed the Council of Nicæa. Arianism had started with a vigour promising a great career, and in a few years seemed no unequal claimant for the supremacy of the East. But its strength collapsed the moment the Council met, withered up by the universal reprobation of the Christian world. The fathers at

Nicæa condemned it all but unanimously, and their subscription held them to their decision. The very creed of Christendom was amended in order to exclude the heresy for ever, and its few faithful defenders were sent into exile as the penalty of stubborn misbelief. Arianism seemed hopelessly crushed when the Council closed.

Yet it instantly renewed the contest, and fought with orthodoxy on equal terms for nothing less than the dominion of the world. It was a hard-fought struggle—more than half a century of ups and downs and stormy controversy—but Arianism for a long time had the best of it. Even when extinguished by Theodosius (379—395) as a political power inside the Empire, it was able to fall back upon its converts among the northern nations. Its future was far from hopeless till the fall of the Gothic power in Aquitaine (507) and Italy (553), and the long contest was ended only by the conversion of the Visigoths and Lombards at the end of the sixth century.

This is the history as it appears on the surface. But why was not Arianism crushed at once by its overwhelming defeat at Nicæa? Where did it find strength for a battle of giants like this? Where were the elements of moral power which so long sustained it? These are the questions which force themselves upon us; and no true student will be content to pass them by. Its extent and duration are enough to shew that it was no mere outbreak of unmeaning wickedness. There must have been historic causes for its victories, historic causes also for its decline and fall.

Few will look to Arian doctrine as a source of Arian strength. Some attractions it certainly had. It seemed simpler than orthodoxy, and was more symmetrical than Semiarianism, more human than Sabellianism, while to the heathen it sounded very Christian. But as a system, Arianism was utterly illogical and unspiritual, a clear step back to heathenism, and a plain anachronism even for its own time. It began by attempting to establish Christian positions, and ended by subverting each and all of them. It maintained the unity of God by opening the door to polytheism. It upheld the Lord's divinity by making the Son of God a creature, and then worshipped him to escape the reproach of heathenism. It lost even his true humanity in a phantastic[1] theory of the Incarnation which refused the Son of Man a human soul. Above all, no true revelation of love could come from a God of abstract infinity and mystery, condemned to stand aloof for ever from the world lest it perish at his touch; no true atonement from a created mediator, neither truly God nor truly man; no true sanctification from a subject Spirit far beneath the dignity even of the first of creatures. In a word, there could be no intrinsic strength in a system which covered the whole field of Christian doctrine with the ruins of its pretentious failures.

Some again will answer that Arianism ceased to be a religious belief when its defenders signed a creed at the bidding of a heathen emperor, and that it was henceforth nothing better than a court faction dependent on back-stairs intrigues, so that we shall waste our time if we condescend to enquire whether its leaders had any definite belief at all. On this theory the Arian reaction was nothing more than as it were an accident of history, an outbreak of imperial wickedness and tyranny against an orthodox and unoffending church.

There is an element of truth in this, for all authorities are agreed that Arian successes began and ended with Arian command of the palace. We might disregard the complaints of zealots like Lucifer of Calaris; but Athanasius puts the matter quite as plainly in the writings of his exile, and even Hilary's calmer spirit breaks out a little later in language scarcely falling short of Lucifer's unmeasured violence. It is clear that Arianism worked throughout by court intrigue and military outrage, and that the Semiarian leaders were all infected with the stain of persecution. In the West indeed Arianism scarcely had any legitimate footing at all. The Council of Milan might be overawed with soldiers, that of Ariminum worn out by delays and cajolery; but the victory was

---

[1] So Eustathius of Antioch (Migne *Patrol.* xviii. 694). Homini vero hæc applicanda sunt proprie, qui ex anima constat et corpore; congruit enim ex ipsis humanis et innoxiis motibus demonstrare, quia non *phantastice* et putative, sed ipsa veritate totum hominem indutus est Deus perfecte assumens.

ephemeral, and the conquerors remained isolated in a crowd of hostile bishops.

It is a coarse view of history which can see nothing in it but the flash of swords. We are told in effect that the Empire was a despotism, which we knew before; and that the initiative had to come from the court, which was also clear. But this is all. We get no account of the forces on which the reaction must have depended—for even a despot must have a party of some sort behind him. Nor is it any credit to the Nicene church, or even bare historic justice, to represent it in this manner as a crowd of timeservers and emperor-worshippers. The long resistance, for example, of the Semiarians at Seleucia is in striking contrast to the abject servility of the Eastern bishops in the age of Justinian or Irene. If Constantius carried his point, it was only by deceiving the deputies of the council, not by overcoming the council itself. The long struggle shews that the recalcitrant bishops at least had a belief of their own, independent of the emperor's. Nor are there wanting in the reaction evidently respectable elements to shew that if it was a court intrigue, it was also something more. It was not with a mere synagogue of Satan that men like Cyril of Jerusalem, Dianius of Cæsarea, and Meletius of Antioch so long took part. Nor is it to a conspiracy of atheists and blasphemers that we owe almost all the mission work of Christendom in that age of deep despair when the Empire seemed dragging the whole order of nature after it to ruin.

This may suffice for the present to shew that the Arian reaction was more than a mere court intrigue, and needs a closer analysis of its constituent elements. We must therefore take up the neglected data, examining the initial relation of Arianism to contemporary thought and education, heathen as well as Christian, the actual state of parties in the Nicene Council, and their mutual reactions as far as the Council of Constantinople.

Our first task is to form a clear conception of the development of the doctrine of the Person of Christ at the appearance of Arius—to find out what principles had been already laid down and how far they were generally accepted; what problems came next for solution, how far they were already answered, and what difficulties stood in the way of further progress. A mere sketch of results may suffice for the earlier period[1].

In the first place then Christianity inherited from Judaism together with the scriptures of the Old Testament, their fundamental principle of the unity of God and the distinction of the divinity from the world, in clear opposition to every Hellenic confusion of it with the world, whether as pervading the whole or as distributed among its parts. It was yet to be seen whether it was possible to rest in earlier views of the divine essence as lying in abstract infinity or isolation from the world; but so far as regards its mere unity and distinction from the world, the declarations of the Gospel were as emphatic as those of Judaism.

But side by side with the unity of God, Christianity held as its own fundamental doctrine the historic fact of the coming of the Lord, the Incarnation and the Resurrection, with all their momentous consequences. It was not orthodoxy alone which felt from the first that the Person of the Lord must have a universal and eternal meaning, stretching over history and reaching back to the inmost sphere of the divine. Ebionism shews us the old Jewish spirit struggling with this conviction, and Gnosticism itself in all its varied forms is little more than Oriental thought modified and often mastered by it. And in the third century, when Christianity had lived down early scandal, even heathenism became dimly conscious of the secret of its strength, and would willingly have enrolled the Crucified in its strange Pantheon of the benefactors of mankind, along with Orpheus and Moses, Socrates and Abraham. Far more did the Christian church feel that the fulness of the Lord is more than human fulness, that the life which flows from him is more than human life, that the atonement through him is with the Supreme himself, that the Person of the Lord is the infinite and final revelation of the Father. Thus the Lord's divinity was from the first as fixed an axiom of Christianity as

---

[1] Fuller accounts are given in the histories of doctrine; esp. Dorner, Nitzsch, and Voigt and Atzberger for the doctrines of Athanasius: also Harnack *Dogmengesch.*

the unity of God, while his humanity was plainly declared by the original apostolic testimony, and both together were necessary to give reality to the Incarnation. It remained to reconcile this view of the Lord's Person with the first fundamental principle of the unity of God.

The earliest Christian writers were hardly conscious of the problem before them. Their greatness was in life rather than in thought, and their works are one long hymn of overflowing thankfulness for the gift of life in Christ. Their task was rather to repeat the apostolic testimony than to discuss it, to urge historic facts rather than to deduce their dogmatic consequences. Hence it is on the Lord's divinity that they lay special stress, as the obvious distinction of Christian from Judaic and philosophic belief alike. But they merely insist upon it as a historic fact, and their utmost endeavour is to prove its correspondence with the prophecies and types of the Old Testament. They scarcely seem to see the difficulty of reconciling divinity with suffering—for this rather than the Resurrection was the stumbling-block of their time. "If he suffered," said the Ebionites, "he was not divine." "If he was divine," answered the Docetists, "his sufferings were unreal." The subapostolic Fathers were content to reply that he was divine and that he truly suffered, without attempting to explain the difficulty. Thus the church had yet to pass from the traditional assertion of the Lord's full deity to its deliberate enunciation in clear consciousness of the difficulties involved in it.

But a firmer base was wanted for research. The Old Testament needed the teaching of the Lord for its own interpretation, and even the apostolic tradition became more and more dependent on the evidence of documents. As soon as Christianity had Scriptures of its own, Christian research could work upon them, and soon essayed the central problem of the Person of the Lord. Even the second century was a period of greater literary activity than its scanty relics would seem to shew. The last collector of the Lord's discourses from the lips of his disciples was also the first orthodox commentator on the Gospels. Apologists started up in all directions to defend the truth of Christianity or to put its doctrines in a clearer form. Quadratus, Aristides, Justin,

THE SECOND CENTURY.

Tatian, Theophilus and Athenagoras all belong to this period. Christian antiquities called forth the work of Hegesippus, Christian controversies those of Agrippa Castor, Melito, Miltiades, Claudius Apollinarius and Dionysius of Corinth; and even fiction has its representatives in the *Shepherd* of Hermas, the Clementine writings, and a host of spurious gospels. Scripture also was studied then as well as now, as we see from the commentary of Papias, the Diatessaron of Tatian, and the Muratorian fragment on the Canon. Even the heretics, though their voluminous writings have mostly perished, contributed the labours of Marcion and others[1] to its criticism, those of Basilides, Ptolemæus and Heracleon to its interpretation. And if much of this literature is unsatisfactory, and scarcely any of it reaches the highest excellence, it marks at any rate a period of busy study.

When once investigation reached the doctrine of the Lord's Person, its difficulties became apparent. It also became evident that the method of the subapostolic Fathers was inadequate. As heresy was dislodged from its broad denials of the historic facts of the revelation, so it drove orthodoxy from its bare assertions of them. The appeal to the "rule of faith" or historical[2] tradition which could only urge the reality of the facts, was useless now that the question was of their interpretation. There was nothing left but to fall back more and

---

[1] *Anon.* ap. Eus. *H. E.* v. 28.

[2] Early references to the "rule of faith" are collected by Swainson *Nicene and Apostles' Creeds* pp. 26—47. It is important to notice their historical character and cautious adherence to the bare facts without any attempt to build dogmatic schemes upon them.

Clement of Alexandria may serve as an example. He speaks much like Irenæus of a παράδοσις *Strom.* i. § 11, p. 322, or of a true γνῶσις *Strom.* vi. § 68, p. 774, committed by the Lord to his disciples, and by them delivered in due course to the γνωστικοί (not necessarily the bishops) of later times. He also appeals under variant names to a κανὼν ἐκκλησιαστικός, through neglect of which the Gnostic errors had arisen. But this he defines *Strom.* vi. § 125, p. 803, to be "the agreement of the Law and the Prophets with the covenant given during the Lord's presence on earth"; or, in other words, the traditional principle of the continuity of Scripture. Instead of being an independent source of doctrine, the κανὼν ἐκκλησιαστικός is nothing more than the confession that each part of Scripture is an authoritative commentary on the other. Thus when Clement draws upon tradition, it is only for allegorical embellishments of the Old Testament, of which a large store had by this time been accumulated in the church. Yet he can scarcely mean to say that the whole of his mystical explanation of the decalogue was received from tradition. On these subjects see Kaye *Clement* pp. 362—396; Westcott in *Dict. of Chr. Biogr.*; also Faye's *Clément d'Alexandrie*.

more upon the grammatical meaning of the documents which embodied it, and trust to the abiding presence of the Holy Spirit by whose providence they were first written. And this is the course taken by all the great leaders of the Eastern Church from Irenæus[1] and the School of Alexandria to Athanasius and Cyril. As each fresh theory came forward, it was tested by a new appeal to the living voice of Scripture; and according to the result of that appeal it was either accepted like Origen's theory of the eternal generation, or rejected like the schemes of Arius or Sabellius. Conservative ignorance or indolence might prefer the easier reference to tradition, but only decaying churches endeavour to return to the childish things which Christianity has put away.

From this time forward the combatants appear distinctly. We find two great tendencies, each rooted deep in human nature, each working inside and outside the church, and each traversing the whole field of Christian doctrine. And the battle has lasted from that day to this, beginning with five hundred years of controversy over the Person of the Lord (say till 717), and gradually working over every aspect of his teaching.

The first tendency was distinctly rationalist. Its crude form of Ebionism had denied the Lord's divinity outright. And now that this was accepted, it was viewed as a mere influence or power, or in any case as not divine in the highest sense. Thus the reality of the Incarnation was sacrificed, and the result was a clear reaction to the demigods of polytheism.

The other tendency, already roughly shadowed out in the docetic evasion of the Lord's humanity, was mystic in its character. Accepting the full deity that was in Christ, it reduced it to a mere appearance or modification of the One. Thus the reality of the Incarnation was undermined on the other side, and the result was a clear step back to pantheism.

The first of these tendencies endangered the Lord's divinity, the second his distinction from the Father; and the difficulty was to find some means of asserting both. In the fourth century it became clear that the problem required a distinction to be

---

[1] Eastern by birth, education, and residence till a mature age.

made inside the divine unity: and as the Lord's Baptismal Formula (Matt. xxviii. 19) associated the Holy Spirit as well as the Son with the Father, it followed that the God of Christianity is not personal only but tripersonal. Arianism laid down a merely external, Sabellianism a merely economic Trinity; but neither the one nor the other satisfied the conditions of the problem. It therefore became necessary to fall back on Scripture to revise the idea of a divine personality, and acknowledge, not three individuals but three eternal aspects ($\dot{v}\pi o\sigma\tau\acute{a}\sigma\epsilon\iota\varsigma$) of the divine, facing inward on each other as well as outward on the world[1].

At this point a difficulty was felt, arising from the continuity of revelation with history and nature. The Lord had not descended suddenly from heaven as Marcion imagined, without historic preparation for his coming; neither was Christianity a magic power independent of the laws of God in nature, but a heavenly one working subject to them in the world. The Lord came, as he said, to complete and not to overthrow, to consecrate and not to revolutionize. The disciple was the child of earth as well as heaven, for the Lord accepted him in his ignorance, and left his speculative errors to be dealt with by the moral power implied in a historic revelation[2]. Even on such a subject as the nature of the divinity, he was not required to give up his earlier beliefs except so far as he found them inconsistent with the teaching of the Lord. Yet, from whatever quarter he approached the Gospel, he brought with him conceptions fundamentally at variance with it. So far as the earlier systems distinguished God at all from the world, they placed his essence in abstract simplicity—a view consistent with either an Arian Trinity of one increate and two created beings, or a Sabellian Trinity of temporal aspects ($\pi\rho\acute{o}\sigma\omega\pi a$) of the One, but not with a Trinity of eternal distinctions ($\dot{v}\pi o\sigma\tau\acute{a}\sigma\epsilon\iota\varsigma$) inside the divine nature.

This needs closer examination, for the earlier conception underlay not only Arianism and Sabellianism, but also much

---

[1] Martensen *Dogmatics* § 56.
[2] Readers of Mozley will remember his splendid contrast of Christianity with Mohammedanism upon the basis of the Epistle to the Romans. *Miracles*, Lecture vii.

orthodox thought; and its expulsion from the doctrine of the Trinity is one of our deepest interests in the Arian controversy.

The old Hellenic polytheism was undermined by the commercial empire of Athens, and Alexander's conquests completed its destruction as a system of serious belief. The ancient rites went on for centuries, but henceforth they were sustained by policy or superstition rather than by real belief. Yet even the philosophers did not venture to abolish the Olympic gods entirely; all they did was respectfully to shift them to a region of mysterious serenity beyond the reach alike of human troubles and of human worship. And when the results of the creative age of Greek philosophy came to be discussed, it was found that the problem of human life was still unsolved. Plato's dreams of a future life and of a God and Father of the universe, however hard to find, fared ill in Aristotle's hands, and were at once too glorious and too unsubstantial to cast a light of hope upon the age of anarchy which followed Alexander's death. Their very splendour shewed the more conspicuously their want of a firm basis of historic revelation. And Greek thought had lost nothing of its subtle power of destructive criticism, nothing but its originality and sunny hopefulness. The old alliance of philosophy with politics was loosened even before the Macedonian conquest by the increasing confusion of the Hellenic state system; and when political freedom received its deathblow at Calauria and Sellasia, the philosophers turned away even from physical research, for which Alexander's conquests had provided so rich a store of materials, and betook themselves in sore distress to ethics as a practical guide for the immediate duties of life. The higher questions were adjourned by common consent as hopeless. The Stoics throned Fate, the Epicureans Chance, while the Sceptics left a vacant space where the gods had been: but all agreed in the confession of despair, that if there be a God beyond Olympus, he must be not only hard to find and impossible to explain to the vulgar, but absolutely beyond the power of man to reach at all[1].

Oriental thought contributed its share to the deepening

[1] Zeller *Philosophie der Griechen;* or (E. Tr.) *Stoics, Epicureans and Sceptics* 1—36. Lightfoot *Philippians* 269—275.

gloom. Conquered Persia reacted on Greece almost as powerfully as Greece itself on Rome; and in the further East there was a still mightier spiritual power than Persia. The austerities of Indian asceticism were a spectacle of unearthly awe to Alexander's army, and the pyre of Calanus became a classic marvel. Buddhism also was in the first vigour of that amazing course of victory which has left it even after its defeat in India the faith of a full third of mankind. It was a far cry from the holy land of Kapilavastu to the shores of the Mediterranean, but trade was active and Greek cities lay all along the route. Chandragupta's elephants decided the battle of Ipsus, and the Greek kings of Syria and Egypt are named on Asoka's monuments in India. And Alexandria lay open even more than Syria to the superstitions of the furthest East[1]. Thus Oriental thought entered largely into Stoicism, formed the groundwork of all the Gnostic systems and almost dominated the theology of Neoplatonism. Its lofty spirituality and its sombre view of Nature were equally attractive to minds disgusted with the vulgar polytheism. Its harsh contrast of the good God with the world of matter was exactly the result towards which the Greeks were already tending. Its formal dualism might be qualified, its endless emanations dropped; but its conception of the divinity as pure Being high above the attributes of character, of passion and of contact with our lower world, remained as an axiom of all philosophy.

Even the stern monotheism of Israel was corroded by Oriental influences. They are as clear in the philosophic Philo

[1] Greek influence in further Asia seriously underestimated by Grote viii. 472—474 (criticised by Freeman *Hist. Essays* ser. II. p. 193). If not permanent, it had a fair amount of strength and duration. Against the mutiny of the colonists after Alexander's death must be set the continuance of Greek kingdoms in Bactria and the Punjab as late as B.C. 126. City of Euthydemia on the Hydaspes. Bactrian conquest of Guzerat. Menander of Sangala in Buddhist legend. Greek inscriptions on coins of Cabul, Guzerat and Magadha. And if the Parthian government was essentially as anti-Hellenic as the Turkish (Rawlinson *Sixth Great Oriental Monarchy* 42, 60, 88), its administration was as dependent on Greek help. Yet this is scarcely just to Parthia: no Turkish sultan ever listened to Greek plays or struck Greek money with the legend φιλέλλην.

For trade, it is enough to compare the accounts of India given by Herodotus and Strabo.

The period contemplated in the text is that of the Seleucidæ. The later intercourse of India with the Roman Empire is a distinct question.

and even in the orthodox Talmudists as in the contemplative self-annihilation of the Essenes. An age of growing formalism put far away the glorious and awful Name, while men of sober piety retraced the ancient records in quest of mediating angels or a mystic Word. The Alexandrine translators softened many of the Old Testament anthropomorphisms, and their ὁ ὤν was altered in its turn by Philo to τὸ ὄν[1]. Even the faithful Onkelos is ever on the watch to smooth away every semblance of irreverence to the spirituality and singleness of God[2]. If Israel never formally forsook Jehovah, we see traces everywhere of a transcendental deism (easily convertible into a Kabbalistic pantheism) which "refined away personality itself as too anthropomorphic."

Those therefore of the philosophical systems which connected God with the world lost their hold on his personality, while those which insisted on his personality removed him into transcendental isolation. In either case there could be no true contact of God and man, for the antithesis of infinite and finite personality was essential, and neither side could do away with it. Man as man might perhaps become a human demigod; but if he was to be united with the divine, he must leave his human self behind.

But if God is removed far from man, then man will have to wander in the darkness far from God. Therefore philosophy was confronted with a more than equal rival in the Eastern superstitions which claimed to satisfy his need of personal communion

---

[1] It is needless to give more than a specimen or two of Philo's language: i. p. 53, δεῖ γὰρ...ἄποιον αὐτὸν εἶναι. p. 148, ἀσωμάτων ἰδεῶν ἀσώματος χώρα. p. 282, ὁ δ᾽ ἄρα οὐδὲ τῷ νῷ καταληπτός, ὅτι μὴ κατὰ τὸ εἶναι μόνον. p. 425, ᾧ πανταχοῦ τε καὶ οὐδαμοῦ συμβέβηκεν εἶναι μόνῳ. His *Quod omnis probus liber* and (but surely spurious: Lucius, *Die Therapeuten*) *De Vita Contemplativa*, with their unbounded admiration of Calanus, Diogenes and the Essenes, are utterly alien from the spirit of the Old Testament. His ideal is nearer that of the Stoics. See Keim, *Jesus of Nazara*, E. Tr. i. 280—296, and works quoted.

[2] Whatever be the date and country of the Targum of Onkelos, and whatever the relation of its text to the Alexandrian version, its general spirit shews few traces of Greek influence. Yet changes traceable to "reverence" for the divine form at least eleven of the 32 classes of alterations reckoned up by Luzzatto (אוהב גר pp. 1—25; or Deutsch's compilation in *Bible Dict.* Art. *Versions*). We constantly find expressions like י"י רוחא מן קדם, וירא (for גלי קדמי, ותב י"י במימרה י"י). The other Targums avoid anthropomorphisms more decidedly as such.

with a personal God. Rome fought them manfully till Rome was lost in the world, and the elevation of Elagabalus and the Eastern emperors who followed him proclaimed her subjugation. Philosophy itself was next invaded, and the letter of Porphyry to Anebon marks the final struggle before the representatives of Socrates and Plato were brought upon their knees before the mummeries of Egypt. Nor did those mummeries want for weighty meaning. The nameless writer *de mysteriis Aegyptiorum*[1] is a strange advocate for Christianity, but some of its deepest teachings have never been more nobly defended than by this champion of sorceries and immoralities, of theurgy and brutish idol-worships. We read with reverence his splendid protests that the gods have not abandoned earth, but pervade it like the sunlight[2]; that all worship depends upon and presupposes a direct infinity[3] and true communion of the gods with man[4]; that prayer is no battery to force their will[5], but their own good gift[6], to free us from the evil passions which estrange us from them; that all the gods are good[7], all full of graciousness and loving care for men[8]; that idols are mere obstructions to the beatific vision[9]; that priests have no prerogative of knowledge[10], for the only inspiration is in complete submission to a pure and holy will[11], and the only perfect good is union with the gods, whose service is perfect freedom from the slavery of fate[12]. Of this the philosopher may see the need, but the theurgist alone can shew the way to it[13].

Are not these the loving words of sympathy from heaven for which the philosophers had cried in vain—the blessings of the living gods upon their children? Those who looked to theurgy for guidance were too impatient for a voice from heaven to see that it came from men like themselves, and

[1] It is safer left nameless than assigned to Iamblichus. See Harless *Das Buch von den ägyptischen Mysterien* p. 2, 3.
[2] i. 8, pp. 28—30. These references are to Parthey's edition.
[3] v. 9, p. 209.
[4] i. 14, p. 44.
[5] i. 12, 13, pp. 42, 43.
[6] i. 21, p. 66.
[7] i. 18, p. 53, iii. 31, p. 176.
[8] i. 13, p. 43.
[9] iii. 29, p. 172.
[10] i. 8, p. 28.
[11] iii. 31, pp. 176—179.
[12] viii. 7, p. 270.
[13] x. 4, 5, pp. 289—292. Professor Maurice almost alone seems to have done justice to the ability and importance of the *de Mysteriis*. It is discussed by Zeller, but Ueberweg (*Hist. of Phil.* § 69) dismisses it with a summary contempt it scarcely deserves.

that the whole system was almost avowedly a mass of mere assertions, encumbered at every turn with the grossest immoralities.

Philosophy on one side, superstition on the other—the ancient world was tossed from side to side between them. No philosophy could climb the heights of heaven, no incantations bring down God to earth. No speculation, no intuition— nothing less than a historic incarnation could firmly link together earth and heaven, for none but the incarnate Lord of all could claim to be the Light of East and West alike.

Now historic Christianity leaned to the philosophic side. Thither it was attracted by high and holy interests, for its noblest spirits were the most anxious to trace our Master's teaching in the splendid past of Greece, while those like Tertullian who most disliked philosophy were even more repelled by the practical immoralities of magic and polytheism. Hence all parties held the philosophic view, forgetting that no incarnation can effectually reveal a God whose essence lies in mystery and abstract isolation. The struggles of the third century disclosed the difficulty in all its magnitude. Tertullian shifted the field of battle, gathering it no longer round the shadowy doctrine of the Logos but the more definite personality of the Son of God. Origen cleared up the idea of a divine generation by shewing that it denotes no finite act either temporal or pretemporal, but an eternal or intemporal process or relation. The correspondence of the Dionysii seemed to settle the unity of essence, the condemnation of Paul of Samosata to establish the Lord's divinity as eternal in the past as well as in the future.

But every advance led into fresh difficulties while the base of operations was unsecured. No minor successes were of the least avail as long as heathenism held the key of the position, and constantly threatened an attack at the decisive point which might recover all that it had lost. It was impossible to stand still without falling back into polytheism, impossible to advance with any safety till the central doctrine of the divine nature had been remodelled to accord with revelation.

This however was beyond the power of the third century. The immediate force which shaped all Christian thought upon the subject was the necessity of reasserting the unity of God[1]. Now that heresy had to be confronted with Scripture, it was found that the plan of insisting on the Lord's divinity without explaining his relation to the Father was leading back to polytheism. The movement was wider than the church, and heathenism itself contributed to it by its persevering efforts to call forth the shadowy Supreme from the dim background of mythology[2]. Hence all parties were monarchian. After a period of hesitation represented by Tertullian and Zeno of Verona[3], the West settled down towards a view, which without renouncing the subordination of the Son, so emphasized the eternal unity as to obscure the distinction of Persons[4]. But the Easterns, also after some hesitation, made theories of subordination their chief reliance, attempting to distinguish the derivative from the absolute divine (θεὸς from ὁ θεὸς or the δόξα from τὸ ὄν behind it), and viewing our Lord as a sort of secondary God, or δευτερεύων θεός.

---

[1] Dorner ii. 5.

[2] Fialon *Saint Athanase* 14—19 draws a parallel of the Christian and Neoplatonic schools of Alexandria from this point of view. The converse is well given by Rendall *Julian* 99.

[3] I have not examined the question of Zeno's date, but place him here on Dorner's authority, ii. 187, as a younger contemporary of Tertullian. The usual arguments for a later date (cir. 380: Dorner has not noticed some of them) seem very weak, and cannot be reinforced from Symmachus *Ep.* i. 93.

[4] So Dionysius of Rome, discussed by Zahn *Marcellus* 14. Dittrich, *Dionysius der Grosse* 91—115, is worth comparison.

CHAPTER II.

THE COUNCIL OF NICÆA.

THE appearance then of Arianism about the year 318 was no historical accident, but a direct result of earlier movements, and an inevitable reaction of heathen forms of thought against the definite establishment of the Christian view of God. In the West the Christians were fewer and more rigid, more practical and more inclined to stand aloof from heathenism, so that the genuine Christian conception had more room to unfold itself, and Subordinatianism was confined within narrower limits. But in the East, where the church had always been stronger, more learned and more disposed to mix with the world[1], heathen influences found it easier to assert their power, so that in the second half of the third century the demoralization of the church kept pace even with its rapid spread[2]. Persecution might weed out the timeservers and the weak; but it hardened the strong, and left behind the abiding mischief of an inhuman ideal of discipline. We fix our eyes too much on the heroic scenes enacted in the heathen courts of justice, and forget the odious assize which followed, when the remnant of the faithful came to sit in judgment on the renegades who had denied their Lord.

---

[1] Notice e.g. the reputation of Origen's learning and the wider knowledge of Christianity, as shewn by the disappearance of old slanders and the antagonism of the Neoplatonists. Notice the splendour of the churches, like that of Nicomedia; the increasing frequency of Christians in high place, like the *ducenarius* Paul and the chamberlains of Diocletian; and above all, the action of the emperors. On one side the friendly interest of Alexander Severus and Philip, the concessions of Gallienus and the favour so long accorded to the Church by Diocletian; on the other, the desperate efforts of Decius and Galerius, the threatening tone of Aurelian, and the more systematic cruelties of Valerian and Maximin Daza—all combine to shew that Christianity was felt to be a political force of the first importance, and that the signs of its approaching victory were plain enough to all who cared to read them.

[2] Indications of this are summed up by Dorner ii. 201; but he scarcely alludes to some of its worst features.

It was not good for human pride that men should presume to impose on their fallen brethren long periods of shameful penance. The Decian persecution stands alone in ecclesiastical history for the number of apostates; and if there were fewer scandals in that of Diocletian, it was only because more warning was given of its coming. And now that persecution seemed to have passed away for ever, it was inevitable that heathen thought inside the church should endeavour to seize for itself the central doctrine of the faith.

Nor was it even accidental that Arianism broke out at Alexandria rather than elsewhere. It is not clear that Lucian of Antioch was heretical, whatever his disciples may have been[1]: and if Arius carried away questionable opinions from his school, so did others. If therefore it was at Alexandria that they grew into open Arianism, we may suppose that circumstances were more favourable to their growth at Alexandria than elsewhere. And this was the case. Origen and Dionysius must be acquitted of heresy; but their language leaned to Arianism quite as much as Lucian's[2]. The Jewish influence was as strong at Alexandria as at Antioch, the heathen much stronger. If we contrast the quiet desolation of Apollo's shrine at Daphne as early as Julian's time[3] with the repeated riots of the heathen populace at Alexandria, the murder of George of Cappadocia, and the tumults of 390, culminating in the bloody struggle

---

[1] Against the statement of Alexander of Alexandria (Theod. i. 4), that Lucian remained outside the church for a long time under three successive bishops, we may set (1) his high character with all parties—even Athanasius never attacks him—and (2) in particular the creed ascribed (it seems rightly) to him at the Council of the Dedication. It is substantially as orthodox a creed as could be written without the gift of prophecy to foresee the adoption of the word ὁμοούσιον. (3) The reckless tone of Alexander's letter, which throws serious doubt on statements in which he might easily have been mistaken.

The further charge of Epiphanius, *Ancoratus* 33, that Lucian denied the Lord's human spirit, may refer to his disciples, and is no clear case for a charge of heresy in Lucian's own time.

There is really nothing against him but the leaning of his disciples to Arianism: and we shall see presently that this can be otherwise accounted for. *Infra* ch. III.

Harnack *D. G.* ii. 184 counts him "*der Arius bevor Arius.*" So Robertson *Ath.* Int. xxviii.

[2] Especially Dionysius has ποίημα τοῦ Θεοῦ, ξένον κατ' οὐσίαν, οὐκ ἦν πρὶν γένηται—all of them watchwords of Arianism.

[3] Julian *Misop.* 362. It was burnt during his visit (Ammianus xxii. 13), and lay in ruins in the time of Chrysostom (*De S. Babyla* passim). The case is not much altered if Christian hands had helped its decay. Julian would have found the temples better kept in Egypt.

round the Serapeum, we shall see which of the two cities offered more encouragement to a heathenized form of Christianity[1].

No doubt Syria seemed Arian and Egypt orthodox in the later years of the controversy; but this case was very different at its outbreak. We underrate the popularity of Arius at Alexandria, especially among the women and the common people, to whose decision he appealed in his *Thalia*. His austere life and novel doctrines, his dignified character and championship of common sense in religion, all helped to make him the idol of the multitude. Part of the clergy followed him[2]; and Alexander's hesitation in so plain a case is enough to shew that the heresiarch's position was too strong to be rashly attacked. From this point we can almost statistically trace its decline before the commanding influence and skilful policy of Athanasius. The election in 328 was the work of a section[3], possibly a minority, of the Egyptian bishops, and was for many years disputed by a strong opposition. However, Arianism was eliminated from the episcopate before the year 339, and the last relics of its early popularity must have been destroyed by Gregory's tyranny and arbitrary interference with the corn distributions. In any case, the triumphal return of Athanasius in 346 clearly marks its extinction as an indigenous power in Egypt[4]. The later intruders, George and Lucius (356 and 373), appear to have

---

[1] Notice also the prominent part taken by the heathen in the Arian troubles at Alexandria. Also the statement of Libanius (*Or. pro Templis* II. 180 sq.), that sacrifice was still allowed at Rome and Alexandria in the time of Theodosius. He does not mention his own city of Antioch.

[2] Six presbyters were excommunicated by Alexander: but what proportion of the city clergy did they form? Comparing the statement of Cornelius in Eus. *H. E.* vi. 43, that there were forty-six presbyters in Rome cir. 260, with that of Optatus ii. 4, that there were rather more than forty churches in Rome some fifty years later, we may accept the inference of Valesius that there was a presbyter to each church. Now Epiphanius *Hær.* 69. 2 enumerates ten churches ("and there were more") at Alexandria, and tells us (also *Hær.* 68. 4; so too Soz. i. 15) that they were assigned separately to presbyters; while Eutychius (a late authority) says that there were only twelve presbyters as late as cir. 300. If so, the number must since have been increased: for sixteen presbyters sign Alexander's encyclical, and sixteen also sign the Alexandrian protest to the Mareotic commissioners in 335. If, as is most likely, the vacancies were already filled up, we may perhaps take sixteen for the whole number of presbyters in Alexandria, not including the Mareotis: if not, we must increase the total to twenty-two. There were sixty at Constantinople in Justinian's time. Of course the total staff of ecclesiastics would be very much larger.

[3] Fialon *Athan.* 104—110.

[4] It is significant that when the Arians and Meletians were afterwards fused together, the party was popularly called by the latter name. Soz. ii. 21.

ARIANISM NOT FROM ANTIOCH.

brought most of their partizans with them[1]. At Antioch on the other hand Arianism was instantly confronted with the most determined opposition from Philogonius and Eustathius, and this at a time when the Syrian bishops of the second rank mostly leaned the other way[2]. Armed force was needed for the expulsion of Eustathius in 330, and the episcopates of Leontius[3] and Meletius complete the proof that the Arians were outnumbered at Antioch from first to last[4]. Thus neither the orthodoxy of Alexandria nor the heresy of Antioch was an original feature of the controversy. Alexandria was at first more favourable to Arianism than Antioch, and might have continued so but for the influence of Athanasius.

As the earlier school of Antioch was not the germ of Arianism, so neither was the later school in any sense its outgrowth. Diodorus of Tarsus and Theodore of Mopsuestia were zealous defenders of the Nicene faith, and their followers never adopted any of the characteristic doctrines of Arianism. If it be heresy to protest against the mutilation of the Lord's humanity, the Antiochenes are heretics indeed, but the Arians are clear. It is one thing to invent a heathen idol in order to maintain a heathenish Supreme in heathen isolation; surely quite another to insist on the Lord's true manhood in order to prevent its effacement by the overpowering splendour of his deity. The Antiochenes erred in their sharp separation of the Lord's two natures; but the Arians impartially abolished both, and

---

[1] Amongst other indications, the soldier's words to Jovian. Ath. p. 624, οὗτοι γάρ εἰσι τὰ λείψανα καὶ ἡ παραβολὴ τῆς Καππαδοκίας, τὰ ὑπόλοιπα τοῦ ἀνοσίου ἐκείνου Γεωργίου.

[2] On the side of Arius we have Eusebius of Cæsarea, Paulinus of Tyre, Theodotus of Laodicea, Gregory of Berytus (successor and probably nominee of the other Eusebius), and Patrophilus of Scythopolis; on the other only Macarius of Jerusalem and Hellanicus of Tripolis. Magnus of Damascus and Anatolius of Emesa are not mentioned in this connexion, but Alphius of Apamea joins (Eus. V. C. iii. 62) in the deposition of Eustathius. One may conjecture the existence of a jealousy of Antioch parallel to the Meletian schism in Egypt, and equally struck at by the Council of Nicæa Can. 6; which is followed Can. 7 by a stipulation in favour of Jerusalem, practically at the expense of Cæsarea.

[3] Infra ch. IV.

[4] The fact would be clearer if the Arian intruders were either omitted from the episcopal succession of Antioch or inserted in that of Alexandria. It is simply misleading to say that Athanasius ruled at Alexandria for nearly fifty years, and the Arians for about an equal time at Antioch. Soz. vi. 21 tells us that Antioch very nearly became wholly Arian during the residence of Valens: but the exaggeration is characteristic. So vi. 28 Syria very nearly Apollinarian, Asia inside Taurus Eunomian.

left an idolatrous abomination in their place. Again, it was from very different motives that Arians and Antiochenes rejected the effeminacies of mystical interpretation. Because Arianism was essentially heathen, the Arians leaned on philosophy, and kept up their formal connexion with Christianity by means of the obsolete appeal to tradition; whereas the Antiochenes made revelation supreme, and endeavoured to substitute the scholarly study of Scripture for the irresponsible vagaries of a zeal without knowledge. The only real resemblance of the Antiochene doctrine to Arianism is on the anthropological ground; and that is the common property of the whole Eastern church. So far as regarded the Person of the Lord, they started from antagonistic positions, worked by different methods and came to contrary results.

It is now time to state shortly what Arianism was. Our chief concern is with the form in which it appeared before the Council of Nicæa; but it will be useful also to indicate the course of its earlier growth[1] and history.

Arianism then was almost as much a philosophy as a religion. It assumed the usual philosophical postulates, worked by the usual philosophical methods, and scarcely referred to Scripture except in quest of isolated texts to confirm conclusions reached without its help[2]. Thus Arianism started from the accepted belief in the unity of God, as a being not only absolutely one but also for that reason[3] absolutely simple and absolutely isolated from a world of finite beings. He is alone ingenerate, alone eternal, alone without beginning, alone good, alone almighty, alone unchangeable and unalterable, and from the eyes of every creature his being is hidden in eternal mystery.

So far Arianism agreed with the Jews, the philosophers and the current Christianity of the day, in the common purpose of

---

[1] This is best traced by comparing the earlier letters of Arius to Eusebius and Alexander with the fragments of the *Thalia*. See Dorner ii. 237. Atzberger *Logoslehre* 23.

[2] So Voigt *Athanasius* 192, not very seriously qualified by Atzberger *Logoslehre* 30. It is important to notice the fragmentary treatment of Scripture resulting from this. Hence also one cause for the frequent irreverence of Arianism. Instances are collected by Newman *Ath.Tr.* ii. 213 n.: but it is hard for "heretics" to escape condemnation, if legitimate difficulties are (*id.* 221) summarily denounced as "pretences."

[3] Dorner ii. 234.

spiritualizing the idea of deity by opposing it as sharply as possible to that of manhood. It was not yet clearly seen that if man was made in the image of God, it follows that God is in some true sense the archetype of man ; so that anthropomorphic images are not entirely misleading, and even that flesh of sin in whose likeness the Son of God was sent cannot be entirely foreign to its creator's goodness.

Next came the problem of creation—how to connect the unknown God with a material world. Here again Arius started from philosophic ground. The further the Supreme is removed from the world of matter, the greater the need of a mediator for his intercourse with it. Philo had long ago separated the demiurgic forces as a half personal, half impersonal relation of Jehovah, and the Gnostics under definite Oriental influences definitely opposed the demiurge to the Supreme. There is no real analogy to Christianity in the Neoplatonic Triad[1] of concentric orders of spiritual existence, but the fragments of Numenius of Apamea fairly represent a belief widely current inside and outside the church in the third century. Like Eusebius of Cæsarea, to whom we owe their preservation, Numenius confessed a primary God undefiled by active contact with the world,—an author of being whom men cannot know ; and a demiurgic Power as a second God,—an author of becoming whom men can know. So far, as Eusebius thought, we have common ground for philosophers and Christians : and if Numenius completed his Trinity by the addition of the world as a third God[2], there is a trace even in Eusebius of this practical limitation of the Omnipotent, when he qualifies the idea of creation ἐξ οὐκ ὄντων by regarding the will of the Father as a sort of ὕλη.

The outlines of the scheme being received from the philosophers, a place had to be found in it for the historic revelation of Christianity. Here again Arianism started from conservative positions. The heavenly Father was easily identified with the Supreme of the philosophers, and invested with as many as possible of its attributes of mystery and isolation. That of self-

---

[1] Characteristic is the declaration of Cyril of Alexandria c. Jul. viii. p. 270, that it needs nothing but the ὁμοούσιον to make it Christian. Is this a travesty of Neoplatonism or of Christianity?

[2] So Proclus tells us.

completeness in particular strictly limited the highest deity, so that if a Trinity had to be retained, it must be either phenomenal or heterogeneous. The next step was to connect the demiurgic Power with the historic Person of the Lord[1]. The men who had replaced the Father in heaven by an abstract ὄν would naturally confess a mere minister of creation rather than a conqueror of death and sin. Looking back however on their demiurge in the light of the historic Incarnation and the declaration of the Lord on earth, it was seen that he must have a premundane and real personality, on the one side independent of the Incarnation, on the other distinct from the Father. This excluded the temporary πρόσωπον of Sabellianism, the ἐκ προκοπῆς deified man of Paul of Samosata, and the theory afterwards upheld by Marcellus, of a mere ἐνέργεια δραστικὴ coming forth to create the world. Whatever be the Lord's true dignity, it must be his from the beginning of his existence[2]. It was moreover necessary to represent the Lord's relation to the Supreme in a manner consistent with the spirituality of God. This implied the rejection of the Valentinian προβολή, of the Manichean μέρος ὁμοούσιον, and of the old simile of λύχνος ἀπὸ λύχνου used by Hieracas[3].

[1] Notice the prominence of the idea in Creeds. We find either δι' οὗ τὰ πάντα ἐγένετο or some equivalent clause in every formula of the Nicene period except the Sirmian manifesto of 357, the ἔκθεσις of Athanasius, and the confessions of Adamantius and Germinius. It is also wanting in the Coptic and Ethiopic Confessions.

[2] Thus Arius to Eusebius, Thdt. i. 4, θελήματι καὶ βουλῇ ὑπέστη πρὸ χρόνων καὶ πρὸ αἰώνων πλήρης θεὸς μονογενὴς ἀναλλοίωτος. This disappears in the letter to Alexander; and before the *Thalia* was written, Arius had essentially modified his system by the introduction of τρεπτόν, Dorner ii. 236. Then the reward merited by the obedience of a creature had to be represented as bestowed in advance.

[3] These three heresies, along with the Sabellian and Marcellian schemes, are expressly denounced in the conciliatory letter of Arius to Alexander (Ath. *de Syn.* 16).

The hostile tone of Hilary's comments, *de Trin.* vi. 7—14, is worth notice. He treats the disavowals as fraudulent; maintaining that the real objection in each case is not to the error of the heresy, but to the element of truth contained in it. Thus the Valentinian *prolatio* is not rejected for its polytheistic absurdities, but merely to discredit the doctrine of a real generation; and the Manichean *pars unius substantiæ* for its recognition of the unity of essence and not for its materialism. Then the offence of Sabellius is not his confusion of Persons, but the Lord's divinity implied in his doctrine of the Incarnation. Hieracas comes next for condemnation, not on account of the separation which answers to one view of his metaphor, but for the continuity of nature which represents the other. Lastly, the Marcellian theory is not rejected for its folly in supposing that a divine Sonship can be other than eternal, but merely to make room for a creation ἐξ οὐκ ὄντων by the will of the Father.

THE ARIAN SYSTEM.

The positive meaning of the divine Sonship came next for consideration. Now Arius never deliberately set himself to lower the Person of the Lord. He earnestly pressed its reality as against Sabellianism[1], and was willing to recognize in the Son of God every dignity compatible with the isolation and spirituality of the Father. But on these points there could be no compromise with polytheism. Hence it was necessary to reject the higher view of the divine Sonship. Ingenerateness being the very essence of divinity, there can be no Son of God in any strict and primary sense. Generation moreover implies unity of nature[2]; which at once destroys the singularity of God. It also ascribes to the Father corporeity and passion, which are human attributes[3], and even subjects the Almighty to necessity[4], so that it is on every ground unworthy of the deity. Nor is the difficulty at all removed by Origen's unintelligible theory of an eternal generation; much less by the heathen assumption of preexistent matter. On every ground then there seemed no escape from the conclusion that the divine generation is a definite and external act of the Father's will, by which the Son was created out of nothing.

Yet the Sonship is real. If we eliminate materializing conceptions, two final results are left—that the Son is inferior

---

[1] Dorner ii. 227.

[2] The Anomœan Candidus *de gen. div.* 6 concedes that unity of essence is the necessary consequence of a real generation.

[3] Thus Eusebius of Nicomedia (Theodoret i. 6), ἓν μὲν τὸ ἀγέννητον, ἓν δὲ τὸ ὑπ' αὐτοῦ ἀληθῶς καὶ οὐκ ἐκ τῆς οὐσίας αὐτοῦ γεγονός, καθόλου τῆς φύσεως τῆς ἀγεννήτου μὴ μετέχον, ἢ ὂν ἐκ τῆς οὐσίας αὐτοῦ· ἀλλὰ γεγονὸς ὁλοσχερῶς ἕτερον τῇ φύσει καὶ τῇ δυνάμει, πρὸς τελείαν ὁμοιότητα διαθέσεώς τε καὶ δυνάμεως τοῦ πεποιηκότος γενόμενον.

It is needless to accumulate specimens of an argument which runs through the whole controversy. The Anomœan Candidus puts it as well as anyone—*Omnis generatio mutatio quædam est. Immutabile autem est omne divinum, scilicet Deus......Si igitur Deus, inversibile et immutabile: quod autem inversibile et immutabile, neque genitum est neque generat aliquid.*

[4] Thus the frequent dilemma:—ἐκ τῆς οὐσίας subjects God to necessity, while θελήσει γεννηθέντα can only mean creation. Arius rightly objected to the fatalism of the Gnostic emanations; but his freedom is nothing more than caprice, albeit divine caprice. (Dorner ii. 239.) However, Eusebius *Dem. Ev.* iv. 3, p. 148, ἡ μὲν αὐγὴ οὐ κατὰ προαίρεσιν τοῦ φωτὸς ἐκλάμπει, κατά τι δὲ τῆς οὐσίας συμβεβηκὸς ἀχώριστον· ὁ δὲ υἱὸς κατὰ γνώμην καὶ προαίρεσιν εἰκὼν ὑπέστη τοῦ Πατρός. Βουληθεὶς γὰρ ὁ Θεὸς γέγονεν υἱοῦ πατήρ, καὶ φῶς δεύτερον κατὰ πάντα ἑαυτῷ ἀφωμοιωμένον ὑπεστήσατο, and again *de Eccl. Theol.* i. p. 67 he emphasizes the distinction of υἱὸς from κτίσμα.

Athanasius answers (*Or.* iii. 62. 66) by asking whether the divine goodness is θελήσει or not; and proceeds to shew that φύσει belongs to a higher sphere than that of choice. Indeed there is no guarantee for the permanence of the Trinity, unless it expresses the divine *nature*.

in rank to the Father, and that he is not strictly eternal. As however we must not materialize the divine generation by introducing the idea of time, all that we can safely say is that there was, when the Son was not. "There was," though there was not a time[1], when the Father was not yet Father, and the Son existed only potentially (δυνάμει) in his counsel, in a sense in which all things are eternal. The Father alone is God, and the Son is so called only in a lower and improper sense[2]. He is not the essence of the Father, but a creature essentially like other creatures[3], albeit μονογενής or unique among them[4]. His uniqueness may imply high prerogatives[5], but no creature can be a Son of God in the primary sense of full divinity. Instead of sharing the divine essence, he does not even comprehend his own. He must depend like every creature on the help of grace. In other words, he must have free will like us and a nature capable like ours of moral change, whether for evil or for good. He was morally as well as physically liable to sin; and nothing but his own virtue kept him as a matter of fact sinless[6].

---

[1] Hence ἦν ποτὲ ὅτε οὐκ ἦν. Though χρόνος is omitted, the argument goes on as if it were inserted. Athanasius notes the evasion, e.g. *c. Ar.* i. 14, p. 330.

[2] Arius in *Thalia* Ath. *Or.* i. 6 εἰ δὲ καὶ λέγεται θεός, ἀλλ' οὐκ ἀληθινός ἐστιν.

[3] Notice the space devoted to this in Alexander's letter in Theodt. i. 4. It is one of the few points we certainly know to have been raised at Nicæa, and figures prominently at Ancyra.

[4] See Hort *Two Diss.* 16, 63 on the meaning of μονογενής as only-*begotten* (*unigenitus* not *unicus*). Cases like Eus. *V. C.* iii. 50 μονογενές τι χρῆμα, of Constantine's church at Antioch, are not common.

The Arians evaded its force mainly by means of the old confusion between the ideas of generation and creation caused by such passages as Prov. viii. 22, Rom. i. 4. Thus Arius to Eusebius, Theodoret i. 5, πρὶν γεννηθῇ ἤτοι κτισθῇ ἢ ὁρισθῇ ἢ θεμελιωθῇ οὐκ ἦν· ἀγέννητος γὰρ οὐκ ἦν, and his list of synonyms is almost copied by Eusebius to Paulinus κτιστὸν εἶναι καὶ θεμελιωτὸν καὶ γεννητὸν τῇ οὐσίᾳ. Their meaning is frequently discussed by Athanasius, e.g. *Fragm.* in Job iii. 1344 Migne. Earlier instances in Möhler *Ath.* 96.

In this connexion notice the Anomœan explanation of μονογενῆ by μόνου ἐκ μόνου, in the Dated Creed (also those of Nicé and Constantinople) replacing the Nicene τουτέστιν ἐκ τῆς οὐσίας τοῦ Π. The clause occupies a less offensive position in the Lucianic Creed.

[5] The Arians varied in their explanation of this uniqueness. Arius himself maintained after Asterius (Ath. *de Decr.* 8, p. 169) that he is the only creature directly created by the Father, others held that he alone partakes of the Father. There are traces of a third view, explaining it by Matt. xxviii. 18.

[6] Eustathius as quoted by Eulogius in Phot. *Bibl.* Cod. 225 was perhaps mistaken (one reading inserts μὴ) in saying that some Arians considered the Lord sinful; but Athanasius of Anazarbus comes very near it in his comparison (Ath. *de Syn.* 17, p. 584) of him to one of the hundred sheep. So the early Arians unhesitatingly declared that the Lord might have fallen like the devil.

THE ARIAN SYSTEM.

Here we get another view of the Pelagianism which is an essential element of the Arian system. Both schemes depend on the same false dualism of God and man, the same rigid and mechanical conception of law, the same heathenizing and external view of sin, the same denial of the Christian idea of grace[1] as a true communication of a higher principle of life. The same false freedom which Arius claims for God he also vindicates for man; but the liberty of God is nothing but caprice, the freedom of man a godless independence. God and man must stand apart eternally; for Arianism can allow no real meaning to the idea either of a divine love which is the expression of the divine nature, or of its complement in a human service which is perfect freedom[2].

Arianism did not stop here. It was not enough to take away from the Person of the Lord every trace of deity but an idle name. It was not enough to make the son of God a creature, and a creature not even of the highest type, but still subject to the risks of a contingent will[3]. Even his true humanity was not to be left intact. Now that the Logos was so far degraded a human spirit was unnecessary, and only introduced the needless difficulty of the union of two finite spirits in one person[4]. It was therefore simpler to unite the Logos directly to a human body, and sacrifice the last relics of the original defence of the Lord's true manhood[5].

Upon the whole the system was at least a novelty. The

---

[1] Möhler *Ath.* 179.
[2] Dorner ii. 239; or for Pelagianism, Mozley, *Predestination* 53. Notice the high view taken by Arianism of the divine free will in contrast to Neoplatonism. Conversely, its assertion of human freedom comes round to nothing better than ἰδού, τοσαῦτα ἔτη δουλεύω σοι.
[3] Arius ad Alex. in Ath. *de Syn.* 16, p. 583, εἰς ἕνα Θεὸν......γεννήσαντα δὲ οὐ δοκήσει, ἀλλ' ἀληθείᾳ· ὑποστήσαντα ἰδίῳ θελήματι ἄτρεπτον καὶ ἀναλλοίωτον κτίσμα τοῦ Θεοῦ τέλειον, ἀλλ' οὐχ ὡς ἓν τῶν κτισμάτων κ.τ.λ. Dorner ii. 235 and Hefele *Councils* § 21 join ἰδίῳ θελήματι with ὑποστήσαντα, so that the clause is equivalent to θελήματι καὶ βουλῇ ὑπέστη πρὸ χρόνων καὶ πρὸ αἰώνων πλήρης θεὸς μονογενὴς ἀναλλοίωτος of the letter to Eusebius in Theodoret i. 4. But a better point is given to ἰδίῳ θελήματι if we connect it with ἄτρεπτον καὶ ἀναλλοίωτον. The result is nugatory; but it exactly agrees with other expressions of Arius, e.g. Ath. *c. Ar.* i. 5, 9, pp. 323, 326, τῷ ἰδίῳ αὐτεξουσίῳ ἕως βούλεται μένει καλός, τρεπτός ἐστι φύσει, τρεπτῆς ὢν φύσεως.
[4] Dorner ii. 243.
[5] There is no dispute that this was the later Arian view. That it dates from an early period of the controversy is proved by the fragments of Eustathius, confirmed by the direct statement of Epiphanius that it was derived from Lucian. Passages are collected by Möhler *Ath.* p. 178, Dorner ii. Note 59.

Arian idol was as much "a wonder in heaven" as the Romish. The Lord's deity had been denied often enough before, and so had his humanity; but it was reserved for Arianism at once to affirm and to nullify them both. The doctrine is heathen to the core, for the Arian Christ is nothing but a heathen demigod. But of the Jewish spirit it had absolutely nothing. It agreed with Judaism only where it agreed with philosophy also, while its own characteristic creature-worship utterly contradicted the first principles of unbelieving Judaism. A transitory halo of divinity encircled Messiah's name in the Apocalypse of Enoch; but it had long since disappeared, and for the last three hundred years the Jew had stumbled "because thou being a man makest thyself God." Nor had the Ebionite Christ ever been more than a mere man. In short, the Arian confusion of deity and creaturedom was just as hateful to the Jew as to the Christian. Whatever sins Israel may have to answer for, the authorship of Arianism is not one of them.

The relation of the Holy Spirit to the Son is scarcely touched by the early Arians, but so far as we can find, they considered it not unlike that of the Son to the Father. If they never drew from St John's "all things were made by him" the logical inference that the Holy Spirit is a creature of the Son their whole system required it[1]. Thus the Arian Trinity of divine Persons forms a descending series separated by infinite degrees of honour and glory, not altogether unlike the Neoplatonic Triad of orders of spiritual existence extending outward in concentric circles[2].

Sooner or later Arius always comes round to a contradiction of his own premises. He proclaims a God of mystery beyond the knowledge of the Son himself, yet argues throughout as if human relations could exhaust the significance of the divine. He forgets first that metaphor would cease to be metaphor if

---

[1] It was drawn by Eusebius *de Eccl. Theol.* iii. p. 174: also by his disciple Acacius, if we may trust Athanasius *ad Serap.* iv. 7, p. 560.

[2] So Arius himself ap. Ath. *c. Ar.* i. 6, p. 323, ὅτι μεμερισμέναι τῇ φύσει, καὶ ἀπεξενωμέναι καὶ ἀπεσχοινισμέναι, καὶ ἀλλότριοι καὶ ἀμέτοχοί εἰσιν ἀλλήλων αἱ οὐσίαι τοῦ Π. καὶ τοῦ Υἱ. καὶ τοῦ ἁγ.

Πν., καί, ὡς αὐτὸς ἐφθέγξατο, ἀνόμοιοι πάμπαν ἀλλήλων ταῖς τε οὐσίαις καὶ δόξαις εἰσὶν ἐπ' ἄπειρον. Fialon, *Saint Athanase* 42, compares the Arian to the Neoplatonic Triad, the Sabellian (he means the Marcellian) πλατυσμὸς to the Stoic. The latter point has not escaped Athanasius, *c. Ar.* iv. 13, p. 496.

there were nothing beyond it; then that it would cease to be true if its main idea were misleading. He begins by pressing the metaphor of Sonship, and works round to the conclusion that it is no proper Sonship at all. In his irreverent hands the Lord's divinity is but the common right of mankind, his eternity no more than the beasts themselves may claim. The Lord is neither truly God nor truly man, but a heathen demigod[1]. He is the minister of the first creation and the prophet of the second[2], but the Lord of life in neither[3].

It is not a mere affair of logic when skilled dialecticians stumble thus from one blunder to another. The Arians had made their problem impossible by neglecting its spiritual conditions[4]. A true creator must be divine, but a created being cannot be divine. Far from spanning the infinite abyss which philosophy, not revelation, had placed between God and sinless man, the Arian Christ is nothing but an isolated pillar in its midst. His witness is not to the love of God, but to a gulf beyond the power of almighty Love to close. Heathenism might hope for a true communion with the Supreme, but for us there neither is nor can be any. Our only privilege is to know the certainty that God is darkness, and in him is no light at all. Revelation is a mockery, atonement an idle phrase; and therefore Christ is dead in vain[5].

No false system ever struck more directly at the life of Christianity than Arianism. Yet after all it held aloft the Lord's example as the Son of Man, and never wavered in its worship of him as the Son of God. On its own principles, this was absolutely heathen creature-worship. Yet the work of Ulphilas is an abiding witness that faith is able to assimilate

[1] Arian degradation of the idea of deity to a heathen scale is frequently noticed by Athanasius, e.g. *Or.* i. 10, p. 327.
[2] Ath. *Or.* ii. 68, p. 424.
[3] The self-contradictions of Arianism are summed up by Dorner ii. 243.
[4] The poverty of Arian ethics is most significant. Fragment after fragment of the *Monumenta Vetera* is purely polemical; and the *Skeireins* of Ulphilas is almost the sole remaining Arian document which is not so. But Ulphilas was only accidentally an Arian. Streams rise above their source in mission work; and we cannot judge of Ulfilas by Eudoxius and Demophilus, any more than of Wilfrid and Boniface by the image-worshipping popes of the eighth century.

Contrast the depth of Athanasius *Or.* ii. 69, p. 424 of the Son, and *ad Ser.* i. 24, p. 537 of the Holy Spirit, on the impossibility of any true life or sanctification through a creature.

So far the case is well put by Baur *Kgsch.* ii. 97.
[5] Gal. ii. 21 (but $δωρεάν$).

the strangest errors; and the conversion of the northern nations remains in evidence that Christianity can be a power of life even in its most degraded forms.

Arius was but one of many who were measuring the heights of heaven with their puny logic, and sounding the deeps of Wisdom with the plummet of the schools. Men who agreed in nothing else agreed in this practical subordination of revelation to philosophy. Sabellius, for example, had reduced the Trinity to three successive manifestations of the one God in the Law, the Gospel, and the Church; yet even he agreed with Arius in a philosophical doctrine of the unity of God which was inconsistent with a real incarnation. Even the noble work of Origen had helped to strengthen the philosophical influences which were threatening to overwhelm the definite historic revelation. Tertullian had long since warned the churches of the danger; but a greater than Tertullian was needed now to free them from their bondage to philosophy. Are we to worship the Father of our spirits or the Supreme of the philosophers? Arius put the question: the answer came from Athanasius. Though his *De Incarnatione Verbi Dei* was written in early manhood, before the rise of Arianism, we can already see in it the firm grasp of fundamental principles which enabled him so thoroughly to master the controversy when it came before him. He starts from the beginning, with the doctrine that God is good and not envious, and that His goodness is shewn in the creation, and more especially by the creation of man in the image of God, whereby he was to remain in bliss and live the true life, the life of the saints in Paradise. But when man sinned, he not only died, but fell into the entire corruption summed up in death; for this is the full meaning of the threat "ye shall die with death[1]." So things went on from bad to worse on earth. The image of God was disappearing, and the whole creation going to destruction. What then was God to do? He could not take back his sentence that death should follow sin, and yet he could not allow the creatures of his love to perish. Mere repentance on man's side could not touch the law of sin; a word from God

[1] Gen. ii. 17, LXX.

forbidding the approach of death would not reach the inner corruption. Angels could not help, for it was not in the image of angels that man was made. Only he who is himself the Life could conquer death. Therefore the immortal Word took human flesh and gave his mortal body for us all. It was no necessity of his nature so to do, but a pure outcome of his love to men and of the Father's loving purpose of salvation. By receiving in himself the principle of death he overcame it, not in his own person only, but in all of us who are united with him. If we do not yet see death abolished, it is now no more than the passage to our joyful resurrection. Our mortal human nature is joined with life in him, and clothed in the asbestos robe of immortality. Thus, and only thus, in virtue of union with him, can man become a sharer of his victory. There is no limit to the sovereignty of Christ in heaven and earth and hell. Wherever the creation has gone before, the issues of the incarnation must follow after. See, too, what he has done among us, and judge if his works are not the works of sovereign power and goodness. The old fear of death is gone. Our children tread it underfoot, our women mock at it. Even the barbarians have laid aside their warfare and their murders, and live at his bidding a new life of peace and purity. Heathenism is fallen, the wisdom of the world is turned to folly, the oracles are dumb, the demons are confounded. The gods of all the nations are giving place to the one true God of mankind. The works of Christ are more in number than the sea, his victories are countless as the waves, his presence is brighter than the sunlight. "He was made man that we might be made God[1]."

The great persecution had been raging but a few years back, and the changes which had passed since then were enough to stir the enthusiasm of the dullest Christian. These splendid paragraphs are the song of victory over the defeat of the Pharaohs of heathenism and the deliverance of the churches from the house of bondage. "Sing ye to the Lord, for he hath triumphed gloriously." There is something in

---

[1] Ath. *De Inc.* 44: αὐτὸς γὰρ ἐνηνθρώπησεν ἵνα ἡμεῖς θεοποιηθῶμεν. Bold as this phrase is, it is not too bold a paraphrase of Heb. ii. 5—18.

them higher than the fierce exultation of Lactantius over the sufferings of the dying persecutors, though that too is impressive. "The Lord hath heard our prayers. The men who strove with God lie low; the men who overthrew his churches have themselves fallen with a mightier overthrow; the men who tortured the righteous have surrendered their guilty spirits under the blows of Heaven and in tortures well deserved though long delayed—yet delayed only that posterity might learn the full terrors of God's vengeance on his enemies." There is none of this fierce joy in Athanasius, though he too had seen the horrors of the persecution, and some of his early teachers had perished in it. His eyes are fixed on the worldwide victory of the Eternal Word, and he never lowers them to resent the evil wrought by men of yesterday. Therefore neither lapse of time nor multiplicity of trials could ever quench in Athanasius the pure spirit of hope which glows in his youthful work. Slight as our sketch of it has been, it will be enough to shew his combination of religious intensity with a speculative insight and a breadth of view reminding us of Origen. If he fails to reach the mystery of sinlessness in man, and is therefore not quite free from a Sabellianising view of the Lord's humanity as a mere vesture of his divinity, he at least rises far above the barren logic of the Arians. We shall presently have to compare him with the next great Eastern thinker, Apollinarius of Laodicea.

Yet there were many men whom Arianism suited by its shallowness. As soon as Christianity was established as a lawful worship by the edict of Milan in 312, the churches were crowded with converts and inquirers of all sorts. A church which claims to be universal cannot pick and choose like a petty sect, but must receive all comers. Now these were mostly heathens with the thinnest possible varnish of Christianity, and Arianism enabled them to use the language of Christians without giving up their heathen ways of thinking. In other words, the world was ready to accept the gospel as a sublime monotheism, and the Lord's divinity was the one great stumbling-block which seemed to hinder its conversion. Arianism was therefore a welcome explanation of the difficulty.

Nor was the attraction only for nominal Christians like these. Careless thinkers—sometimes thinkers who were not careless—might easily suppose that Arianism had the best of such passages as "The Lord created me[1]," or "The Father is greater than I[2]." Athanasius constantly complains of the Arian habit of relying on isolated passages like these without regard to their context or to the general scope and drift of Scripture.

Nor was even this all. The Lord's divinity was a real difficulty to thoughtful men. They were still endeavouring to reconcile the philosophical idea of God with the fact of the incarnation. In point of fact, the two things are incompatible, and one or the other would have to be abandoned. The absolute simplicity of the divine nature is consistent with a merely external Trinity, or with a merely economic Trinity, with an Arian Trinity of one increate and two created beings, or with a Sabellian Trinity of three temporal aspects of the one God revealed in history; but not with a Christian Trinity of three eternal aspects of the divine nature, facing inward on each other as well as outward on the world. But this was not yet fully understood. The problem was to explain the Lord's distinction from the Father without destroying the unity of God. Sabellianism did it at the cost of his premundane and real personality, and therefore by common consent was out of the question. The Easterns were more inclined to theories of subordination, to distinctions of the derivately from the absolutely divine, and to views of Christ as a sort of secondary God. Such theories do not really meet the difficulty. A secondary God is necessarily a second God. Thus heathenism still held the key of the position, and constantly threatened to convict them of polytheism. They could not sit still, yet they could not advance without remodelling their central doctrine of the divine nature to agree with revelation. Nothing could be done till the Trinity was placed inside the divine *nature*. But this is just what they could not for a long time see. These men were not

[1] Prov. viii. 22, LXX. mistranslation.　　[2] John xiv. 28.

Arians, for they recoiled in genuine horror from the polytheistic tendencies of Arianism; but they had no logical defence against Arianism, and were willing to see if some modification of it would not give them a foothold of some kind. To men who dreaded the return of Sabellian confusion, Arianism was at least an error in the right direction. It upheld the same truth as they—the separate personality of the Son of God— and if it went further than they could follow, it might still do service against the common enemy.

The controversy broke out about the year 318. Arius was now[1] presbyter at Alexandria, in charge of the church of Baucalis, and in high favour[2] with bishop Alexander. He was a grave ascetic character, a man of learning[3] as became a disciple of Lucian, a skilful dialectician, and a master of dignified and stately language. When he publicly disputed some of Alexander's expressions as Sabellian, the quarrel spread at once. He had many supporters in the city, and Alexander was slow to move, needing perhaps to be stirred up by younger men[4], so that it was not till after a considerable period of disquiet that he summoned a full council of the bishops of Egypt, by whom his heterodox presbyter was unanimously excommunicated[5].

---

[1] We may pass over earlier disputes. The first stage of the controversy is discussed by Dorner ii. 231.

[2] Soz. i. 15.

[3] Theodoret's words, i. 2, τὴν τῶν θείων γραφῶν πεπιστευμένος ἐξήγησιν do not necessarily imply that he was ever president of the catechetical school. Of his personal disciples we find Ursacius and Valens, Ath. *ad episc. Æg.* 7, p. 218: also Eustathius of Sebaste, if we may trust Basil's explicit statements, *Epp.* 223, 244, 263.

[4] Newman *Hist. Treatises* 297, after Möhler *Ath.* 174, makes Athanasius the real author of Alexander's Encyclical, and is followed by Robertson *Ath.* 68. Newman's arguments are weighty, but it is not safe to set down all that resembles Athanasius as his genuine work. Alexander must have powerfully influenced his young deacon, but upon the whole it is better to accept the Encyclical as substantially Athanasian.

[5] Arianism seems to have had an important influence on the history of church government in Egypt. The consecration of the bishop of Alexandria by bishops instead of presbyters, would appear to have been already accepted by all parties, for we hear of no difficulties connected with it at the election of Athanasius. But the case of Ischyras, like the ambiguous position of the *chorepiscopi* (some sign at Nicæa and Chalcedon: yet stricter views creeping in *Can.* Ancyr. 13, Antioch 10), seems to shew that the Eastern conservatives still held no very rigid views of the need of episcopal ordination.

Arianism was also by force of circumstances a protest against the authority of the patriarchal see; and therefore easily made common cause with the Meletians, whose system was *essentially* such another protest. The one was a Greek attack on the doctrine of Alexandria, the other a Coptic revolt

Arius was too much in earnest to be expelled without a contest. He held his services in defiance of the bishop, stirred up the zeal of women, and gained supporters by canvassing (he would call it pastoral visiting) from house to house[1]. He next appealed from the church to the people in a multitude of theological songs. Their popularity was immense, and culminated in the publication of the *Thalia* or *Spiritual Banquet*[2], for which he could find no better metre than one commonly appropriated to the foulest immoralities. The excitement reached every village in Egypt, and Christian divisions became a grateful subject for the laughter of the heathen theatres[3].

Alexandria was no place for an outcast presbyter; and Arius betook himself like Origen to Cæsarea. He next wrote letters, and with a fair measure of success, to the Eastern bishops generally. His doctrine fell in with the prevailing dread of

---

against its discipline. The Meletian bishops (Ath. *Apol. c. Ar.* 71, p. 148) come from every part of Egypt, but are more sparsely scattered far up the Nile, near heathen Philæ.

The Council of Nicæa upheld the authority of Alexandria (*Can.* 6), and Athanasius finally established it. It is curious to notice the marvellous unanimity which succeeds the discords of his early years. Every bishop in Egypt must have signed the Sardican decisions in 346. Later on, about 369, they all join in the *Ep. ad Afros*. Some of them, it is true, were not present; but, as Athanasius adds (c. 10, p. 718) with charming simplicity, "we are all agreed, and always sign for each other if anyone chances to be absent."

The supremacy of Alexandria is clear enough at the well-known scene in the Council of Chalcedon. Is it too much to see a foreshadowing of it in the omission of the Egyptian bishops from the censures of Seleucia? Ten of them had signed the Acacian creed, and some of these, like Seras and Heliodorus, were decided Anomœans: yet only George of Alexandria was deposed, and none of the others were even suspended.

Many causes prevented the rise of a similar patriarchal tyranny in Syria. Instead of standing alone in the land like Alexandria, Antioch was checked on every side by the venerable memories of Cæsarea, Jerusalem and Edessa, and moreover never had a bishop whose ability will bear comparison with that of Athanasius, or even Cyril.

[1] Alexander ap. Theodoret i. 4, δικαστήρια συγκροτοῦντες δι' ἐντυχίας γυναικαρίων ἀτάκτων ἃ ἠπάτησαν......τὸν χριστιανισμὸν διασύροντες ἐκ τοῦ περιτροχάζειν πᾶσαν ἀγυιὰν ἀσέμνως τὰς παρ' αὐτοῖς νεωτέρας......ἑαυτοῖς σπήλαια λῃστῶν οἰκοδομήσαντες ἀδιαλείπτως ἐν αὐτοῖς ποιοῦνται συνόδους. So Theodoret i. 2, οὐ μόνον ἐν ἐκκλησίᾳ......ἀλλὰ κἂν τοῖς ἔξω συλλόγοις καὶ συνεδρίοις, καὶ τὰς οἰκίας περινοστῶν ἐξηνδραπόδιζεν ὅσους ἴσχυεν. Epiph. *Hær.* 68. 4, πλῆθος πολὺ ...παρθενευουσῶν καὶ ἄλλων κληρικῶν; so 69, 3.

[2] No doubt the meaning Arius intended. See Fialon *Athan.* 65, who lays much stress on the political aspect of its popularity, and on the offence it gave to Constantine. "Ce qui excitait la mauvaise humeur du grand archevêque, c'était moins l'indignité que le succès d'un poème, qui, de son propre aveu, 'donnant à des blasphèmes les couleurs de la piété,' popularisait l'hérésie......Elle n'était rien moins qu'une futilité et une bouffonnerie. Elle n'avait de léger que le titre."

[3] Socr. i. 6.

anything like the doctrines of Sabellius and Paul of Samosata, his personal misfortunes excited interest[1], his dignified bearing commanded respect, and his connexion with the school of Lucian secured him learned and influential sympathy. He received more or less decided encouragement from the great Syrian bishops Eusebius of Cæsarea, Paulinus of Tyre and Theodotus of Laodicea: and when Eusebius of Nicomedia, the ablest court-politician of the East, took up his cause and held a Bithynian synod[2] to demand his recall, Arius might feel himself Alexander's equal. Learned men defended and improved his teaching, and before long he was able to boast[3] that the Eastern bishops held with him, except a few "heretical and ill-taught" men like Philogonius of Antioch or Macarius of Jerusalem[4].

The emperor Licinius let the dispute take its course. He was a barbarous old heathen soldier, as ignorant of religion as possible, and drifted into a policy of annoyance to the Christians late in his reign, and merely out of rivalry to Constantine[5]. If

---

[1] Soz. i. 15, ὡς ἠδικημένους ἐλεοῦντες καὶ τῆς ἐκκλησίας ἀκρίτως ἐκβεβλημένους.

[2] Soz. i. 15.

[3] Arius ad Eus. πάντες οἱ κατὰ τὴν ἀνατολὴν......δίχα......ἀνθρώπων αἱρετικῶν ἀκατηχήτων.

[4] The supporters of Arius as far as the council of Nicæa may be classified thus: (I) Disciples of Lucian—Eusebius of Nicomedia, Menophantus of Ephesus, Theognius of Nicæa, Maris of Chalcedon, Athanasius of Anazarbus (Philost. iii. 15), the sophist Asterius and Leontius (Epiph. Hær. 69. 4) the future bishop of Antioch. These are all the Lucianists whom we can trace; for Antonius and Eudoxius were not yet promoted to Tarsus and Germanicea respectively, and we know nothing of Numenius and Alexander. All these except Athanasius are named by Philostorgius ii. 14. (II) Disciples of Dorotheus—Eusebius of Cæsarea and probably his friend Paulinus of Tyre. (III) (a) From Egypt and Libya—Theonas of Marmarica, Secundus of Ptolemais, and the presbyter George of Alexandria. Philostorgius Fragm. ap. Nicetam adds Daches of Berenice, Secundus of Tauchira, Sentianus of Boræum, Zopyrus of Barca, and by a clear mistake Meletius of Lycopolis. A few of these may have been Lucianists like Arius himself. (b) From various parts—Patrophilus of Scythopolis, Narcissus of Neronias, Theodotus of Laodicea, Gregory of Berytus and Ætius of Lydda. Philostorgius supra names Tarcodimantus of Ægæ, and Eulalius of Cappadocia: but when he adds Basil of Amasea, Meletius of Sebastopolis, Amphion of Cilicia (Sigedonis Philost.) and Leontius and Longianus of Cappadocia, there must be some mistake, deliberate or otherwise. Basil was dead before 323 (Görres Licin. Chrverf. 115—120, against Valesius), and all five are expressly claimed as orthodox by Athanasius ad episc. Æg. 8, p. 220; Leontius also by Greg. Naz. Or. xviii. 12, p. 338, and Moses of Chorene, ii. 89. Meletius is identified by Valesius on Eus. Hist. Eccl. vii. 32, § 26, with the historian's old teacher Meletius of Pontus, who was living at least as late as 310; and with the orthodox Meletius named by Basil de Sp. Sancto 29.

[5] It was a local policy of annoyance (Socr. i. 3, τοπικός, ἔνθα γὰρ ἦν Λικίννιος, ἐκεῖ μόνον ἐγένετο), rather than a systematic persecution. There were frequent cruelties against bishops and soldiers,

Eusebius of Nicomedia endeavoured to use his influence in favour of Arius, it was not to much purpose. But when the battle of Chrysopolis (Sept. 323) laid the Empire at the feet of Constantine, he found it necessary for his own purposes to bring the controversy to some decision.

In some respects he was well qualified for the task. There was no want of ability or earnestness in Constantine, or of genuine interest in Christianity. His life was pure, and his legislation everywhere shews that he could appreciate its lofty morals. In political skill he was a match for Diocletian, while his military successes were unequalled since the triumph of Aurelian. The heathens saw in him the restorer of the Empire, the Christians their deliverer from persecution. Even the feeling of a divine mission which laid him so open to flattery gave him also a sense of responsibility which lifts him far above the level of a vulgar Bonaparte. But Constantine had spent his life in camps, and was above all things a practical statesman keenly alive to the social miseries of the time. There are few nobler pages in the statute-book of Rome than those which record his laws. Their cruelty was a passing evil, while their genuine Christian aim was a landmark for ever[1]. He had seen with

but the Edict of Milan was never formally repealed. See Görres *Licin. Chrverf.* esp. 56.

[1] Constantine's character as a Christian legislator can scarcely be sustained by his unsteady policy of toleration; still less by his elevation of Sunday to the rank of the heathen *feriæ*. But his aim at Christian ends is clear from his action in social matters.

I. Slavery. Freedom put beyond prescription (314). Laws against kidnappers (315), against extreme cruelty, &c. (319; yet compare law of 326 *Cod. Theod.* IX. xii. 2,—"correction is not murder") and separation of families by sale (334? *Cod. Theod.* II. xxv. 1). Easy form of manumission (321), placed under the guardianship of the church. The Antonine jurists had done something against excess of cruelty, but Constantine first ventured clearly to reverse the old heathen policy (*vicesima* B.C. 357, *lex Ælia Sentia* B.C. 3, *lex Furia Caninia* A.D. 7) of checking the growth of the vile class of freedmen. Yet he retains the old contempt for slaves; keeps up the system of severer legal punishments for their offences, and restores to slavery (332) freedmen guilty of disrespect to their *patroni*. Mutilation of runaway slaves. Laws embodying older ones and substantially repeated by later emperors against connexion of senators, priests, &c. with low women (336). *Cod. Theod.* IV. vi. 3 (Haenel), *ex ancilla vel ancillæ filia, vel liberta vel libertæ filia, sive Romana facta seu Latina, vel scenica vel scenicæ filia, vel ex tabernaria vel ex tabernariæ filia, vel humili vel abjecta, vel lenonis aut arenarii filia, vel quæ mercimoniis publicis præfuit.* The list is quoted by Marcian in 454 Nov. tit. 4, 1, but the changed tone of his law is significant. Such marriages forbidden also to *curiales* under penalty of *deportatio in insulam* by law of 319 (*Cod. Theod.* XII. i. 6, *cum ancillis non potest esse connubium, nam ex hujusmodi contubernio servi nascuntur*). This however partly a fiscal measure to prevent *curiales*

his own eyes the martyrs of Nicomedia: and as he watched the evil ends of the persecutors, the conviction grew[1] upon him that the victorious antagonist of the Empire must owe its strength to the protection of the heavenly Power. He learned to recognize the God of the Christians in his father's God, and in the Sun-god's cross of light to see the cross of Christ. Accepting the witness of the gospel to his old belief, he forgot that a revelation may have new truths to declare as well as old ones to confirm. He lingered on the threshold of the church, coining money with the Sun-god's name, and preaching the vanity of idols to his courtiers. Thus with all his interest in Christianity, he could never reach the secret of its inner life. Its imposing monotheism he could appreciate; but surely the Person of the Lord was something secondary. Constantine understood his own age because he shared its heathen

from escaping their burdens. Savage regulations against marriage of free women with slaves (326; or mitigated 331 by a return to the law of 314).

II. Women. Laws (312) to save their appearance in court. Restriction of divorce (331) to three specified cases on each side, not including the husband's adultery. Prohibition of concubinage (321 or 324) to married men. Savage though not unprecedented punishments (320) of fornication. Partial repeal (320) of the *lex Papia Poppæa* (Eus. *V. C.* iv. 26, Soz. i. 9, and esp. Niceph. Call. vii. 46) notwithstanding the Empire's sore need of fighting men. Yet strong class feeling against low women—*supra*, and contemptuous exemption (326) from the penalties of adultery of tavern servants, *quas vilitas vitæ dignas legum observatione non credidit*.

III. Poor Laws. The hasty edict (Guizot's note on Gibbon ch. xiv.) of 315, and the more carefully drawn one for Africa of 322, directing immediate relief of destitute parents at the expense of the *fiscus*. Nerva's law Aur. Victor *Epit.* 12, and Trajan's Dio C. 68, 5, were limited to Italy: they are discussed by Marquardt *Röm. Alterthümer* v. 137—141, and further references given by Hatch *Organization*, 34. Whoever reared a foundling was allowed to retain it (313, 329) as a slave, or (331) as a son.

IV. Respect for human life. Laws regulating prisons (320) and prohibiting branding on the face (315) *quæ ad similitudinem pulchritudinis cælestis est figurata*. Gladiatorial games used for punishment of slaves 315, but ineffectually forbidden 325. Crucifixion of slaves 314. His abolition of it Soz. i. 8, Aur. Victor *Cæs.* 41 is very doubtful.

A special account of Constantine's legislation is given by Chawner. The laws themselves are mostly collected in Migne VIII. from the *Codex Theodosianus*.

[1] If the best mirror of the emperor's mind is found in the language of his flatterers, it becomes important to notice the distinctly and increasingly monotheistic (not definitely Christian) tone of his Gaulish panegyrists. See Freeman *Hist. Essays, Third Series*, 100, 120. His Christianity may be compared from some points of view with the tolerance of Cyrus or of Messer Marco's Kublai.

On the sun-worship of the time, see refs. collected by Keim. *Uebertritt Constantins* 92—97, and on the cross Zahn *Constantin der Grosse* 11—15, and Wietersheim (Dahn) *Völkerwanderung* i. 406—414. The best general account of Constantine is by Wordsworth in *Dict. Chr. Biogr.* On his relation to the church, Loening *Kirchenrecht* i. 20 sq.

superstitions and its heathen class-feeling; and Christianity to him was nothing more than a monotheistic heathenism. Arianism therefore came up to his ideal of religion, and he could not see what was lacking in it. The whole question seemed a mere affair of words.

But if the emperor had no special theological interest in the matter, he could not overlook its political importance. Old experience warned him of the danger of a stir in Egypt; and he had himself seen with what difficulty the revolt of Achilleus had been crushed. These Arian songs might cause a bloody tumult any day at Alexandria; and if the Christians went down into the streets, they could hardly be allowed to fight it out like Jews. Nor was the danger confined to Alexandria. The dispute was not on a question of local interest like the consecration of Cæcilian, but was already tearing all the East in sunder. The unity of Christendom was at peril; and with it the support which the shattered Empire looked for from an undivided church. Even Aurelian had seemed to feel that a *religio licita* must have no divisions; and though the edict of Milan had proclaimed toleration for every form of heresy, the more substantial gifts of Constantine were the reward of orthodox belief, or rather of communion with the leading bishops of the Christian corporation. Law after law gives honours and immunities to the church, but law after law excludes the sectaries from its benefits. The Empire could deal with a church, but not with miscellaneous gatherings of self-willed schismatics. Thus when Constantine's efforts failed to satisfy the Donatists of their duty to obey Cæcilian, he next endeavoured in the interest of unity to crush them, and only gave up the attempt when experience had shewn its uselessness.

In this temper Constantine approached the Arian difficulty. His first step was to send Hosius of Cordova to Alexandria with a characteristic letter to Alexander and Arius. It presents "a strange mixture of a master's pride, a Christian's submission, and a statesman's disdain[1]." But the very strangeness of the document guarantees its sincerity. If Eusebius

[1] So Broglie i. 380. The best summary of the letter is given by Baur E. Tr. ii. 223.

of Nicomedia had any hand in its despatch[1], he cannot have done more than give the final impulse to the emperor's purposes. Constantine treats the dispute as a mere word-battle about mysteries beyond our reach, arising out of an overcurious question asked by Alexander, and a rash answer given by Arius. They were agreed on essentials, and ought to forgive each other the past as our holy religion enjoins, and for the future to avoid these vulgar quarrels[2]. The dispute was most distressing to himself, and really quite unnecessary.

At that stage of the controversy such a letter was unavailing[3]. The excitement at Alexandria grew worse, though Hosius succeeded in healing one of the minor schisms. Whether it was during this mission (Socr. iii. 7), or somewhat later at Nicomedia (Philost. i. 7), that he came to an understanding with Alexander, we cannot say.

Constantine enlarged his plans. If Arianism divided Alexandria, the Meletian schism was giving quite as much trouble higher up the Nile. The old Easter controversy[4] too had not been effectually settled at Arles; and there were minor questions about Novatian and Paulianist baptism, and the treatment of the Licinian *lapsi*. He therefore issued invitations to all Christian bishops to meet next summer at Nicæa in Bithynia (an auspicious name[5]), in order to make a final end of all the disputes which rent the unity of Christendom[6]. The restoration of peace was a holy service, and would be a noble preparation for the solemnities of the great emperor's *Vicennalia*.

---

[1] As Dr Reynolds thinks, *Dict. Chr. Biogr.* Art. *Eusebius of Nicomedia*.

[2] Socr. i. 7, δημώδη ταῦτ' ἐστί, καὶ παιδικαῖς ἀνοίαις ἁρμόττοντα μᾶλλον, ἢ τῇ τῶν ἱερέων καὶ φρονίμων ἀνδρῶν συνέσει προσήκοντα.

[3] After this failure Broglie i. 388, following Tillemont, *Mém.* vi. 742, places the emperor's angry letter to Arius, preserved by Gel. Cyz. iii. 1.

[4] The wild theory that the Asiatic school of Quartodecimans had died out before 276, and a perfectly new one arisen since under Jewish influences at Antioch, is sufficiently refuted by the direct statement of Eusebius *V. C.* iii.

[5] μακροῖς ἤδη χρόνοις τῶν ἀπανταχοῦ λαῶν διενηνεγμένων, that the dispute was both ancient and general. It is the subject of the very first decision at Arles in 314, and was quite as conspicuous as Arianism at Nicæa.

[5] So Eusebius *V. C.* iii. 6 πόλις ἐμπρέπουσα τῇ συνόδῳ, νίκης ἐπώνυμος. On the choice of Nicæa, Stanley *Eastern Church*, 88—91.

[6] We hear nothing of the Donatists. They had been tolerably quiet for some years; and Constantine was wise enough to leave them out of the Nicene programme.

THE COUNCIL OF NICÆA.

The idea of an œcumenical council may well have been Constantine's own. It bears the stamp of a statesman's imperial and far-reaching policy, and is of a piece with the whole of the emperor's life. Smaller councils had been a constant resource in smaller disputes; and Constantine hoped (notwithstanding his experience at Arles) that if the bishops could only be brought to some decision, all the churches would follow it.

It is needless here to analyse the imposing list of bishops present from almost every province of the Empire[1], and some from beyond its frontiers in the far East and North. We need only note the Eastern character of the assembly[2], and the large number of confessors present[3]. And if the bishops were not usually men of learning, they were not on that account any the less competent witnesses to the actual belief of their churches[4]. Little as the issue of the council satisfied him, Eusebius is full of genuine enthusiasm over his majestic roll of churches far and near, from the extremity of Europe to the furthest ends of Asia. Not without the Holy Spirit's guidance did that august assembly meet. Like the apostolic choir, like the Pentecostal gathering the fathers of Nicæa seemed to their own contemporaries; and we cannot wonder if the old historian turned away from the noisy bickerings of after years to recall the glorious hope which gathered round the council's meeting[5]. Nor was that day a day of hope for the church of God alone, but also for the world. The Empire seemed to forget its ancient sickness now that it was at last confronted with its mysterious antagonist. The old world faced the new, and all was ready for

---

[1] Every diocese was represented except Britain, though we know only of single bishops from Spain, Gaul, Africa, Italy, Illyricum and Dacia. From outside the Empire we have John the Persian, Cathirius (name corrupt) of Bosporus, and Theophilus the Goth.

[2] We can only trace seven bishops from the West; and in any case there cannot have been very many.

[3] We can name for certain Hosius of Cordova, Paul of Neocæsarea, Paphnutius and Potammon. Eustathius of Antioch is vouched for by Athanasius, *Hist. Ar.* 4, p. 274, Macedonius of Mopsuestia by the Eusebians at Philippopolis (Hilary *Fragm.* III.); and the only reflection on the confessorship of Eusebius of Cæsarea is Potammon's taunt at Tyre, which is rejected by Semisch in Herzog *Realencycl.*, and with emphasis by Lightfoot, *Eusebius of Cæsarea.* A few more are given by Niceph. Call. viii. 14, but some of them at least are unhistorical.

[4] The ignorance of the bishops was exaggerated (Socr. i. 8) by Sabinus of Heraclea. It is also alluded to by the Homœans at Sirmium.

[5] Eus. *V. C.* iii. 5—9.

the league which joined the names of Rome and Christendom, and made the sway of Christ and Cæsar one.

All parties seem to have agreed to deal with the controversy by issuing a new creed; by no means for popular use, but as a universal test of orthodoxy to be signed by bishops upon occasion. Christendom as yet had no authoritative creed at all. There was a traditional Rule of Faith, and there was a final standard of doctrine in Scripture; but there was no acknowledged and authoritative Symbol. Different churches had varying creeds ($\pi l \sigma \tau \epsilon \iota s$[1]) for catechetical use, besides the proper baptismal professions made by the catechumen with his own lips. Some of these were ancient, and some of widespread use[2], and all were couched in the words of Scripture, and all variously modelled on the Lord's Baptismal Formula (Matt. xxviii. 19). But there was no universal Symbol. With existing forms it was not proposed to interfere; but it was none the less a momentous change to draw up a single document as a standard of orthodoxy for the whole of Christendom, to put an end not only to this but to all future controversies. The plan seems Constantine's own, like that of the œcumenical council itself; but all parties entered into it, and only the wording remained to be decided upon.

The Arians had come full of hope to the council. They were confident that the bishops would accept or at least allow their doctrine. They had powerful friends at court, and an influential connexion in the learned Lucianic circle. They reckoned also on the unwillingness of the conservatives to exclude opinions which tradition had never expressly condemned. Their confidence must have received some rude shocks in the preliminary conferences[3], but few could have foreseen that on the day of the decisive meeting, the great heresy could not muster twenty votes in support of an Arianizing creed presented by Eusebius of Nicomedia. The bishops raised an angry

---

[1] The Nicene Creed itself is regularly called $\pi l \sigma \tau \iota s$ or $\mu \acute{a} \theta \eta \mu a$: never $\sigma \acute{\nu} \mu \beta o \lambda o \nu$ (except in *Can. Laod.* 7) till its conversion into a baptismal profession in the next century. See Caspari *Quellen* i. 24.

[2] The Roman creed of Marcellus is an instance, if we can accept Caspari's theory (*Quellen* iii.) of its origin.

[3] Required by the duration of the council, and implied by Soz. i. 17, $\dot{\eta} \mu \acute{\epsilon} \rho a \nu$ $\ddot{\omega} \rho \iota \sigma \epsilon$, $\kappa a \theta$' $\ddot{\eta} \nu$ $\dot{\epsilon} \chi \rho \hat{\eta} \nu$ $\lambda \hat{\nu} \sigma a \iota$ $\tau \grave{a}$ $\dot{a} \mu \phi \iota \sigma \beta \eta \tau o \acute{\nu} \mu \epsilon \nu a$. $\pi \rho \grave{o}$ $\delta \grave{\epsilon}$ $\tau \hat{\eta} s$ $\pi \rho o \theta \epsilon \sigma \mu \acute{\iota} a s$ $\sigma \nu \nu \iota \acute{o} \nu \tau \epsilon s$ $\kappa a \theta$' $\dot{\epsilon} a \nu \tau o \grave{\nu} s$ $o \dot{\iota}$ $\dot{\epsilon} \pi \acute{\iota} \sigma \kappa o \pi o \iota$, $\kappa . \tau . \lambda$.

clamour, and tore it in pieces. Thereupon we are told that Arius was abandoned by all but five of his supporters[1].

This was decisive. Arianism was condemned by a crushing majority; and it only remained to formulate the decision. But here began the difficulty. The conservatives[2] were really shocked at what had been read before them, and could not refuse to agree with Athanasius, that such 'blasphemies' were not to be allowed. Their doubt was rather whether sound policy[3] required their conclusions to be embodied in the new creed, and whether any direct condemnation of Arianism might not involve dangers on the Sabellian side.

At this point Eusebius of Cæsarea came forward. Though neither a great man nor a clear thinker, he was much the most learned member of the council. He occupied an important see, stood high in the emperor's favour, and with regard to doctrine held a conservative position which commanded general respect by its safe moderation[4]. He agreed with Arius in the current belief that God is absolutely one, essentially mysterious and entirely separate from a world which cannot bear his touch. He agreed again that the idea of divinity is complete in the Father, so that the Trinity is from the will only of God. Hence if the separate personality of the Son is to be maintained against Sabellius, it was impossible to allow him full eternity. So far Eusebius went with Arius; but here he stopped. Instead of drawing the inference that the Lord is only a creature, he preferred to regard him as the personal copy of the divine attributes, as the $\delta\epsilon\upsilon\tau\epsilon\rho\epsilon\acute{\upsilon}\omega\nu$ $\theta\epsilon\grave{o}s$ begotten

---

[1] Eustathius ap. Theodoret, i. 7, 8. De Broglie ii. 36 has a theory that the rejected creed was that of Eusebius of Cæsarea. But this, as Neander iv. 22 decisively remarks, contained nothing which could offend the conservatives.

[2] It may be convenient here to dissociate my use of the word *conservative* from Dr Abbott's in his *Oxford Sermons*, 1879. I am transferring to ecclesiastical matters the broad meaning which the word is supposed to bear in English politics, as indicating a class of men more inclined than others to acquiesce in an existing state of things. In the Nicene age the new idea which claimed admittance was that of hypostatic distinctions: in our own (according to Dr Abbott) it seems to be the full coordination of Nature with Revelation. His division therefore turns on questions unknown to the Nicene age, where he would have to set down all parties as substantially conservative.

[3] So Hort *Two Diss.* 56 n, though referring to the next stage of the debate.

[4] His position at the council is well drawn from one point of view by Fialon *Saint Ath.* 122.

ineffably of the Father's will before the ages. Thus the eternal generation was no longer an intemporal relation as Origen had understood it, but a pretemporal act of will; and the only escape from the Arian ἦν ποτὲ ὅτε οὐκ ἦν was to lay stress on its mysterious nature, and to contemplate it from the side of cause rather than from that of time.

To a man of this sort it seemed a natural course to fall back upon the authority of some older creed such as all could sign. Eusebius therefore laid before the council that of his own church of Cæsarea, which he had himself learned as a catechumen and since taught as presbyter and bishop. It is a short and simple document, admirably recommended to conservative feeling by its scriptural language and prudent evasion of the question before the council. In character[1] it belongs to the previous century, going back even behind Tertullian in emphasizing the Logos doctrine rather than the eternal Sonship. Arianism it ignored. Its πρωτότοκον πάσης κτίσεως and its πρὸ πάντων τῶν αἰώνων might mean "begotten (not eternally, but) before other things were created[2]." Its θεὸν ἐκ θεοῦ was no more than Arius had repeatedly confessed, while its solitary σαρκωθέντα left the whole doctrine of the Incarnation in uncertainty[3]. To this document Eusebius added a protest of his own (Πατέρα ἀληθῶς Πατέρα κ.τ.λ., quoting Matt. xxviii. 19) modelled on the creed of Lucian[4], and directed mainly against the Sabellianism he most feared.

Had the council been drawing up a creed for popular use, a short and simple document of this kind would have been

---

[1] The Cæsarean creed is best discussed by Hort *Two Dissertations* 54—71. His account of the council seems unassailable, and we can only regret that a complete narrative of it was no part of his plan.

[2] προαιώνιον rather than ἀΐδιον.

[3] The word σαρκωθέντα by itself is very rare in creeds. It occurs as a various reading in the confession of Arius and Euzoius. The other reading is σάρκα ἀναλαβόντα, which is found in the Apostolical Constitutions and (with a change of construction) in the first creed of Antioch, and in that of Seleucia. The dated creed of Sirmium has γεννηθέντα, to which (τὸ) κατὰ σάρκα is added at Nicé and Constantinople. It is usually qualified by ἐναν-θρωπήσαντα, as in the Nicene Creed. The Arian view is clearly given in the confession of Eudoxius (discussed by Caspari, *Alte u. neue Quellen* 176—185), where we have σαρκωθέντα οὐκ ἐναν-θρωπήσαντα.

[4] As Eusebius was dead before 341, this is more likely than the converse, that the Lucianic passage was adopted from him at Antioch. He also has it in view *ctra Marcellum* i. p. 4. Asterius had it *id.* p. 19.

suitable enough. The undecided bishops received it with delight. It contained none of the vexatious technical terms which had done all the mischief—nothing but familiar Scripture, which the least learned of them could understand. So far as Arianism might mean to deny the Lord's divinity, it was clearly condemned already, and the whole question might now be safely left at rest behind the ambiguities of the Cæsarean creed. So it was accepted at once. Marcellus himself could find no fault with its doctrine, and the Arians were glad now to escape a direct condemnation. But unanimity of this sort, which really decided nothing, was not what Athanasius and Marcellus wanted. They had not come to the council to haggle over compromises, but to cast out the blasphemer, and they were resolved to do it effectually.

Hardly a more momentous resolution can be found in history. The whole future of Christianity was determined by it; and we must fairly face the question whether Athanasius was right or not. Would it not have been every way better to rest satisfied with the great moral victory already gained? When heathens were pressing into the church in crowds, was that a suitable time to offend them with a solemn proclamation of the very doctrine which chiefly kept them back? It was, moreover, a dangerous policy to insist on measures for which even Christian opinion was not ripe, and it led directly to the gravest troubles in the churches—troubles of which no man then living was to see the end. The first half century of prelude was a war of giants; but the main contest opened at Nicæa is not ended yet, or like to end before the Lord himself shall come to end it. It was the decision of Athanasius which made half the bitterness between the Roman and the Teuton, between Christianity and Islam to this day. Even now it is the worst stumbling-block of Western unbelief. Many of our most earnest enemies would gladly forget their enmity if we would only drop our mysticism and admire with them a human Christ who never rose with power from the dead. But we may not do this thing. Christianity cannot make its peace with this world by dropping that message from the other which is its only reason for existence. Athanasius was clearly right. When Constantine had fairly put the question, they could not refuse to answer. Let the danger be what it might, they could not deliberately leave it open for Christian bishops (the creed was not for others) to dispute whether our Lord is truly God or not. Those may smile to whom all revelation is a vain thing; but it is our life, and we believe it is their own life too. If there is truth or even meaning in the gospel, this question of all others is most surely vital. Nor has history failed to justify Athanasius. That heathen age was no time to trifle with heathenism in the very citadel of Christian life. Fresh from the fiery trial of the last great persecution, whose scarred and mutilated veterans were sprinkled through the council-hall, the church of God was entering on a still mightier conflict with the spirit of the world. If their fathers had been faithful unto death or saved a people from the world, their sons would have to save the world itself and tame its Northern conquerors. Was that a time to say of Christ, "But as for this man, we know not whence he is[1]"?

The Cæsarean creed being adopted in substance, the controversy could be fought out in the searching discussion to which its details were subjected. Constantine proposed only to add the word ὁμοούσιον, but it was found impossible to stop there. Ill-compacted clauses invited rearrangement, and older churches like Jerusalem or Antioch[2] might claim to share with Cæsarea the honour of giving a creed to the whole of Christendom. Above all, the Athanasian party could urge that several of the Cæsarean phrases decidedly favoured the opinions which

---

[1] See Harnack *D. G.* ii. 220.
[2] Hort *Two Diss.* 59 points this out, and calls attention to the prominent part taken in the council by Eustathius and Macarius. It may be added that we find more than one trace of the Lucianic creed in the discussions at Nicæa. The protest of Eusebius has been mentioned before. It would also seem that one of the forms proposed at the next stage of the debate was a modification of the Lucianic creed. Athanasius speaks of the bishops as discussing such phrases as ὅς ἐστιν οὐκ ἐξ οὐκ ὄντων ἀλλ' ἐκ τοῦ Θεοῦ, καὶ Λόγος ἐστὶ καὶ σοφία, ἀλλ' οὐ κτίσμα οὐδὲ ποίημα, ἴδιον δὲ ἐκ τοῦ Πατρὸς γέννημα... δύναμιν ἀληθινὴν καὶ εἰκόνα τοῦ Πατρὸς τὸν Λόγον, ὅμοιόν τε καὶ ἀπαράλλακτον αὐτὸν κατὰ πάντα τῷ Πατρί, καὶ ἄτρεπτον καὶ ἀεὶ καὶ ἐν αὐτῷ εἶναι ἀδιαιρέτως *de Decr.* 19. 20, and again οὐ κτίσμα ἀλλὰ δύναμιν, σοφίαν μόνην τοῦ Πατρὸς καὶ εἰκόνα ἀΐδιον ἀπαράλλακτον κατὰ πάντα τοῦ Πατρὸς καὶ Θεὸν ἀληθινόν, *ad Afros* 5. Is it too much to see behind these passages a reference to the Lucianic creed, especially to its central phrase οὐσίας ἀπαράλλακτον εἰκόνα? Of course οὐσίας would be dropped at this stage of the debate.

THE NICENE CREED.

it had been agreed to condemn. Ultimately changes were made, falling conveniently into six groups.

(*a*) Its τὸν τῶν ἁπάντων ὁρατῶν τε καὶ ἀοράτων ποιητήν, which might imply the creation of the Son and the Holy Spirit[1], was softened by the substitution of πάντων.

(*b*) The Sonship was thrown to the front, referring all subsequent clauses to the Son instead of the Logos. We find no trace of any objection to this, though the council might have divided strangely on it, with Arius and Athanasius on one side, Eusebius and Marcellus on the other.

(*c*) As this brought the words γεννηθέντα ἐκ τοῦ πατρὸς μονογενῆ next to θεὸν ἐκ θεοῦ, it was decided to qualify *both* by the insertion of the new clause τουτέστιν ἐκ τῆς οὐσίας τοῦ Πατρός, as a parenthesis which "while chiefly limiting the sense of ἐκ τοῦ πατρός, limited also the sense of μονογενῆ, as against the Homœousians, and at the same time compelled μονογενῆ into a subsidiary limitation of ἐκ τοῦ πατρός, as against the Anomœans[2]."

(*d*) Dropping ζωὴν ἐκ ζωῆς and πρωτότοκον πάσης κτίσεως, the Nicene Creed inserts θεὸν ἀληθινὸν ἐκ θεοῦ ἀληθινοῦ : then, parallel to γεννηθέντα ἐκ τοῦ πατρός, it resumes—γεννηθέντα οὐ ποιηθέντα, ὁμοούσιον τῷ πατρί, carefully contrasting the two participles which the Arians so industriously confused.

(*e*) The dangerous σαρκωθέντα was explained by the addition of ἐνανθρωπήσαντα. Thus the Lord took something more than a mere human body : but it was left undecided whether he assumed human nature or merely entered into union with a man. Nestorian error on the Incarnation is still left open, but Arian is shut out[3].

(*f*) The anathemas were added—τοὺς δὲ λέγοντας ὅτι ἦν ποτὲ ὅτε οὐκ ἦν, καὶ πρὶν γεννηθῆναι οὐκ ἦν, καὶ ὅτι ἐξ οὐκ ὄντων ἐγένετο, ἢ ἐξ ἑτέρας ὑποστάσεως ἢ οὐσίας φάσκοντας εἶναι, ἢ κτιστὸν ἢ τρεπτὸν ἢ ἀλλοιωτὸν τὸν υἱὸν τοῦ θεοῦ, ἀναθεματίζει ἡ καθολικὴ ἐκκλησία.

---

[1] The suggestion is due to Swainson *Dict. of Chr. Biogr.* Art. *Faith*. It is confirmed by the significant avoidance of ἁπάντων in other documents, except the *Apostolical Constitutions* and the confession of Adamantius. Its importance is as shewing how carefully the Council did its work.
[2] Hort *Two Diss.* 69.
[3] Swainson *Nicene Creed* 77.

Our accounts of the Nicene debates are too fragmentary to let us trace many of the objections made before the council: but knowing as we do that they were carefully discussed, we may presume that they were the standing difficulties of the later Arianizers. These are four in number—

1. The expressions ἐκ τῆς οὐσίας and ὁμοούσιον are materialist, tending to a Manichean view of the Son as a part of the divine essence[1], or else imply a third essence prior to both[2]. This objection would carry weight even in the East, and be a serious difficulty in the West, where οὐσία was translated by the materializing word *substantia*.

2. The word ὁμοούσιος is Sabellian. It implies the common possession of the divine essence, and fairly admits the doctrine of Marcellus, that the unity of Person is like that between man and his reason. If we consider its derivation and follow its use in the early part of the controversy, there is no escape from the conclusion that the word *was* Sabellian, and that the sense ultimately given to it was a result of Seminarian influence[3]. In the creed however it was balanced by the more important[4] ἐκ τῆς οὐσίας τοῦ Πατρός; and it was soon turned into a comprehensive mode of asserting a complete identity of attributes. It was needed as a direct condemnation of Arianism, and formed a first approximation to the mysterious doctrine of the περιχώρησις, by which the metaphor of triune personality was afterwards explained and

---

[1] So Arius ad Al. in Ath. *de Syn.* 16, p. 583. Arianizers usually press μέρος ὁμοούσιον.

[2] Annulling the idea of γέννησις, as Hilary notices *de Syn.* 68.

[3] The word is best discussed by Zahn *Marcellus* 11—27, 87, followed by Harnack *D. G.* ii. 214 and Robertson *Ath. Int.* xxxii.; against Dorner ii. 247, Voigt *Ath.* 46, and Atzberger *Logoslehre* 84.

[4] Athanasius always laid more stress on ἐκ τῆς οὐσίας τοῦ Π. than on ὁμοούσιον. The latter indeed, as is well known, he uses sparingly. Even in his *Exp. Fidei* it comes in only once, and that indirectly (c. 2, p. 80 ὡς οἱ Σαβέλλιοι λέγοντες μονοούσιον καὶ οὐχ ὁμοούσιον—yet ἐκ τῆς οὐσίας is replaced by periphrases in the style of the Lucianic creed). In his conciliatory *de Synodis* he avoids it: also in his *Orationes* (written shortly after: see Newman *Ath. Tr.* ii. 227 n) where it is only found i. 9, p. 325. He uses it freely elsewhere, esp. *Epp. ad Ser., de Inc. et c. Ar.*, and *ad Afros*. One remarkable passage is *ad Ser. Ep.* II. 3, p. 547, where he says that a father and son are ὁμοούσιοι, also man and man, and hence the Son is ὁμοούσιος with the Father (this is the meaning of ὁμ.), but not with created beings (contrast *Def.* Chalcedon), for no created being is either (1) παντοκράτωρ, (2) ἄτρεπτος, (3) increate, or (4) φύσει θεός, not μετουσίᾳ only. So *de Sent. Dion.* 10, p. 197.

checked: yet conservative instinct pointed to a real danger. On the accepted theory of the absolute simplicity of the divine nature there was no room for a hypostatic Trinity; and as all parties repudiated tritheism, it was hard to see how the Lord's full deity admitted of any but a Sabellianizing defence: and if Marcellus shewed his leanings in that direction, we may presume that he was not condemned at Nicæa by the party which refused to disavow his developed scheme at Sardica.

3. The words οὐσία and ὁμοούσιος are not found in Scripture. This is the argument which seems to have influenced the conservatives most of all. The policy of Athanasius was pivoted on these words: yet the use of ἄγραφα in an authoritative creed was a positive revolution in the church. It was a mere *argumentum ad hominem* to answer[1] that the Arians had set the example. At any rate, they had not attempted to put their ἐξ οὐκ ὄντων, ἦν ποτὲ ὅτε οὐκ ἦν κ.τ.λ. into the creed.

4. The use of ὁμοούσιος is contrary to tradition, having been condemned by the council of Antioch in 269 against Paul of Samosata. It is not clear whether he used the word or not[2]; but the council certainly rejected it. The danger from the Manichean side had not passed away in 325; but this the Arians had already urged. Their insistence on the fact apart from the motives of the decision at Antioch was an appeal from Scripture to tradition. In fact, it is not too much to say that the victors of Nicæa leaned on Scripture, the Arians on tradition[3]. Both sides indeed accepted Scripture as the paramount authority; but when the interpretation of Scripture was

---

[1] Athanasius *de Syn.* 36, p. 600.
[2] Athanasius *de Syn.* 45, p. 606 (followed by Nitzsch *Grundriss* 205) says that he objected to it as implying a prior essence. On the other hand, Hilary *de Syn.* 81, 86, 88 and Epiphanius *Hær.* 65, 5 (followed by Dorner ii. 12) declare that he accepted it, apparently in the Sabellianizing sense in which Marcellus understood it. In this case the authority of Athanasius is impaired by the fact that he wrote in exile, and without his books.
[3] Justice is not always done to the ground of Scripture, on which the fathers of Nicæa specially took their stand.

Westcott *Canon* 422—426 need not have condescended to quote Gelasius of Cyzicus in proof of what we may find on almost every page of Athanasius. Voigt *Ath.* 192—3 is not too decided on this point, though he seems to forget that the question was never *formally* placed on the ground of Scripture as against tradition. Athanasius never raises the question in this exact shape, for he never contemplates the possibility (how could he?) of the whole church having worshipped a mere creature from the first. On the council, Stanley *Eastern Church* 117.

disputed, it became a question whether a word not sanctioned by tradition could be rightly made a test of orthodoxy. If tradition gave them a foothold (and none could deny it), the Arians thought themselves entitled to stay in the church. If Scripture condemned them (and there could be no doubt of that), Athanasius thought himself bound to turn them out. His works are one continuous appeal to Scripture[1]. In this case his principal argument is that if the word ὁμοούσιος is not found in Scripture, the doctrine is. This was enough; but if the Arians referred to tradition, they might be met on that ground also[2]. Athanasius claims the authority of Origen and Theognostus, and shews that even the incautious Dionysius of Alexandria freely recognized the disputed word when it was pressed upon him by his Roman namesake. With regard to its rejection by the Syrian churches, he refuses all mechanical comparisons of numbers or antiquity between the councils of Antioch and Nicæa, and endeavours to shew that while Paul of Samosata used the word in one sense, Arius denied it in another[3].

The council paused. The confessors in particular were an immense conservative force. Some of them, like Hosius and Eustathius, had been foremost in denouncing Arius; but few of them can have been eager for changes in the faith which had sustained them in their trial[4]. Now the plan proposed was nothing less than a revolution—no doubt in its deepest meaning conservative, but none the less externally a revolution. So the council paused[5]. It was an immense change to issue a single

---

[1] The mere number of his quotations is significant. The *de Decretis* contains 105 in 24 pages, the three *Orationes c. Arianos* 918 in 181 pages, and the *de Incarnatione et c. Ar.* as many as 186 in 15 pages. The *de Synodis* is a narrative of events, so that it contains fewer; but the instant a doctrine has to be established (c. 49), he gives a series of thirty quotations. And these are not merely ornamental, as when he quotes Hermas, but substantial parts of his argument.

[2] The traditional side of his teaching is seen in passages like *Encycl.* 1, p. 88; *de Decr.* 27, p. 183; *Or.* i. 8, p. 325; *ad Serap.* i. 28, p. 540; *ad Afros* 7, p. 716. Möhler *Ath.* 110—117 and Atzberger *Logoslehre* 46 have made the most of them.

[3] In the conciliatory *de Syn.* 43, p. 604: but his arguments at Nicæa have not come down to us.

[4] Rufinus i. 2 *Cumque in eodem concilio esset Confessorum magnus numerus sacerdotum, omnes Arii novitatibus adversabantur.* This may be formally true: but it needs qualification for Eusebius of Cæsarea and (no doubt) Macedonius of Mopsuestia.

[5] Soz. i. 17 must be noticed here.

CONSERVATIVE SCRUPLES.

test creed for all the bishops of Christendom: and though the entire council had agreed to do it, and was actually sitting for the purpose, the conservatives were sure to make it as innocent as they could. Again, it was a serious step positively to exclude Arianism; and though they had consented to this also, they had not done so without misgiving. But when it was proposed to make everything depend on a word not found in Scripture, of materialist tendency and savouring not a little of Sabellianism, and lying moreover under the condemnation of an earlier council of high and orthodox authority, it would have been strange indeed if the conservatives had not looked for some escape.

But there was no other method of excluding Arianism. As the dispute was not of the canon, but of the interpretation of Scripture, it was quite indifferent how much Scripture was put into the creed. If Scripture was to be limited to any particular meaning, they must go outside Scripture for technical terms to define that meaning. Athanasius of course understood this, but others were less acute, and needed to be convinced of it by a fruitless search for some alternative. We have a curious account[1] of the Arian evasions of every Scriptural expression proposed. If it were Of God, the answer was "All things are of God." If the Lord were described as the Image of God, "So are we, for In the image of God made he man." If as the Son, "We too are sons of God." If as the Power of God, "There are many such powers, the locust and the caterpillar for example[2]." If as True God of True God, even this was evaded, for the Arians recognized him as true God *in their sense* from his creation. Thus the conservatives were ultimately driven back on ἐκ τῆς οὐσίας and ὁμοούσιον only by experience of the impossibility of excluding the non-Scriptural expressions of Arianism in any other way.

The reluctance with which they accepted the insertions is clear from the action of some conspicuous members of the council. Some subscribed almost openly as a formality to please

---

[1] Ath. *ad Afros* 5, p. 714. Robertson *Ath. Int.* xx. puts the scene before the proposal of the Cæsarean creed.

[2] The allusion is to Joel ii. 25 ἡ δύναμίς μου ἡ μεγάλη.

the emperor. "The soul," said they, "is none the worse for a little ink[1]." Others like Eusebius of Nicomedia and Theognius of Nicæa, who were more Arian than conservative, put their own meaning on the words and signed with a deliberate mental reservation. This, if we can trust their admirer Philostorgius[2], was the course advised by their protector Constantia.

The sorest disappointment was reserved for Eusebius of Cæsarea. Instead of giving a creed to Christendom, he received back his confession in a form which at first he could not consent to sign at all. He was not without ground for his complaint that under pretence of inserting the single word ὁμοούσιον, the council had in effect replaced it by a composition of their own[3]. It was a venerable document of stainless orthodoxy; but they had laid rude hands on almost every clause of it. Instead of a truly conservative confession which commanded the assent of all parties by deciding nothing, they forced upon him a stringent condemnation, not indeed of his own belief, but of opinions held by many of his friends, and separated by no clear logical distinction from his own. He felt that an apology for his signature was due to the people of his diocese, and explained his conduct in a letter preserved by Socrates and Theodoret[4]. It was an unpleasant necessity[5], but he made the best of it, interpreting the council's decisions from his own point of view, to shew that he had signed it with a good conscience. First he gives the creed of Cæsarea, then records its unanimous acceptance subject to the insertion of the word ὁμοούσιον, which Constantine explained as directed against materializing

---

[1] The expression is from Greg. Naz. *Or.* xviii. 17, p. 342; quoted by Fialon *Ath.* 116.

[2] Philostorgius i. 9. He calls her Constantina: but no doubt the widow of Licinius is meant. Socr. i. 25.

[3] Eus. ap. Theodoret i. 12 ταύτης ὑφ' ἡμῖν ἐκτεθείσης τῆς πίστεως, οὐδεὶς παρῆν ἀντιλογίας τόπος. Ἀλλ' αὐτός τε πρῶτος ὁ θεοφιλέστατος ἡμῶν βασιλεὺς ὀρθότατα περιέχειν αὐτὴν ἐμαρτύρησεν· οὕτω τε καὶ ἑαυτὸν φρονεῖν συνωμολόγησε, καὶ ταύτῃ τοὺς πάντας συγκατατίθεσθαι ὑπογράφειν τε τοῖς δόγμασι καὶ συμφρονεῖν τούτοις αὐτοῖς παρεκελεύετο· ἑνὸς μόνου προσεγγραφέντος ῥήματος τοῦ ὁμοουσίου, ὃ καὶ αὐτὸ ἡρμήνευσε λέγων......καὶ ὁ μὲν σοφώτατος ἡμῶν καὶ εὐσεβέστατος βασιλεὺς τὰ τοιαῦτα διεφιλοσόφει· οἱ δὲ προφάσει τῆς τοῦ ὁμοουσίου προσθήκης τήνδε τὴν γραφὴν πεποίηκασιν (followed by the creed of the council).

[4] Socr. i. 8. Theod. i. 12.

[5] Notice ἀναγκαίως twice repeated, as in *H. E.* iii. 39, where he cannot escape the subject of Papias. The prominence given to Constantine's action will not bear de Broglie's invidious inference (v. 32 n): for it would not impair the council's authority with any but the Donatists.

views. But it emerged from the debates in a form so altered that he could not sign it without more precise assurances of its orthodox import. The first questionable expression was ἐκ τῆς οὐσίας; but this he accepted on the statement that it was not meant in a Manichean sense. Next γεννηθέντα οὐ ποιηθέντα was explained as declaring that the Son has nothing in common with the creatures, but is of a higher essence ineffably begotten from the Father. Then ὁμοούσιον τῷ Πατρὶ implies that the divine generation is not like that of creatures, allowing as it does of neither division nor separation, nor change nor passion[1], but separates the Son from the creatures as a being in all respects like the Father and from no other essence than the divine, and really amounts to no more than ἐκ τοῦ Πατρός. This was reasonable, especially as there was learned authority[2] for using the word. The anathemas were directed against the non-scriptural expressions whose use had caused nearly all the mischief. Finally, the denunciation of οὐκ ἦν πρὶν γεννηθῆναι is discussed. The paragraph is omitted by Socrates; but as it is given by Theodoret and alluded to by Athanasius[3], we have no reason to doubt its genuineness. In it he first explains the anathema his own way as merely asserting the Lord's Sonship even before the Incarnation, in opposition to the view afterwards taken up by Marcellus, and already glanced at by Arius[4]. Then he gives a strange interpretation of the emperor's own, as referring to mere virtual (δυνάμει) existence. On either theory the anathema asserted what Arius had never attempted to deny[5].

The case of Eusebius is a fair specimen of the explanations to which the conservatives were driven before they could accept the amended creed, for he is all the more representative for his want of originality.

[1] Similarly *Dem. Evang.* iv. 3, p. 149, and *de Eccl. Theol.* i. p. 73. Here however, as he tells us himself (Thdt. i. 12), Eusebius was following the emperor's lead.
[2] No doubt Dionysius of Alexandria was one of the authorities to which Eusebius most readily deferred. He was a disciple of Origen, and we know the weight of his doubts on the authorship of the Apocalypse.
[3] Athanasius *de Decr.* 3, p. 166.
[4] Ath. *de Syn.* 16, p. 583.
[5] So Ath. *de Decr.* 3, p. 166. It must however be observed that an opinion resembling the second theory is ascribed to Theognius by Philost. ii. 15.

However, they did accept it. With whatever reluctance and under whatever reserves, all signed except a few. Then it was time for Constantine to interpose. He had summoned the council as a means of union, and opened it with a discourse on unity enforced by the conflagration of the letters; and to that text he still adhered. There is no reason to accuse him of any undue interference with its deliberations up to this point. He understood too little of the controversy to have any very strong personal leaning to either side; and the court influence which might have guided him was divided, for if Hosius of Cordova leaned to the Athanasian side, Eusebius of Nicomedia was almost Arian. Constantine had purposes of his own in his comprehensive effort to heal the divisions of Christendom; but we cannot doubt that he was really aiming to restore the imposing unity which had more than anything attracted him to Christianity, and not merely balancing[1] the parties against each other. If he had any real feeling on the subject—dislike for example of the popularity of Arius—we may credit him with shrewdness enough not to risk offence to the council by declaring it too openly. If he attempted to force a view of his own on the undecided centre, half Christendom might resent the effort; but if he left the field clear for the strongest force inside the council to assert its supremacy, he might safely step in at the end to coerce the recusants. And this is what he did. Whatever pleased the council pleased the emperor too. When they tore up the Arian creed, he approved: when they accepted the Cæsarean, he accepted it too; when the morally strong Athanasian minority pushed the bishops to insert the disputed clauses, Constantine did his best to smooth the way[2]. At last, always in the interest of unity, he proceeded to put pressure on the few who still held out. Ultimately all signed except the Egyptian bishops Theonas and Secundus. These, as well as Arius himself, were exiled to Illyricum and Galatia; while the subscriptions

---

[1] So Fialon *Saint Athanase*.
[2] Constantine at least understood conservative difficulties, as we see from his explanation of ὁμοούσιον (Eusebius ap. Thdt. i. 12) ὃ καὶ αὐτὸ ἡρμήνευσε λέγων, ὅτι μὴ κατὰ τὰ τῶν σωμάτων πάθη λέγοιτο ὁμοούσιος, οὔτε κατὰ διαίρεσιν, οὔτε κατά τινα ἀποτομὴν ἐκ Πατρὸς ὑποστῆναι. μηδὲ γὰρ δύνασθαι τὴν ἄϋλον καὶ νοερὰν καὶ ἀσώματον φύσιν σωματικόν τε πάθος ὑφίστασθαι· θείοις δὲ καὶ ἀπορρήτοις λόγοις προσήκει τὰ τοιαῦτα νοεῖν.

of Eusebius of Nicomedia and Theognius of Nicæa only saved them for the moment[1]. Constantine also ordered the heretic's writings to be burnt, and his followers to be called Porphyrians—a convenient mode of refusing them the Christian name. This done, and the rest of the business disposed of, the emperor dismissed the council with the great feast of his *Vicennalia* (July 25, 325), somewhat profanely compared by Eusebius[2] to the kingdom of heaven.

Let us now sum up the results of the council. From one point of view the victory was complete. Arianism was defeated all along the line—in logic, on the ground of Scripture, and even in its chosen domain of tradition. So utterly was it defeated that even the conservatives recoiled from it; and its supporters never ventured to avow their real belief for many years. To the Athanasian cause, on the other hand, the gain was enormous. It was an invaluable advantage to have begun the contest by obtaining a definite condemnation of Arianism from the highest authority. In the West, this was enough to array conservative feeling in steady defence of the great council. Even in the East, the authority of Nicæa was decisive as against Arians and conservatives alike. Its creed was a watchword for the next half century. The Atha-

---

[1] Reynolds in *Dict. Chr. Biogr.* Art. *Eusebius of Nicomedia*, has shewn that Eusebius and Theognius must have signed the whole of the Nicene formula; and if so we have no choice but to reject their letter to the bishops in Socr. i. 14, Soz. ii. 16, in which they excuse themselves on personal grounds for not having subscribed the anathemas. With this letter falls its reference to Arius as having been restored before them.

But surely Constantine's allusion in Theod. i. 20 οὗτοι οἱ καλοί τε καὶ ἀγαθοὶ ἐπίσκοποι, οὓς ἅπαξ ἡ τῆς συνόδου ἀλήθεια πρὸς μετάνοιαν τετηρήκει is to Eusebius and Theognius themselves rather than to the Meletians. In the first place, the Meletians could scarcely have sheltered the Arian heretics ἐνταῦθα, for Constantine was not east of Nicomedia in Nov. 325: and if they did, the emperor has not hinted that Eusebius had anything to do with the matter. Moreover, the Meletians were restored on honourable terms, and not reserved for penance by the council.

It follows that Eusebius and Theognius were exiled for sheltering the Arians, not for intriguing with the Meletians. The plots mentioned by Socr. i. 27, Soz. ii. 21, Epiph. *Hær.* 68, 5 p. 721 were after the elevation of Athanasius. We can see from *Cod. Theod.* ix. 1, 4 dated Oct. 1, 325 that Constantine was already falling into the mood of morbid suspicion which issued in the execution of Crispus.

Jerome *c. Lucif.* (*Opp.* II. 193) is certainly mistaken if he means to say that Arius himself was received by the council.

[2] Eus. *V. C.* iii. 15. The feast however, like the *Tricennalia* in 335, was probably not held till some time after the anniversary.

nasian doctrine could now be made to wear a conservative aspect as the actual faith of Christendom, and its enemies could always be represented as disturbers.

On the other hand were serious drawbacks. The victory of Nicæa was rather a surprise than a solid conquest. As it was not the spontaneous and deliberate purpose of the bishops present (almost all Eastern, it must be noticed), but a revolution which a minority had forced through by sheer strength of clearer Christian thought, a reaction was inevitable as soon as the half-convinced conservatives returned home. This we find joined, not only by the known malcontents of Nicæa, such as Eusebius of Nicomedia, Menophantus, Maris, Theognius, Patrophilus, &c. but by men whom the records of the council never class among the Arianizers, like Macedonius of Mopsuestia, Flaccus of Hierapolis, and Cyrion of Philadelphia[1]. In other words, Athanasius had pushed the Easterns further than they wished to go, and his victory recoiled on him. But he had made retreat impossible by inserting the disputed expressions in the creed. They were a "monument against all heresy[2]" in more ways than Athanasius quite intended; for they could not be effaced, whatever offence they might give to men who were anything rather than heretics[3].

---

[1] From the Sardican (Philippopolis) signatures. Hil. *Fragm.* III.

[2] Ath. *ad Afros* 11, p. 718 στηλογραφία κατὰ πάσης αἱρέσεως.

[3] With all the veneration of Athanasius for the Nicene decisions, his writings give us no trace of the mechanical theory of conciliar infallibility. His belief is plainly independent; and if "the great and holy synod" had decided the other way, he would undoubtedly have treated it as a gang of blasphemers. So when he discusses *de Syn.* 43, 47, pp. 604, 608 the rejection of ὁμοούσιον by the council of Antioch in 269, he says "it is wrong to prefer the one council as the larger, or the other as the earlier, for they are all fathers and all fell asleep in Christ"; and proceeds to shew that the word was used in different senses at Antioch and Nicæa. So *de Syn.* 5, p. 574 and *ad Afros* 2, p. 713 he urges the weighty reasons for the assembly at Nicæa and the evil designs of its enemies; and presses its wide reception rather as a reason against unsettling it, than as a proof of its infallibility. So *de Decr.* 4, p. 166.

Nor does he consider it inconsistent with his respect for the council to hint *Apol. c. Ar.* 59, p. 140, and to express *id.* 71, p. 148, ὡς μήποτ' ὤφελον his decided disapproval of its reception of the Meletians.

He is as independent of its canons, and nowhere discusses any of them. He considers indeed *Or.* ii. 43, p. 403 Paulianist baptism invalid (*Can.* XIX.): but on the same principle extends his condemnation to Arians, Manichees and Montanists, as using the name of an illusory Trinity. He also denounces the scandal of Leontius e.g. *de Fuga,*

RESULTS OF THE COUNCIL.

If the policy which won the victory was doubtful, the use made of it was deplorable. The exile of Arius and his friends was the immediate work of Constantine, but we find no sign of objection to it on the part of the Athanasian leaders[1], either at the time or afterwards, so that much of the discredit must fall on them. Orthodoxy is as responsible for this persecution as Arianism is for that of Valens. It was not a severe one if measured by the barbarous penal code of the Empire after Diocletian; but it was enough seriously to embitter the controversy. The example of persecution once set by the Nicene party was followed and improved upon by Arians and conservatives alike, till the whole contest threatened to degenerate into a series of personal quarrels and retaliations. The process was only checked by the common hostility of all parties to Julian, and the growth of a more moderate spirit among the Nicene leaders, evident in the later writings of Athanasius and in those of Hilary, and especially in the decisions of the council of Alexandria (362).

26, p. 266 (see *Can.* I. III.), the hasty or corrupt ordinations of the ignorant Meletians *Hist. Ar.* 78, p. 309, and compare *Epp. Æg.* 19, p. 110 κατα- στάσεις ἀλόγους καὶ σχεδὸν ἐθνικῶν (see *Can.* II., and also *Can* x. Sardica), and of the Arians *Encycl.* 2, p. 89 ἐξ ἐμπορίας καὶ προστασίας, and *Hist. Ar.* 73, p. 306, and the translations of bishops, e.g. Eusebius of Nicomedia *Hist. Ar.* 7, p. 275 (see *Can.* xv.). But in none of these cases does he appeal to the decisions of the great council.

Julius of Rome is worth comparison. His direct purpose (*Ep. ad Danium Flaccillum*, &c.) is to shew that the decisions of councils are always liable to revision, and says that this was expressly admitted at Nicæa. If however conciliar decisions were really final, Nicæa should be preferred to Tyre. He also attacks Eusebius for his translation to Nicomedia, Gregory for his intrusion at Alexandria (μήτε ἐκεῖ βαπτισθέντος), and comes very near to an appeal to *Can.* 14. Yet Vincent the Roman legate at Nicæa appeared at Sardica as bishop of Capua, and in that quality consented for a second time to a canon against episcopal translations (*Can.* 1, Sardica).

[1] The council itself forbade Arius to enter Alexandria Soz. i. 20. The council of Tyre imposed a similar prohibition ten years later on Athanasius himself, Soz. ii. 25.

CHAPTER III.

THE LATER YEARS OF CONSTANTINE.

WE are now in a position to see some causes of the reaction which followed the council. If the church was not definitely Arian, it does not follow that it was yet definitely Nicene. If it was Arian, no account can be given of the council itself; if Nicene, no cause can be shewn for the resistance its decisions encountered. In fact, Christendom as a whole was neither the one nor the other. If the East was not Nicene, neither was it Arian, but conservative: and if the West was not Arian, neither was it Nicene, but conservative also. Conservatism however had different meanings in East and West[1]. Heresies in the East had always gathered round the Person of the Lord, and more than one had already partly occupied the ground of Arianism, so that Eastern conservatism inherited its doctrine from the age of subordination theories, and feared the Nicene definition as a needless innovation. Thus it was not a fall from the faith but a hesitation to define it more closely. But the controversy scarcely reached the Western bishops till it was forced upon them by Constantius. Warmly as they took up the personal questions of Marcellus and Athanasius at Sardica, they were not fully involved in the doctrinal controversy till the reaction was in a position to persecute them at home. They had no great literature on the subject, and knew but little of its history or meaning[2]. Even its technical terms were so unfamiliar that

---

[1] So Harnack *D. G.* ii. 19.
[2] Western ignorance of the affairs of the East is conspicuous throughout the controversy, and was constantly taken into account on both sides. Rufinus puts the council of Tyre in the reign of Constantius, omits the first exile of Athanasius, and confuses the exile of 339 with that of 356. Sulpicius Severus prolongs the reign of Constantine to the council of Sardica, and confuses the first and second exiles

many difficulties encumbered their translation into Latin. Therefore Western conservatism fell back upon the august decisions of Nicæa. No later meeting could ever rival the authority of "the great and holy council" where Christendom had once for all pronounced the condemnation of Arianism. Thus it was not so much a positive attachment to orthodoxy as a determination to maintain the existing faith of Christendom which committed the West to the defence of the Nicene definition. In other words, East and West were alike conservative; but while conservatism in the East went behind the council, in the West it was content to start from it.

The Eastern reaction was therefore in its essence not Arian but conservative. The Arians were merely the tail of the party: its leaders were either genuine conservatives like Eusebius of Cæsarea, or court politicians like Ursacius and Valens, who found it convenient for the time being to profess conservatism[1]. As nothing short of the Nicene definition was of any avail to exclude the Arians, conservative hesitation kept open the back door of the church for their return. For a long time they sheltered themselves behind their powerful protectors, and only endeavoured to obtain their personal restoration without having to sign the obnoxious formula. It was not till 357 that they could venture to challenge conservative supremacy by the issue of the Sirmian manifesto.

The contest was not, as some seem to think, between persecuted innocence and meaningless diabolism, but between a higher and a lower level of Christian thought and feeling, not to add of life and practice also. On one side was an advance into new ground along the lines of Scripture; on the other a fantastic theory which collected together and brought to their logical results all the still unrepudiated elements of heathenism in the current Christian thought. Arianism was supported partly by conservative timidity, partly by the heathen influences

---

of Athanasius. Even Hilary *de Syn.* 91 solemnly declares that he had not studied the Nicene Creed till shortly before his exile. His words may mean more than this, but they cannot mean less. Augustine repeatedly *c. Cres-conium* iii. § 38, iv. § 52 sets aside the council of Sardica as Arian.

[1] Socr. ii. 37 of Ursacius and Valens, οὗτοι γὰρ ἀεὶ πρὸς τοὺς ἐπικρατοῦντας ἐπέκλινον.

around. Agreeing as it did with the philosophers in its conception of the divinity, and with the vulgar in its worship of a demigod, it usually found ready sympathy among the heathen. The case was exceptional when the common oppressor George of Alexandria was murdered by a heathen mob, or when Julian attacked both Arians and Nicenes in undistinguishing hatred of everything that bore the Christian name. And heathenism was still a living power in the world; strong in numbers, especially in the West, and even stronger in the imposing memories of history. Christianity was still an upstart on Cæsar's throne. The favour of the gods had built up the Empire, and men's hearts misgave them that their wrath might overthrow it. Heathenism was still an established religion, receiving state support till the time of Gratian, a vast and venerable system. The emperor was still its official head during life; and even Theodosius was formally placed among the gods at his death[1]. Old Rome was still devoted to her ancient deities, her nobles still recorded their priesthoods and augurships among their proudest honours, and the senate itself still opened every meeting with an offering of incense on the altar of Victory. The public service was largely heathen, from its lowest ranks up to the prefectures of Rome and Constantinople[2]. The army was full of heathens, both Roman and barbarian, though Christians were not a few even among the paladins of Julian[3]. Education also was mostly heathen, turning on

[1] References are given by Sievers *Studien* 333. Claudian's picture of the apothesis is a passage few readers will forget.

[2] It will be enough to name the Roman prefects Vettius Prætextatus, Olybrius and Symmachus, Themistius and Optatus of Constantinople, and the Eastern prefect Sallust, to whom the Empire was offered at the death of Julian.

[3] Their coryphæus, the Gothic hero Arinthæus, died a Christian (Basil *Ep*. 269, to his widow). Sebastian the *dux Aegypti* in 357, of whom Eunapius p. 110 and Ammianus xxx. 10, 3 speak so well, was a Manichee, as Athanasius continually reminds us (e.g. *Hist. Ar*. 59, p. 300, Μανιχαῖον ὄντα καὶ ἀσελγῆ

νεώτερον), and perished on the field of Hadrianople just in time to escape the Theodosian persecution. Victor, the cautious Sarmatian who almost alone drew off a remnant from the slaughter, was a Christian some years before (Basil *Epp*. 152, 153); and Theodoret *H. E.* iv. 33 joins him with Arinthæus and Trajan in an orthodox remonstrance to Valens. Palladius *Hist. Laus*. c. 145 gives Trajan an ascetic wife Candida: but Palladius is more often romancing than not. The cases of Jovian the *primus domesticorum* and of Valentinian are well known: if their confessorship is doubtful, their faith is not. With them legend joins the Persian refugee Hormisdas. Lupicinus the persecutor of the Massalians .

heathen classics and taught by heathen rhetoricians[1] like Themistius, "the king of eloquence," or Libanius, the honoured friend of Basil as well as Julian[2]. Above all, society in the Nicene age was heathen to an extent we can scarcely realize. The two religions were often so strangely intermingled that it is hard to say which was which. The heathens on one side never quite understood the idea of an exclusive worship; while on the other, crowds of nominal Christians thought it quite enough to appear in church once or twice a year, and lived exactly like the heathen round them, steeped in superstitions like their neighbours, attending freely their immoral games and dances[3], and sharing in the sins resulting from them. This free intercourse had its good side in the easy transition from one system to the other[4]; but it undoubtedly heathenized the church. The penitential discipline helped to increase the evil by its impolitic severity. One set of men merely deferred indefinitely the baptism which

in Melitene was a Christian, if we can trust the allusion of Theodoret *Hist. Rel.* p. 1213. Nothing seems recorded of Dagalaifus, of the traitor Agilo, or of Constantine's veteran Arbetio, who rose from the ranks to be the conqueror of Procopius, though the Chalcedon commission (Ammianus xxii. 3. 1) was hardly the place for a Christian. Julian's barbarian (Ammianus xxi. 10. 8) consul Nevitta was pretty certainly a heathen, and it is not easy to see how his heathen colleague Mamertinus has found a place in Migne's *Patrologia*. We may also set down Procopius as at least suspected of heathenism.

Sievers *Libanius* 109 notices the barbarian element in the army as a heathen influence. But it was hardly so before the battle of Hadrianople. Bacurius the Iberian was a zealous Christian; and we have already named Victor and Arinthæus. The barbarian generals are more decidedly heathen in the time of Theodosius. Fravitta, Bauto, Richomer, Saul and Arbogast may more than balance the Christians, Gaïnas, Modarius and Stilicho.

[1] Proæresius at Athens and Marius Victorinus at Rome were the only Christian rhetoricians of note. Hardly one of the Bordeaux professors named by Ausonius can be identified as a Christian; and the Christianity of Ausonius himself is the very thinnest whitewash.

The expulsion of the Apollinarii Socr. ii. 46, Soz. vi. 25 by Theodotus of Laodicea will illustrate Christian scruples.

[2] Sievers *Libanius* 294 accepts part of the correspondence with Basil as genuine, and points out p. 291 a letter to Amphilochius of Iconium.

[3] Heathen feasts scandalously immoral. Objected to by better class of heathens Friedländer *Sittengesch.* i. 473, e.g. Julian at Antioch. Clergy ordered *Can.* Laod. 54 to withdraw before the performers came in. Passages collected by Mayor on Juv. xi. 162. For the time of Theodosius, a good summary of superstitions will be found in P. E. Müller *Comm. Historica de Genio Moribus et Luxu ævi Theodosiani*, Hafniæ 1797, pp. 34—37.

[4] The change was easy to philosophers like Hecebolius (and plenty more in Julian's time, if we may trust Asterius of Amasea), or to men of the world like Modestus or Elpidius. Reversely, Synesius and Chrysostom had no difficulty in exchanging their ambiguous life for an unequivocal profession of Christianity.

brought them under it, while another caused much confusion by their efforts to escape from it[1]. Arianism therefore found a large class of superstitious or undecided men to whom it seemed to impart the strength of Christianity without requiring them entirely to abandon their heathen thoughts and lives. So far then as heathen influences were enlisted in the strife, they decidedly supported Arianism.

Nor was the leaning of the philosophers a trifling advantage on the Arian side. We undervalue the philosophy of the fourth century, if we measure its charm for the imagination by its want of power to control the multitude. Its chosen votaries could still compare with the ancient worthies. If Plotinus and Iamblichus cannot rank with Plato, they rise above many intervening generations. Nor had it wholly lost its moral power. With all its wavering superstition and unclean frivolity[2], heathen society was hardly so corrupt in the Nicene age as in that of Tacitus. Humanity and truth still flourished in the common life of mankind, and vice and cruelty were still noted by the common conscience of the world. Even from the gloomy record of Ammianus we can see that the Empire never wanted yet for brave and faithful soldiers to keep alive the old tradition of Roman discipline and self-devotion —men too good for a jealous and ungrateful master like Constantius[3]. Libanius could intercede for Antioch as well as Flavian; and if we are to honour uprightness and purity, we must confess that Julian himself was not wholly an unworthy servant of the Lord he scorned. What philosophy had lost in originality and vigour, it had gained in antiquity and imposing comprehensiveness, now that it had leagued together all the failing powers of the ancient world against a rival not of this world. The Pantheon of Iamblichus was huge and irregular, with halls for the philosopher and shrines for the devotee— buildings of every age piled and heaped together, and forming

---

[1] Arian discipline was probably none of the strictest: and we hear much of their reception of black sheep like Asterius and Leontius. Each camp most likely contained abundance of deserters.

[2] It is not for nothing that the Apostle puts idolatry next to ἀκαθαρσία and ἀσέλγεια. On this as the *practical* meaning of heathenism, Rendall *Julian* 255—262.

[3] Merivale *Romans under the Empire* vi. 454 has a fine protest against the depreciation of heathen morality even in the *colluvio Neroniani sæculi*.

JEWISH INFLUENCE.

a colossal whole whose incongruities are lost in sheer awe of its stupendous vastness. Its porch bore Plato's name, but Egyptian sphinxes guarded its approach, and clouds of Oriental incense floated through its endless colonnades. Philosophers of every school could walk its ample courts, and all the gods of earth find room in its innumerable sanctuaries. Even the Galilean God was welcome also to his honourable place in the host of heaven. Neoplatonism still confronted Christianity on equal terms. It was not yet clear that heathenism was a beaten enemy. Its slow retreat was covered by a formidable rearguard; and on a world-wide field of battle, it was hard to say but that the chance of war might still sway round again to the side of the immortal gods. Waverers abounded in an unsettled age of languid half-beliefs and superstitions lightly held and lightly thrown aside; and no waverer could face the terrors of that mighty gathering of infernal powers. Saints and councils strove in vain to break the spell. Emperors and statesmen dealt with magic, and sometimes even fathers of the church were not ashamed to tamper with the spirits of the nether world[1].

The Jews also usually took the Arian side. They were still a power in the world, though it was long since Israel had challenged Rome to seventy years of internecine contest for the dominion of the East. Half overcome themselves by the spell of the eternal empire, they never ceased to look vaguely for some Eastern deliverer to break the yoke of "Impious Rome[2]," who had destroyed Jehovah's sanctuary. It was Persia now; in after ages Islam. Fiercely the great rabbis resented the advances of the *Roman* queen Zenobia. "Happy the man that shall live to see the fall of Tadmor[3]." And if one Sapor had not executed Jehovah's vengeance on "Edom[4]," the second might. The Christian Empire was settling into a steady policy

---

[1] Notice for example the patronage of Sopater, Valens and Prætextatus by Constantine, and the savage laws of Constantius against magic. Somewhat later we have Valens meddling with the black art, and the doings of Pompeianus with the Etruscan soothsayers in the siege of Rome—a crisis where Innocent himself seems to have lost his head. Many of the later emperors were students of omens.

[2] רומי רשיעא.

[3] Athanasius (*Hist. Ar.* 71, p. 305: so Philastrius and Chrysostom) makes Zenobia a Jewess: but there are many indications (collected by Grätz *Gesch. d. Juden* iv. 336) that Jewish feeling was on Sapor's side, and against the destroyer of Nehardea.

[4] So they frequently call Rome, with a glance at Isa. xxxiv. or Ps. cxxxvii.

of persecution, while its wars with Persia were becoming wars of religion. The revolt of 352 may have been provoked by the exactions of Gallus, but it was scarcely unconnected with the disasters on the Eastern frontier. Rome's distress was Israel's opportunity. While Roman armies destroyed each other on the Save, the hills of Galilee were held against the weakened legions, and the flames of war spread south as far as Lydda. The last of the Jewish wars called for the ablest general of Rome to stamp it out; but the books are lost in which Ammianus recorded the victories of his old friend and captain Ursicinus[1]. The Jewish cities[2] were laid in ruins, and the massacre of Sepphoris formed no unworthy epilogue even to the overwhelming tragedy of Bethar[3].

The Jews were a sort of caricature of the Christian church. They made every land their own, yet were aliens in all. They lived subject to the laws of the Empire, yet gathered into corporations governed by their own. They were citizens of Rome, yet strangers to her imperial comprehensiveness—in a word, they were as a spirit in the body like the Christians[4], but a spirit of uncleanness and of sordid gain. If they hated the Gentile, they were not above learning his vices[5]. If the old

---

[1] So T. H. *Jebam* 15, col. 3 (the ref. is due to Jost).

ביומי דארסקינס מלכא הוון ציפוראי מחבעין

The *magister peditum* was more likely to manage the military than the fiscal oppression.

[2] Sepphoris, Tiberias, Capernaum and Nazareth were Jewish cities till the time of Constantine. Epiph. *Hær.* 30, 11; a good authority here. Eusebius *V. C.* iii. 25—53 mentions no new churches at any of these places, but surely Peter of Alexandria (ap. Theodoret iv. 22) is behind the times in making Sepphoris a Jewish city as late as 373. It was destroyed together with Tiberias, Lydda and other places in 352.

[3] Socr. ii. 33, Soz. iv. 7, Jerome *Chron.* 355, Aurelius Victor *Cæs.* 42, and Jewish authorities in Grätz (*Gesch. d. Juden* iv. 392—396). The rising in 352 bears a close resemblance to Bar Coziba's, though Jost (*Gesch. d. Isr.* iv. 199) and Grätz do not fully recognize its national character. Aurelius Victor most likely blunders between *patriarcham* and *Patricium* when he tells us that the insurgents even proclaimed a king of the Jews—*qui Patricium nefarie in regni specie sustulerant*. In any case the victories of Ursicinus must have been won almost on the old battlefields of Julius Severus, for in both wars the revolt had its headquarters in Galilee. May we venture to find traces of a ferment among the Jews as early as 348 (the year of Singara) in the marked emphasis of Cyril's warnings?

The attempt on Jerusalem in Constantine's time, mentioned only by the inaccurate (Renan, *supra*) Chrysostom *adv. Jud.* v. 11, Migne xlviii. 900 (we need not notice Cedrenus and Nicephorus Gregoras) and very vaguely even by him, may safely be rejected as unhistorical. So Jost (*supra* p. 181).

[4] *Epist. ad Diognetum* 5, 6.

[5] On the demoralization of the foreign Jews even in our Lord's time, see passages collected by Keim *Jesus of Nazara* i. 278 (E. Tr.).

missionary zeal of Israel was extinct, they could still purvey impostures for the world. Jewish superstitions were the plague of distant Spain, the despair of Chrysostom at Antioch[1]. And though Arianism sprang from heathen rather than from Jewish influences, its generally lower moral tone and in particular its denial of the Lord's divinity were enough to secure it a fair amount of Jewish support as against orthodoxy. At Alexandria, for example, the Jews were always ready for lawless outrage at the call of Gregory or George[2].

The court also leaned to Arianism. The genuine Arians, to do them justice, were not more pliant than the Nicenes: Aetius and Eunomius were as little disposed as Hilary or Lucifer to accept the dictation of the Emperor in questions of doctrine[3]. But convinced Arians were only one section of the motley coalition which endeavoured to reverse the Nicene decisions. Their conservative patrons and allies were extremely open to court influence, for some forms of conservatism are the natural home of the impatient timidity which looks round at every difficulty for a Saviour of Society, and would fain turn the whole work of government into a crusade against a series of scarecrows. This time Sabellianism was their terror, so that as long as the emperor was ready to put it down for them, the conservatives were glad to make him Pontifex Maximus for Christianity as well as heathenism. Thus when

---

[1] The councils are very earnest in their efforts to check intercourse with the Jews. For example, that of Elvira forbids eating with Jews, *Can.* 50, giving in marriage to Jews or heretics, *Can.* 16 (or pagans, *Can.* 15), or calling in the Jews to bless the crops, *Can.* 49. That of Laodicea prohibits acceptance of εὐλογίαι from Jews, *Can.* 37 (or heretics, *Can.* 32), and attendance on Jewish feasts, *Can.* 38 (also pagan, *Can.* 39). The fourth of Carthage joins in one denunciation, *Can.* 89 auguries and incantations, Jewish feasts and superstitions.

Chrysostom's homilies *adv. Judæos* are full of this subject. A few of his phrases may be noted—"Synagogue no better than the theatre. Jewish fasts only an excuse for gangs of harlots and stageplayers. A whole day not enough to tell of their extortions, avarice, thefts and cheating. Synagogues abode of demons, full of fornication. Feast of Trumpets worse than the races."

The last expression means a good deal from Chrysostom.

[2] Jews at Alexandria let loose by Gregory Ath. *Encycl.* 3, p. 89; by George (who even "gave up orthodox churches for synagogues") Ath. *Hist. Ar.* 71, p. 305, Lucifer *pro S. Athan.* ii. p. 916; by Lucius Theodoret iv. 21. It reads like the old days of Polycarp or Apollinarius of Hierapolis. They seem also to have taken their share in outrages under Julian.

[3] Fialon *Athan.* 115, one of the few writers who have noticed this important point.

Constantius turned against them, their leaders were found wanting in the clearness of conviction which kept both Nicene and Anomœan chiefs from condescending to a battle of intrigue with masters of the art like Valens or Acacius.

But for thirty years the intriguers found it their interest to profess conservatism. It would be unjust to compare Constantius personally with Louis XV—there was no *Parc aux Cerfs* at Constantinople—but his court was as full of selfish cabals as that of the old French monarchy. Behind the glittering ceremonial on which the treasures of the world were squandered were fighting armies of placehunters great and small, cooks and barbers[1], women and eunuchs, courtiers and spies and adventurers of every sort, for ever wresting the majesty of law to private favour, for ever devising new oppressions for the single class on whom the exactions of the Empire already fell with crushing weight. The noblest bishops, the ablest generals, were their fairest prey; and we have no surer testimony to the greatness of Athanasius and Hilary, of Julian and Ursicinus, than the pertinacious hatred of this odious horde. Constantius was as callous and as selfish as Louis XV; and his court was like himself. Intriguers of this kind found it a pleasanter and more promising task to unsettle the Nicene decisions, in the interest of conservatism forsooth, than to maintain them in the name of truth. There were many ways of upsetting them, and each might lead to gain; only one of defending them, and that through suffering and exile.

Nor were Constantius and Valens without reasons of their own for the course they took. Established near Constantinople, Constantius had conservative Asia behind him when he struck on one side at orthodox Egypt, on the other at orthodox Rome[2]. No doubt it was a miscalculation when he transferred

---

[1] Julian's clearance of the palace is well known. The story is told a little too favourably for him by Rendall *Julian* 154—156.
We may mention, for cooks, the case of Demosthenes under Valens. For barbers, Julian's experience. For women and eunuchs Socr. ii. 2, the interference of Basilina (Ath. *Hist. Ar.* 5, p. 274), the women on the Semiarian side (Philost. iv. 8), and the repeated complaints of Athanasius, e.g. *Hist. Ar.* 6, p. 275 τὴν πρὸς βασιλέα παρὰ τῶν γυναικῶν σύστασιν, *id.* 38, p. 290 σπαδόντων αἵρεσιν. For the *curiosi*, Godefroy on *Cod. Theod.* vi. 29, 1. For the adventurers, Ammianus xxii. 4, 3 may suffice.

[2] This point may be reserved for a while. See ch. iv.

his support to the Homœans; but an abler sovereign than Constantius might have mistaken the strength of parties in 358. In any case, it was not altogether a mistake. Homœan Arianism won its victory in 360, and kept it for twenty years.

Upon the whole, we may say that Arian hatred of the council would have been powerless if it had not rested on a formidable mass of conservative discontent; while the conservative discontent might have died away if the court had not supplied it with the means of action. In other words, the ultimate power lay with the majority, which was conservative, while the initiative rested with the court, which leaned on Asia; and therefore the reaction went on as long as they were both agreed against the Nicene doctrine. It was suspended as soon as Julian's policy turned another way, and became unreal when conservative alarm subsided.

The contest may be divided into two main periods, separated by the council of Constantinople in 360, when the success of the reaction seemed complete. We have also a minor break at the death of Constantine in 337, and halts of more importance at the return of Athanasius in 346 and of the death of Julian in 363[1].

Our first period is a fight in the dark, as Socrates calls it[2], where no man knows whether he strikes friend or foe. But upon the whole the conservative coalition steadily gained ground, in spite of Nicene reactions after Constantine's death in 337 and the detection of Stephen's plot in 344. We can trace in it three successive efforts of Eusebian policy, somewhat overlapping in point of time, but well marked in sequence. At first, perhaps down to the death of Arius in 336, it was enough to obtain the recall of the Arian leaders on meagre and evasive confessions, and general declarations of adhesion to the council. The next step, first seen in the deposition of Eustathius of

---

[1] For a sketch of the history, Nitzsch *Grundriss* 210—214, or from a more doctrinal point of view, Dorner ii. 261—271. Of the general historians, Neander is still without a rival for impartiality and keen appreciation of character. Baur is careless as usual, but always suggestive. The Roman catholic version is best given by Möhler *Athanasius*, or with less of its characteristic unfairness by Hefele *Councils*.

[2] Socr. i. 13 νυκτομαχίας τε οὐδὲν ἀπεῖχε τὰ γινόμενα· οὐδὲ γὰρ ἀλλήλους ἐφαίνοντο νοοῦντες, ἀφ' ὧν ἀλλήλους βλασφημεῖν ὑπελάμβανον. The whole summary is most instructive.

Antioch about 330, was to get rid of the Nicene chiefs on any convenient charges. First one was exiled, then another, and at last Athanasius was deposed at Tyre in 335, Marcellus a few months later. They were both restored after Constantine's death, and both expelled again in 339. After this the way stood open for a third advance, dating from the Council of the Dedication in 341. Hitherto the Nicene definition had only been threatened from a distance; but it now seemed possible to replace it by something else. The task however was not an easy one. The conservatives indeed were not fastidious, and would have been fairly suited by almost any symbol which confined itself to the words of Scripture. But if they abolished the old formula because it had caused some divisions, they could not stultify themselves by failing to secure the consent of all parties to the new one. Here the Arians gave no difficulty. They could not expect any direct sanction for their doctrine; but they could return to the church as soon as it had ceased to be expressly forbidden. But if the Arians came in at one door, the Nicenes went out at the other. There was no alternative; for when once the controversial clauses had been solemnly inserted in the creed, it was impossible to drop them without making the Lord's divinity an open question. Athanasius had staked the future of the church upon them, and cut off all retreat. The conservative creed of Lucian was therefore as much a failure as the less orthodox one sent to Constans in Gaul a few months later.

The council of Sardica in 343 pronounced at all points for the Nicene party: but its authority was impaired partly by the Eastern secession to Philippopolis, partly by its own imprudent support of Marcellus. However, some concessions were made on both sides, and political events enforced an uneasy truce for several years, during which conservatism was softening into a less hostile Semiarian form, while Arianism was growing into a more offensive Anomœan doctrine. Thus the conservatives were less interested in the contest when Constantius resumed it in 353, and took alarm outright at the Sirmian manifesto of 357. Civil war arose in the Eusebian camp; and victory fell at first to the Semiarians, who utterly abused it. Acacius and

Valens were thus enabled to form a Homœan or professedly neutral party, supported by the Anomœans and the court. Repulsed at Seleucia by a new alliance of the Semiarians with the Eastern Nicenes, they cajoled the orthodox West at Ariminum, and established their supremacy by the exile of the Semiarian leaders in 360.

The second period, from the council of Constantinople in 360 to that in 381, falls into two unequal stages. First comes the reign of Julian (361—363), whose policy was to give the Galileans full scope for their intestine quarrels by restoring the exiles. He might have done more mischief by supporting the faction Constantius had left in power; but if he really intended to set the Christians by the ears he overreached himself. Conservatism, pressed by Homœan tyranny, was already swaying over to the Nicene doctrine; so that when Julian invited the Galileans to fight out their difference for themselves, the reconciliation made rapid progress. Bishop after bishop went over to the Athanasian side, creed after creed was remodelled on the Nicene, and everything bade fair for the restoration of peace.

The death of Julian deferred it for nearly twenty years. Disregarding for the present the short career of Jovian, the remainder of this period is mostly occupied with the reign of Valens (364—378) in the East. The Western emperor Valentinian let things take their own course; but Valens was a tool of the Homœans. With a feebler character and a weaker position, he resumed the disastrous policy of the last years of Constantius. But even imperial power could not wholly arrest the natural course of events. The return of the conservatives to the Nicene faith was delayed partly by the continuance of Western sympathy with Marcellus, partly by personal questions like that of Meletius at Antioch, but chiefly by the emergence of new difficulties in the doctrine of Apollinarius and the advance of the Nicene party to the co-essential deity of the Holy Spirit. Homœan Arianism was maintained by Eudoxius and Demophilus till the death of Valens; but its dominion became purely artificial. The old age of Athanasius on one side, the life of Basil on the other, were devoted to the work of conciliation. The issue of the strife was a foregone conclusion even before the veteran of Alexandria was taken to his rest in 373. Afterwards his Western friends gave up Marcellus and learned to recognize the newer or modified Nicene conservatism of Antioch and Cappadocia represented by Meletius and Basil. This schism at Antioch remained a fertile source of jealousies; but it was not suffered to disturb the substantial harmony of doctrine which at last united Rome and Gaul with Pontus and Syria. The instant the Nicene faith was proclaimed by the Spanish Theodosius, the Homœan supremacy fell of itself and fell for ever. The remnant of the Homœans were reduced to beg for the communion of Eunomius, and henceforth a riot at Constantinople was the limit of Arian power inside the Empire. A few of the Semiarians under Eleusius of Cyzicus refused to share the victory; but when the alliance of orthodoxy and conservatism, made for a moment at Nicæa, was permanently renewed at Constantinople, the long contest was at an end. Arianism soon ceased to be a political power inside the Empire; and if Teutonic converts prolonged its existence till the sixth century, their fitful persecutions availed little to recover for their faith its lost dominion of the world.

Returning however to the immediate sequel of the council of Nicæa, let us trace the history more in detail, that we may see how far it confirms our account of the aims and meaning of the Arian reaction.

If Constantine expected the council to restore peace in the East, he soon found out his mistake. The literary war was resumed almost where his summons interrupted it. Eustathius of Antioch and Marcellus of Ancyra were opposed by Eusebius of Cæsarea, Patrophilus of Scythopolis and the "many-headed" sophist Asterius. The battle was still fought round Origen's name, and charges of heresy were flung in all directions; but the great council seemed almost forgotten. Its creed was signed and done with, and for the present we hear more of Lucian's. To Athanasius and perhaps to Eustathius it may have been a watchword from the first; but it had scarcely yet become so to Marcellus, much less to the conservatives. Eusebius for example had signed it in good faith and still maintained[1] his adhesion to it; but henceforth the less said the better about a document of such questionable policy. Even Marcellus was more inclined to get rid of all philosophical terms than to lay stress on those the council sanctioned. But the creed was nowhere openly repudiated. Both parties had learned caution at Nicæa. Marcellus disavowed Sabellianism and Eusebius avoided Arianism, as though it were agreed on all hands that both the rival heresies had been for ever rejected by the church of Christ[2].

Meanwhile the contest went on in Egypt. The Arians were not overawed by the authority of the council, much less conciliated by the exile of their leaders[3]. The Meletians also accepted the council's compromise with no good will, and so slowly that the list of their clergy was not delivered to Alex-

---

[1] Socr. i. 23, copied by Soz. ii. 18.

[2] So well understood was the condemnation of Sabellius that Marcellus *Fr.* 38, p. 76 thought it necessary expressly to denounce him, and is accused by Eusebius p. 60 of inconsistency for the disavowal.

The other side was equally cautious. When Marcellus wanted to fix on his enemies a clear statement that the Lord is no more than a creature, he was obliged *Fr.* 33, p. 27 to go back to Paulinus of Tyre, who was dead before the council met. (Lightfoot *Eus. Cæs.* p. 322.)

With regard to Eusebius himself, it is significant that his loose half-Arianizing expressions mostly belong to his earlier works, while his strongest passages on the Nicene side are mostly found in his *c. Marcellum, de Eccl. Theol.*, and the *Theophania*. Thus we have pp. 66—69 a direct confutation of the Arian ἐξ οὐκ ὄντων, closely connected with his explanation of ὁμοούσιον at the council: p. 109 explains οὐκ ἄναρχον by ἀρχὴν τὸν Π. κεκτημένην; hence the Lord's divinity not ditheist: p. 22 τὸ μὴ χρόνῳ πρὸ πάντων δὲ τῶν αἰώνων τὸν υἱὸν γεγεννηκέναι: p. 121 πάντη τε καὶ κατὰ πάντα ὁμοιότατον τῷ γεγεννηκότι. Even Möhler *Ath.* 333 has noticed his more cautious tone, though Dorner seems to overlook the change, and only Lightfoot has given him full credit for it.

[3] Others were exiled besides Arius and the two bishops. Constantine denounces (Theodoret i. 20) the intrigues of Eusebius with certain Alexandrian heretics who had been sent to Nicomedia. As Eusebius was exiled three months after the council, his friends can scarcely have escaped sharing his fate. Euzoius was undoubtedly a companion of Arius in exile; and the sentence would most likely include Achillas, Carpones, and the rest of the heretics deposed by Alexander.

ander till November 327. Five months later Alexander died[1], and his church was thrown into confusion over the choice of a successor[2]. The Nicene party put forward the deacon Athana-

[1] The election of Athanasius is clearly fixed for June 8, 328 by the Index to the *Festal Letters*. The only doubt is about his own statement *Apol. c. Ar.* 59, p. 140 ἐν τῇ κατὰ Νίκαιαν συνόδῳ ἡ μὲν αἵρεσις ἀνεθεματίσθη, καὶ οἱ Ἀρειανοὶ ἐξεβλήθησαν, οἱ δὲ Μελιτιανοὶ ὁπωσδήποτε ἐδέχθησαν· οὐ γὰρ ἀναγκαῖον νῦν τὴν αἰτίαν ὀνομάζειν. οὔπω γὰρ πέντε μῆνες παρῆλθον, καὶ ὁ μὲν μακαρίτης Ἀλέξανδρος τετελεύτηκεν κ.τ.λ., at which Theodoret i. 26 seems to glance when he dates Alexander's death five months after the council. Epiphanius also *Hær.* 69, 11 says ἐν τῷ αὐτῷ ἔτει.

Putting aside the hopeless theories of a three years' session of the council, or of a two years' interval between Alexander and Athanasius, we come to Larsow's conjecture *Festbriefe* 26 that there was a long delay in the formal ratification of the Nicene decisions. Sievers *Einl.* § 20 looks upon it with some favour, noticing that the acts of Ephesus were not ratified till September 443, and that a similar delay will explain the date 347 assigned to the council of Sardica by Socrates and Sozomen.

But in the cases of Ephesus and Sardica there are distinct historical circumstances to explain the long delay: in that of Nicæa we know of nothing analogous. It is therefore better to suppose that Meletius and Alexander were in no hurry to carry out a compromise which neither of them much liked.

[2] The various accounts of the election may be summarized as follows:—
(1) The bishops of Egypt in Ath. *Apol. c. Ar.* 5, p. 101, writing to Julius of Rome in 339. Election regular and unanimous, though Arians said it was done secretly by six or seven bishops.
(2) Epiphanius (*a*) *Hær.* 68, 7 says that the Meletians chose Theonas to succeed Alexander during the absence of Athanasius, who was elected on the death of Theonas three months later:
(*b*) *Hær.* 69, 11. Meletians chose Theonas, Arians Achillas, during absence of Athanasius, who was elected on the death of Achillas three months later. (3) Index to *Festal Letters*. Alexander died April 17, 328; Athanasius chosen to succeed him June 8. (4) Rufinus i. 14. The boy-baptism: Athanasius designated by Alexander. (5) Socrates i. 15 merely copies Rufinus. (6) Sozomen ii. 17. Longer account from "Apollinarius the Syrian" of the designation by Alexander: then Arian story (? from Athanasius *supra*): then copies Rufinus. (7) Theodoret i. 26 is very meagre. (8) Philostorgius ii. 11. Athanasius cut short a disputed election by coming late one evening to the church of Dionysius and compelling a couple of bishops who were there to consecrate him with closed doors. For this he was excommunicated by the other bishops; but he obtained the emperor's confirmation by means of forged letters.

There were three parties at Alexandria, for the Meletians had hardly yet made common cause with the Arians; and it is not unlikely that there was a triple election. In that case the Egyptian bishops will by no means be "telling a *public* falsehood" but merely ignoring the acts of minorities. If however Arianizers and Meletians acted together, the Nicenes themselves may have been the minority. Bright *Hist. Treatises* p. xxi. seems to have overlooked this possibility.

Epiphanius is an intolerable blunderer: but he has Meletian accounts in *Hær.* 68, and his story of the Meletian election of Theonas is not at all unlikely. Only Athanasius must have been chosen in direct opposition to him, and not after his death. There is more difficulty in his mention of Achillas. It may be a truly Epiphanian confusion with Alexander's predecessor: but it may refer to the presbyter Achillas, who was twice excommunicated with Arius. In that case we are in a region of conjecture. Was Achillas exiled with Arius and Euzoius? If so, was he restored before Alexander's death? If so, would the Arians have ventured to elect him?

Upon the whole it seems best to accept the elections of Athanasius and Theonas, and leave that of Achil-

sius, "the people" shouted for him, and he was duly consecrated in the face of a determined opposition from Meletians and Arians.

And now that we stand before the greatest of the Eastern fathers, let us see how he was fitted by his character and training to fight the hardest of the battle against Arianism.

Athanasius was a Greek by birth and education; Greek also in subtle thought and philosophic insight, in oratorical power and supple statesmanship. Though born almost within the shadow of the mighty Serapeum, he shews hardly a sign of Coptic influence. His very style is clear and simple, without a trace of Egyptian involution and obscurity. His character had nothing of the Egyptian love of mystery and reverential awe; and his fearless understanding, Greek as that of Arius himself, recognized the limit of its powers in no superstitious dread of undefined irreverence, but in the voice of Scripture only[1]. Athanasius was born at Alexandria about the time of its capture by Diocletian in 297[2], so that he must have well remembered the worst days of the persecution under Maximin Daza. The tales of the boy-baptism[3] and of his intercourse with the legendary Antony[4] may be safely rejected. He may have been a lawyer for a short time[5]; but in any case his training was

las in uncertainty. This is the conclusion of Fialon *Saint Athanase* 104—110.

[1] The *Greek* character of Athanasius is best drawn by Fialon *Saint Athanase*—a work of marked independence, but wanting in detail and attention to recent research.

On Athanasius, Harnack *D. G.* ii. 24; Robertson *Ath.* xiv.—lxxx.

[2] The date of his birth can be fixed within very narrow limits. On one side we have (1) his *contra Gentes* and *de Incarnatione*, written before the rise of Arianism about 318; and (2) his statement *de Inc.* 56, p. 77 that some of his teachers perished in the persecution. On the other side we have (1) the charge of his enemies, Index to *Festal Letters*, that he was under age at his consecration in 328—a charge which must have had a semblance of truth; and (2) his statement (implied in *Hist. Ar.* 64, p. 302 ἤκουσα τῶν πατέρων) that he could not himself remember the persecution "in the days of Maximian." So he calls it (and again *de Syn.* 18, p. 584 ἐν τῷ κατὰ τὸν πάππον τοῦ Κωνσταντίου; so too Philost. iii. 12), though the expression comes more naturally from the Western bishop Hosius, ap. Ath. *Hist. Ar.* 44, p. 292.

Here then are two lines of argument, converging pretty nearly on the year 297.

[3] Note A. *The Authority of Rufinus.*
[4] Note B. *The Legend of Antony.*
[5] This is de Broglie's view, iii. 37. It is quite possible, though there are few direct traces of it in his works; and Sulph. Severus ii. 42 *episcopum jurisconsultum* is no great authority for the fact. But if so, he cannot have been in constant attendance on Alexander, much less a scholar of Antony.

neither Coptic nor monastic[1], but Greek and scriptural, as became a disciple of the school of Alexandria. In his earliest works he refers to Plato; in later years he quotes Homer, and models his notes on Aristotle, his Apology to Constantius upon Demosthenes[2]. He seldom refers to Egyptian

---

[1] Athanasius is called an ascetic by the bishops of Egypt and Libya, *Apol. c. Ar.* 6, p. 102 ἕνα τῶν ἀσκητῶν, but the expression need not imply very much. He had something of the ascetic spirit of the next generation, but its traces are remarkably scarce in his writings, though the subject frequently comes before him. He claims for example no superiority for the monastic life in his letter to Dracontius, and betrays no ascetic leanings at *Or.* ii. 69, p. 425, or in the discussion on fasting in his *Festal Letter* for 329. He avoids the ascetic interpretations of 1 Cor. vii. 1, Ps. lxviii. 6, 23, explaining (*Fragm.* III. 1404 Migne) the first passage spiritually, passing over the second (*Exp.* III. 293), and referring the dogs in the third (*Exp.* III. 300) to the clergy instead of the monks. Neither can much be made of such a commonplace as *Or.* iii. 52, p. 476 ἀφίστασθαι τῶν αἰσθητῶν. His praise of the moral miracles of chastity *de Inc.* 48, 51, pp. 71, 73, and *ad Drac.* 7, p. 210 (see also refs. to ἄσκησις *ad Marcell.* I., *Fragm. in Matt.* III. 1381 Migne, where he names the ascete after the deacon) are no more than anyone might have written who contrasted them with the slough of heathen immorality. The rejoicing *ad Mon.* 25, p. 283 goes a little further. The *Vita Antonii* and *de titulis Psalmorum* being spurious, the *Sermo de Patientia* very doubtful, the strongest passages in his writings are (1) *Exp.* in Ps. l. 7, where marriage is declared to have been no part of God's original purpose in paradise, but a consequence of sin—the very opinion so strongly rejected by Augustine. (2) *ad Amunem*, p. 766 μακάριος ὃς ἐν νεότητι, ζυγὸν ἔχων ἐλεύθερον, τῇ φύσει πρὸς παιδοποιΐαν κέχρηται...... δύο γὰρ οὐσῶν ὁδῶν ἐν τῷ βίῳ περὶ τούτων, μιᾶς μὲν μετριωτέρας καὶ βιωτικῆς, τοῦ γάμου λέγω· τῆς δὲ ἑτέρας ἀγγελικῆς καὶ ἀνυπερβλήτου, τῆς παρθενίας· εἰ μέν τις τὴν κοσμικήν, τοῦτ' ἐστι τὸν γάμον, ἕλοιτο, μέμψιν μὲν οὐκ ἔχει, τοσαῦτα δὲ χαρίσματα οὐ λήψεται. The married man will bear thirtyfold, and receive gifts in proportion: εἰ δὲ τὴν ἁγνήν τις καὶ ὑπερκόσμιον ἀσπάσοιτο, his share will be a hundredfold. To this we may add his praises of παρθενία, *Fragm. in Luc.* III. 1393 Migne, τὸν νόμον ὑπερβᾶσα...γνώρισμα μέν ἐστι τοῦ μέλλοντος αἰῶνος, εἰκὼν δὲ τῆς τῶν ἀγγέλων καθαρότητος, *Apol. ad Ctium* 33, p. 251, εἰκόνα τῆς τῶν ἀγγέλων ἁγιότητος ......νύμφας τοῦ Χριστοῦ as the church is wont to call them, and perhaps *Exp.* in Ps. xliv. 16, τῆς γὰρ παρθενίας πλησίον ἡ ἐγκράτεια, and the conspicuous position given to complaints of Arian misconduct towards these μέλη τοῦ Σωτῆρος.

But this is a scanty gleaning from works of such extent. A glance at a genuine ascetic like Basil or Jerome is enough to shew that if Athanasius had been very zealous in the cause he would have contrived to let us hear more of it.

The ascetic spirit is better marked in Cyril of Jerusalem, in whose *Cateches* we find i. 5, iii. 6 general references to ἄσκησις. vi. 35 παρθενίας ἰσάγγελον ἀξίωμα. xv. 23 τὰ πρωτεῖα ἔχει παρθενία. xii. 6, 15 Eve a virgin in paradise (a frequent inference from Gen. iv. 1). iv. 24 μοναζόντων καὶ παρθένων τάγμα (implied again xii. 33), τῶν τὸν ἰσάγγελον βίον ἐν κόσμῳ κατορθούντων. xii. 25 ὁ καλῶς ἱερατεύων ἀπέχεται γυναικός. xvi. 12, 22 ascetic continence among the gifts of the Spirit, even in the case of κόρη παρὰ παστάδας. Yet neither marriage iv. 25 nor even second marriage iv. 26 to be despised. Ascetic poverty xvi. 19 a gift of the Spirit, and xiii. 5 a teaching of the Lord himself—a statement Cyril has left unproved.

It may be noted here that the passage above given from *ad Amunem* is hardly so strong as the closely allied statement of Eusebius (*Quæstiones ad Marinum* III. 1007 Migne) which Suidas under βίος has quoted with it.

[2] A few parallels may be given, though this is no place for a full discussion of the relation of Athanasius to the great

classical writers. His quotations from them are rare and mostly indirect, but imply familiarity so far as they go. From Homer we have only a few stock phrases like μοῦνος ἐὼν ἀγαπητὸς (*Or.* iv. 29, p. 507) and ἀθάνατον κακόν. From Demosthenes a good many expressions are borrowed in the *Apol. ad Ctium*: list in Fialon *Saint Athanase* 285. For imitation of Aristotle Newman *Ath. Tr.* 501. But the most important parallels come from Plato. Thus *c. Gentes* 41 and *de Inc.* 3 ὁ θεὸς γὰρ ἀγαθός ἐστι κ.τ.λ. are modelled on *Timæus* 29 E, while *de Inc.* 43 directly quotes *Politicus* 273 D, and *c. Gentes* 10, p. 9 alludes to the opening of the *Republic.* The argument *c. Gentes* 33 for the immortality of the soul from its self-moving nature is on the model of *Phædrus* 245 C, or more likely *Laws* x. 896; that for the credibility of the Incarnation *de Inc.* 41, p. 66 from the analogy of the world-soul in the *Timæus*. We have further direct references to Stoic pantheism *Or.* ii. 11, p. 378, cycles and πλατυσμοὶ *Or.* iv. 13, 15, pp. 496, 497; to pre-existent ὕλη *Or.* ii. 22, p. 387; to the Neoplatonic Triad *de Inc.* 28, p. 184. In *de Inc.* 2, p. 38 he discusses the Epicurean, Platonic, and Gnostic theories of the origin of the world, and alludes again to the former *de Decr.* 19, p. 176.

The exegesis of Athanasius is far from faultless, but it is usually suggestive. He has a greater leaning to the literal meaning than we should expect to find at Alexandria. Allegory with him is secondary and ornamental, and never long kept up.

He frequently urges the necessity of considering the speaker, the circumstances and the context of a passage, and the general drift (σκοπὸς) of Christian doctrine; thus *de Decr.* 14, p. 173, and his complaint *ad Episc. Æq.* 18, p. 228 of Arian misinterpretation. As a critic however he does not stand very high. Various readings he seldom if ever discusses, though some remarkable ones might be gathered from his pages, like *Exp. Fid.* 4, p. 81 δ ἐγεννήθη for ὃς ἐγενήθη in 1 Cor. i. 30 (noticed by Swainson, p. 78 n), and the addition *Fragm. in Matt.* Migne III. 1380 of the clause βλέπετε τοὺς χοίρους in Phil. iii. 2—a reminiscence of Matt. vii. 6. Both readings seem unique.

In the Old Testament Athanasius hardly ever goes behind the words of the Septuagint version; and of this, at least in his *c. Gentes*, he is nearer to the Vatican than to the Alexandrine text. We find only an occasional reference to Aquila *Exp. Fid.* 3, p. 80, *Exp. in Pss.* xxx. 12, lix. 5, lxv. 18; to Theodotion *Exp. in Ps.* xvii. 36; or to Symmachus *Exp. in Ps.* xxxviii. 6. His ignorance of Hebrew is evident, and often causes him serious difficulty. The whole discussion on Prov. viii. 22, LXX. Κύριος ἔκτισέ με κ.τ.λ. might have been avoided by a glance at the original קָנָנִי יְ״י. Even Aquila, Theodotion and Symmachus all have ἐκτήσατο, Eusebius *de Eccl. Theol.* iii. 2, pp. 152, 153 mentions the fact, refers to the Hebrew and compares Gen. iv. 1, xlix. 30: so also Dionysius of Rome (Ath. *de Decr.* 26, p. 182) and Basil *c. Eunom.* ii. 20, p. 256.

His mistakes are not uncommonly grotesque; like *de Inc.* 37, p. 63, where Deut. xxviii. 66 (thy life hang in doubt before thee) is referred to the crucifixion, after the example of Irenæus IV. xx. 2, and others. In *ad Afros* 4, p. 714 he interprets φωνὴ ὑπάρξεως (voice of the cattle) instead of the divine ὕπαρξις, and *Or.* ii. 29, p. 392, refers Isa. i. 11 πλήρης εἰμὶ (ὁλοκαυτωμάτων) to the divine perfection.

Other instances might be given from the treatise *de titulis Psalmorum*, if this could be accepted as a genuine work of Athanasius. Its translations of Hebrew words seem derived from some such *onomasticon* as Philo's, as we see from the characteristic rendering of *Ps.* 1 Βηρσαβεὲ (Bathsheba) by φρέαρ πλησμονῆς (בְּאֵר שָׂבָע or בְּאֵר שֶׂבַע); but they are quite independent of the *Exp. in Pss.*, and are not even tolerably consistent with themselves. For some words indeed a different rendering is given almost every time of their occurrence. Ephraim for example is translated *Ps.* lxxvii. (24) ηὐξημένος, and a few verses further on (151) καρποφόρος; while of David's name at least a dozen renderings might be collected. Its exegesis differs widely from the *Ep. ad Marcellinum*, as will be seen in such Messianic passages as *Pss.* xiv. 1, 11; cix. 3; xxxii. 6. It is equally independent of the *Exp. in Pss.*, and seems to breathe another spirit. Specimens will be

idolatry[1], but is quite at home in Greek mythology and Greek philosophy.

As a man of learning and a skilful party-leader Athanasius was not beyond the rivalry of Acacius or Cyril. But he was more than this. He had a deep conviction wanting in Acacius, and it moulded his character in a way unknown to Cyril. His whole spirit seems penetrated by his vivid faith in the reality and eternal meaning of the Incarnation. His earliest works rise high above the level of Arianism and Sabellianism; and throughout his long career we catch glimpses of a spiritual depth which few of his contemporaries could reach. And Athanasius was before all things a man whose whole life was consecrated to a single purpose. If it was spent in controversy, he was no mere controversialist. And if he listened too easily to the stories told him of Arian misdeeds, his language is at worst excused by their atrocious treachery[2]. As for the charge of persecution, we must in fairness set against the Meletians who speak through Epiphanius[3] the explicit denial of the Egyptian bishops[4]. And if we take into account his own pleas for toleration and the comprehensive charity of his *de Synodis* and of the council of Alexandria, we must pronounce the charge unproved. If we could forget the violence of his friends at Tyre, we might say more.

Such a bishop was sure to meet and overcome a bitter opposition. Egypt soon became a stronghold of the Nicene faith, for

found in their comments on viii. ὑπὲρ τῶν ληνῶν, on xxi. where the *Exp.* is more dogmatic throughout, esp. v. 15 ὅστᾶ which is *Exp.* the Jews, *de tit.* Christian doctrine. Add the reference in *de tit.* of cxxxviii. 11 (21) to baptism, ciii. (45) σκύμνους to trine immersion; lxxxviii. 38 (74) of the faithful witness in heaven to the Trinity; lxvii. 6 (14) —μονοτρόπους—and 23 (53)—thy dogs —to the monks. All these are wanting or otherwise explained in the *Exp.*, which in its turn has an ascetic comment on l. 7 (10) not found in the *de tit.* The parallels between the *de tit.* and the genuine works of Athanasius collected by Antonelli *Præf.* xxxviii. (Migne III. 643) are mostly obvious *loci communes*. Nor can much stress be laid on Jerome's mention of such a work *de viris illustr.* 87, in company with *de virginitate, de persecutionibus Arianorum*, and the Life of Antony.

[1] Chiefly *c. Gentes* 9, 10, 23. Significant is the reference to *Greek* legend in *Or.* ii. 32, p. 395 πῶς οὐ κατὰ τοὺς μυθευομένους γίγαντας καὶ αὐτοὶ νῦν θεομαχοῦσι; and again *Or.* iii. 42, p. 468.

[2] We can scarcely blame Athanasius for his language towards Constantius. The transition to abuse is not more sudden than the emperor's treachery: and that treachery would have done credit to the vilest of his predecessors.

[3] Epiph. *Hær.* 68, 7.

[4] Ath. *Apol. c. Ar.* 5, p. 100.

Athanasius could sway the heart of Greek and Copt alike. The pertinacious hatred of a few was balanced by the enthusiastic admiration of the many. The Meletians dwindled fast[1], the Arians faster still, and only outside persecution was wanting to establish Nicene orthodoxy as the national faith of Egypt[2].

It is needless to give more than an outline of the events of the next few years. They concern us chiefly so far as they explain the formation of a reaction against the great council.

Eusebius of Nicomedia and Theognius of Nicæa were exiled by Constantine in Nov. 325, on the eve of his tragic journey to Rome. But they had a powerful friend at court in the princess Constantia; and as they had in fact signed the creed[3] and only been exiled for suspicious intimacy with the Arians, they were able in course of time to satisfy the emperor of their substantial orthodoxy. Constantine was not unforgiving, and policy as well as easy temper forbade him to scrutinize too closely the professions of submission laid before him. Once returned from exile, Eusebius recovered his influence at court, and became the centre of intrigue against the council. He was obliged indeed to abstain from direct attacks upon it as long as Constantine lived; but as a test of orthodoxy he had disposed of it once for all by signing it. And if the creed itself could not be assailed, its defenders might be got rid of one by one.

Eusebius is a man of whom we should like to know more[4]. His influence in his own time was second to none, his part in history for many years hardly less than that of Athanasius; yet we have to estimate him almost entirely from the allusions of his enemies. However, it is clear that Eusebius was one of the ablest politicians of his time, and that he carried out his policy by a systematic perversion of justice. His own account, if we

---

[1] Athanasius appears to have gained over many of the Meletian bishops. Of the 29 names given in by Meletius in 327 (Ath. *Apol. c. Ar.* 71, p. 148), nine reappear at Tyre (*id.* c. 79) in 335, and three can be traced as far as the *Festal Letter* for 347. On the other side was John Archaph; also Eudæmon, Ision and Callinicus, who accused Athanasius in 331 (*Festal Letter* for 332), and are found at Philippopolis in 343.

[2] Alexandria included. Stanley *Eastern Church* 230 makes Arianism chiefly Greek and Alexandrian, orthodoxy Coptic and Egyptian. For his fact he leans too much on the Coptic names of apocryphal monks; but so far as Arianism was an exotic in Egypt, it was necessarily Greek and Alexandrian.

[3] *Supra*, p. 49.

[4] Much the best account of him is given in the thoughtful article of Dr Reynolds in *Dict. Chr. Biogr.*

had it, could hardly excuse his conduct, though it might help to explain it. But given his nefarious means, we have still to find the purpose they were meant to serve. Mere revenge on the authors of his exile is not a likely aim for a great diplomatist like Eusebius. Mere ecclesiastical rivalry between the capital[1] and Alexandria belongs rather to the next generation, and might have been satisfied with fewer victims. Mere sycophancy and emperor-worship might surely have let the creed alone and found itself less dangerous fields of action. The court chaplain for example might have raised a cry against the Jews. Upon the whole it seems that even the unjust judge had a conscience of some sort. Arius and he were Lucian's disciples; and the Lucianists had a strong *esprit de corps*. Asterius[2] for one was far from full agreement with Arius, and others may have cared more for their old companion than for his doctrine. And when the Lucianists as a body defended him before the council, the council trod them underfoot. They felt his exile as a common wrong, and naturally made his doctrine their common faith.

---

[1] It will be remembered that Nicomedia was the capital till 330, and that Eusebius obtained Constantinople at the first vacancy. But it was some time before Constantinople fairly asserted its position. It did not become the settled residence of the emperors till the time of Theodosius.

[2] Our knowledge of Asterius is soon summed up. He was a converted sophist who sacrificed in the persecution "of Maximian," and was restored to the faith (Philost. ii. 10) by his master Lucian. Some years later he composed a συνταγμάτιον in favour of Arius, and made many journeys on behalf of his old friend. He also defended (Marcellus *Fr.* 29) the letter of Eusebius of Nicomedia to Paulinus. Afterwards we find him using the Lucianic creed, and (so his enemies said) in great hope of a bishopric for his services. We last meet him at Antioch (339 or 341), in attendance on Dianius of Cæsarea Mazaca.

The fragments of the συνταγμάτιον are decidedly Arianizing. We have from Athanasius, (*a*) *Or.* i. 30, pp. 343 sq.—the Lord ποίημα by implication, and contrasted with the ἐν ἀγενήτον and the divine σοφία on the strength of the anarthrous Θεοῦ δύναμις καὶ Θεοῦ σοφία in 1 Cor. i. 24. (*b*) *de Syn.* 18, p. 584—another contrast with the σοφία. Socrates i. 36 seems dependent on this passage. (*c*) *Or.* ii. 28, p. 392—the Lord κτίσμα, καὶ τῶν γενητῶν, and learned as a workman to create: where however we must take into account the disavowal of the word by Eusebius *de Eccl. Theol.* i. 9, p. 67.

On the other hand, all this was written before the council, and is hardly consistent with his later views. He spoke certainly of the Father as ὁ μόνος ἀληθινὸς Θεός, though Eusebius also defended this. But no thorough Arian could have come forward so conspicuously in defence of the Lucianic creed as even to be accused by Philostorgius of interpolating the decisive οὐσίας ἀπαράλλακτον εἰκόνα. So also on the Nicene side Epiphanius *Hær.* 76, 3 contrasts him with the Anomœans. Account in Zahn *Marcellus* 38—41, who takes the same view of him.

Eusebius himself was the ablest of the Lucianists, and had fared the worst of all. He had strained his conscience to sign the creed, and it had not even saved him from exile. What marvel if he brought back a firm determination to restore his less fortunate friends and to abolish the council's hateful creed?

A party was easily formed. The Lucianists were its nucleus, and all sorts of malcontents gathered round them. The Meletians of Egypt joined the coalition, and the unclean creatures of the palace rejoiced at the prospect of fresh intrigue. Above all, the conservatives gave extensive help. The charges against the Nicene leaders were often more than plausible, for men like Asterius or Eusebius of Cæsarea dreaded Sabellianism above all heresies, whereas Marcellus of Ancyra was practically Sabellian, and the others aiders and abettors of his misbelief. Some even of the darker charges may have had some ground, or may at least have seemed truer than they were. Thus Eusebius had a very heterogeneous following; and it would be scant charity if we transferred its leader's infamy to all its members.

They began with Eustathius of Antioch—" the great Eustathius," as Theodoret calls him. He was an old confessor and a man of eloquence, and enjoyed great and lasting popularity in the city. He was a strong opponent of Origen[1] and one of the foremost enemies of Arianism at Nicæa, and had since waged an active literary war with Eusebius, Patrophilus and the Arianizing clique in Syria. In one respect they found him a specially dangerous opponent, for his connexion with Antioch enabled him to insist on the important consequences of the Arian denial of the Lord's true human soul. Eustathius was therefore deposed in 330, and exiled with many of his clergy to Thrace[2]. The vacant see was offered to Eusebius

---

[1] Socrates vi. 13 couples him with Methodius, Apollinarius and Theophilus to form a κακολόγων τετρακτὺς for their attacks on Origen.

[2] The chief passages bearing on the deposition of Eustathius are Ath. *Hist. Ar.* 4, p. 274 (where Tillemont and Neale were misled by the reading Κωνσταντίῳ), Socrates i. 24, ii. 9, Sozomen ii. 18, Theodoret i. 21, 22, Philostorgius ii. 7. Eusebius *V. C.* iii. 59—62 (as Photius remarks) gives us little help, Chrysostom *de S. Eustathio* still less.

The subject is beset with difficulties, but they are mostly connected with the nature of the charge against him. Of this four different accounts are given. Athanasius speaks only of disrespect to Helena, who was now some years dead. Socrates, on the authority of George of Laodicea, mentions a charge

of Cæsarea, and finally accepted by the Cappadocian Euphronius[1].

Party spirit ran high at Antioch, and the count Musonianus was hardly able to prevent a bloody riot. Armed force was needed for the removal of Eustathius; and his departure was followed by an open schism when the Nicene party refused to communicate with Euphronius. Nor were they conciliated by a

of Sabellianism made by Cyrus of Berœa, but demurs to it on the ground that Cyrus himself was deposed for Sabellianism, according to George. He therefore prefers another account, that it was δι' ἄλλας οὐκ ἀγαθὰς αἰτίας· φανερῶς γὰρ οὐκ εἰρήκασιν, as was usual when bishops were deposed. Sozomen has οὐχ ὁσίαις πράξεσι, but afterwards alludes to the literary quarrel with Eusebius of Cæsarea. Philostorgius mentions a charge of seduction, alluded to by Jerome c. Ruf. iii. 42 (II. 569 Migne); and Theodoret records it in full detail, at the same time indicating a fourth accusation of episcopal tyranny (ὡς μοιχὸν ὁμοῦ καὶ τύραννον), possibly akin to the case of Ischyras. At least we are told by Ath. Hist. Ar. v. p. 274 that Eustathius refused to ordain Leontius, Eudoxius and others. We hear nothing of his translation from Berœa.

These various accounts are not inconsistent with each other, for the Eusebians were quite in the habit of stringing together heterogeneous accusations. But it would seem that the charge of fornication was really made. Theodoret indeed is not the soberest of historians; and in this case his credit is specially damaged by his tale of the journey of Eusebius *of Constantinople* and the rest to Jerusalem. Still, his evidence is often important for the affairs of Antioch, and his account is confirmed by the cautious words of Socrates and Sozomen, by the less important allusions of Philostorgius and Jerome, and perhaps by the expression of Constantine (Eus. V. C. iii. 60) τὸν ῥύπον ἐκεῖνον ἀπωσάμενοι.

The silence of Athanasius is a serious difficulty; but we may connect it with the further question, why the council of Sardica did nothing for Eustathius. The Eusebian charge from Philippopolis (Hil. *Fragm.* iii., sed et Eustasio et Quimatio Hosius adhærebat pessime

et carus fuit, de quorum vitæ infamia turpi dicendum nihil est: exitus enim illorum eos omnibus declaravit) may be accepted in proof that Eustathius was a personal friend of Hosius, perhaps even that the question was raised at Sardica, as it ought to have been when Stephen of Antioch was deposed. Yet nothing was done. Was his case only not formally brought before the council? Was there truth in one or another of the charges against him? The simplest solution is that he was dead; but even this is not free from difficulty. Jerome and Chrysostom (*De S. Eustathio* 2, Opp. ii. 600) place his death in Thrace, i.e. before Julian's recall of the exiles in 362. Theodoret iii. 4 puts it before the consecration of Meletius in 361. In any case Socrates iv. 14, 15 and Sozomen vi. 13 are clearly mistaken in telling us that he was alive in 370. Yet Athanasius in 356 (De Fuga 3, p. 253) gives no hint of his death, though he notices that of Eutropius in the same list of exiles. There is no mention of him at Seleucia in 359, when the Semiarians deposed Eudoxius; but this is not surprising. The passage already quoted from the encyclical of Philippopolis would settle the question (so Tillemont VII. 654) if his name were not coupled with that of Cymatius (of Paltus—an exile, Ath. supra), who was certainly (Ath. *ad Antiochenos* 19, p. 619) alive in 362. We also have some fragments from a work of his against Photinus (Cowper *Syr. Misc.* 60) who did not come into prominence till near 343. Moreover it is not likely that his adherents at Antioch remained headless for twenty years before the consecration of Paulinus in 362. These considerations would seem to place his death about 356—360, and reopen the question why the council of Sardica neglected him.

[1] So Lightfoot *Eusebius of Cæsarea*.

wholesale promotion of the Arianizers Eustathius had refused to ordain[1].

Once begun, the system was vigorously followed up. Asclepas of Gaza may have been exiled about the same time as Eustathius, Eutropius of Hadrianople shortly after. Other bishops shared their fate within the next few years[2].

But Alexandria and Ancyra were the real strongholds of the Nicene party; and the Eusebians still had their hardest work before them, to obtain the expulsion of Athanasius and Marcellus. The natural course would have been to raise a charge of heresy; but Athanasius might have met the intriguers with a dangerous retort. Doctrinal questions were therefore avoided except in the case of Marcellus, whom they found it possible to assail without an open disavowal of the Council. As Marcellus even more than Athanasius was the champion of the Nicene party in the period preceding the council of Sardica, it will be convenient here to review his peculiar doctrinal position[3].

Marcellus of Ancyra was already in middle life when he came forward as a resolute enemy of Arianism at Nicæa[4]. Nothing

---

[1] Athanasius *Hist. Ar.* 4, p. 274 names Stephen and Leontius of Antioch, George of Laodicea, Theodosius of Tripolis, Eudoxius of Germanicea and Eustathius of Sebaste. George however was originally ordained by Alexander of Alexandria, and seems from Eus. *V. C.* iii. 62 to have been serving in 330 as presbyter at Arethusa. Here again I cannot feel satisfied with the authority of the *Hist. Ar.*

[2] Athanasius *Hist. Ar.* 5, p. 274 names ten in all. Macarius of Jerusalem was the only leading member of his party who seems to have been left unmolested. His influence with Constantine would partly shield him; and (Soz. ii. 20) he did not altogether escape annoyance. On the see of Jerusalem in the Nicene age, Couret *La Palestine sous les empereurs grecs* 10—82.

In the case of Eutropius we get a note of time, for the princess Basilina, whose influence was used against him, only survived a few months her son Julian's birth, Nov. 6, 331.

The only difficulty about Asclepas is the statement of the Easterns at Philippopolis (Hilary *Fragm.* III. 11) that he was deposed seventeen years before. But there must be some error in the numeral, for the council of Sardica cannot be dated after 343.

[3] The fragments of Marcellus are mostly contained in the replies of Eusebius *c. Marcellum* and *de Eccl. Theol.* They are collected by Rettberg, *Marcelliana.* The best modern account of him is the monograph of Zahn *Marcellus von Ancyra:* and to this work I am much indebted in the next few pages. See also Harnack *D. G.* ii. 237. His Eastern origin is discussed by Caspari *Quellen* iii. 44 n. He is also discussed by Dorner ii. 271—285, and an excellent summary of the controversy is given by Nitzsch *Grundriss* 223—225. Passages are also collected by Newman *Ath. Treatises* 504—511.

[4] The data for his age are (1) his share in the council of Ancyra about 314, confirmed by a doubtful signature; (2) his presence at Nicæa; (3) Eusebius *de Eccl. Theol.* ii. p. 140 εἰ καὶ καταγηράσας ἐν ἐπισκοπῇ, written about 338; (4) Athanasius *Hist. Ar.* 6, p. 275 τὸν γέροντα, written in 358 but referring to his exile in 336, or more likely 339; (5) his death in 373, Epiph. *Hær.* 72, 1.

is known of his early life and education, but we can see some of the influences which surrounded him in riper years. Ancyra was a strange diocese, full of uncouth Gauls and chaffering Jews, and overrun with Montanists and Borborians and Manichees and votaries of endless fantastic heresies and superstitions[1]. In the midst of this turmoil Marcellus spent his life; and if he learned too much of the Galatian party spirit, he learned also that the Gospel is wider than the forms of Greek philosophy, and that its simpler aspects may better suit a rude flock. The speculations of Alexandrian theology were hardly better appreciated by the Celts of Asia than is the stately churchmanship of England by the Celts of Wales. They were the foreigner's thoughts, too cold for Celtic zeal, too grand for Celtic narrowness. Fickleness is not inconsistent with a true and deep religious instinct, and we may find something austere and high behind the ever-changing phases of spiritual excitement. Thus the ideal holiness of the church contended for by Montanists and Novatians attracted kindred spirits at opposite ends of the Empire, among the Moors of the Atlas[2] and the Gauls of Asia; and thus too Augustine's high Calvinism proved a dangerous rival to the puritan exclusiveness of the African Donatists. Such a people will have sins and scandals like its neighbours, but there will be very little indifference or cynicism. It will be more inclined to make the liberty of Scripture an excuse for strife and debate. The zeal for God which carries the Gospel to the loneliest

We may therefore fix his birth 280—290.

In any case the allusions of Eusebius and Athanasius to his old age are remarkable. Zahn *Marcellus* 84 supposes the latter somehow ironical; but Marcellus, like Latimer, may have looked much older than he was.

[1] So Eusebius *c. Marcellum*, p. 1 τὸ πολὺ στίφος τῶν αἱρεσιωτῶν, Jerome vii. 429 and other passages collected by Lightfoot *Galatians*, p. 32, to which add Greg. Nyss. *Ep.* xix. (Migne III. 1076) τὸ σύνηθες αὐτοῖς περὶ τὰς αἱρέσεις ἀρρώστημα. His popularity in his diocese is clear from the trouble it took to eject him (so Julius ap. Ath. *Apol. c. Ar.* 33, p. 119), from the continual references of Eusebius to his supporters, and from the attachment of his followers till the end of his life. He was perhaps not born of Christian parents. The Greek learning shewn in his discussions of heathen proverbs may not be very deep; but his ignorance of Scripture seems to indicate a heathen origin. Deductions must be made from the list of errors collected by Eusebius, pp. 10—14; but it is clear that Marcellus was not merely entangled in a bad exegesis, but had not even a student's knowledge of the text as a whole.

Fragm. 52, p. 40 can hardly be taken to shew an acquaintance with Athanasius *de Inc.* Such speculations were not much to the mind of Marcellus.

[2] Allusions to the *leves Mauri* are not unfrequent.

mountain villages will also fill them with the jealousies of endless quarrelling sects. And the Galatian clung to his scriptural separatism with all the more tenacity for the secret consciousness that his race was fast dissolving in the broader and better world of Greece. Thus Marcellus was essentially a stranger to the wider movements of the time. His system was an appeal from Origen to St John, and a defence of the simplicity of Scripture from philosophical refinement or corruption[1]. Nor can we doubt the high character and earnest zeal of the man who for years stood side by side with Athanasius. The more significant therefore is the failure of his bold attempt to cut the knot of controversy.

Marcellus agreed with Arius that the idea of sonship involves those of beginning and inferiority, so that a Son of God is neither eternal nor equal to the Father. Now that which is not eternal is creature, and that which is inferior to the Supreme is also creature. On both grounds therefore Arius drew the conclusion that the Son of God must be a creature. The conservatives replied[2] that the idea of sonship excludes that of creation, and implies a peculiar relation to and origin from the Father. But they could form no consistent theory of their own. Let them say what they might, their secondary God was a second God, and their eternal generation seemed no real generation at all, while their concession of the Son's origin from the will of the Father made the Arian conclusion irresistible[3].

Marcellus was as far as possible from accepting any such result. The Lord's true deity was none the less an axiom of faith because the conservative defence of it had broken down. It was only necessary to review the position and take back the admissions which led to creature-worship. Turn we then to Scripture. "In the beginning was" not the Son, but the Logos. And who can tell us of the Lord so well as his own disciple and evangelist, the inspired apostle John? It is no secondary or accidental title which St John throws to the front of his Gospel, and repeats with deliberate emphasis three times

---

[1] Notice his attacks on Origen *Fr.* 32—78, p. 23. Here he agreed with Eustathius, and consequently both were opposed to Eusebius.
[2] Eusebius, pp. 66—68.
[3] Eus. pp. 20, 27, 29.

over in the first verse. In other words, the primary relation of the Lord to the Supreme is as the Logos. This is his strict and proper title and the only one which expresses his eternity, so that it must govern the meaning of such merely secondary names[1] as the conservatives had accumulated in their Lucianic formula. Then the Logos will not be only the silent[2] thinking principle[3] which is in God, but also the active creating principle, the ἐνέργεια δραστική which comes forth from God, and yet remains with God[4]. That is to say, the Logos is not only eternally immanent (for the Father alone does not complete the idea of deity any more than the Logos alone[5]), but also comes forth for the dispensation of the world[6]. In this Sabellianizing

[1] *Fr.* 28, 36—46 are devoted to this one doctrine, which is indeed the key of the Marcellian position. Thus *Fr.* 28, p. 37 τῆς ἀϊδιότητος αὐτοῦ μνημονεύων......οὐδὲν γεννήσεως ἐνταῦθα μνημονεύων τοῦ Λ., ἀλλ' ἐπαλλήλαις τρισὶ μαρτυρίαις χρώμενος ἐβεβαίου ἐν ἀρχῇ τὸν Λ. εἶναι. *Fr.* 37, p. 81 ὥστε πανταχόθεν δῆλόν ἐστι, μηδὲν ἕτερον τῇ ἀϊδιότητι τοῦ Λόγου ἁρμόττειν ὄνομα, ἢ τοῦθ' ὅπερ ὁ ἁγιώτατος τοῦ Θεοῦ μαθητὴς καὶ ἀπόστολος Ἰωάννης ἐν ἀρχῇ τοῦ εὐαγγελίου εἴρηκεν. *Fr.* 40, p. 116 οὐ καταχρηστικῶς ὀνομασθεὶς...ἀλλὰ κυρίως καὶ ἀληθῶς ὑπάρχων Λ. *Fr.* 41, p. 36 quotes Old Test. passages.

Eusebius answers pp. 83 sq.— (1) St John avoids the word elsewhere, and does not even keep to it in his prologue. (2) Our Lord calls himself by other names, even in St John's Gospel. (3) It is also avoided in other parts of Scripture. Elsewhere he complains p. 116 that Marcellus has seized upon a single word, and that not even the Lord's own. Similarly p. 68 the Arians have made the most of the single word ἔκτισεν in Prov. viii. 22.

Rettberg complains of this "*longa ac nugacissima diatribe.*" The discussion might have been shorter: but surely it was important to reduce to its proper place as one title amongst others the name on which the whole Marcellian system depended. If all titles but one were used καταχρηστικῶς, we should expect to hear more of the single exception.

Matt. xi. 27 πάντα μοι παρεδόθη ὑπὸ τοῦ Πατρός μου was limited by Marcellus and Athanasius (*In illud* 1, p. 82) to the Incarnation. On the other side, Asterius and the Eusebians (Eus. p. 6) connected it with the δόξα προαιώνιος or προκόσμιος of John xvii. 5, for the purpose of establishing (1) the premundane reality of the Sonship as against Marcellus, and (2) the inferiority of the Son, to whom things παρεδόθη. See Marcellus *Fr.* 93, pp. 39, 104; *Fr.* 97, p. 49.

[2] Hence Eusebius p. 114 invidiously compares the Valentinian Σιγή.

[3] *Fr.* 55, p. 39 parallels the divine with the human Logos. The comparison is taken up by Eusebius p. 4 from a hostile point of view.

[4] Thus *Fr.* 47, p. 37 δυνάμει ἐν τῷ Πατρί...—ἐνεργείᾳ πρὸς τὸν θεόν. This last point Eus. p. 113 fails to understand, when he asks τί οὖν ἐν τῷ μεταξὺ χρόνῳ, ὅτε ἐκτὸς ἦν ὁ Λόγος τοῦ Θεοῦ, προσήκει νοεῖν;

[5] Notice the advance of Marcellus on both Arians and conservatives, in that he does *not* identify the Father with the Monas. See *Fr.* 58, p. 138, and passages discussed by Zahn, 142.

In the same sense Eugenius uses language closely allied to that of the creed ascribed to Gregory of Neocæsarea—οὐδὲν ἐπείσακτον οὐδὲ κτίσμα ἐστὶν ἐν τῇ Τριάδι.

[6] Thus he says *Fr.* 31, 32, pp. 22, 36 προελθόντα, καὶ τοῦτον (Gaisford omits μή) εἶναι τὸν τῆς γεννήσεως ἀληθῆ τρόπον, and agrees with Arius in rejecting the Valentinian προβολή as implying corporeity, though it seems alluded to by Ath. *Or.* iv. 11, p. 495. *Fr.* 54,

sense Marcellus accepted the Nicene ὁμοούσιον[1], holding that the Logos is one with God as man with his reason[2].

The divine Sonship presents no difficulty now that it can be limited to the Incarnation. The Logos as such is pure spirit, invisible and ingenerate; and it was only as the Son of Man that the Logos became the Son of God[3]. Even the Arian identification of generation with creation only needed to be transferred from the Lord's higher nature to the flesh, which was undoubtedly created[4]. Then too the invisible Logos first became the visible "Image of the invisible God[5]." In the same way the "Firstborn of all Creation," as well as other titles which seem to contradict the Lord's eternity, are explained as denoting relations which had no existence before the Incarnation[6].

The eternal Logos then came forth from the Father to realize the idea of creation, though yet remaining in inseparable union with the Father, and in due time descended into true created human flesh. It was only in virtue of this humiliating separation from the Father that the Logos acquired a sort of independent personality. Thus the mediator of God and man was truly human as the apostle declared, but not a mere man as

---

p. 41; *Fr.* 62, p. 107 ἐνεργείᾳ μόνῃ πλατύνεσθαι δοκεῖ, where note the Stoic (not Sabellian: Zahn, 203) πλατυσμός. Eusebius p. 108 turns round the charge of materialism on this πλατυσμός, as a slander ἐπὶ τῆς ἀσωμάτου καὶ ἀλέκτου καὶ ἀνεκφράστου οὐσίας, and again pp. 114, 167 on the ἐντὸς καὶ ἐκτὸς as breaking up the divine simplicity. Athanasius *Or.* iv. 14, p. 497 also takes the deeper argument (already urged against the Arians, *Or.* i. 17, p. 333) that distinctions inside the divinity are either materializing or meaningless unless they express the divine nature.

[1] The word is not found in the fragments preserved by Eusebius, but Marcellus must have used it on occasion.

[2] It must be noted that one main object of Marcellus was to obliterate every trace of Subordination. In *Fr.* 64, p. 37 he presses John x. 30 as implying something more than the unity of will imagined by Asterius. Eusebius p. 211 argues on the other side from John xiv. 28, v. 30.

[3] *Fr.* 42, p. 35. In *Fr.* 36, p. 81 and often elsewhere he explains Old Test. references to the Sonship as prophecy. Thus Ps. cx. 3 is a prophecy of the Incarnation. So Prov. viii. 22 is of the flesh created, the Logos established (not begotten) before this present age (not before all ages) as the ground of the church. So here Athanasius; except that γεννᾷ with him refers to the eternal generation.

Eusebius p. 7 rightly quotes Gal. iv. 4 to shew that the Sonship was previous to the Incarnation.

[4] *Fr.* 44, p. 43, and the comment of Eusebius. *Fr.* 10, p. 44.

[5] He argues *Fr.* 80, 82, pp. 47, 15 that whereas the Logos as such is invisible, an εἰκὼν is necessarily visible. Eusebius pp. 47, 142, 175 endeavours by a gross misunderstanding to fix upon him the absurdity of making the mere σὰρξ the εἰκών. See Zahn, 110. It is not a fair inference from *Fr.* 83, p. 47.

[6] *Fr.* 4—8, pp. 20, 43, 44. Compare Zahn, 102.

Eusebius (so he says) maintained[1]; for the Logos was not joined to a man but assumed impersonal human nature, and therefore remained the mediating person[2].

And though the whole work of mediation was conditioned by the presence of this human nature, the Logos remained unchanged. Not for his own sake but merely for the conquest of Satan was the Logos incarnate. "The flesh profiteth nothing"; and even the gift of immortality cannot make it worthy of permanent union with the Logos[3]. God is higher than immortality itself, and even the immortal angels cannot pass the gulf which separates the creature from its Lord. The Logos cannot wear a servant's form for ever. That which is of the earth is unprofitable for the age to come. Hence it must be laid aside[4] when its work is done and every hostile power overthrown. Then the Son of God shall deliver up the kingdom to the Father, that the kingdom of God may have no end[5]; and then the Logos shall return, and be immanent as before[6].

A universal cry of horror rose from the conservative ranks to greet the new Sabellius or Samosatene, the Jew and worse than Jew, the shameless miscreant who had forsworn the Son of God, made indiscriminate war upon his servants and assailed even the sainted dead with every form of slander and reviling[7].

---

[1] *Fr.* 89, p. 29 he accuses Eusebius of confessing μόνον ἄνθρωπον. Eusebius replies p. 29 that he has not gone beyond 1 Tim. ii. 5, and retorts p. 54 that Marcellus said πρὸ ἐτῶν οὐδ' ὅλων τετρακοσίων διὰ τῆς ἀναλήψεως τῆς σαρκὸς γεγεννῆσθαι κάτω of the Son of God. The phrase may be chosen as an allusion to the κάτωθεν of Paul of Samosata.

[2] Compare Zahn, 164. Eusebius p. 8 replies from Gal. iii. 20 and 1 Tim. ii. 5 that a ψιλὸς Θεοῦ Λόγος ἀνυπόστατος, ἐν καὶ ταὐτὸν ὑπάρχων τῷ Θεῷ could not be a mediator.

[3] *Fr.* 107, 104, pp. 52, 177. Contrast Ath. *de Inc.*

[4] This was one of the worst offences to the conservatives. Did Marcellus abandon it as Rettberg p. 105 suggests? It is omitted in the Sardican letter, nor is it found either in the Roman confession, or in that of Eugenius; yet it seems essential to his system.

[5] 1 Cor. xv. 28. This (not Lu. i. 33) is the passage alluded to in his Roman confession. In *Fr.* 101, p. 50 he puts his doctrine clearly. Zahn, 182.

[6] *Fr.* 108, p. 41.

[7] Even the bad language of Eusebius will repay study. Thus pp. 18 μονονουχὶ πάμμαχον συνιστάμενος ἀγῶνα πρὸς πάντας, 19 εἶτα ἐπὶ τὸν τοῦ Θεοῦ ἄνθρωπον, τὸν ὡς ἀληθῶς τρισμακάριον, τρέπεται Παυλῖνον...... καὶ τοῦτον μακαρίως μὲν βεβιωκότα, μακαρίως δὲ πεπαυμένον, πάλαι τε κεκοιμημένον, 42 γυμνῇ τῇ κεφαλῇ τὸν Υἱὸν τοῦ Θεοῦ ἐξωμόσατο, 85 ὁ νέος Σαβέλλιος, 105 'Ιουδαῖον ἄντικρυς, 63 πόσῳ δὲ ἑκατέρων βελτίων ὁ 'Ιουδαῖος;

Acacius is even more violent than his master. A few fragments of his work against Marcellus are preserved by Epiph. *Hær.* 72, 6—10.

It was not unprovoked. Marcellus is accused by Eus. p. 1 of "cursing like quarrelling women," and puts into the mouth of Eusebius of Nicomedia a bitterly ironical confession *Fr.* 88, p. 26 ἡμάρτομεν, ἠσεβήσαμεν, ἠνομήσαμεν, καὶ τὸ πονηρὸν ἐνώπιόν σου ἐποιήσαμεν.

REVIEW OF MARCELLIAN SYSTEM.

The system of Marcellus was a confusion of heterogeneous errors. From the mire of Sabellianism came his doctrine of a single divine essence under a triple name and triple mask. Paul of Samosata contributed the heresy of an impersonal Logos descending into human flesh, while the idea of a Son of God no better than a Son of Man was nothing but a Jewish dotage[1]. The Trinity becomes an idle name, and the Lord is neither God nor man, nor even a personal being of any sort. The faith itself was at peril if blasphemies like these were to be sheltered behind the rash decisions of Nicæa.

The conservative panic was undignified from the first, and became a positive calamity when it was taken up by political adventurers for their own disinterested purposes. Yet the danger from Marcellus was not imaginary. As far as doctrine went, there was not much to choose between him and Arius. Each held firmly the central error of the conservatives and rejected as illogical the modifications and side-views of it by means of which they were finding their way to something better. If Eusebius hung back from the advance of Athanasius, Marcellus receded even from the position of Eusebius. Instead of destroying Arianism by the roots, he returned to something very like the obsolete error of Sabellianism[2]. In his doctrine the Son of God is a mere phenomenon of time; and even the Logos is as external to the divine essence as the Arian Son. "He that hath seen me hath seen the Father": but if the Arian Son can only reveal in finite measure, the Marcellian Logos gives only broken hints of an infinity beyond[3]. Yet this shadowy doctrine was the key of his position. For it he rejected not only Origen's theory of the eternal generation, but even Tertullian's establishment of the divine Sonship as the

---

[1] Eus. p. 175. Μάρκελλος δὲ πάντα φύρας, ποτὲ μὲν εἰς αὐτὸν ὅλον τοῦ Σαβελλίου βυθὸν χωρεῖ, ποτὲ δὲ Παύλου τοῦ Σαμοσατέως ἀνανεοῦσθαι πειρᾶται τὴν αἵρεσιν, ποτὲ δὲ Ἰουδαῖος ὢν ἄντικρυς ἀπελέγχεται· μίαν γὰρ ὑπόστασιν τριπρόσωπον ὥσπερ καὶ τριώνυμον εἰσάγει τὸν αὐτὸν εἶναι λέγων τὸν Θεόν, καὶ τὸν ἐν αὐτῷ Λόγον, καὶ τὸ ἅγιον Πνεῦμα. So also p. 33.

[2] Marcellus Fr. 38, p. 76 disavows Sabellianism, but his system is essentially much the same, and Eusebius was not likely to be conciliated by the statement that "Sabellius knew not the Son, that is the Logos." So Athanasius calls the Marcellians not indeed Σαβελλιανοί but Σαβελλίζοντες.

[3] Compare the ἀναλόγως τοῖς ἰδίοις μέτροις οἶδε of Arius with the σημαντικὴ δύναμις of Marcellus.

centre of the Christian problem. Resting on the doctrine of the Logos like the apologists and Irenæus[1], Marcellus abandoned the eternal Sonship—the one solid conquest of the last generation, and brought back the whole question into the old indefiniteness from which a century of toil had hardly rescued it.

He scarcely even kept his hold on the Lord's humanity. He confessed it indeed, but the incarnation became a mere theophany with him, the flesh a useless burden to be one day laid aside. Marcellus reaches no true mediation, no true union of God and man, only a $\sigma\eta\mu\alpha\nu\tau\iota\kappa\grave{\eta}$ $\delta\acute{\upsilon}\nu\alpha\mu\iota\varsigma$ taking human flesh for a time. The Lord is our redeemer and the conqueror of death and Satan, but there is no room for a second Adam, the organic head of regenerate mankind. The deliverance becomes a mere intervention from without, not also the planting of a power of life within, which will one day quicken our mortal bodies too. He forgets that if the body is for the Lord, the Lord is also for the body, and even our life in the flesh is wholly consecrated by the resurrection of the Son of Man.

No doubt Eusebius has the best of the dispute, so far as concerns the mere proof that the theory of Marcellus was a failure. Yet he laid himself open to more than one keen retort when the controversy came before a master's eye. The gleanings of Athanasius[2] are better than the vintage even of Eusebius. Both parties, he says, are equally inconsistent. The conservatives who refuse eternal being to the Son of God will not endure to hear that his kingdom is other than eternal, while the Marcellians who deny his personality outright are equally shocked[3] at the Arian limitation of it to the sphere of time. One party rests on the Sonship, the other on the doctrine of the Logos; so that while each accepts one half of the truth, neither can attack the other without having to confess the other half also. Athanasius then goes on to shew that the Marcellian system is involved in much the same difficulties as

---

[1] This is noted by Zahn *Marcellus* 227, Nitzsch *Grundriss* 224.
His return to the old distinction of the Logos as $\grave{\epsilon}\nu\delta\iota\acute{\alpha}\theta\epsilon\tau o\varsigma$ and $\pi\rho o\phi o\rho\iota\kappa\grave{o}\varsigma$ is significant.

[2] The reference of Ath. *Or.* iv. 8—24 to the Marcellian controversy was long ago pointed out by Rettberg. It is illustrated by Newman *Ath. Treatises* 497—511, and has recently been more satisfactorily discussed by Zahn 198—208, who adds an analysis of the whole book.

[3] Eusebius, pp. 34, 55.

Arianism. If for example the idea of an eternal Son is polytheistic, nothing is gained by transferring the eternity to an impersonal Logos[1]. If a divine generation is materializing, so also is a divine expansion. If the work of creation is unworthy of God, it matters little whether it is delegated to a created Son or to a transitory Logos. The one theory logically requires an infinite series of mediators, the other an infinite series of cycles of creation; for if the procession of the Logos was needed for the work of creation, it follows that the present cycle must come to an end with the return of the Logos.

Marcellus had fairly exposed himself to a doctrinal attack; but other methods were used against Athanasius. There was abundant material to work upon in the disputed election, the complaints of the Meletians and miscellaneous charges (they were all found useful) of oppression, of magic and of political intrigue[2]. At first the Meletians could not even obtain a hearing from the emperor[3]; and even when Eusebius took up their cause, they found it prudent to defer the main attack to the winter of 331. Even then their charges were partly refuted by two presbyters of Athanasius who chanced to be at Nicomedia; and when the bishop himself was summoned to the *comitatus*, it was only to complete the discomfiture of his enemies and return in triumph to Alexandria shortly before Easter 332. The intriguers had to wait awhile, especially as Constantine was occupied on the frontiers.

We are not here concerned with the intricate details of the Gothic war[4]; but the peace which ended it claims our attention

---

[1] So Eusebius, p. 29.
[2] Ammianus xv. 7, 7 sums them up in the form which reached the heathen. He notices (1) ambition, *ultra professionem altius se efferentem*; (2) magic, *scitarique conatum externa, ut prodidere rumores adsidui*, mentioning his skill in augury—*quæve augurales portenderent alites scientissime callens, aliquotiens prædixisse futura* (compare his interpretation of the crow's *cras* in Soz. iv. 10); (3) *alia quoque a proposito legis abhorrentia, cui præsidebat,* which may mean immorality, or perhaps oppression.
[3] Epiph. *Hær.* 68, 5—6.

[4] The *Anon. Valesii* relates the Gothic war after 330, and Jerome and Idatius fix the decisive battle for Apr. 20, 332. The *Anon. Val.* and Julian, *Or.* i., p. 9 D (see Spanheim's note), ascribe the victory to the younger Constantine. This is not unlikely, for we have no trace of him in the West between July 1, 331 and July 27, 332: yet we find his father dating a law Apr. 12, 332 from Martianopolis, the headquarters of Valens in the Gothic war of 367, and of Lupicinus in 376.

It is the repeated complaint of Joannes Lydus *de magistr.* ii. 10, iii. 31, 40 that Constantine's removal of

as the last of Constantine's great services to the Empire. The Edict of Milan had removed the standing danger of Christian disaffection in the East, the reform of the administration completed Diocletian's work of reducing the army to permanent obedience, the foundation of Constantinople made the seat of power safe for centuries; and now the consolidation of the northern frontier seemed to enlist all the most dangerous enemies of Rome in her defence. The Empire gained three hundred thousand settlers for its Thracian wastes, and a firm peace of more than thirty years with the greatest of the northern nations. Henceforth the Rhine was guarded by the Franks, the Danube covered by the Goths, and the Euphrates flanked by the Christian kingdom of Armenia. The Empire already leaned too much on barbarian help within and without its frontiers; but the Roman peace was never more secure than when the skilful policy of Constantine had formed its barbarian enemies into a ring of friendly client states[1].

The emperor returned to his well-earned rest, the intriguers to their work of mischief. Athanasius was ordered in 334 to appear before a new council. As the trial was to be held at Cæsarea, we may suppose that the bishop of the place was intended to preside over it. But Athanasius was far from sharing the emperor's confidence in the moderation of Eusebius[2]. He treated the assembly as a cabal of his enemies and declined its jurisdiction.

Next year (335) the Eastern bishops gathered to Jerusalem

the frontier troops from the Danube to lower Asia left Europe open to the barbarians; and with this step Schmidt *De auct. Zosimi* 16 proposes to connect the outbreak of the Gothic war. Now Joannes says that it was done ἄκων...... δέει τυραννίδος, which can only mean the Persians, and fixes the date by the words Κωνσταντίνου μετὰ τῆς τύχης τὴν 'Ρώμην ἀπολιπόντος which points to the year 326. Cedrenus p. 516 Bonn edition, who also denounces the transfer, puts the Persian war in 326—7, and relates at length its origin through a fraud of the philosopher Metrodorus. He seems dependent on Joannes, and has his date ten years too early; but we may very well suppose that a Persian war was threatening in 326—7, and that the withdrawal of troops from the Danube gave an opening to the Goths.

[1] Compare Bethmann-Hollweg *Römische Civilprozess* iii. 25.

[2] This is the reason given by Soz. ii. 25 for his refusal to attend. It is confirmed from his own hints by Lightfoot, *Eusebius of Cæsarea*, whose narrative is very suggestive about this part. Hefele, *Councils* § 48, has entirely failed to explain the thirty months' delay mentioned by Sozomen. The council of Cæsarea may have been held in the autumn of 333, but no manipulation will bring it thirty months before that of Tyre.

III.]   THE COUNCIL OF TYRE.   89

to keep the *Tricennalia* of Constantine and to dedicate the splendid church on Golgotha, which Eusebius enthusiastically compares[1] to the new Jerusalem of prophecy. But first it was a work of charity to restore peace in Egypt. A synod of about 150[2] bishops was therefore held at Tyre; and this time the attendance of Athanasius was secured by peremptory orders from the emperor. The Eusebians had the upper hand in it, though there was a strong minority. Athanasius had brought forty-eight bishops from Egypt: and others like Maximus of Jerusalem and Alexander of Thessalonica were willing to hold an impartial trial. Athanasius was not accused of heresy, but with more plausibility of episcopal tyranny. His friends replied with reckless violence, and the Eusebians might have crushed him altogether if they had only kept up a decent semblance of truth and fairness. But nothing was further from their thoughts than an impartial trial. Scandal succeeded scandal[3], till the iniquity culminated in the despatch of an openly

[1] Eusebius, *V. C.* iii. 33.
[2] The number is nowhere given, but 150 seems a fair estimate. The council at Jerusalem consisted according to the *Acts* of Basil of Ancyra of 230 bishops: and this number exactly suits the language of Eusebius, which implies that the gathering was a very large one, not indeed equal to that of Nicæa, but quite beyond comparison with any other meeting of his times. Now the council of Tyre was a mere preliminary to the ἐγκαίνια at Jerusalem, and must have been considerably smaller.

On the other hand it is clear that the Eusebians had a real majority. Athanasius had at least fifty friends; and if there had been only a knot of intriguers on the other side, he would have been quite able to defend himself. Indeed, we nowhere find any indication that the council was coerced by a mere minority. Its misdeeds were at least its own.

These considerations require fully double the number of sixty bishops given by Socrates i. 28.

It is therefore not likely that Athanasius brought with him eighty-nine Egyptian bishops to Tyre as early as 335. As there were in all only "about ninety" (Ath. *ad Afros* c. 10, p. 718) or "nearly a hundred" (Ath. *Apol. c. Ar.* c. 71, p. 147) bishops in Egypt and Libya, they cannot have been so numerous at Tyre, even if the Meletians and Arians had been already weeded out of the list. In fact, their protest to the Count Dionysius (Ath. *Apol. c. Ar.* c. 78, p. 154) is signed by only forty-eight. Socrates i. 28 gives sixty as the total number of the council; but this is too low. Even if the Egyptians are not included, as Hefele (*Councils* § 49) evidently supposes, Athanasius' treatment of it as a mere cabal of his enemies is not easy to explain, especially as he had supporters or at least neutrals outside Egypt, like Maximus of Jerusalem and Alexander of Thessalonica. And if he brought with him an actual majority of the council, his conduct becomes simply foolish.

[3] The charge of fornication seems apocryphal. It is found in Rufinus i. 17, and from him in Soz. ii. 25 ("not in the synodical acts, for it was too absurd to insert"), and heavily retouched in Theod. i. 30. Philostorgius ii. 11 has it with the parts reversed.

This is outweighed by the silence of Athanasius himself, of later councils, and of Socrates, who had it before him in Rufinus, and deliberately left it out.

partizan commission to superintend the manufacture of evidence in the Mareotis. Maximus of Jerusalem left the council, the Egyptian bishops protested, and Alexander of Thessalonica warned the imperial commissioner of the plot. Athanasius himself took ship for Constantinople, and the council condemned him by default[1]. This done, the bishops went on to Jerusalem for the proper business of their meeting.

The concourse on Golgotha was a brilliant spectacle. Ten years had passed since the still unrivalled gathering at Nicæa, and the veterans of the great persecution must have been deeply moved at their meeting once again in this world. The stately ceremonial suited the old confessors of Jerusalem and Cæsarea much better than the noisy scene at Tyre, and may for the moment have soothed the swelling indignation of Potammon and Paphnutius. It was the second time that Constantine had plastered over the divisions of the churches with a general reconciliation; but this time Athanasius was condemned and Arius received to communion.

The heretic had long since left Illyricum, though it seems impossible to fix the date of his recall[2]. However, one winter

---

Lightfoot notices the suspicious circumstance that Eusebius of Cæsarea appears as the presiding bishop, both in the incident of Potammon (Epiph. *Hær.* 68, 7) and in the story of the seduction (Philost. ii. 12). If Athanasius had objected to him the year before, Constantine would not have committed so open a piece of injustice as to put him at the head of the council. It seems indicated by Ath. *Apol. c. Ar.* 81, p. 156 that Flacillus presided, to whom Eusebius dedicated his three books *de Eccl. Theol.*

[1] Athanasius stayed at Tyre as long as possible. The Egyptian protest is dated Sept. 7, and was written before he left.

The fact of his condemnation at Tyre is established by Socr. i. 32, Soz. ii. 25, though no stress can be laid on the encyclical of Philippopolis (Hil. *Fragm.* III. *in præsentem Ath.*) or on the apocryphal dialogue in Theodoret ii. 16. If Julius of Rome ap. Ath. *Ap. c. Ar.* 23, p. 113 seems to deny it, he only means (as the next sentence shews)

that the decision was invalid. A condemnation by default at Tyre would be a useful *præjudicium* when the merits of the case were supposed to be discussed on the return of the Mareotic commission to Jerusalem.

[2] It seems impossible with our present materials to clear up the chronology of the few years which followed the Nicene council. We have not a single certain landmark till we reach the election of Athanasius in 328, his stay at Nicomedia in 332, and the exile of Eutropius before Basilina's death.

Rejecting the apparently spurious letter of Eusebius and Theognius in Socr. i. 14, Soz. ii. 16, the following are our chief data. (1) The recall of Eusebius and Theognius, which most likely preceded that of Arius. Philostorgius ii. 7 dates it in 328, and this is likely enough: but he stands alone, and the chapter is a jumble of blunders. (2) The letter of Constantine to Arius and Euzoius, which bears date Nov. 27. But we cannot fix the year, for the emperor seems to have been at or near

the emperor invited Arius and Euzoius to Constantinople, where they laid before him their confession of faith. It was a simple document, which observed a prudent silence on all the disputed questions[1]. If it abstained from contradicting the Nicene decisions, it also failed to withdraw the *Thalia*. However, it was enough for Constantine. It was not unorthodox as far as it went: nor were they bishops, that the Nicene symbol should be forced upon them. They were therefore sent to lay it before the council at Jerusalem, which in due course approved it, and received its authors to communion. In order to complete the work of peace, Athanasius was condemned afresh upon the return of the Mareotic commission, and proceedings were begun against Marcellus of Ancyra, who had alarmed the whole conservative party by his attack upon Asterius[2], and might also be supposed to have given personal offence to the emperor by his absence from the council.

Meanwhile Constantine's dreams of peace had been rudely dissipated by the sudden appearance of Athanasius before him in the streets of Constantinople. Whatever the bishops had done, it had plainly caused dissensions just when the emperor was most anxious for harmony. An angry letter summoned the whole assembly straight to court. But there came only a

---

Constantinople every winter from 327 to 334 inclusive. Socrates i. 26 gives the letter after the exile of Eustathius, while Sozomen ii. 27 connects it more nearly with the council of Tyre. In this he may be right, for we know that Arius went to Jerusalem with a confession of faith. But the friendly tone of Constantine's letter to him suggests that it was written *after* his recall. Altogether, our data are hopelessly deficient.

We may perhaps get a glimmer of light from the mention of Ursacius and Valens as personal disciples of Arius, and as young men in 335, though already bishops. But where did Arius meet with them? Their dioceses were in Pannonia; but we see from the cases of Photinus and Germinius that they were not necessarily themselves Pannonians. At the same time there is nothing to connect them with Egypt: and if we take into account the uncertain life of Arius, it will be most likely that they were his disciples during his exile. If so, he must have spent some time in Illyricum.

[1] Socr. i. 26, Soz. ii. 27. They merely say εἰς κύριον Ἰ. Χ. τὸν υἱὸν αὐτοῦ, τὸν ἐξ αὐτοῦ πρὸ πάντων τῶν αἰώνων γεγενημένον θεὸν λόγον...τὸν κατελθόντα καὶ σαρκωθέντα (σάρκα ἀναλαβόντα Soz.) καὶ παθόντα κ.τ.λ. They end with desires for peace, &c. which might almost have been copied from Constantine's letter to Alexander and Arius.

[2] The bishops (Socr. i. 36) refused to discuss the counter-charge against Asterius, on the ground that he was only a layman. It is well to notice the numerous indications that the Nicene faith was not intended to bind in all its strictness any but the bishops.

deputation[1]; and in truth it would have been very inconvenient to transfer so large a council to the palace. Once confronted with the accused, the Eusebians dropped the old charges of sacrilege and tyranny, and brought forward a new one of political intrigue. Athanasius was allowed no reply to this, but summarily sent away to Trier in Gaul, where he was honourably received by the younger Constantine. The emperor refused either to restore him to Alexandria or to fill his place, and exiled the Meletian John Archaph "for causing divisions." Upon the whole, success was not unequally divided between the two parties. To Constantinople also came Marcellus. He had avoided the councils at Tyre and Jerusalem, and only appeared now to invite the emperor's decision on his book[2]. Constantine as usual referred the case to the synod, which at once condemned it and deposed the author[3].

There remained only the formal restoration of Arius to the

---

[1] As the church was consecrated in September, and Athanasius only reived formal audience Nov. 7, it is likely that the council had mostly dispersed before the emperor's letter arrived. In that case the relics of it would largely consist of Eusebians, who would at least wait for the return of the Mareotic commissioners.

[2] Soz. ii. 33 says that Marcellus objected to the proceedings at Tyre, and left Jerusalem before the dedication, while Socr. i. 36 tells us that he promised at Jerusalem to burn his book. The silence of Eusebius (Zahn 45) seems to disprove both accounts. Eus. c. Marcellum, p. 56 "when nobody asked him." It must have been a strange book if Eusebius of all men could denounce its flattery of Constantine.

[3] Was Marcellus twice in Rome? Caspari Quellen III. 28—30 assigns him a stay of fifteen months in 336—7, in addition to a somewhat longer one in 339—341.

Marcellus presents a creed of his own accord to Julius in Epiph. Hær. 69, 2 ἀναγκαῖον ἡγησάμην......ὑπομνῆσαί σε......ἐμοῦ ἐνιαυτὸν καὶ τρεῖς ὅλους μῆνας ἐν τῇ Ῥώμῃ πεποιηκότος, ἀναγκαῖον ἡγησάμην, μέλλων ἐντεῦθεν ἐξιέναι, ἔγγραφόν σοι τὴν ἐμαυτοῦ πίστιν...ἐπιδοῦναι; whereas Julius in Ath. Apol. c. Ar. 32, p. 118 ἀπαιτούμενος παρ' ἡμῶν εἰπεῖν περὶ τῆς πίστεως, οὕτως μετὰ παρρησίας ἀπεκρίνατο δι' ἑαυτοῦ, ὡς κ.τ.λ. tells us that Marcellus made his defence when called upon. So Athanasius himself Hist. Ar. 6, p. 275 καὶ αὐτὸς μὲν ἀνελθὼν εἰς τὴν Ῥώμην ἀπελογήσατο, καὶ ἀπαιτούμενος παρ' αὐτῶν, δέδωκεν ἔγγραφον τὴν ἑαυτοῦ πίστιν. Caspari declares this a contradiction, and refers the Epiphanian document to an earlier visit.

The necessity of this arrangement is not very clear. Marcellus was ready enough for another fray with the misbelievers he "had exposed at Nicæa"; and if pressure had to be put upon him to declare his belief, he was not bound to tell us the fact. Even if Julius had required him to make a plain statement before leaving Rome, he might still prefer to say only that he himself thought one necessary. A couple of minor points may be noticed—(1) The words of Athanasius supra δέδωκεν ἔγγραφον τὴν ἑαυτοῦ πίστιν may be an echo of the Epiphanian document, (2) as Marcellus cannot have reached Rome before the spring of 336, an interval of fifteen months will bring us some time past the death of Constantine. Would Marcellus have merely said μέλλων ἐντεῦθεν ἐξιέναι, without a hint of his expected restoration?

Zahn Marcellus 64 passes over Caspari's difficulty in silence.

communion of Constantinople; for it seems[1] that Alexandria had once again refused him since the council of Jerusalem. This was prevented by his sudden death the evening before the appointed day[2].

The chief interest of these events is in the strange wavering of Constantine. Had he really deserted the Nicene faith? Had the fatigues of the Gothic war broken down his strength, and left him an impatient invalid? Was he at the mercy of the last speaker? Was he merely balancing parties in order fully to control them all? Or was he still deliberately acting in the interest of unity?

He had not turned Arian. Whatever might be his policy towards the outside sects, there is no indication that he ever allowed the authority of the Nicene decisions to be openly repudiated inside the church[3]. If he exiled Athanasius, it was not for heresy; if he invited Arius and Euzoius to court, it was only that they might clear themselves from the imputation. In this case no doctrinal charge came before him. The quarrel ostensibly lay amongst orthodox bishops, for the Eusebian leaders had all signed the Nicene decisions. Nor indeed does any writer accuse him of Arianism[4]. There is more to be said for the theory[5] that he was balancing the parties against each other; and if he had not struck so hard at Nicæa, we might be

---

[1] Soz. ii. 29.

[2] The earliest account of the death of Arius is given in the letter of Athanasius *de morte Arii;* the next is an allusion of Epiphanius *Hær.* 68, 6. Rufinus i. 13 improves the story by putting the catastrophe during the procession on the Sunday morning. Socrates i. 38 is independent, and avoids the error; while Sozomen ii. 29, 30 and Theodoret i. 14 quote Athanasius.

[3] Thus Sozomen iii. 1 says that the Nicene doctrine only came into dispute again after Constantine's death, τοῦτο γὰρ εἰ μὴ πάντες ἀπεδέχοντο Κωνστ. ἔτι περιόντος τῷ βίῳ οὐδεὶς περιφανῶς ἐκβαλεῖν ἐτόλμησεν. Even the Antiochene council of 341 adopted a respectful tone (Socr. ii. 10) to that of Nicæa—the compliment was repaid to itself by the Acacians at Seleucia.

It is too much to say (Chawner, p. 71) that he made the Nicene symbol the test and touchstone of orthodoxy. The Novatians were perfectly orthodox in doctrine: yet they are included in the severe law given by Eus. *V. C.* iii. 64 and alluded to by Soz. ii. 32, which seems to have been issued about 332. In this notice the omission (1) of the Donatists, whose dangerous temper was well known, (2) of the Manichees. This must have been deliberate, for Constantine took pains (Ammianus xv. 13, 2) to have their books translated for him by Strategius (Musonianus).

[4] Except Jerome *Chron.* for 337, *Constantinus extremo vitæ suæ tempore ab Eus. Nicom. episcopo baptizatus, in Arianum dogma declinat:* and Lucifer *pro S. Ath.* p. 857, Migne, *Athanasium perosum habitum a patre tuo.* These however are scarcely serious exceptions.

[5] Fialon *Saint Athanase* 114, 143.

inclined to adopt it. Perhaps again[1] he was really irresolute, and at the mercy of the last speaker. But Constantine was still in vigorous health[2]; and there is no need to throw away the clue which has guided us through his policy hitherto. Upon the whole, he seems to have aimed at unity throughout. If he had believed the charge of delaying the corn ships, he would have sacrificed Athanasius as he sacrificed Sopater. Better risk a rebellion at Alexandria than a riot at Constantinople. His refusal to listen to any defence looks like a decision already made rather than a real explosion of rage. Athanasius was sent out of the way as a troublesome person. It was not easy to find out the merits of the case; but he was plainly, for some reason or other, a centre of disturbance. The Asiatic bishops disliked him; and this was enough for Constantine. As we have here a clue to the Arianizing policy of Constantius and Valens, it will be well to explain it further.

Nature has indeed marked out Constantinople as the head of a great empire; but in some respects it matters little whether the body is European or Asiatic. It may make a great difference to the happiness of Europe; but the state itself may flourish in either case. In Roman times the heart of the Empire was the tract of country from Mount Taurus to the Bosphorus and the wall of Anastasius; and as long as that was unsubdued by its invaders, the Empire remained upon the whole the strongest power on earth. It outlived the rise and fall of kingdoms without number; and even the splendour of the great Karl was hardly more than a meteor-flash across the all but everlasting firmament of the eastern Roman Empire. Visigoths, Avars, Bulgarians, and Russians[3] might sweep the European provinces from end to end; they only dashed themselves in pieces on the walls of Constantinople. As long as the Empire had the solid strength of Asia to fall back upon, it never failed to recover its losses. Even in the eleventh and twelfth centuries, the Roman army held the Danube for Basil II

[1] Lightfoot *Eus. Cæs.*
[2] Eusebius *V. C.* iv. 53, 61 particularly notices that Constantine enjoyed unbroken health till the spring of 337.
[3] The Russians mostly came by sea: yet Sviatoslav (Σφενδοσθλάβος) reached Arcadiopolis before his repulse by Bardas Sclerus, and would undoubtedly have driven almost any Emperor but John Zimisces to the shelter of Constantinople.

or Manuel Comnenus much as it had done for Constantine or Julian. The recovery of Asia from the European side was a harder task; yet this too was more than once accomplished. The Persians held Chalcedon for years together, but it was not long before Heraclius returned their defiance on the battle-field of Nineveh. The Saracens besieged Constantinople twice; but within a few years the Iconoclasts were defending the old frontier of Mount Taurus, and a time was yet to come when the Byzantine labarum was borne in one victorious campaign from the sources of the Tigris through the Lebanon passes to the walls of Berytus. The Empire sustained its first irreparable injury in the establishment of the Seljukian Turks at Iconium; and its fate was never hopeless till the ravages of Michael Palæologus deprived it of its last firm resting-ground in Asia, among the Bithynian archers who had rescued it from its deep humiliation, and won back Constantinople from the chivalry of Latin Europe.

Now Asia in 336 was neither Nicene nor Arian, but conservative. There was a good deal of Arianism in Cappadocia; but we hear little of it in Asia. We find indeed a knot of Asiatic Lucianists at Nicæa, who held prominent sees and must have had much influence; but they left no successors. Cecropius and Germinius are the only Asiatic bishops denounced by Athanasius, and even they seem (like Eugenius of Nicæa) to have been violent men rather than extreme in doctrine. Much less was Asia Nicene. Setting aside Marcellus as Sabellian, we can hardly name an Asiatic Nicene before the reign of Valens. Thrace and Syria contribute largely to the lists of exiles deplored by Athanasius, but there is only one obscure name from Asia. The ten provinces "verily knew not God[1]" in Hilary's time, and even the later Cappadocian orthodoxy rested on a conservative rather than a Nicene basis. Upon the whole, Asia seems to have been indifferent to the controversy. And indifference is always conservative. If it will not fight for creeds, it is usually willing to strike at such a "disturber" as Athanasius.

In the unconscious predominance of Asia we find a clue to the policy of the Arianizing emperors. There was no Greek

[1] Hilary *de Syn.* 63.

national feeling in the matter, for such Greek national feeling as existed in the Nicene age was certainly not Arian. Constantine moreover was as Western as an emperor could be, while Julian's Greek tastes led to an entirely different line of action. Neither was the Arianizing policy originally due to any Byzantine jealousy of Alexandria. The New Rome was at first hardly more than a great and favoured colony of the Old; and the consciousness of its imperial mission took fully half a century to gather shape. The city was neither a permanent residence of the emperors nor a patriarchal see of Christendom till the age of Theodosius[1]; and in the Arian controversy it played a very secondary part before the elevation of Eudoxius in 360. Meanwhile Constantius and his eunuchs pursued for many years a distinctly Asiatic policy, striking with one hand at orthodox Egypt, with the other at orthodox Rome. Even the change of front at Sirmium in 359 corresponded to a change in Asiatic feeling, and was no unskilful bid for support in Asia. The camarilla was dispersed and the Asiatic policy broken off by Julian, but Valens restored both; and when a greater than Valens came in as a stranger from the Spanish West, he too soon fell under the Asiatic influence[2].

The action of Constantine is therefore best explained by a reference to the conservatism of Asia. The bishops were not all of them either Arians or intriguers. The Asiatics were hardly prepared to reverse the Nicene decisions, much less to record themselves followers of Arius. It was not always furtive sympathy with heresy which led them to regret the heresiarch's expulsion for doctrines he had disavowed: neither was it always partizanship which could not see the innocence of Athanasius. Constantine's vacillation is intelligible, if his policy was to seek for unity by letting the bishops guide him[3].

---

[1] It will be noticed that Constantius lived a very wandering life, and that Valens avoided Constantinople throughout his reign. On the *gradual* rise of the city, Hertzberg *Gesch. Griech.* i. 28, or more fully in his *Griech. u. d. Römern* iii. 252—272.

[2] At this point I owe a special obligation to Hort, whose indication of Asiatic influence at work on Theodosius has been the clue to many other parts of the history. In February 380 the emperor names Damasus of Rome and Peter of Alexandria as his standards of orthodoxy; but in July 381 he replaces Damasus of Rome by Nectarius of Constantinople, and adds other Eastern bishops (*Cod. Theod.* xvi. 1, 1 and 2). We cannot mistake the Asiatic influence; which by this time had found a centre in Constantinople. Hort *Two Diss.* 97 n.

[3] Note C. *The Index to the Festal Letters of Athanasius*.

NOTE A.

THE AUTHORITY OF RUFINUS.

We shall be in a better position to estimate the credibility of Rufinus after a review of the legends and uncertain stories copied by later writers from his *Historia Ecclesiastica*. It will be borne in mind that copying is no confirmation if there is no trace of independent knowledge. Omitting then all reference to the *Historia Monachorum*, which is past defence except as a novel, the following are the chief contributions of Rufinus to *history*.

(1) Conversion of the Philosopher at Nicæa. Ruf. i. 3; copied by Soz. i. 18, and much expanded by Gel. Cyz. ii. 13—23. Omitted by Socrates and Theodoret.

(2) Spyridon and the miracles of the Thieves and the Deposit. Ruf. i. 5; Socr. i. 12 (names Ruf., and mentions hearsay in Cyprus); Soz. i. 11 more fully, and adds two other stories. Gel. Cyz. ii. 10, 11 follows Ruf., but could have told more stories.

(3) *Inventio Crucis*, with miracle of the sick woman. Ruf. i. 7, 8, copied by Socr. i. 17, Soz. ii. 2, Theod. i. 19. Eusebius and the author of the *Itinerarium Burdigalense* say nothing of the cross; Cyril, Ambrose and Chrysostom, nothing of the miracle. Yet Sulpicius Severus *Chron.* ii. 34 and Paulinus of Nola have a variant account of the raising of a dead man.

(4) Conversion of Ethiopia. Ruf. i. 9, copied by Socr. i. 19 (naming Ruf.), Soz. ii. 24, Theod. i. 23. According to "this delightful history" (Ebrard *Kgsch.* i. 166), the philosopher Meropius went on a scientific voyage to India (some confused geography here) in imitation of Metrodorus, who had made a similar journey a few years before. On his return he was killed in Ethiopia with the whole ship's company except two boys (*puerulos*, or in one MS. *pueros*), Frumentius and Edesius. When Frumentius was grown up, he became regent of

the country; and when his ward was grown up too, he returned to Egypt, where Athanasius, *nam is nuper sacerdotium acceperat*, consecrated him as bishop for Ethiopia. These words point to a date cir. 329; but one MS. of Rufinus omits them. Meanwhile Edesius became a presbyter at Tyre; and from his lips Rufinus professes to have heard the story, not before 378.

Bearing on this narrative are (α) The letter of Constantius in 356 (given by Ath. *Apol. ad Ctium* 31, p. 250) to the Ethiopian kings Aizanas and Sazanas, which implies that Frumentius had recently (say 354 or 355) been consecrated by Athanasius, and would need fresh instruction from "the most reverend bishop George." Constantius seems *Cod. Theod.* xii. 12, 2 to have sent an embassy to Ethiopia in Feb. 356, and forbids it to delay at Alexandria. (β) Ammianus xxv. 4, 23 *sciant docente veritate perspicue, non Julianum sed Constantinum ardores Parthicos succendisse, cum Metrodori mendaciis avidius acquiescit, ut dudum retulimus plene* (in lost books), *unde cæsi ad internecionem exercitus nostri, &c.*, referring to the disasters of 359—363. Here Tillemont *Mémoires* vii. 710 and Priaulx *Indian Travels of Apollonius of Tyana* 180—188 argue upon the reading *Constantium* of Valesius p. 295 and Wagner. Gardthausen however silently substitutes *Constantinum*: and internal evidence is on his side, for events connected with the outbreak of the war in 358 ought not to have been related in the lost books of Ammianus. (γ) Jerome *Chronica* names Metrodorus as flourishing in the year 328. Joannes Lydus frequently refers to him, but I cannot find that he gives us any hint of his date. (δ) Photius *Bibl.* Cod. 116 tells us that one Metrodorus (of whom he knows nothing more) drew up a Paschal canon for 533 years from the time of Diocletian. If we may assume that the writer lived when the controversy was at its height, we have a tempting identification. Jerome's date may even be that of the work in question. (ε) Cedrenus p. 516—7, and from him (Leo Grammaticus) p. 86, Bonn edition, relate at length the fraud of Metrodorus, but the former puts the outbreak of the war in the year 326—7, which is ten years too early. I cannot but suspect that the story comes from Joannes Lydus.

The narrative of Rufinus requires an interval of fully twenty years from the capture of Edesius to the consecration of Frumentius about 329. But if he was already *puerulus* about 305, he can scarcely have lived to converse with Rufinus after 378. One chief difficulty is the clause *nam is nuper sacerdotium acceperat*, which seems genuine, but cannot be true. On this point the letter of Constantius and the silence of Eusebius are decisive. If however we venture to set it aside and to read *Constantinum* in Ammianus (it is a bold venture), we may put the return of Metrodorus about 335, the voyage of Meropius soon after (not earlier as in Benedictine *Life* of Athanasius 330, and as suggested by Tillemont), and the consecration of Frumentius in 355, so that the age of Edesius in 378 would be about 50.

This is at best a harsh scheme, but it seems considerably better than the duplication of Frumentius by Baronius: yet it may well be doubted whether even in this case the interval of twenty years from the return of Metrodorus to the consecration of Frumentius is enough for all that has to be crowded into it. There is still a minor difficulty in the letter of Constantius, which is addressed to *two* kings, whereas Rufinus speaks of one only. However, we know from an inscription (Boeckh 5128) that Aizanas reigned alone in the days of his heathenism, and Sazanas his brother was his general. In any case the error is trifling.

Upon the whole, the story is very doubtful, but if we make these two alterations, it may just fall short of physical impossibility.

(5) Conversion of Iberia, with two miracles. Ruf. i. 10, from the lips of Bacurius, then *Palæstini limitis dux* at Jerusalem. Copied by Socr. i. 20 (naming Ruf.), Soz. ii. 7, with considerable variation by Theod. i. 24, and almost too independently by Moses of Chorene ii. 86. As Bacurius fought at Hadrianople (Ammianus xxxi. 12, 6), he cannot have told the story to Rufinus in Palestine till his return from the Gothic war. A dozen years or so later he was at Antioch (Libanius *Epp.* 963, 964, 980). He perished in the battle of the Frigidus in 394.

(6) Constantine's Will entrusted to the Arian presbyter. Ruf. i. 11, copied by Socr. i. 39, Soz. ii. 34. Philostorgius ii. 16 has a story that it was committed to Eusebius of Nicomedia. But Constantine's arrangements had been publicly made long before, and there is no sign that he wished to alter them. So Manso *Leben Constantins* 163, and de Broglie ii. 376 n; but the silence of Eusebius *V. C.* iv. 55—70 is of little weight, if we consider how delicately he passes over the dangerous interval which followed Constantine's death, without anywhere even naming Dalmatius and Hannibalianus.

(7) The boy-baptism of Athanasius. First by Rufinus i. 14, who relates it *sicuti ab his qui cum illo vitam duxerant accepimus.*

Quoted from him by Socr. i. 15, with the remark, "and not unlikely, for other cases of the sort have been known." Copied in full by Soz. ii. 17, who improves Antony's single visit to Alexandria into several. Besides minor difficulties, the story involves a fatal anachronism, for the anniversary of Peter's death cannot have been earlier than 313, when Athanasius must have been too old for such childish games. Had the great bishop's surviving companions nothing better to tell of him than this? Even Tillemont *Mém.* viii. 651 rejects the story.

(8) The story of Arsenius is in outline undisputed. But de Broglie ii. 331 urges the silence of Athanasius in disproof of the dramatic scene at Tyre related by Ruf. i. 17.

Here however Socrates i. 29 does not mention Rufinus, and has not copied him. His account seems discriminating and independent, omitting the charge of fornication and the final tumult. Soz. ii. 25, and Theod. i. 30, relate the affair shortly, but follow Rufinus. Upon the whole, it seems safer to reverse de Broglie's decisions, and reject the charge of fornication while we accept the scene with Arsenius on the authority of Socrates and leave it an open question whether the charge of murder was formally repeated at Tyre.

(9) Rufinus confuses the two first exiles of Athanasius and puts the council at Tyre in the time of Constantius, the third exile during the Magnentian troubles. After this comes the story of Theodore in Julian's time. Rufinus i. 36 relates it (with a miracle) from the confessor's own lips. From Rufinus it is quoted by Socr. iii. 19 (naming Rufinus), and copied by Soz. v. 20, Theod. iii. 11. It is also alluded to by Augustine *de Civ. Dei* xviii. 52.

The story is likely enough in itself, for Ammianus xxii. 13, 2 tells us that Julian was furious, used torture freely, and closed the great church at Antioch. Still the tale rests entirely on the evidence of Rufinus; and we may set against him the silence of Gregory and Chrysostom, who were credulous enough as against Julian. The miraculous part must be an invention either of Theodore himself (Rode), or more likely of Rufinus.

(10) Refusal of Jovian to rule a heathen army, and cry of the soldiers—*et nos Christiani sumus.* Rufinus ii. 1; copied by Socr. iii. 22, Soz. vi. 3, Theod. iv. 2. If the story be taken seriously, it is disposed of (so Gibbon, not Wagner) by a single phrase of Ammianus xxv. 6, 1, *hostiis pro Joviano extisque inspectis.*

(11) Stories of monks. Ruf. ii. 4, *quæ præsens vidi loquor, et eorum gesta refero, quorum in passionibus socius esse promerui.*

Quoted by Socr. iv. 23, but simply on the testimony of Rufinus. These however we may pass over, though they make a greater figure in the histories than all the rest put together.

(12) Account of the woman at Edessa. Ruf. ii. 5, copied by Socr. iv. 18 (omitting paganism of Modestus), Soz. vi. 18 (calling him ἑτερόδοξος), Theodoret iv. 17 (shorter, and adding a long story of one Eulogius).

(13) The peace with Mavia and consecration of Moyses as bishop for the Saracens. Ruf. ii. 6, copied by Socr. iv. 36, who adds that Count Victor married Mavia's daughter. Also by Soz. vi. 18, with a long account of the Saracens, who were his neighbours in Palestine; also by Theodoret iv. 23, who shortens the whole story.

Some of these tales appear to be true enough, and it would be most uncritical to charge Rufinus with deliberate invention in every case of error. But it cannot be denied that his history contains a large element of mere romance. Credulity and carelessness of truth are here; but do they amount to downright falsehood? If Rufinus was a man of truth, he met with a strange series of deceivers; for we can only clear him by throwing the blame on his informants— Edesius, Theodore and Bacurius, a man in whose praise all writers (including Libanius and Zosimus) are agreed. Rufinus reached Egypt before the death of Athanasius, and claims to have enjoyed the intimacy and shared the sufferings of the great archbishop's surviving friends. Their hearts must have been full of the hero they had lost: yet Rufinus retails nothing but the boy-baptism, two or three scandals, and a wretched muddle of the bishop's exiles. Jerome *ctra Ruf.* ii. 3, scoffs at the confessorship of Rufinus—*miror quod non adjecerit: Vinctus Jesu Christi, et liberatus sum de ore leonis, et Alexandriæ ad bestias pugnavi, et cursum consummavi, fidem servavi, superest mihi corona justitiæ. Quæ exsilia, quos iste carceres nominat? Pudet me apertissimi mendacii; quasi carceres et exsilia absque judicum sententiis irrogentur. Volo tamen ipsos scire carceres, et quarum provinciarum se dicat exsilia sustinuisse,* &c.

This time perhaps Jerome's *quidquid in buccam venerit* is not far wrong, though the charge comes with a bad grace from the writer of the *Vita Pauli*. Meanwhile it is important to notice that, with the exceptions already mentioned, these stories are absolutely uncorroborated. Rufinus must stand or fall by them, and they by him.

Socrates follows Rufinus, but with some discretion; omitting for example the miracles of Paphnutius, the conversion of the philosopher at Nicæa, the paganism of Modestus, and the charge of fornication against Athanasius at Tyre. But he follows with evident uneasiness, roundly denouncing (ii. 1) Rufinus for his gross mistakes of chronology, and carefully throwing back upon him the responsibility of the more romantic stories.

Sozomen is less cautious, usually following Socrates with slight revision. He never names Rufinus, but seems to have had independent access to his work, giving for example (i. 18) the story of the philosopher at Nicæa, and restoring more than one account judiciously passed over by Socrates. Theodoret usually follows in the same track, commonly adding many rhetorical improvements to the account before him.

If Rufinus is a liar at all, he is a liar circumstantial. And it is just this wealth of detail which has enabled him to deceive better men than himself, from Socrates and Sozomen to Neander and Keim. Uncritical historians to whom the Fathers are nothing but "the Fathers" from Clement of Rome to Bernard of Clairvaux can hardly be expected to distinguish Rufinus from the rest; and writers of another sort who have their doubts are too often daunted by the spurious authority of a long line of copyists. Perhaps the climax of the mischief is reached when a historian like Keim (*Aus dem Urchristenthum* 204—211) quotes Socrates and Sozomen as independent evidence for his most important facts when they are merely retailing the stories of Rufinus.

NOTE B.

THE LEGEND OF ANTONY.

Professor Weingarten of Breslau *Ursprung des Mönchthums im nachconstantinischen Zeitalter* (first in *Zeitschrift f. Kirchengesch.* for 1876, and since separately) has shewn that Antony as we know him is no more than an ideal of the generation after Athanasius. His results are discussed by Hilgenfeld *Zeitschr. f. wissensch. Theol.* xxi. 139—150, Gass *Zeitschr. f. Kirchengesch.* ii. 254—275, and Cropp *Jahrb. f. deutsche Theol.* for 1878, p. 342, but without any very serious modifications on this question. Even Keim *Ursprung des Mönchswesens* in *Aus dem Urchristenthum* 204—220 depends much on statements ultimately derived from Rufinus and Jerome; and if these be omitted, his case assumes a very different aspect. As no

English writer (except references by Hatch *Organization* 155—157) seems yet to have noticed these important researches, it will be convenient to give a summary of his arguments, with such changes and additions as have fallen in my way in the course of a review of the subject.

Weingarten begins by shewing that Jerome's accounts of Paul of Thebes and Hilarion of Gaza are mere romances unconfirmed by any independent evidence; and in this he has since been supported by W. Israël in *Zeitschr. f. wissensch. Theol.* for 1880, pp. 129—165. This done, he goes on to the life of Antony. Here our knowledge ultimately depends on Eusebius and Athanasius, for there is no trace of Antony's existence in any other writer of that generation. The silence of Cyril of Jerusalem (not without significance in passages like *Cat.* xvi. 19) may be allowed to pass; and even that of Didymus, though the legend more than once connects his name with Antony. But it is remarkable that the ascetic Basil never mentions the great anchorite, even in *Epp.* 207, 227, where he is expressly speaking of monasticism in Egypt. Later references are abundant, but there is nothing of any consequence which can be considered independent evidence. These allusions we can take into account in the course of our investigations.

Now (I.) with regard to Eusebius. The existence of monastic communities in Egypt seems unknown to him. (1) He mentions none in his Life of Constantine, and has to go back to the apostolic communism in his defence (*H. E.* ii. 17) of the Therapeutæ, whom he discusses without any suspicion that Philo's *de Vita Contemplativa* is only a novel of the third century. (2) Carefully as he describes the persecution of Maximin at Alexandria, he says nothing of Antony's visit, though *Vita* c. 4 implies that it was not a short one. In fact, he nowhere seems aware of the great saint's existence. (3) The references in his *Chronica* to Constantine's letter in 335 and to Antony's death in 356 are due to Jerome, who inserted them to suit the *Vita Antonii*.

Next (II.) as regards Athanasius. The account given *Hist. Ar.* 14, p. 278 of Balacius, of his contempt (καταπτύσαι) for the letter of (the illiterate) Antony and of his sudden death, is dependent on the *Vita* c. 86, and scarcely consistent with facts. Nestorius of Gaza did not become Prefect of Egypt till after Easter (or more likely August) 344 (Index to *Festal Letters*), and the summer of the same year is the extreme limit for the duration of Gregory's persecutions. The whole incident is wanting in the parallel narratives of the *Ep. Encycl.*

In the rest of the works of Athanasius, there is no trace of Antony's existence. Considering the grandeur of the saint's position and his intimate relations with the bishop of Alexandria, this fact alone should be decisive. Even in the letter to Dracontius, written within a year of Antony's death, where Athanasius gives a list of ascetics who had not thought ecclesiastical preferment any hindrance to the highest sanctity, there is not a word of the great hermit's deep reverence (*Vita* c. 67) for the lowest clerics, though his authority would have been conclusive. There remains only the *Vita Antonii*: and this, though in substance written, and perhaps at Alexandria (c. 12 πέραν), and even translated before 375 (Jerome *Vita Pauli*), is not a genuine work of Athanasius, much less an authentic history.

(1) It is inscribed πρὸς τοὺς ἐν ξένῃ μοναχούς—namely to the Westerns, as is clearly shewn in the Benedictine preface. Some may set aside this passage as a later addition, though it is found in the Evagrian translation; but c. 93 agrees with it in assuming the existence of monks in the West as early as 356—362, the professed date of the *Vita Antonii* (c. 82 ἡ νῦν ἔφοδος τῶν Ἀρειανῶν). Now monasticism was not imported to Rome by Athanasius in 339. Jerome indeed *Ep.* 127, *ad Principiam* has a very confused statement which seems to say so, but he is plainly romancing when he introduces the name of his friend Marcella, who survived the capture of Rome in 410, and died in no extreme old age. Athanasius moreover gives a very different account *Apol. ad Ctium* 4, p. 236 of his stay in Rome τῇ ἐκκλησίᾳ τὰ κατ' ἐμαυτὸν παραθέμενος (τούτου γὰρ μόνου μοι φροντὶς ἦν), ἐσχόλαζον ταῖς συνάξεσι. Indeed monasticism was unknown in Europe in the reign of Valentinian (Soz. iii. 14), and at Rome in particular when Jerome went into the East in 373; and at Milan it had only lately been introduced by Ambrose at the time of Augustine's visit in 385 (Aug. *Conf.* vii. 6).

(2) Apart from its numerous miracles, the general tone of the *Vita* is unhistorical. It is a perfect romance of the desert, without a trace of human sinfulness to mar its beauty. The saint is an idealized ascetic hero, the *mons Antonii* a paradise of peaceful holiness (c. 44, 49). We cannot pass from the *Scriptores Erotici* to the *Vita Antonii* without noticing the same atmosphere of unreality in both. From Athanasius there is all the difference of the novel writer from the orator,—of the *Cyropædia* from the

III.] NOTE B. THE LEGEND OF ANTONY. 105

de Corona. Accordingly Gregory of Nazianzus *Or.* 21, p. 383 calls it τοῦ μοναδικοῦ βίου νομοθεσίαν ἐν πλάσματι διηγήσεως. So Fialon *Saint Ath.* 237, 249, "c'est l'épopée du désert......Telle est cette vie, ou plutôt ce panégyrique, ou mieux encore, puisque j'ai risqué le mot, ce poëme de saint Antoine : c'est moins, en effet, la vie et l'éloge d'un homme, qu'un tableau idéal d'une grande institution." Yet he writes without any suspicion of its spuriousness.

(3) Though Athanasius had ample room for miracles in the adventures of his long life, he never records anything of the sort. The death of Arius is not a case in point, not being in itself miraculous; the revelation of Julian's death to the abbot Theodore is integrally connected with the *Vita Antonii;* and the σημεῖα mentioned *ad Drac.* 9, p. 211, are the moral miracles of continence *id.* 7, p. 210 : compare also *de Inc.* 48, p. 71. But miracles, often of the most puerile description, are the staple of the *Vita Antonii,* and some of them, c. 70, 71, are said to have been done before the eyes of Athanasius himself, who could not have omitted all reference to them in the writings of his exile.

(4) Antony is represented (c. 1, and everywhere implied) as an illiterate Copt, dependent on memory even for his knowledge of Scripture (c. 3, ὥστε...λοιπὸν αὐτῷ τὴν μνήμην ἀντὶ βιβλίων γενέσθαι: so understood by Augustine *de Doctr. Chr.* Prol. 4, discussed by Neander E. Tr. iii. 325). He preaches in Coptic (c. 16), and needs an interpreter (c. 72, 74, 77) for his conversation with the Greeks. Yet he alludes to Plato (c. 74, τὴν ψυχὴν φάσκετε πεπλανῆσθαι καὶ πεπτωκέναι ἀπὸ τῆς ἀψῖδος τῶν οὐρανῶν εἰς σῶμα— a plain reference to the language of *Phædrus* 247), combats an abstruse doctrine of Plotinus (c. 74 ὑμεῖς δὲ εἰκόνα τοῦ νοῦ τὴν ψυχὴν λέγοντες), discusses Stoic or rationalizing theories of *Greek* mythology (c. 76), investigates Arianism (c. 69), explains the origin of oracles (c. 33), speculates on the Incarnation (c. 74), and in general reasons like a learned philosopher. Much of this display may be due to his biographer, but it all helps to form the great Antony with whom we are familiar. And in this case it is worth notice that Athanasius would scarcely quote the *Phædrus* in preference to the *Timæus,* which refers the descent of the soul to a universal cosmic law (Zeller E. Tr. *Plato* 391, or Plotinus *Enn.* IV. viii. 1). The *Phædrus* would seem in the fourth century to have been much less used than the *Timæus.* Eusebius *Præp. Ev.* quotes it twice, the *Timæus* 21 times, while the *Laws* appear in Gaisford's index no less than

57 times. The proportion is similar in Plotinus, as regards the *Phædrus* and the *Timæus*.

(5) The *Vita Antonii* has coincidences with Athanasius in language and doctrine, as we should expect in any professed work of his: e.g. "the very uncatholic-sounding declaration of the sufficiency of Scripture" (Schaff E. Tr. ii. 182), which begins the *c. Gentes* (c. 1), as well as Antony's sermon (*Vita* c. 16). This however is a commonplace. The divergences are serious. Antony's shame of the body is not in the spirit of the writer of *ad Amunem*. The stress on φιλοπτωχία, c. 17, 30, is more like Cyril of Jerusalem. The demonology in particular resembles (c. 22, 35) that of the *de mysteriis*, and is utterly foreign to Athanasius, who keeps the powers of evil in the background instead of allowing them familiar intercourse with men. In his writings there is nothing in the least resembling the varied and grotesque appearances of evil spirits and the substantial combats with them which fill the pages of the *Vita Antonii*.

(6) The early intercourse of Athanasius with Antony is unhistorical. The saint loved dirt (c. 47, 93) much too well to endure the defilement of water poured on his hands (*Proœm.* p. 632, reading παρ' αὐτοῦ). Athanasius on his part shews neither trace nor recollection of it in his works, nor is there any room for it (Tillemont viii. 652) in his early life. This however we have discussed elsewhere.

(7) It is implied throughout the *Vita Antonii* (e.g. c. 41, 44) that the monks were extremely numerous throughout the East during Antony's lifetime. Now there were monks in Egypt, monks of Serapis, long before; but Christian monks there were none. Rufinus of course has novels in abundance, but Eusebius (*supra*) mentions no monks, nor Athanasius in 338 (*Festal Letter*); and they seem new to Basil *Ep.* 207 as late as 375. And if Athanasius speaks of monks in 355 *ad Dracontium* 9, p. 211, the context shews that they were ascetics of the old type, who refrained neither from marriage nor from social life. Nor can anything else be inferred from the inscription of Ath. *Hist. Ar.* p. 271, τοῖς ἀπανταχοῦ κατὰ τόπον—referring to the τόποι of Egypt (Kuhn *Verfassung* ii. 495, Marquardt *Rom. Alterth.* iv. 291). As regards Syria and Pontus, it may be that Weingarten has gone too far in denying the existence of monks outside Egypt before the reign of Julian. (Gass, pp. 266—271 or Keim, pp. 204—211.) The council of Gangra, which may be as early as 340, defeated an

attempt to introduce the monastic life into Pontus; but the vexation of the Massalians by Lupicinus Epiph. *Hær.* 80, 2, shews it actually established in Melitene about 365. But the rescript of Valens *Cod. Theod.* xii. 1, 63, in 373 is one of our first signs that the monks were becoming numerous enough to attract the attention of a jealous administration in the direst want of fighting men.

Against all this there seems nothing but the ascription of the *Vita Antonii* to Athanasius by Gregory of Nazianzus *Or.* 21, written soon after 380. But this seems copied from the work itself. It is anonymous to Augustine in 385, to Rufinus, and to Jerome in 375—6, who first names Athanasius as its author *de Scriptt. Eccl.* about 393. Its translation into Latin by Evagrius before 389, or perhaps before 375, proves nothing but its antiquity, which is fully conceded. Of other writers who ascribe it to Athanasius, Socrates (appealed to by Keim, p. 207) is not independent. About the allusions of Ephraem Syrus I can find nothing certain; but even Tillemont viii. 138 seems doubtful of them.

It will be noticed that many of these difficulties belong to the structure of the *Vita Antonii*, and are not removed by any theory of interpolations.

NOTE C.

The Index to the Festal Letters of Athanasius.

The value of the Index to the *Festal Letters* of Athanasius has hardly been sufficiently recognized. It has its numerical slips and occasional traces of legend; but its general good faith and accuracy seem unimpeachable. Hefele, *Councils* § 54 (whom others seem to copy), has collected a serious list of errors; but a little care in reading the Index itself will shew that they are all his own. We may take the opportunity to discuss some of the chief dates connected with the two first exiles of Athanasius (335—346). There are two points to be noticed.

(1) Cassian's statement, that the Festal Letter was not sent till after Epiphany, may be true for his own time, but needs modification for that of Athanasius. The Letters for 330, 345 and 346 were written as early as the preceding Easter; but we cannot say the same of those for 333 and 334. The Letter for 329 was written after his election the preceding June 8, that for 347 after his return

the preceding Oct. 21, that for 338 after his release from Trier in June 337. That for 332, which begins with an apology for its lateness, is dated from the court at Nicomedia, whence he reached Alexandria about the middle of March. As it records the failure of the Meletian plots, it probably arrived only a little in advance of the writer. Similarly, the Letter for 363 was sent after his flight to Upper Egypt, the preceding Oct. 24, and that for 364 was written from Antioch, for which he started Sept. 5, 363, and whence he returned Feb. 20.

It follows that we must date his expulsion by Philagrius in 339, not in 340. We have the Letters for 338 and 339, and one from Rome for 341; but that for 340 is expressly stated to be wanting, and the Index tells us that none was written. As Athanasius fled only three weeks before Easter, the Festal Letter for the year must have been already sent. Hence it was in 339. This agrees with the statement of the *Hist. Acephala* §§ 1, 12 (both passages are emended by Sievers, *Einl.* § 19) that the second exile of Athanasius lasted seven years and six months, not six years. So also Jerome *Chron.*, but he is full of mistakes. We reach the same result if we compare Theodoret's account *H. E.* ii. 4, that Gregory "devastated the flock worse than a wild beast" for six years, with the notice in the Index of Gregory's death June 26; which, as we shall see, will have to be placed in the year 345. It is possible however that Theodoret is confusing Gregory with George, who really was murdered.

(2) The writer of the Index not only counts by the Egyptian months, but usually follows the Egyptian reckoning of the year, beginning it Aug. 29. He also loosely groups together connected events without caring whether they are strictly included in any single year, whether Julian or Egyptian.

Thus (*a*) under the consuls of 336 we find the departure of Athanasius July 11 for Tyre, his arrival at Constantinople Oct. 30, and his exile to Gaul Nov. 7. But these events are given as the reason why no Festal Letter was written for 336, and are therefore clearly intended to belong to our year 335. Again (*b*), under the consuls of 338, we are told that Constantine having died May 22, Athanasius returned from Gaul to Alexandria Nov. 23, and that Antony paid a two days' visit to the city, leaving it July 27. As Athanasius was there to receive him, according to the legend in the *Vita Antonii* 69—71, Constantine's death as well as the bishop's return must be intended for 337. Again (*c*) under the year 343, we have first the Council of Sardica, then the notice of continued troubles; then the recantation of Ursacius and Valens, which cannot well be dated on any theory within twelve months of the meeting at Sardica. Similarly (*d*), Gregory's death June 26 and the return of Athanasius from Italy Oct. 21 are both recorded under the year 346. Now there was an interval of more than a year between these events. Gregory's death being (Ath. *Hist. Ar.* 21, p. 282) ten months after the deposition of Stephen, which was itself three years after the Council of the Dedication in the summer of 341, is firmly fixed for 345. On the other hand, the return of Athanasius is settled for 346 by the concurrent evidence of the *Hist. Aceph.* §§ 1, 12, emended as before, and the Letters themselves—that for 347 having been finished after his arrival. Hence it follows that the whole of the Egyptian year beginning Aug. 29, 345 falls within the interval. One more instance (*e*) may be given. Under the year 363 we have the flight of Athanasius Oct. 24 (no doubt 362), the death of Julian "eight months later," and the departure of Athanasius Sept. 5 (a new Egyptian year begun) to meet Jovian.

On the other hand, it is the Letter for 332, not that for 331 as the Index tells us, which was written from the *Comitatus*. There is an error also in the elevation of Gallus, which the Index places in 352. The *Chron. Pasch.* dates it Mar. 15, 351; and in any case it was before and not after the battle of Mursa.

CHAPTER IV.

THE COUNCIL OF SARDICA.

CONSTANTINE'S part on earth was done. His worldly dispositions were already made; and when the hand of death was on him, the great emperor laid aside the purple, and the ambiguous position of a Christian Cæsar with it, and passed away (May 22, 337) in the white robe of a simple neophyte. In that last impressive scene we hardly recognize the man who had shocked heathenism itself with the great beast-fights at Trier thirty years before. Darkly as his memory is stained with isolated crimes, Constantine must for ever rank among the greatest of the emperors. If it were lawful to forget the names of Licinius and Crispus, we might also let him take his place among the best. Others equalled—few surpassed—his gifts of statesmanship and military genius. Fewer still had his sense of duty, though here he cannot rival Julian or Marcus. But as an actual benefactor of mankind Constantine stands almost alone in history. It was a new thing for an emperor to declare himself a lover of peace for its own sake, and not merely because the Empire needed peace. The heathens could not understand it, and Zosimus[1] calls it sloth or cowardice—a strange reproach to bring against a soldier like Constantine, who had fought in almost every country from Caledonia to Egypt. Constantine had seen too much of war and social misery not to be a reformer and a man of peace. He was no mere administrator like Tiberius, but seemed to feel that Christianity had laid on him a new duty and given him a new power to strike at the root of social evils. Nor were his efforts wholly vain. The Nicene Council is unique in history; for its

---

[1] Zos. ii. 32. He repeats against Theodosius this unfortunate charge of sloth and cowardice. His own narrative is enough to refute it in either case.

record really sounds as if for a moment Constantine had roused the East from the deep despair of ages. In that great crisis every eye was fixed on the strange upstart church which had fought its way from the mines and the catacombs to the throne of the world, and in every heart the question rose, whether the power which had overcome the Empire had also a spell from heaven to cure its ancient sickness. Statesmen and soldiers had tried in vain, and it was now the bishops' turn. The flattery of Eusebius is not indiscriminate[1], and is at least disinterested after his master's death. It may sound fulsome to us, but we have not lived in times like his. We might not think it overstrained if our eyes had seen like his the years of shame and outrage when the Evil Beast ran riot in the slaughter of the saints of God, and every whelp of Satan drank his fill of Christian blood. Even our cold spirit might kindle with enthusiasm if we had shared like him the final victory, and stood like him by Constantine's side on the great day when hope for the world for once flashed out like a burst of sunlight on the sombre glory of the Empire[2].

[1] Thus Eusebius *V. C.* iv. 54 speaks of the ἄλεκτος εἰρωνεία of the courtiers, and condemns the easy temper of Constantine in listening to flatterers.

In his *Chronica* we find *Licinius contra jus sacramenti privatus occiditur*, and *Crispus et Licinius junior crudelissime interficiuntur:* but these entries seem the work of Jerome, like the mentions of Antony, of Quirinus of Siscia, and of Helena (*concubina*, contrast Eus. *H. E.* viii. 13, παῖδα γνήσιον).

[2] The orthodoxy and good faith of Eusebius have recently been defended by a much abler hand than mine; and I cannot pretend to add much to Lightfoot's argument. It will however be somewhat strengthened if we adopt the dates really given by the Index to the *Festal Letters*.

No complaint of the historian's enemies is more frequent than that if he had not been secretly inclined to Arianism, he would have given more prominence to the subject in his Life of Constantine. In answer to this, it would be enough to refer to the purpose of the work, or to the distinctly orthodox declarations scattered through his writings. But if Eusebius was of opinion that Sabellianism was the more pressing danger of the two, he is fully justified in assigning to Arianism the secondary position he does. It will not be denied that such was his belief: and it was not unreasonable at the time he wrote. We may question his foresight, but we are not therefore entitled to dispute his orthodoxy.

The Life of Constantine was written between September 337 and the death of Eusebius. This Lightfoot dates probably May 30, 339, or not later than the beginning of 340. We may shift it a year earlier, for the ejection of Athanasius by Philagrius must be placed in March 339 (not 340); and no writer connects Eusebius with the appointment of Gregory shortly before it. Upon the whole, we may pretty safely place the Life of Constantine somewhere in the course of 338, during an interval of the strife.

Looking back from that date, he might almost think Arianism an extinct controversy. The matter had always been very much of a personal quarrel, Arius himself long ago had

The sons of Constantine shared the world among them like an ancestral inheritance[1]. Thrace and Pontus had already been assigned to their cousins Dalmatius and Hannibalianus; but the army at Constantinople promptly rose and gave them six feet of earth apiece. With them perished almost the whole family of Constantius Chlorus by his second marriage[2]. From the confusion three *Augusti* emerged, to represent on earth the Trinity in heaven[3]. The division of the Empire was completed some time later. Constantine II. added Africa to his Gaulish prefecture, the legions of Syria obtained the East for Constantius, and Italy and Illyricum were left as the share of Constans[4]. Thus neither Rome nor Constantinople fell to the eldest brother.

renounced his heresy, and Eusebius had seen his restoration by the council at Jerusalem. It had a few adherents left at Alexandria, whom it might be well some day to restore to communion; but for thirteen years it had scarcely troubled the peace of Christendom. Athanasius on the other hand had gravely misconducted himself at Alexandria; and not the least of his offences was the attempt to raise a cry of heresy against his accusers. However, even he had been allowed by imperial clemency to return (November 337, not 338), and might rule better in the future. There had also been a terrible scandal at Antioch, where a great bishop had been deposed for fornication. But the doctrinal troubles (so Eusebius would say) had come entirely from the Sabellians; and the chief offender was the universal enemy Marcellus.

[1] So Eusebius *V. C.* iv. 51, 63 ὥσπερ τινὰ πατρικὴν ὕπαρξιν.

[2] Six princes were killed (Rendall *Julian* 36). Of the whole house of Theodora none escaped but Gallus, Julian and Nepotianus.

[3] Such was the demand of the army (Eus. *V. C.* iv. 68), curiously repeated in the time of Constantine IV. (668—685).

[4] Questions of chronology become very intricate about this point, and I have given no more than a summary of results.

Constantine's death is settled firmly enough for May 22, 337, and Idatius names September 9 for the proclamation of the three *Augusti*, while the meeting in Pannonia (Julian *Or.* i. p. 22) is fixed for the summer of 338 by the laws (a) *Cod. Theod.* x. 10, 4 dated by Constantine II. from Viminacium June 12, and (b) *Cod. Theod.* xv. 1, 5, dated by Constans from Sirmium July 27.

The massacre is placed by de Broglie iii. 10 soon after Constantine's death, while Tillemont (*Empereurs* iv. 664) defers it to the next year. Now Eusebius *V. C.* iv. 68 tells us that as soon as the soldiers heard of the emperor's death, they decided unanimously that none but his sons should succeed him, and that not long afterwards they demanded three *Augusti* to represent on earth the heavenly Trinity. Reading between the lines, we may pretty safely assume that the massacre was the form in which the army expressed its decision, and that it took place some time before September 9. So Zosimus ii. 40.

The outbreak is only too easy to account for. The soldiers were devoted to Constantine's memory; and if the inheritance of his sons was any way threatened by the house of Theodora, the sooner it was exterminated the better. Hatred of Ablavius may also have played a part in the matter, if we can trust a hint of Greg. Naz. *Or.* iv. 21 ἡνίκα τὸ στρατιωτικὸν ἐξωπλίσθη κατὰ τῶν ἐν τέλει, καινοτομοῦν φόβῳ καινοτομίας, καὶ διὰ νέων προστατῶν καθίστατο τὰ βασίλεια (discussed

IV.]   CONSTANTIUS.   113

The exiled bishops were restored before these things were settled. The younger Constantine had received Athanasius in all honour, and now released him the moment his father's death was known at Trier. Athanasius travelled by way of Hadrianople, and reached Alexandria Nov. 23, 337[1], to the joy of Greeks and Copts alike. Marcellus, Paul and the rest were restored about the same time, but not without much disturbance at Ancyra, which each party ascribed to its enemies[2].

The reign of Constantius lies before us. But before we trace a miserable record of oppression and exhaustion in the state, of confusion and misrule in the church, let us cast a glance at the emperor himself.

Constantius had something of his father's character. In temperance and chastity, in love of letters and in dignity of manner, in social charm and pleasantness of private life, he was no unworthy son of Constantine; and if he inherited no splendid genius for war, he had a full measure of soldierly courage and endurance. Nor was the statecraft contemptible, which might have boasted that no mutiny had disturbed the East for four and twenty years, and no revolt except the Jewish war. It was no trifling merit to have maintained the Roman peace so well without undue favour to the army[3].

But Constantius was essentially a little man, in whom his father's vices took a meaner form. Upon occasion Constantine

by Wietersheim *Völkerwanderung* iii. Anm. 91). Ablavius may also be the unworthy favourite of Constantine whose punishment is cautiously alluded to by Eus. *V. C.* iv. 54, 55.

Beugnot's theory of a pagan reaction is needless; and is moreover contradicted by the curiously theological form in which the army couched its demand for three *Augusti*.

The share of Constantius in it is another disputed question. Rendall *Julian* 36 sums up the evidence and declares his guilt unproved. It may be added that the silence of Lucifer is a strong argument for a complete acquittal; but it is weakened by the fact that he does not refer to the murder of Gallus—unless an allusion be found in *Cain, carnifex, homicida*, &c. In any case it makes little difference to our estimate of Constantius.

[1] Note CC. *The Return of Athanasius in* 337.
[2] Zahn *Marcellus* 65.
[3] Considering that no mutiny followed his defeats in the East, we may safely reject (Tillemont notwithstanding) the story of his abject cowardice at Mursa, told by Sulpicius Severus, *Chron.* ii. 38.

Ammianus xxi. 16, 2—3 notices his care to secure a due supremacy to the civil power. The consular *Fasti* in his reign are in striking contrast to the appointments of Valentinian, for Arbetio is the only general we find in them. Men of letters on the other hand often reached the highest offices, like Anatolius and Musonianus.

G.   8

could break his oath and strike with ruthless cruelty; but the whole spirit of Constantius was corroded with fear and jealousy of every man better than himself. The executioner had a busy time, and the assassin[1] was always in reserve. Thus the easy trust in unworthy favourites which marks even the ablest Flavian emperors became in Constantius nothing less than a public calamity. It was bad enough when the uprightness of Constantine or Julian was led astray by Sopater or Maximus, Ablavius or Mamertinus; but it was incomparably worse when Eusebius and Florentius[2] found a master too weak in moral courage to stand alone, too jealous and too vain to allow an able counsellor about him, too easy-tempered[3] and too indolent to care what oppressions were committed in his name. In war it was the standing weakness of the Empire, that a good general was nowhere safe but on the throne[4]; and in peace imperial suspicion made a paradise for the spies and eunuchs of the palace. The peculiar repulsiveness of Constantius, like that of Charles I., is not due to flagrant personal vice, but to the combination of cold-blooded treachery with the utter want of any inner nobleness of character. But Constantius was altogether an abler plotter. Instead of playing with half a dozen schemes of treachery at once, he aimed his blow at Athanasius once for all, and with a consummateness of perfidy Alexius Comnenus might have envied. Almost alone of the Christian emperors, he scarcely made an effort to check the decay which Diocletian had bequeathed to his successors. More than one noble law of Constantine was aimed at the evil, Julian fought it with unremitting energy, Valentinian and Theodosius have left an honourable record, and the Empire may owe something even to Honorius, but the

---

[1] As in the case of Silvanus.

[2] For the chamberlain Eusebius, the sarcastic reference of Ammianus xviii. 4, 3 *apud quem, si vere dici debeat, multa Constantius potuit*. For Florentius, the indignant words of Julian *Ep.* 17, rightly referred by Rendall *Julian* 131 to the Gaulish prefect rather than the chamberlain. Julian *ad S. P. Q. R. Athen.* scarcely bears out Clinton's objection that Florentius was on good terms with Julian till after the recall of Sallust in the autumn of 357.

[3] Theodoret *H. E.* v. 7 contrasts the εὐκολία of Constantius with the μοχθηρία of Valens and ii. 2 εὐρίπιστον τοῦ Κ. τὴν γνώμην. So Epiph. *Hær.* 69, 12. Eutropius x. 15 *ad severitatem tum propensior, si suspicio imperii moveretur, mitis alias*. His unsteady purpose is clear enough in the history: but see Ath. *Hist. Ar.* 69 p. 304. Theodoret ii. 3, 31.

[4] Silvanus, Julian and Ursicinus may serve as examples for the reign of Constantius.

services of Constantius are overshadowed by the iniquities of miscreants like Apodemius and Paul *Catena*[1].

Yet Constantius was a pious emperor in his own way. He loved the ecclesiastical game, and was easily won over to the conservative side. The growing despotism of the Empire and the personal vanity of Constantius were equally suited by the episcopal timidity which cried for an arm of flesh to fight its battles. It is not easy to decide how far he acted on his own preferences and superstitions, how far he merely allowed his flatterers to guide him, and how far he saw that it was good policy to follow them; but so far as we can see, his opinions seem to have kept pace with those professed by Acacius of Cæsarea. Thus without ever being a genuine Arian, he began with a thorough dislike of the Nicene council, continued for many years to hold conservative language, and ended by adopting the vague Homœan compromise[2].

Eusebian intrigues were soon resumed. Fresh troubles were raised at Alexandria, and a new prefect[3] sent to make the most of them. Now that Constantine was dead, a schism could be established; so the Arians were encouraged to hold assemblies of their own, and provided with a bishop in the person of Pistus, one of the original heretics deposed by Alexander. No fitter consecrator could be found for him than Secundus of Ptolemais, one of the final recusants at Nicæa. Charges new and old were made against Athanasius, and the presbyter Macarius was sent on behalf of Pistus to lay them before Julius of Rome. Athanasius on his side assembled the Egyptian bishops at Alexandria, and forwarded to Rome their solemn witness in his favour. Macarius fled at the first rumour of its coming, and his deacons could only escape exposure for the moment by asking Julius to hold a council, and undertaking to produce full evidence before it.

Meanwhile the Eusebians had deposed Athanasius in a

---

[1] Note D. *The Legislation of Constantius.*
[2] The character of Constantius is drawn by Ammianus xxi. 16, of the moderns by Reinkens *Hilarius* 86—99, Wietersheim (Dahn) i. 461.
[3] Correcting the title of the *Festal* Letter for 338 after Sievers, *Hist. Aceph.* § 7. Philagrius must have been appointed for a second term (Ath. *Hist. Ar.* 51, p. 296), before the end of the Egyptian year in August, 338. The disturbances are alluded to in the Index for 338 and in the *Letter* for 339.

council held at Antioch, where Constantius had fixed his quarters for the winter of 338—9[1]. But we hear nothing of heresy—only the old charges of sedition and intrigue, with a few more of the same sort, and a new one of having allowed the civil power to restore him after his deposition at Tyre[2]. Pistus was not appointed in his place. The see of Alexandria was offered to the learned Eusebius of Edessa, afterwards bishop of Emesa. But Eusebius had seen with his own eyes the popularity of Athanasius in Egypt, and had no mind to challenge his supremacy. The council therefore chose Gregory of Cappadocia, a student of Alexandria like Eusebius, and a fitter agent for the rough work to be done. Athanasius was expelled by the apostate prefect Philagrius[3] in Lent 339, and Gregory installed by military violence in his place. Scenes of outrage were enacted all over Egypt[4].

Athanasius fled to Rome, and his example was followed by Marcellus of Ancyra, and ejected clerics from all parts of the East. Julius at once took up the high tone of judicial impartiality which became an arbiter of Christendom. He received the fugitives with a decent reserve, and invited the Eusebians to the council they had asked him to hold. For a long time there came no

---

[1] As the departure of Athanasius for Rome is clearly fixed for 339, we must distinguish this council from that of the Dedication, which is as clearly fixed for 341. So in the main Hefele *Councils* § 54: but both he and de Broglie iii. 33 are led astray by the initial error of placing his first return from exile in 338 instead of 337. Hence de Broglie brings him to Rome first in 339, in obedience to the pope's summons, and again in 341, on his expulsion by Philagrius. For the return from Rome between the Council of the Dedication and the beginning of Lent 342, he gains time by the unique mistake (iii. 38, 47, 53) of dating the Council "dès les premiers jours de 341."

[2] Soz. iii. 2. Socrates and Sozomen confuse the council with that of the Dedication. But a charge plainly alluded to by the latter (*Can.* 4 and 12) was probably raised at the earlier assembly.

[3] On Philagrius, Sievers *Libanius* 209.

In the Index to the *Festal Letters* it is said that Athanasius "fled from the church of Theonas" on the morning of March 19, three days before Gregory's arrival. Athanasius himself, *Encycl.* 5, p. 91, says that he stayed in the city for some time after the outrages had begun, whereas *Hist. Ar.* 10, p. 277, we are told that Athanasius fled to Rome, πρὶν γενέσθαι ταῦτα, καὶ μόνον ἀκούσας.

The last statement may be explained by referring ταῦτα to the general summary of outrages made just before, while the other two are quite consistent with each other. If Athanasius went into hiding (ὑπέκλεψα ἐμαυτὸν τῶν λαῶν *Encycl.*) Mar. 19, it might be April before he found a ship of Alexandria sailing into Italy.

[4] Athanasius (*Hist. Ar.* 11, p. 277) had his accounts from his partizans at Alexandria. They would not lose in the telling; but there is no reason to doubt their substantial truth.

answer from the East. The old heretic Carpones appeared at Rome on Gregory's behalf; but the envoys of Julius were detained at Antioch till January (340), and at last dismissed with an unmannerly reply[1]. After some further delay, a synod of some 50 bishops met at Rome in the autumn of 340. The cases were examined, Athanasius and Marcellus acquitted; and it remained for Julius to report their decision to the Easterns.

His letter to Dianius[2], Flacillus, Eusebius and the rest is one of the ablest documents of the entire controversy. Nothing can be more skilful or more prudent than the calm and high judicial tone in which he lays open every excuse of the Eusebians. He was surprised, he says, to receive so discourteous an answer to his letter, and had kept it to himself for some time, in hopes that some of them might even yet return to a better mind. But what was their grievance? If it was (1) his invitation to a synod, they could not have much confidence in their cause. Even the great council of Nicæa had decided (and not without the will of God) that the acts of one synod might be revised by another[3]. Their own envoys had asked him to hold a council; and the men who set aside the authority of Nicæa by using the services of heretics like Secundus, Pistus and Carpones were hardly entitled to claim finality for their own decisions at Tyre. If the decisions of the councils against Novatus and Paul of Samosata were to be respected, much more those of the great council against the Arians. They complained (2) that he had given them too short a notice—a very good reply, if only the appointed time had found them on the road to Rome. "But this also, beloved, is only an excuse." They had detained his envoys for months at Antioch, and plainly did not wish to come.

---

[1] Reconstructed by Bright *Hist. Treatises* xxiv. from the answer of Julius.

[2] The letter *ad Danium Flacillum* &c. is given by Ath. *Apol. c. Ar.* 21, p. 111. Montfaucon identifies the unknown Danius with Theognius of Nicæa; but it seems better to follow Tillemont *Mém.* vi. 322, who understands the venerated bishop of Cæsarea Mazaca. Dianius was present at Philippopolis; and also (Soz. iii. 5) at the Council of the Dedication, or more likely that which deposed Athanasius in 339. He is not indeed named as an enemy by Athanasius, but from all accounts appears to have been rather conservative than Arian.

Hefele *Councils* § 55 gives a summary of the letter. I have omitted a few of the minor arguments.

[3] Not in the extant canons. Robertson *Ath.* iii. suggests that it is "a free use of *Can.* v."

As for (3) the reception of Athanasius, it was neither lightly nor unjustly done. The Eusebian letters against him were inconsistent, for no two of them ever told the same story; and were moreover contradicted by letters in his favour from Egypt and elsewhere. The Mareotic commission was a travesty of justice; and with regard to the murder of Arsenius, he was alive and well, and actually a friend of Athanasius. The accused had come to Rome when summoned, and waited for them eighteen months in vain; whereas the Eusebians had uncanonically appointed an utter stranger in his place at Alexandria, and sent him with a guard of soldiers all the way from Antioch, to break up the peace of Egypt with horrible outrages. With regard to (4) Marcellus, he had denied the charge of heresy and presented a very sound confession of his faith. The Roman legates at Nicæa had also borne witness to the honourable part he had taken in the council. Thus the Eusebians had no ground for their complaint that Athanasius and Marcellus had been hastily acquitted at Rome. Rather their own doings had caused the division, for complaints of their violence arrived from all parts of the East. In this state of things it was strange to hear that there was peace in the church. The authors of these outrages—rumour said they were all the work of a few intriguers—were no lovers of peace, but of confusion. It was sad that petty quarrels should be allowed to go on till bishops drove their brethren into exile. If there were any complaint against the bishop of Alexandria, they should not have neglected the old custom of writing first to Rome, that a legitimate decision might issue from the apostolic see. It was time to put an end to these outrages, as we must answer for it in the day of judgment.

Severe as the letter is, it is free from needless irritation, and in every way contrasts well with the disingenuous querulousness of the Eusebians. Nor is Julius unmindful of his own authority. The weak point is his support of Marcellus; for Julius must have deliberately intended to accept his teaching as at least permissible[1].

---

[1] Socrates *H. E.* ii. 17 (among other mistakes) says that he wrote μὴ δεῖν παρὰ γνώμην τοῦ ἐπισκόπου ῾Ρώμης κανονίζειν τὰς ἐκκλησίας. No passage of his letter goes nearly so far as this.

The Eusebians replied in the summer of 341[1], when some ninety bishops[2] met at Antioch to consecrate the Golden Church of Constantine[3]. Hence the council is usually called that of the Dedication (ἡ ἐν τοῖς ἐγκαινίοις). Its character is one of the most disputed points of the history before us. Hilary calls it an assembly of saints[4]; and its canons were not only ranked with those of the œcumenical councils, but largely drawn upon in the collection ascribed to the apostles. Yet its chief work was to confirm the deposition of Athanasius and to draw up creeds in opposition to the Nicene. Was it orthodox or Arian? As its canons contain nothing distinctive[5], the question must be decided by an examination of its creeds. As we find no complaints of court influence, we may fairly assume that the council represented the real belief of a majority of the bishops

---

[1] In the fifth year after Constantine's death (Socr. Soz.), and in the 14th Indiction (Ath.): i.e. some time between May 22 and September 1. Hefele *Councils* § 56. We might fix it at once for May 22 if we could assume with Möhler *Ath.* 350 that it was the fifth anniversary of the accession of Constantius.

[2] Schelstraten's list *Sacr. Ant. Conc.* 58—98 of 51 bishops needs much revision. Of his authorities, the letter of Julius *ad Danium Flacillum* &c. refers to the earlier council, and the later Latin translations of the Synodical Acts are worthless, the sees being copied from the Nicene signatures. We may also omit the name of Marcellus, who had indeed left Rome more than a year before, but would hardly have ventured into the lion's mouth at Antioch. Gregory of Alexandria (expressly named also by Socr. ii. 10: but contrast *Festal Letters*) and Eusebius of Emesa seem also due to the confusion between the two councils.

There remain from Sozomen the names of Dianius of the Cappadocian and Acacius of the Palestinian Cæsarea, Eusebius of Constantinople, Theodore of Heraclea, Eudoxius of Germanicea, Patrophilus of Scythopolis and George of Laodicea; and from Ath. *de Syn.* 24, p. 588, Theophronius of Tyana. The *Prisca*, which is usually confirmed by the Syriac list in Cowper *Syr.*

Miscell. 43, mentions also Tarcondimantus (of Ægæ in Cilicia Philost. ap. Nicetam *Thes. Ord. Fid.* v. 7, and signs at Nicæa), Eustathius (signs at Philippopolis for Epiphania in Syria), Anatolius (not of Emesa—Schelstraten's ingenious theory *Sacr. Ant. Conc.* 674 is not convincing) and 14 others. To these we may reasonably add the name of Flacillus of Antioch; also those of Narcissus of Neronias, Maris of Chalcedon and Mark of Arethusa, who were certainly present a few months later. And if the corrupt lists are to be used at all, they may be allowed to suggest the Mareotic commissioner Macedonius of Mopsuestia, who is addressed by Julius *ad Danium* &c., and is favourably mentioned in the Encyclical of Philippopolis, signed by him alone under the honourable title of *confessor*.

[3] It was to be μονογενές τι χρῆμα ἐκκλησίας μεγέθους ἕνεκα καὶ κάλλους ἀφιέρου, Eus. *V. C.* iii. 50, and had taken at least ten years in building. The sister church at Constantinople was not consecrated till 360. *Chron. Pasch.*

[4] Hilary *de Syn.* 32 *Sanctorum synodus.*

[5] Nothing can be inferred from the confirmation of the Nicene rule respecting Easter in the first canon, except that the Quartodecimans were still flourishing in Syria.

present. Its successive creeds admirably reflect the anarchy of parties in it.

The first of these is an encyclical of the Eusebians[1]. They begin by declaring themselves not followers of Arius (for that would be inconsistent with episcopal dignity), but his independent adherents. The creed itself is meagre and evasive, much resembling the confession of Arius and Euzoius. The main controversy is dismissed with the words εἰς ἕνα Υἱὸν τοῦ θεοῦ μονογενῆ, πρὸ πάντων αἰώνων ὑπάρχοντα, καὶ συνόντα τῷ γεγεννηκότι αὐτὸν Πατρί[2].

The Arianizers had overshot their mark, and brought suspicion on themselves[3]. It was not by this sort of evasion that a great controversy could be settled. Moreover, the conservatives had older standards of their own, and were not prepared obediently to record themselves adherents of Arius. Instead therefore of composing a new creed, they put forward a work of the venerated martyr Lucian of Antioch. Such at least it was said to be, and such in the main it probably was. In any case it was the creed of Lucian's disciple Asterius, which Eusebius had defended from the attacks of Marcellus[4].

It is an elaborate and highly scriptural creed, in some respects akin to that which bears the name of Gregory of Neocæsarea[5]. Its most prominent feature is a direct attack on Arianism[6] in the words ἄτρεπτόν τε καὶ ἀναλλοίωτον, τὴν τῆς θεότητος οὐσίας τε καὶ δυνάμεως καὶ βουλῆς καὶ δόξης τοῦ

[1] Socr. ii. 10 says οὐδὲν μὲν τῶν ἐν Νικαίᾳ μεμψάμενοι κ.τ.λ. So Soz. iii. 5, who notices the evasive character of the document.

[2] Socr. ii. 10, Soz. iii. 5, who notices its evasive character. The only other clauses which call for any remark are the Arianizing σάρκα...... ἀνειληφότα, and the attack on Marcellus in διαμένοντα βασιλέα καὶ θεὸν εἰς τοὺς αἰῶνας.

[3] Hilary de Syn. 29 heads it Expositio......cum in suspicionem venisset unus ex episcopis, quod prava sentiret. Baronius conjectures that this was Gregory of Alexandria; Schelstraten p. 118, Marcellus. One guess is usually as good as another; but these are certainly wrong: so Tillemont vi. 757.

[4] We can recognize its characteristic sentences in Eus. c. Marcell. esp. p. 24. Philostorgius ii. 15 accuses Asterius of interpolating the clause οὐσίας ἀπαράλλακτον εἰκόνα. So also the Macedonian is charged with adding to it in Pseudo-Ath. Dial. iii. p. 441 (=Theodoret v. p. 992)—a work claimed by Garnerius (ditto p. 420) for Theodoret, but in any case later than 451 from its mention of orthodox additions to the Nicene creed.

Caspari Alte u. Neue 42 discusses Lucian's authorship, but without positively deciding the question.

[5] Caspari Alte u. Neue 42.

[6] So Zahn Marcellus 73; against Hefele Councils § 56, who follows Hilary de Syn. 32, in supposing it directly aimed at Marcellus. Such

Πατρὸς ἀπαράλλακτον εἰκόνα. So strong are these that Athanasius himself might have been glad to accept them if there had been any possibility of retreat from the Nicene decisions. The clause bore the stamp of Origen, and had been used by Alexander in an early stage of the controversy; Hilary accepted it in after years, while Athanasius himself had used it before and was to use it yet again[1]. However, there are a few points to be noticed.

(1). It was illogical for men who objected to the Nicene ὁμοούσιον as not found in Scripture themselves to use the equally non-scriptural οὐσίας ἀπαράλλακτον εἰκόνα. Athanasius takes full advantage of the mistake[2].

(2). Arius himself had used the words ἄτρεπτον καὶ ἀναλλοίωτον in his letter to Alexander, but with the all-important qualification ἰδίῳ θελήματι or τῷ ἰδίῳ αὐτεξουσίῳ. In the Lucianic creed they are a direct denial of the Arian τρεπτὸς καὶ ἀλλοιωτός.

(3). The phrase οὐσίας ἀπαράλλακτον εἰκόνα emphasizes the absence of any change of essence in the transition from the Father to the Son[3]; and is therefore equivalent to ὁμοούσιον, though the conservatives only intended by it the unphilosophical ὁμοιούσιον[4]. Thus they not only meant to say what was illogical, but they did not even succeed in expressing it.

was hardly its main purpose; but it might have been a useful sideblow at Marcellus to ratify the creed of Asterius.

[1] We have Origen *Comm. in Joann.* xiii. 36 (quoted by Caspari) ὥστε εἶναι τὸ θέλημα τοῦ θεοῦ ἐν τῷ θελήματι τοῦ υἱοῦ ἀπαράλλακτον τοῦ θελήματος τοῦ πατρός, εἰς τὸ μηκέτι εἶναι δύο θελήματα, ἀλλ᾽ ἓν θέλημα......καὶ τάχα διὰ ταῦτα εἰκών ἐστι τοῦ θεοῦ τοῦ ἀοράτου· καὶ γὰρ τὸ ἐν αὐτῷ θέλημα εἰκὼν τοῦ πρώτου θελήματος, καὶ ἡ ἐν αὐτῷ θεότης εἰκὼν τῆς ἀληθινῆς θεότητος. Alexander (to Alexander of Byzantium) in Theodoret i. 4 ἀπαράλλακτος εἰκὼν τοῦ Π. τυγχάνων, καὶ τοῦ πρωτοτύπου ἔκτυπος χαρακτήρ......ἄτρεπτον τοῦτον καὶ ἀναλλοίωτον. ὡς τὸν Π.,... εἰκὼν γάρ ἐστιν ἀπηκριβωμένη καὶ ἀπαράλλακτος τοῦ Π. Hilary *de Syn.* 33. Athanasius *c. Gentes* 41, p. 32, and esp. his peroration 46, 47, p. 37 συνελόντι φράσαι, εἰκὼν ἀπαράλλακτος τοῦ Π....... ἔστι γὰρ ὥσπερ τοῦ Π. λόγος καὶ σοφία, οὕτω καὶ...γίνεται...αὐτοαγιασμὸς καὶ αὐτοζωὴ καὶ θύρα καὶ ποιμὴν καὶ ὁδὸς καὶ βασιλεὺς καὶ ἡγεμὼν καὶ ἐπὶ πᾶσι σωτήρ, καὶ ζωοποιὸς καὶ φῶς, καὶ πρόνοια τῶν πάντων. *Or.* i. 26, p. 339 ἴδιον τῆς οὐσίας καὶ ἀπαράλλακτον ἔσχεν εἰκόνα, ii. 33, p. 396, iii. 5, p. 439 ἀπαράλλακτος γάρ ἐστιν ἡ ἐν τῇ εἰκόνι τοῦ βασιλέως ὁμοιότης, and iii. 11, p. 443 he argues that if the unity is not of nature, the Son is not ἀπαράλλακτος εἰκών. But he avoids the phrase in his equally conciliatory *de Synodis*, except to point out its inconsistency with the objection to ἄγραφα, for himself preferring ἴδιον τῆς οὐσίας γέννημα.

[2] Ath. *de Syn.* 36. So also Soz. iii. 5.

[3] Hilary *de Syn.* 33, discussing *essentiæ incommutabilem imaginem*.

[4] This is well put by Pseudo-Ath. supra.

There were two features of the Lucianic creed which might of themselves have indisposed the Nicenes to accept it, notwithstanding the strength of the controversial clause. The first of these is the expression τῇ μὲν ὑποστάσει τρία, τῇ δὲ συμφωνίᾳ ἕν, which recalls the Arian evasion of Jno. x. 30 ἐγὼ καὶ ὁ Πατὴρ ἕν ἐσμεν as a mere reference to unity of will[1]. The other is the weakness of the anathemas. The insertion of χρόνος in that against ἦν ποτὲ ὅτε οὐκ ἦν seemed a loophole expressly made for the escape of the blasphemers; while the addition of ὡς ἓν τῶν κτισμάτων to that against κτίσμα might have been copied from the letter of Arius to Alexander[2].

The conservatives were well content with the Lucianic creed, and more than once referred to it in after years with a veneration akin to that of Athanasius for the Nicene[3]. But the wirepullers were determined to upset it. Their chief argument was the danger from Sabellianism, as we see from the direct attack on Marcellus "and those who communicate with him" in the confession next presented by Theophronius of Tyana. It obtained a momentary approval, but the meeting broke up without adopting it in the place of the Lucianic formula[4].

---

[1] Hilary in his conciliatory *de Syn.* 32 explains it by reminding us that the council was convened (so he says) solely against Sabellianism. He also calls attention to the difference between ὑπόστασις and *substantia* (= οὐσία); and suggests that the reference to will might have been thought a more spiritual way of expressing the likeness. This would agree with the conservative rejection of ἐκ τῆς οὐσίας as unspiritual in favour of θελήσει γεννηθέντα.

It was the usual conservative explanation of Jno. x. 30 ἐγὼ καὶ ὁ Πατὴρ ἕν ἐσμεν. Thus in Eus. c. *Marcellum* pp. 28, 37, Asterius says καθ' ὃ ἐν πᾶσι συμφωνοῦσιν, and διὰ τὴν ἐν ἅπασιν λόγοις τε καὶ ἔργοις ἀκριβῆ συμφωνίαν; and Marcellus replies that this is not the force of the words, and that there was no such συμφωνία at Gethsemane. Athanasius de *Syn.* 48, p. 608 objects on the ground that mere agreement of will might be claimed by a creature. In the spurious Sardican definition (Theodoret ii. 8) we find διὰ τὴν συμφωνίαν καὶ τὴν ὁμόνοιαν set aside in favour of διὰ τὴν τῆς ὑποστάσεως ἑνότητα, ἥτις ἐστὶ μία τοῦ Π. καὶ μία τοῦ Υἱοῦ.

The phrase, as Huet points out *Origeniana* III. ii. 3, is derived from Origen c. *Celsum* viii. 12 θρησκεύομεν οὖν τὸν πατέρα τῆς ἀληθείας, καὶ τὸν υἱὸν τὴν ἀλήθειαν, ὄντα δύο τῇ ὑποστάσει πράγματα, ἓν δὲ τῇ ὁμονοίᾳ, καὶ τῇ συμφωνίᾳ, καὶ τῇ ταυτότητι τοῦ βουλήματος.

The Sabellianizing counterpart would be such a phrase as that used (perhaps ἀγωνιστικῶς only: Caspari *Alte u. Neue* 37) by Gregory of Neocæsarea, as quoted by Basil *Ep.* 210 ἐπινοίᾳ μὲν εἶναι δύο, ὑποστάσει δὲ ἕν, or as the Marcellian οὐσίᾳ καὶ ὑποστάσει ἕν denounced by Eusebius c. *Marc.* p. 5, and glanced at by Athanasius *Or.* iv. 3, p. 491.

[2] Ath. *de Syn.* 16, p. 583.

[3] Notice the words of Silvanus and of Sophronius at the council of Seleucia, Socr. ii. 39, 40: also those of the Semiarian synod in Caria, Soz. vi. 12. They all ignore the other Antiochene creeds.

[4] The above view of the Council of the Dedication seems best to suit the

THE FOURTH CREED.

Defeated in a free council, the wirepullers a few months later assembled a cabal of their own (δῆθεν περὶ πίστεως, comments Athanasius[1]) and drew up a fourth creed, which a deputation of notorious Arianizers presented to Constans in Gaul as the genuine work of the council[2]. It seems to have suited them better than the Lucianic, for they repeated it with ever-increasing anathemas at Philippopolis in 343, at Antioch the next year, and at Sirmium in 351. It was not till 359 that the dated creed was drawn up to supersede it.

We can see why it suited them. While in substance it is less opposed to Arianism than the Lucianic, its form is a close copy of the Nicene, even to the adoption of the anathemas in a

facts of the case. If we consider (1) that the majority must have been conservative, (2) that there are no direct complaints of court influence, (3) that the Arianizing first creed was decidedly rejected, (4) that the conservatives in later times constantly refer to the Lucianic creed as the permanent work of the council, (5) that the meeting broke up without accepting that of Theophronius in its place, (6) that the next step of the wirepullers was to draw up a fourth creed—the inference seems irresistible, that the council substantially resulted in a conservative victory over the intriguers.

Zahn *Marcellus* 74 regards the Lucianic creed as decidedly anti-Nicene, but agrees that it went far enough for the majority, and that it was and remained the confession of the council. He also declares it more than doubtful whether the fourth creed came from the council; but does not press the question further.

Ebrard *Kgsch.* i. 212 maintains a peculiar theory. He makes the first creed Semiarian or Eusebian (convertible terms with him), the second absolutely orthodox, the third intermediate, and the fourth a formula of concord agreed upon by all parties in the presence of Constantius. This last detail by the way has no support from Ath. *de Syn.* 25, p. 589.

[1] Ath. *de Syn.* 25, p. 589.
[2] There are several indications that the fourth creed of Antioch was drawn up in opposition to the conservative Lucianic, and in the interest of a more decided though still cautious opposition to the Nicene.

As Athanasius wrote *de Syn.* 25, p. 589 in exile, he might well have failed to distinguish the different classes of "Arian maniacs." Yet he notices the interval of time, gives the names of the envoys, and uses language (ὡς ἀπὸ συνόδου πεμφθέντες) not inconsistent with the direct charge of fraudulent suppression made by Socr. ii. 18 and Soz. iii. 18. Hilary *de Syn.* gives the Lucianic creed alone as the work of the council, and then passes on to that of Philippopolis. So also *c. Ctium* 23. It was the Lucianic creed which Silvanus and Sophronius defended (Socr. ii. 39, 40, Soz. iv. 22) at Seleucia. It is also mentioned with a certain respect by the Acacians, though they amended the dated creed by inserting a clause from the fourth of Antioch; and to the Lucianic creed does Athanasius *de Syn.* 36, p. 600 refer in his address to the Semiarians. The Lucianic creed was also ratified (Socr. iii. 10) by frequent councils in the reign of Julian, and a few years later (Soz. vi. 12) by one in Caria about 366. Epiphanius *Hær.* 73, 1 is therefore quite entitled to treat it as the recognized creed of the Semiarians. We may also infer from Pseudo-Ath. *de S. Trinitate Dial.* iii. p. 441 that it was long retained by the Macedonians.

There seems nothing on the other side but the argument of the Semiarians at Ancyra from Eph. iii. 15 ἐξ οὗ πᾶσα πατριὰ κ.τ.λ., which may suggest the fourth creed rather than the Lucianic.

weakened form. Upon the whole it might fairly pass for such a revision of the Nicene as Eusebius of Cæsarea might have been glad to see. On one side it omitted Lucian's controversial clauses and dropped the word οὐσία[1]; on the other it left out the offensive reference of the unity to will.

The direct blow at Julius of Rome in the third creed is quite enough to shew that its authors had no wish to conciliate the West. But Western suspicion was already roused by the issue of the Lucianic creed. There could be no doubt now that the intriguers were striking at the Nicene faith. Before the Eastern envoys reached Constans in Gaul, he had already written to his brother from Milan to demand that a new general council should be assembled. As Constantius was occupied with the Persian war, he was in no condition to refuse. After some delay, it was summoned to meet in the summer of 343[2]. To the dismay of the Eusebians, the place chosen was Sardica in Dacia, just inside the dominions of Constans, where they could not ply their usual court intrigues. After their

[1] This must be taken in connexion with the Western destination of the creed.

[2] The Council of Sardica is placed in the year 343 (beginning Aug. 29, 342) by the Index to the *Festal Letters*, and seems fixed for the summer of that year by several convergent lines of argument.

(1) Athanasius having completed his Letter for 347 after his arrival at Alexandria, we must place his return in the autumn of 346, independently of the direct statement of the Index. As Constantius wrote at one time that he had already waited a whole year for him, the negotiations for his return must have occupied at least a year and a half. We must therefore carry back Stephen's plot, which we know was laid at Easter, to the year 344, and consequently the Council of Sardica cannot be placed later than the autumn of 343.

(2) It is not clear whether Athanasius *Apol. ad Ctium* 4, p. 236 reckons from his leaving Alexandria in April, 339 or from his arrival at Rome during the summer, but he tells us that three years had passed and a fourth was begun when Constans sent for him to Milan and told him that it was proposed to hold a council. Its meeting therefore cannot be placed before the spring of 343.

(3) We reach the same result another way if we assume that the negotiations for a council were not begun till news reached the West that the intriguers at Antioch had been tampering with the faith. The Council of the Dedication was held between May 22 and September 1, 341, the fourth creed drawn up a few months later. As however it only reached Constans in Gaul, it would seem that he took action on the Lucianic creed in the winter of 341—2 or following spring, and sent for Athanasius before starting on his Frankish war. As campaigns often began late (e.g. Probus in 277, or Constantius in 354) there is no difficulty in placing the Milan interview in May. The *ludi Francici* of the Calendar of 354 seem to indicate a victory of Constans on July 15, and it seems in this year. Mommsen *Ueber den Chronographen vom J.* 354, p. 571 places it in 345, but Jerome *Chron.* connects it with the murder of Hermogenes in 342. In any case it need cause no difficulty.

failure at Antioch, they could not hope for success if the council was allowed to debate freely.

So to Sardica the bishops came. The Westerns were about 96[1] in number, "with Hosius of Cordova for their father[2]," bringing with him Marcellus, Athanasius, and Asclepas[3], and supported by the chief Westerns—Gratus of Carthage, Protasius of Milan, Maximus of Trier, Fortunatian of Aquileia and Vincent of Capua, the former legate at Nicæa. For once the Easterns were outnumbered. They therefore travelled together in one body, lodged together in one house[4] at Sardica and agreed to act together under the protection of the accomplished count Musonianus[5]. Their first demand was that the deposition of Marcellus and Athanasius at Antioch should be accepted without discussion. They urged that one council had no right to revise the acts of another, and that in this case many of the witnesses were dead. But on any theory of the authority of councils, there was no reason[6] why the deposition at Antioch should be ratified rather than the acquittal at Rome. They had

---

[1] The number of the majority is reckoned by Socr. ii. 20 and Soz. iii. 12 at about 300 ὥς φησιν 'Αθανάσιος; by Theodoret ii. 7 at 250, ὡς διδάσκει τὰ παλαιὰ διηγήματα. But Athanasius *Apol. c. Ar.* 50, p. 132 expressly includes later subscriptions in his list of 282 signatures. This is also clear from internal evidence. The Palestinians for example (as Athanasius notices *supra* 57, p. 139) are just those whom Maximus assembled to meet him at Jerusalem on his return in 346. The Egyptians again could not possibly have mustered 94 at Sardica, for there were not more than 100 bishops in the whole of Egypt, so that the number leaves no margin for the infirm who could not have undertaken so long a journey. The list moreover corresponds with the new bishops mentioned by Athanasius in his Festal Letter for 347, and not with the old ones whose places they took.

Elsewhere Athanasius (*Hist. Ar.* 15, p. 278) gives "170, more or less, from East and West together" as the number actually present; and Sabinus of Heraclea (Socr. *supra*, confirmed by Hilary, *Fragm.* iii.—see also Hefele *Councils* § 60) estimates the Eusebians at 76. The majority was therefore about 94. Piecing all authorities together, the Ballerini (Migne *Patrol.* lvi. 53—61) reach a list of 96, which cannot be far wrong. The distribution is natural: we have from Spain seven, Gaul three, Britain none, Africa four, Italy eight, Illyricum three, Dacia nine, Macedonia (as far as Crete) thirty-three, Thrace four, Asia one, Pontus one (Marcellus), Syria three, Egypt one (Athanasius), Unknown nineteen. Fuller discussion in Robertson *Ath.* 147.

[2] Ath. *Hist. Ar.* 15, p. 278.

[3] Not Paul of Constantinople.

[4] Ath. *ad Mon.* 15 ἀποκλείουσιν ἑαυτοὺς ἐν τῷ παλατίῳ. As Dacia belonged to the Western part of the Empire, the *Palatium* at Sardica was under the control of Constans, and they must have been lodged in it merely for convenience.

[5] On Musonianus Reinkens *Hilarius* 124. Sievers *Libanius* 22. He had assisted at the deposition of Eustathius in 330, Eus. *V. C.* iii. 62, and afterwards held the Eastern prefecture 354—358.

[6] As Hefele points out *Councils* § 61.

an express commission to reopen the whole case; and if they were not to do so, they might as well go home[1]. The demand was clearly unreasonable, and its only interest is as shewing the peculiar view of conciliar authority which the Eastern conservatives were expected to support.

The Westerns were determined to sift the whole matter to the bottom. But they invited the attendance of the Eusebians in vain—none came but Asterius of Petra and Arius of Palestine[2]. It was in vain that Hosius asked them to communicate their proofs at least privately to himself; in vain he promised that if Athanasius were acquitted and they were still unwilling to receive him, he would take him with him away to Spain. There was no choice but to let the accused take their seats and stand their trial. The Easterns left Sardica by night in haste, under pretence of news arrived from Constantius of a victory on the Persian frontier.

The Westerns examined the charges afresh, and acquitted all the accused. Doctrinal questions were formally raised only in the case of Marcellus; but when his work was read before the council, it was found that the Eusebians had quoted as his deliberate opinions views which, as the context shewed, he had put forward merely for examination ($\zeta\eta\tau\hat{\omega}\nu$), and thus falsely charged him with denying the eternity of the Logos in the past and of his kingdom in the future. Did the council forget to ask whether he also confessed the eternal Sonship, or were they indifferent about it? In either case the Eastern grievance was ignored.

Though the charges against Athanasius were not doctrinal, they notoriously indicated a doctrinal quarrel. One party therefore in the council was for issuing a new creed, fuller than the Nicene; but the proposal was wisely rejected. It would have made the fatal admission that Arianism had never yet been clearly condemned, and thrown upon the Westerns the odium of innovation, and all to no purpose, for the council

---

[1] Julius of Rome *ad Danium* &c. (Ath. *Apol. c. Ar.* 22, p. 112) says that the Council of Nicæa expressly admitted that its decisions might be revised. No traces of the fact remain; but the mere assertion must have had weight at Sardica. The Easterns mentioned (*id.* c. 25) the councils against Novatus and Paul of Samosata: the latter may glance at $\delta\mu oo\acute{v}\sigma\iota o\nu$.

[2] Unless we reckon Olympius of Ænos among the Easterns.

could no longer look for acceptance in the East[1]. All that could be done was to pass a series of canons to check the worst scandals of late years[2]. This done, the council issued an encyclical letter, another to the church of Alexandria, and a report to Julius of Rome.

Meanwhile the Easterns (such was their haste) halted for some weeks[3] at Philippopolis to issue their own encyclical, falsely dating it from Sardica. It is addressed to Gregory of Alexandria, Donatus of Carthage[4], and others. They begin

---

[1] This is the account given by Athanasius *ad Antiochenos* 5, p. 616 and confirmed *id.* 10, p. 619 by Eusebius of Vercellæ in his subscription. The story of Socrates ii. 20 and Sozomen iii. 12, that the council issued an explanation of the Nicene definition, is therefore erroneous; and that appended to the encyclical by Theodoret ii. 8 and in Latin by the Ballerini from the Maffeian MSS. (Leo iii. 605 = p. 840 Migne) cannot be accepted as an official document of the council, though it may be that against which Athanasius warns the church of Antioch.

It ascribes to Ursacius and Valens a strange mixture of heresies, ὅτι ὁ Λόγος καὶ ὅτι τὸ Πνεῦμα καὶ ἐσταυρώθη καὶ ἀπέθανεν καὶ ἀνέστη· καὶ ὅπερ τὸ τῶν αἱρετικῶν σύστημα φιλονεικεῖ, διαφόρους εἶναι τὰς ὑποστάσεις τοῦ Π. καὶ τοῦ Υἱ. καὶ τοῦ ἁγίου Πν., καὶ εἶναι κεχωρισμένας. The former clause, so distinctly separated from the rest as a private opinion of their own, is Sabellian, unless we follow Newman *Ath. Tr.* ii. 123 in referring it to the Arian doctrine of the passibility of the Logos. The Council of Sardica was not impartial, but it does not follow that there is any mistake here. Timeservers like Ursacius and Valens may very well have professed to hold as confused a doctrine as the Homœan they afterwards defended; Socr. ii. 37 οὗτοι γὰρ ἀεὶ πρὸς τοὺς ἐπικρατοῦντας ἐπέκλινον.

We may notice the clause μίαν εἶναι ὑπόστασιν, ἣν αὐτοὶ οἱ αἱρετικοὶ οὐσίαν προσαγορεύουσιν, for which the Latin has unam esse substantiam, quam ipsi *Græci* Usiam appellant. This and other references to the μία ὑπόστασις seem directly aimed at the Lucianic τῇ μὲν ὑποστάσει τρία, τῇ δὲ συμφωνίᾳ ἕν, with a further allusion to the original passage of Origen *c. Cels.* viii. 12, whom they follow in quoting Jno. x. 30, and in restoring the word ὁμόνοια. But the main attack is not on the Antiochian creeds. We cannot fully trace the allusions, but the first position condemned (ὅτι Θεός ἐστιν ὁ Χριστὸς δηλονότι, ἀλλὰ μὴν ἀληθινὸς Θεὸς οὐκ ἔστιν) was an expression of Eusebius of Cæsarea (ap. Ath. *de Syn.* 17, p. 584 and *Or.* i. 37, p. 348, also ap. Marcellum *Fr.* 74, p. 27). The stress laid on the Incarnation shews that the writers had in view the Christological side of the controversy; but their language is very undeveloped. The Ballerini consider it a draft prepared by Hosius and Protogenes, rejected by the council but erroneously attached to some copies of the encyclical. The curious equation αὐτοὶ οἱ αἱρετικοὶ = *Græci* may be illustrated from Hosius *ad Ctium* ap. Ath. *Hist. Ar.* 43, p. 292 μὴ φρόνει τὰ ᾿Αρείου, μηδὲ ἄκουε τῶν ἀνατολικῶν; or on the other side from the Semiarian Sophronius of Pompeiopolis (Socr. iii. 10) οἱ κατὰ τὴν δύσιν ἐνόσουν τὸ ὁμοούσιον.

[2] *Can.* 1 against translations of bishops, refusing offenders even lay communion. 3—6 against unjust depositions. 10 against hasty ordinations. They are not mentioned by Athanasius, but I have not examined recent doubts of their genuineness.

[3] They must have stayed some time, for their encyclical relates the Western decisions.

[4] Notice the bid for African support. It was not ineffectual. Augustine *ctr. Cresconium* iii. § 38 iv. § 52 and elsewhere has to set aside the Council of "Sardica" as Arian. But there are very few traces of Arianism in Africa. See Hefele *Councils* § 67.

with their main argument, that the decisions of one council cannot be revised by another. They then recount the charges against Marcellus and Athanasius. Next they record the action of the Westerns at Sardica, denouncing Hosius[1], Julius and others (not including Gratus of Carthage) as associates of heretics and patrons of the detestable errors of Marcellus; and adding against some of them a few of the charges of immorality which the Eusebians always had at hand. They conclude with a confession of faith substantially identical with the fourth creed of Antioch, but enriched with a longer series of denunciations, against several Arianizing positions, against tritheism[2], against confusion of the Persons, and against those who deny that the Son is of the will of the Father. The last is aimed at the Nicene ἐκ τῆς οὐσίας τοῦ Πατρός. At the head of the signatures is the name of Stephen of Antioch, followed by Acacius of the Palestinian and Dianius[3] of the Cappadocian Cæsarea, and most of the Eusebian leaders except George of Laodicea, who had kept away from the council.

The quarrel was worse than ever. The Eusebians had made a discreditable exhibition of themselves, but they had at least escaped the condemnation of a general council, and secured for the first time a recognition of the fourth creed of Antioch from a large body of Eastern conservatives[4]. They now went home to devise extreme measures. They exiled the deserter Asterius of Petra to the unhealthy mine of Phæno, forbade all communication with Julius of Rome, and seemed resolved to push the contest to extremities.

But a reaction followed. When the Western envoys Vincent of Capua and Euphrates of Cologne reached Antioch towards Easter 344, their "truly diabolical" reception[5] by bishop Stephen

---

[1] Eusebius *V. C.* ii. 63, 73 alludes to Hosius in terms of high praise. But this was in 338: the change marks the increasing bitterness of the controversy.

[2] Dorner ii. 182 and Note 38 connects tritheism with Marcion. To his refs. add the direct statement of Cyril *Cat.* xvi. 7.

[3] Dion in the corrupt Latin text of Hilary *Fragm.* iii.

[4] This may be why Hilary (*de Syn.* 34) omits it at its first composition, and only gives it as issued at Philippopolis.

[5] Stephen's nefarious attempt to get up a charge of fornication against them is related by Ath. *Hist. Ar.* 20, p. 281, and more fully by Thdt. ii. 8—10. Theodoret's account seems independent: and it is worth notice that if the Council of Sardica had been held in

was too gross an outrage for the Eastern conservatives. A new council was called, by which Stephen was deposed[1] and Leontius the Lucianist, himself the subject of an old scandal, raised to the vacant see. At the same time a creed was issued, the fifth of the Antiochene series, called also μακρόστιχος from its excessive length. It is a reissue (with a few tenses varied) of the creed of Philippopolis, including (1) its condemnation of Arian positions, (2) its anathemas against those of the Tritheists, Paul of Samosata, Marcellus and Sabellius, and (3) indirectly against the Nicene ἐκ τῆς οὐσίας τοῦ Πατρός. It is however followed by long conciliatory explanations for the Westerns. In these they begin (1) by maintaining the Lord's eternal Sonship against the Arians, whose favourite phrases ἐξ οὐκ ὄντων, ἐξ ἑτέρας ὑποστάσεως and ἦν ποτὲ ὅτε οὐκ ἦν are rejected as non-scriptural and dangerous; the latter as also inconsistent with the mystery (ἀνεφίκτως καὶ πᾶσιν ἀκαταλήπτως) of the divine generation. And if the subordination is also asserted, it is balanced by the strong words θεὸν κατὰ φύσιν τέλειον καὶ ἀληθῆ, where the opportunity is taken to strike a blow at the old enemy Paul of Samosata for saying ὕστερον αὐτὸν μετὰ τὴν ἐνανθρώπησιν ἐκ προκοπῆς τεθεοποιῆσθαι, τῷ τὴν φύσιν ψιλὸν ἄνθρωπον γεγονέναι. Next (2) Marcellus and "Scotinus[2]" (they seem unaware of the difference between them) are anathematized by name for their denial of the Son's true and pre-existent personality[3] (Gen. i. 26) and eternal kingdom; the Sabellians or Patripassians, to use their Western name, for

347, we should scarcely have found the next year's consul Salia described merely as στρατηγὸς during his term of office. I cannot follow Sievers Einl. § 11 in doubting whether Salia was sent to Antioch.

On the pretended Synod of Cologne against Euphrates Hefele Councils § 69.

[1] Chrysostom de S. Babyla 22 (ii. 568 Migne) says that Julian restored him after the Babylas riot in 362.

[2] Σκοτεινοῦ Ath., but Φωτεινοῦ Socr. The Syriac fragments in Cowper Syr. Misc. 60 translate his name by Murinus. Undignified puns of this sort best suited Lucifer, though he may have mistaken the name; thus de non

parc. p. 972 conscotinum tuum, quem verso ordine Sirmienses vocant Photinum, also 990, 996 qui vere dicitur Scotinus; and even Athanasius c. Apoll. ii. 19, p. 762 has τοῦ λεγομένου Φωτεινοῦ. So Moriendum 830, 1028 Germanicensium Adoxius and others. Athanasius avoids them, though he has Κοστύλλιον and Κωνσταντίου τοῦ ἀσεβεστάτου in the writings of his exile. Controversy had scarcely yet descended to the level of Jerome's Dormitantius.

[3] Here we first find the Semiarian ὅμοιον κατὰ πάντα; but it is used only against the Marcellian doctrine that the Sonship is not eternal.

their subjection of the Father to passion and limitation. This forms the transition to (3) a denunciation of οὐ θελήσει γεννηθέντα (an inference from the Nicene ἐκ τῆς οὐσίας τοῦ Πατρὸς) as a most impious subjection of the divine generation to necessity; whereas it is voluntary (ἑκουσίως καὶ ἐθελοντὴν) and absolutely different from mere creation. Yet (*Par.* ix.) it is not to be understood as impairing the unity of God. Instead of the older τέλειον ἐκ τελείου, we have a strong declaration that the Father and the Son are mutually, inseparably, and as it were organically united in a single deity[1].

This conciliatory move was not without effect. Marcellus indeed was not abandoned by the Westerns; and if Athanasius separated himself[2] from his communion for a time, he was far from explicitly renouncing it. But Photinus of Sirmium had given a new turn to his master's system. He dropped the vital distinction between the two aspects of the Logos as δύναμις and as ἐνέργεια, gave up the whole theory of πλατυσμοὶ and abandoned the supernatural birth, making the Lord a mere man like Paul of Samosata or the Ebionites[3]. There was no excuse to be made for him, so he was frankly given up by Julius of Rome, and condemned by a Western council held at Milan. Two years later (347) his rejection was confirmed by another Milanese council, at which Valens and Ursacius took the opportunity to make their peace with Julius, confessing the falsehood of their charges against Athanasius.

The way stood clear for a general cessation of hostilities. Stephen's misconduct had thrown discredit on the whole gang of Eastern court intriguers, and the genuine conservatives recovered some of their power. The latest measures of persecution were reversed, and the condemnation of Photinus by the Westerns accepted as a sort of compensation for their continued support of Marcellus[4]. Constans pressed the execution of the

---

[1] No translation can fully express the Greek—ὅλον μὲν τοῦ πατρὸς ἐνεστερνισμένου τὸν υἱόν, ὅλου δὲ τοῦ υἱοῦ ἐξηρτημένου καὶ προσπεφυκότος τῷ πατρὶ καὶ μόνου τοῖς πατρῴοις κόλποις ἀναπαυομένου διηνεκῶς.

The μακρόστιχος is also worth comparison with Cyril's *Catecheses*. In each document Marcellus is denounced by name, Arius in silence. Conversely Athanasius attacks Marcellus and Apollinarius without naming them.

[2] Hilary *Fragm.* iii.
[3] Zahn *Marcellus* 189—194.
[4] Zahn *Marcellus* 80.

decrees of Sardica[1]; and Constantius with a Persian war impending[2] was in no condition to refuse compliance. Athanasius and he had fought "like rival kings," and the emperor was utterly defeated. There was no alternative; and Constantius made up his mind to submission even before the last obstacle was removed by Gregory's death in June 345[3]. It was not till the third invitation that Athanasius condescended to return " from his wanderings among the trackless haunts of wild beasts," as Constantius is pleased to call the hospitable West[4]. He had to take leave of his Italian friends; and the tone of the emperor's letters might well have seemed suspicious. However,

[1] Weingarten *Ursprung* 23 summarily rejects the story of Rufinus, Socrates, Sozomen, Lucifer and Philostorgius, that the recall of Athanasius was due to the threats of Constans, wie die Fabel seit Rufinus bis zu Hefele geht, alluding to Hefele *Councils* § 69. Though Rufinus has fables enough to answer for, this is not one of them. No stress can be laid on the dialogue in Theodoret ii. 13, and not much on Ath. *Hist. Ar.* 49, p. 296 where Constantius says that he recalled Athanasius merely to avoid a quarrel with his brother. On the other hand, the passage (Ath. *Apol. ad Ctium* 4, p. 236), on which Weingarten relies, carries little weight, being addressed to Constantius himself.

[2] The second siege of Nisibis was early in 346; and Constantius was in the city in May 345, so that the war must have been seriously threatened, if not actually begun.

[3] Theodoret's account *H. E.* ii. 4, 12 of Gregory's murder after six years' tyranny, may be a relic of the old confusion with George. There is no hint of violence in Ath. *Hist. Ar.* 21, p. 282, or in the Index to the *Festal Letters*, where we find the beginning of Gregory's illness noticed in 341, its continuance in 342, and its natural result in 345.

There are some difficulties here about the exact chronology. Accepting as fixed points already discussed the death of Gregory June 26, 345 and the return of Athanasius October 21, 346, we are obliged to place his interview with Constantius at Antioch (Ath. *Apol. ad Ctium* 5, p. 236: also referred to *Hist. Ar.* 22, p. 282) in March or April 346. This gives six months for his journey through Syria. But the emperor was at Nisibis in May 345, and not likely to leave the East while the siege was pending in the next spring. We also find him at Constantinople in May and August 346, and at Ancyra moving eastward in March 347. It is therefore impossible to fix the interview at Antioch in the summer without assuming an unrecorded and very hurried journey of Constantius to Syria and back; nor can we place it in September, as Sievers *Einl.* § 11 prefers, without the additional objection that no time is left for the meeting at Jerusalem.

Athanasius must have been invited to return before the death of Gregory. One or other of the emperor's letters reached him at Aquileia (*Apol. c. Ar.* 51, p. 135), where (Index to *Festal Letters*) we know that he spent the Easter of 345. Thence he went (*Apol. c. Ctium* 4, p. 235) to see Constans in Gaul (whom we find at Trier May 15), and Julius at Rome. No wonder Constantius told his brother (Ath. *Hist. Ar.* 21, p. 282) that Athanasius had kept him waiting for more than a year.

The passage just mentioned seems to imply that the negotiations for the return of Athanasius were not begun till after Gregory's death, and is so understood by Hefele and Sievers. If so, we have another indication that the *Hist. Ar.* is not an uncorrupted work of Athanasius.

[4] Ath. *Apol. c. Ar.* 51, p. 134. See Fialon *Saint Ath.* 158, 159.

Constantius received him graciously at Antioch, ordered the destruction of all the charges against him, gave him a solemn promise of full protection for the future, and restored to his adherents at Alexandria the substantial privileges accorded by the state to orthodox belief. Athanasius went forward on his journey; and the old confessor Maximus assembled a council of Palestinian bishops[1] to meet him at Jerusalem and to sign the decrees of Sardica. But his entry into Alexandria (Oct. 31, 346) was the crowning triumph of his life. For miles along the road, the whole city streamed out to meet him with enthusiastic welcome; and the jealous police of Constantius could raise no tumult to mar the universal harmony of that great day of *national* rejoicing.

The next few years were an uneasy interval of suspense,—hardly of peace, for the contest had ended in a compromise which decided nothing. The Nicene confessors were restored, but the Eusebian disturbers were not deposed. One side had to put up with Acacius at Cæsarea, the other with Marcellus at Ancyra. Thus while Nicene animosity was not satisfied, the permanent grounds of conservative distrust were not removed. Above all, the return of Athanasius was a personal humiliation to Constantius; and he could not be expected to accept it without watching his opportunity for a final struggle to decide the mastery of Egypt. Still there was tolerable quiet for the present. The court intriguers could do nothing without the emperor; and Constantius was fully occupied with the disastrous Persian war. The defeat of Singara marks the summer of 348, the defence of Nisibis the spring of 350; and the rest of the interval is filled up with the civil war against Magnentius. If there was not peace, there was a fair amount of quiet till the emperor's hands were freed by the victory of Mount Seleucus in the summer of 353[2].

---

[1] It was but a small gathering of 16 bishops (Ath. *Apol. c. Ar.* 57, p. 139), whereas 19 at least had appeared at Nicæa.

[2] Hilary's excuse for him *de Syn.* 78 *homines perversi......fefellerunt ignorantem regem, ut istiusmodi perfidiæ fidem bellis occupatus exponeret, et credendi formam ecclesiis nondum impone-* *ret*—is unfortunate. Constantius made the ecclesiastical game the occupation of his years of peace and the amusement of his winter quarters, and the Sirmian manifesto of 357 fairly marks the culmination of his prosperity. It was only *bellis occupatus* that he could keep out of mischief.

The truce was hollow and the rest precarious, but the mere suspension of hostilities was not without its influence. Nicenes and conservatives were fundamentally agreed upon the reality of the Lord's divinity; and minor jealousies began to disappear as soon as they were less busily encouraged. The Eusebian phase of conservatism, which emphasized the distinction of the Lord's personality, was giving way to the Semiarian, where stress was rather laid on his essential likeness to the Father. The old τέλειον ἐκ τελείου of the Lucianic creed disappears, and ὁμοιούσιον and ὅμοιον κατὰ πάντα become more and more decidedly the watchwords of conservatism. The Nicenes on the other side, warned by the excesses of Marcellus, began to fear that there might be some ground for the conservative dread of ὁμοούσιον as Sabellian. The expression could not be withdrawn, but it might be put forward less conspicuously, and explained rather as an authoritative and emphatic form of ὁμοιούσιον than as a rival doctrine, as denoting absolute likeness rather than common possession of the divine essence[1]. So by the time the war is renewed, we can already see the possibility of a new alliance between Nicenes and conservatives.

We also see the rise of a new[2] and more defiant Arian school, more in earnest than the older generation, impatient of their shuffling diplomacy, and less pliant to imperial dictation[3].

---

[1] Thus Athanasius constantly uses Semiarian paraphrases in the writings of his exile (ὁμοίας οὐσίας, ὅμοιος κατ' οὐσίαν, and his own favourite ἴδιον τῆς οὐσίας γέννημα). The word ὁμοούσιον is found but once in his *Or. c. Ar.*, at i. 9, p. 325.
So Hilary *de Syn.* 68 adopts Semiarian objections, allowing that ὁμοούσιον admits of a wrong use (*a*) in a Sabellian sense—*ut hic subsistens, sub significatione licet duum nominum, unus ac solus sit;* (*b*) in a materializing sense—*ut divisus a se Pater intelligatur, et partem exsecuisse quæ esset sibi Filius;* or (*c*) as implying a prior essence—*ut significari existimetur substantia prior, quam inter se duo pares habeant.*

[2] We may question how far it was really new. The tone of Philostorgius is significant; and Ruf. i. 25 tells us that some of the extreme men refused to receive Arius on his return from exile.

[3] Möhler *Ath.* 405 (whom others seem to copy) thinks that Arianism necessarily leaned on the state. "Every sect has in virtue of its separation from the church a tendency to become a mere state religion. In the case of Arianism, a limited Saviour corresponds to a limited church (viz. a state church), and in the lowering of his dignity is implied the depreciation of his work, which is the church. If men cannot find anchorage on the catholic church, they will seek it on a state church."
The theory is as unhistorical as it can well be. Had Möhler never heard of English or American sects which abhor the idea of a state church as much as he did? In the Nicene age the whole existence of Anomœan Arianism is a standing protest against it.

The Anomœan leaders took their stand on the doctrine of Arius himself, dwelling with special emphasis on those offensive aspects of it which had since been prudently kept in the background. Arius had clearly laid down the absolute unlikeness of the Son to the Father[1]; but for years past the Arianizers had softened it down. Now however ἀνόμοιον became the watchword of Eunomius, and his followers delighted to shock all sober feeling by the harshest and profanest declarations of it. The scandalous jests of Eudoxius must have given deep offence to thousands. But the most striking novelty of the Anomœan doctrine was its audacious self-sufficiency, unrivalled since the days of Gnostic speculation. Arius was merely illogical in reasoning as though human analogies could exhaust the mystery of divine relations, for he still regarded the divine nature as essentially incomprehensible even to the Son himself. But the Anomœans boldly laid down that a God of simplicity cannot be a God of mystery at all, for even man is as competent as God to comprehend simplicity, not to say to rise above it. Such was the new school of Arianism—presumptuous and shallow, quarrelsome and heathenizing, yet not without a directness and a firmness of conviction which gives it a certain dignity in spite of all its wrangling and irreverence. Its conservative allies it despised for their wavering and insincerity: to its Nicene enemies it repaid hatred for hatred, and flung back with retorted scorn their denial of its right to bear the Christian name[2].

What else again was orthodoxy from the time of Theodosius but a state church? It is not sectarians but conservatives who lean upon the state.

[1] In his Thalia (Ath. Or. i. 6, p. 323, and de Syn. 15, p. 582). He does not press it in his letters to Eusebius (Theodoret i. 5) and to Alexander (Ath. de Syn. 16, p. 583). His confession presented to Constantine (Socr. i. 26) of course avoids the subject.

[2] Epiphanius Hær. 76, 5 Εὐνόμιός τις......ἀναβαπτίζει τοὺς ἤδη βαπτισθέντας, οὐ μόνον τοὺς ἀπὸ ὀρθοδόξων πρὸς αὐτὸν ἐρχομένους καὶ αἱρέσεων, ἀλλὰ καὶ τοὺς ἀπ᾽ αὐτῶν τῶν Ἀρειανῶν, with strange forms and ceremonies, perhaps not very exactly reported. So Augustine (perhaps alluding to this very statement) vi. 1008 c, 1030 A, viii. 54 B

Rebaptizari quoque ab his catholicos novimus; utrum et non catholicos, nescio. On the other hand Philostorgius x. 1 seems to imply that Eunomius demanded nothing of the sort from the Homœans of Antioch in 381, though he mentions x. 4 the rebaptism of some Arians by his own party. The reordination of Theodorus of Oxyrhynchus (Faustinus Libell. 26) by George of Alexandria is not a case in point, for George was not an Anomœan.

The Nicene view of the question is not free from difficulty. The nullity of heretical baptism was a settled question in the East during the earlier part of the fourth century, and general declarations of it are frequent, like Apostolic Canons 46, 47 (Drey Untersuchungen 260, where refs. are given).

Let us now examine two subjects which will throw some light on the character of the interval of rest.

The first of these is the *Catecheses* of Cyril of Jerusalem. In 348 Cyril was presbyter in charge of the catechumens in Constantine's great church on Golgotha, and within a couple of years bishop of the city. If it is not a work of any great originality[1], it will shew us all the better what was passing in the minds of men of practical and simple piety who had no taste for the controversies of the day. All through it we see the earnest pastor who feels that all his strength is needed to combat the practical immoralities of a holy city[2], and never lifts his eyes to the wild scene of theological confusion round him but in

---

Cyril *Procatech.* 7 (discussed by Touttée p. cci.). Athanasius *Or.* ii. 42, 43, p. 403. Gregory of Nazianzus *Or.* xxxiii. 16, 17 (specifying Valentinians, Marcionites, Montanists, Manichees, Novatians, Sabellians, Arians and Photinians). Didymus *de Trin.* ii. 15 (Eunomians as using one immersion, Montanists for confusing the Persons). The same doctrine is found even in the West, as Hilary *de Trin.* viii. 40 and other writers, though the Council of Arles *Can.* 8 had enjoined the Roman practice as early as 314. Thus when that of Nicæa (*Can.* 19, where the difficulty is passed over by Hefele *Councils* § 42) rejected the baptism of the Paulianists, it cannot have been intended to make them the solitary exception to a general rule of acceptance. It might as well be argued that the acceptance of the Novatians in *Can.* 8 was meant as the only exception to a rule of rejection. If heretical baptism was to be admitted at all, no reason could be given for refusing the Paulianists which did not apply to others also. Thus when Athanasius *supra* denounces their baptism as mere defilement because given in the name of an illusory Trinity, he extends his condemnation to Arians, Manichees and Montanists.

But if orthodox principles were clear, orthodox practice wavered. Neither the Nicene Council itself nor that of Alexandria in 362 required the rebaptism of Arians, and Liberius of Rome *post cassatum Ariminense concilium* expressly forbade it. The Council of Laodicea (*Can.* 7 and 8) exempts Novatians, [Photinians], and Quartodecimans, but insists on it in the case of Montanists. Basil *Ep.* 188 maintains the general rule, though without express mention of Arians; but by drawing a distinction between heresy and schism, he is enabled to leave the case of the Novatians to local custom. So again substantially *Ep.* 199, reading οὐ τῷ αὐτῷ. Epiphanius, whose errors are not usually on the side of liberality, objects (*Hær. de fide* 13, p. 1095) to the rebaptism of Arians by a Lycian presbyter (1) that no œcumenical council had yet specially decided their case, (2) that parties being still so confused converts frequently had no more Arianism than the misfortune of having met with a heretical teacher. So too the seventh canon of Constantinople, which though spurious is not so much as a century later than its professed date, states that the custom is to rebaptize Eunomians (who use but one immersion), Montanists, Sabellians, and all other heretics except Arians, Macedonians, Sabbatians, Novatians, Quartodecimans and Apollinarians. Hefele's assertion (*Councils* § 98), that the Montanists, &c. had given up the Lord's baptismal formula since 325, seems a mere guess copied from Mattes (*Theol. Quartalschr.* for 1849, p. 580).

[1] Cyril's ἀναγκαῖα δόγματα are closely modelled on Origen *de Principiis*. Caspari *Alte u. Neue* 146—160.

[2] Students will not forget the picture drawn by Gregory of Nyssa *de euntibus Hierosolymam*. It is amply borne out by later experience of holy places like Grätz (Mariazell) or Loretto.

fear and dread that Antichrist is near. "I fear the wars of the nations; I fear the divisions of the churches; I fear the mutual hatred of the brethren. Enough on this. God forbid it come to pass in our days; yet let us be on our guard. Enough concerning Antichrist[1]." Jews, Samaritans and Manichees[2] are his chief opponents, yet he does not forget to warn his hearers against the doctrines of Sabellius and Marcellus[3]. Arius he occasionally contradicts in set terms[4], but without naming him. Of the Nicene party too we hear nothing directly; but it seems glanced at in the complaint that whereas in former times heresy was open, the church is now full of secret heretics[5]. The Nicene creed again he never mentions: but we cannot mistake the allusion when he tells his hearers that their own creed of Jerusalem was not put together by the will of men, and impresses on them that every word of it can be maintained by Scripture[6]. But the most significant feature of his language is its close relation to that of the dated creed of Sirmium. Nearly every point where the latter differs from the Lucianic is one specially emphasized in Cyril's work[7]. Yet the bishop of Jerusalem

---

[1] *Cat.* xv. 18. Compare also xv. 7, 9, xvii. 33 on the divisions of the churches as the sign of Antichrist's coming. Of the Apocalypse however we hear nothing, unless xv. 16 οὐκ ἐξ ἀποκρύφων λέγομεν, ἀλλ' ἐκ τοῦ Δανιὴλ be an allusion to it.

[2] Epiph. *Hær.* 66, 21 names as writers against the Manichees—Archelaus, Origen ὡς ἀκήκοα, Eusebius of Cæsarea (doubted by Lightfoot *Eus. Cæs.* p. 345), Eusebius of Emesa, Serapion of Thmuis, Athanasius, George of Laodicea, Apollinarius of Laodicea, and Titus (of Bostra).

[3] *Cat.* xv. 27 τοῦ δράκοντός ἐστιν ἄλλη κεφαλή, προσφάτως περὶ τὴν Γαλατίαν ἀναφυεῖσα. ἐτόλμησέ τις λέγειν, ὅτι κ.τ.λ.

[4] *Cat.* vi. 6, vii. 5, xi. 8.

[5] *Cat.* xv. 10. So Touttée understands it, p. xi. and *ad loc.*

[6] *Cat.* v. 12. The bearing of this passage has been pointed out by Professor Swainson. *Nicene and Apostles' Creeds* p. 17 n. The appeals to Scripture are continual in Cyril, e.g. Catech. iv. 17, xii. 5.

[7] The following are the chief novelties of the dated creed as contrasted with the Lucianic:—

τὸν μόνον καὶ ἀληθινὸν θεόν] logically implying that the Son is not ἀληθινὸς θεός. This however was the doctrine of Asterius, and Eusebius had defended it against Marcellus.

τὸν πρὸ πάντων τῶν αἰώνων καὶ πρὸ πάσης ἀρχῆς καὶ πρὸ παντὸς ἐπινοουμένου χρόνου καὶ πρὸ πάσης καταληπτῆς οὐσίας γεγεννημένον ἀπαθῶς ἐκ τοῦ θεοῦ......

ὅμοιον τῷ γεννήσαντι αὐτὸν πατρί, κατὰ τὰς γραφάς· οὗ τὴν γέννησιν οὐδεὶς ἐπίσταται εἰ μὴ μόνος ὁ γεννήσας αὐτὸν πατήρ] Compare Cyril, *Cat.* iv. 7 τὸν ὅμοιον κατὰ πάντα τῷ γεννήσαντι· τὸν οὐκ ἐν χρόνοις τὸ εἶναι κτησάμενον, ἀλλὰ πρὸ πάντων τῶν αἰώνων ἀϊδίως καὶ ἀκαταλήπτως ἐκ τοῦ Θεοῦ γεγεννημένον (where Touttée quotes parallels). vi 6 ὁ γεννηθεὶς ἀπαθῶς πρὸ χρόνων αἰωνίων οἶδε τὸν γεννήσαντα, καὶ ὁ γεννήσας οἶδε τὸν γεγεννημένον. xi. 4 υἱὸν ἀεὶ γεννηθέντα ἀπεριεργάστῳ καὶ ἀκαταλήπτῳ τῇ γεννήσει; so next section, where he quotes Isa. liii. 8. xi. 20 ἀρχὴ τοῦ υἱοῦ ἄχρονος, ἀκατάληπτος, ἄναρχος, ὁ πατὴρ ......ὁ γεννήσας αὐτὸν καθὼς οἶδεν αὐτὸς μόνος; so *id.* xi. 8, 11. xi. 10 ἐκ πατρὸς

cannot be supposed to have had any direct hand in it. If therefore the Lucianic creed represents the earlier conservatism, it follows that Cyril expresses the later views which the Acacians were endeavouring to conciliate.

The other subject is the state of the church at Antioch under the episcopate of Leontius (344—357). The Nicene faith was quite as strong in the city as Arianism had ever been at Alexandria. The Eustathians formed a separate and strongly Nicene congregation under the presbyter Paulinus, and held their meetings outside the walls. Athanasius communicated with them on his return from exile; and consented to give the Arians a church in Alexandria as Constantius desired, if only the Eustathians might have one inside the walls of Antioch[1]. His terms were prudently declined, for the Arians were in a minority even in the larger congregation which adhered to Leontius. The old Arian needed all his caution to avoid offence. "When this snow melts," touching his white head, "there will be much mud." When the doxology was sung, Leontius dropped his voice so that it was impossible to guess whether his version of it was Nicene or Arian[2]. His policy was so far successful that he was able to keep out of the Eustathian communion not only the large numbers who had no fixed convictions at all, but also many whose sympathies were decidedly Nicene, like his own successors Meletius and Flavian, and Diodorus the disciple and successor of Silvanus of Tarsus. But they always

ἀϊδίως καὶ ἀνεκφράστως, καὶ ἐν ὑποστάσει γεννηθέντα. vii. 5 πρὸ πάσης ὑποστάσεως, καὶ πρὸ πάσης αἰσθήσεως, πρὸ χρόνων τε καὶ πρὸ πάντων τῶν αἰώνων, τὸ πατρικὸν ἀξίωμα ἔχει ὁ Θεὸς......οὐ πάθει Πατὴρ γενόμενος.

νεύματι πατρικῷ παραγενόμενον...εἰς ἀθέτησιν ἁμαρτίας] This may be Acacian: but Cyril has Cat. x. 9 υἱὸς εὐπειθής; and νεῦμα is a frequent word of his, e.g. Cat. x. 5, xi. 22, xv. 25, xvii. 31. He also speaks xv. 30 of his αὐτοπροαίρετος εὐπείθεια.

πᾶσαν τὴν οἰκονομίαν πληρώσαντα κατὰ τὴν πατρικὴν βούλησιν] Acacian again? Yet Ath. Or. iii. 31, p. 460.

εἰς τὰ καταχθόνια κατελθόντα καὶ τὰ ἐκεῖσε οἰκονομήσαντα· ὃν πυλωροὶ ᾅδου ἰδόντες ἔφριξαν] Cyril mentions this amongst his ten ἀναγκαῖα δόγματα—Cat. iv. 11 κατῆλθεν εἰς τὰ καταχθόνια,

ἵνα κἀκεῖθεν λυτρώσηται τοὺς δικαίους, and explains it fully xiv. 19, where both clauses are found. The doctrine does not figure among the *necessaria* of Origen *de Principiis*, which Cyril is closely following. See Caspari *Alte u. Neue* 152.

καθεζόμενον (instead of καθεσθέντα)] frequent in Cyril, who lays much stress on the eternity of the session, e.g. Cat. iv. 7, xi. 17, xiv. 27.

ἐλευσόμενον...τῇ δόξῃ τῇ πατρικῇ]This also may be Acacian in the emphasis again laid on his derivative glory and subordinate action. The words come from Mark viii. 38.

[1] The story comes from Rufinus i. 19, but is not otherwise improbable.
[2] Sozomen iii. 20. Theodoret ii. 24.

considered him an enemy, and all the more dangerous for
his moderation, so different from the violence of Macedonius
at Constantinople. His appointments were Arianizing, and
he gave deep offence by the ordination of his old disciple the
detested Aetius. It was doubtless under the influence of their
common Lucianist friends[1]; but no genuine conservative would
have done it, and indeed even Euphronius or Flacillus (whichever
it was) had refused to do it. So great was the outcry that
Leontius was forced to suspend him, though he continued to do
him all the service he could in other ways. The opposition
was led by two ascetic laymen, Flavian and Diodorus, who both
became distinguished bishops in later time. They kept alive
orthodox feeling by a vigorous use of hymns, keeping vigil
frequently with night-long services round the tombs of the
martyrs. The practice became so popular that Leontius could
not venture to suppress it. His order to transfer the services
to the church may have been designed quite as much for good
order as for surveillance.

The case of Antioch was not exceptional. Arians and
Nicenes were still parties inside the church rather than distinct
sects[2]. They still used the same prayers and the same hymns,
still worshipped in the same buildings, still commemorated the
same saints and martyrs[3], and still considered themselves

[1] Aetius was a disciple of Paulinus of Tyre, of Athanasius of Anazarbus, and Antonius of Tarsus (both Lucianists); a friend also of Acacius of Cæsarea, and of Eudoxius of Germanicia (another Lucianist). Epiphanius *Hær.* 76, 1 makes George of Alexandria ordain Aetius.

[2] This is the reason given by Sozomen ii. 32 for the omission of the Arians in Constantine's law, dated about 331 and given in full by Eusebius *V. C.* iii. 64, 65, in which we find enumerated as distinct sects the Novatians, Valentinians, Marcionists, Paulianists, Montanists, καὶ πάντες ἁπλῶς οἱ τὰς αἱρέσεις διὰ τῶν οἰκείων πληροῦντες συστημάτων, which Sozomen refers to the relics of earlier heresies.

The relations of Arians and Nicenes are well given by Fialon *Saint Athanase* 124—129.

[3] The Arian acceptance of the earlier orthodox saints is occasionally turned against them by Athanasius, e.g. *de Syn.* 13, p. 581 πῶς Πατέρας ὀνομάζουσιν οὓς διεδέξαντο, ὧν αὐτοὶ τῆς γνώμης κατήγοροι γίνονται; but it was only made a primary argument in the time of Nectarius (381—397), by the advice of the Novatian reader Sisinnius, Socr. v. 10.

We may note here a few points of Arian hagiology, and some legends which seem traceable to Arian sources:

I. (*Third century.*)

Penance of the emperor Philip, a current story in the time of Eusebius (*H. E.* vi. 34), but first connected (so far as we know) with Babylas by Leontius the Eusebian (ap. *Chron. Pasch.* 254). The legend is discussed by Görres in *Zeitsch. f. wiss. Theologie* for 1880, p. 191—195.

Lucian of Antioch, martyr under Maximin. His body carried in true heathen style by a dolphin to Helenopolis (Drepana), Philost. ii. 13.

members of the same church[1]. The example of separation set by the Eustathians at Antioch and the Arians at Alexandria[2] was not followed till a later stage of the controversy, when Diodorus and Flavian on one side and the Anomœans on the other began to introduce their own peculiarities into the service. The lawless alteration of the common worship was the last and not the first resource of party malice in the Nicene age. And if the bitterness of intestine strife was increased by a state of things which made every bishop a party nominee, there was some compensation in the free intercourse of parties afterwards separated by barriers of persecution. Nicenes and conservatives mingled freely in most places long after Leontius was dead; and the Novatians of Constantinople threw open their churches to the victims of Macedonius in a way which drew his persecution on themselves, and was remembered in their favour in the reign of Theodosius, and even by liberal men like Socrates in the next century[3].

II. (*Licinian Persecution.*)
Agapetus confessor and bishop of Synnada, and worker of miracles. Philost. ii. 8. Rejected by Görres *Licin. Christenverfolgung* 231—234. Procopius of Synnada signs at Nicæa, and Agapetus does not appear at Sardica.

Auxentius confessor and μετά τινα χρόνον ὕστερον bishop of Mopsuestia, where he kindly received Aetius in 360. Philost. v. 2, and in Suidas Αὐξέντιος. Discussed by Görres 234—236. Macedonius signs for Mopsuestia at Nicæa and Philippopolis, while Auxentius does not sign the Acacian creed at Seleucia in 359. However the Nicenes adopted both him and Agapetus.

III. (*Reigns of Constantius and Julian.*)
Philostorgius ascribes miracles to Eusebius of Nicomedia (Photius *Bibl.* Cod. 40), to Theophilus the Indian (esp. iv. 7), to Aetius, Eunomius, Leontius of Tripolis, and most of the Anomœan leaders. He is also the chief authority for the legend of Artemius.

From the Homœan writer of the time of Valens we have the stories of the officers of Leontius of Antioch, the exhumation of Patrophilus, the death of Eustathius of Epiphania, and perhaps the evil end of the apostates Hero and Theotecnus, which is also told by Philost. vii. 13.
By George of Laodicea (Socr. ii. 9, Soz. iii. 6) miracles were ascribed to his friend Eusebius of Emesa. Augusti (*Eus. Em. Opuscula* 72—82) connects them with the doubtful reputation of Eusebius as a student of the black art.

[1] This is well put by Fialon *Saint Athanase* 127—129.
[2] As the early insubordination of the Arians at Alexandria (Alexander ap. Theodoret i. 4) was only temporary, their separation is best dated from the consecration of Pistus about 338.
[3] Socrates records the persecutions of his Novatian friends ii. 38 by Macedonius, iii. 12 by Eleusius of Cyzicus, iv. 9 by Valens. They were left undisturbed (Socr. v. 10, 14, 20) by Theodosius. Persecution from the Nicene side was begun by Chrysostom (Socr. vii. 7: compare *C. Th.* xvi. 5, 34 against the Montanists in 398) and Cyril (Socr. vii. 7), and at Rome by Innocent or Celestine (Socr. vii. 9, 11). They are not expressly named in any of the persecuting laws (except the anomalous rescript of Constantine in Eus. *V. C.* iii. 64) before *C. Th.* xvi. 5, 59, dated in 423.

NOTE CC.

THE RETURN OF ATHANASIUS IN 337.

Athanasius was exiled to Gaul shortly after the assembly at Jerusalem; which Eusebius *V. C.* iv. 40, 47 connects with the *Tricennalia* of Constantine, July 25, 335, though without fixing it for the anniversary. Indeed there is reason to think it took place a few weeks later. This is indicated by the departure of Athanasius July 11 for Tyre, by his unexpected arrival October 30 at Constantinople, and by the protest, Ath. *Apol. c. Ar.* 75, p. 152 of the Mareotic presbyters, dated September 7. The dedication of the great church is variously fixed for September 13 (Greek *Menologion*), September 14 (*Chron. Pasch.*; but in the year 333) and September 17 (Niceph. Call. viii. 30).

After relating the arrival of Athanasius October 30 at Constantinople, the Index to the *Festal Letters* records his exile November 7. Since, however, this allows no time for the journey of the bishops summoned by Constantine (Ath. *Apol. c. Ar.* 86, p. 159) from Tyre, we may accept the emendation of Sievers *Einl.* § 5, and shift the date to February 5, 336, by reading *Mechir* 10 for *Athyr* 10.

The return of Athanasius, as we have seen elsewhere, is fixed for the autumn of 337 by the concurrent evidence of the *Festal Letter* for 338, the Index, the *Hist. Aceph.* and Theodoret. The only difficulty is in the letter of the younger Constantine, first given by Athanasius *Apol. c. Ar.* 87, p. 160. It is written after his father's death and dated from Trier, June 17, but the year is not given. Valesius assigns it to 337; and Sievers *Einl.* § 6 follows him, adding (*a*) that Constantine II. would have called himself Augustus after September 9, 337, (*b*) that he would have no right to meddle with Alexandria after it had been definitely assigned to Constantius.

CH. IV.]   NOTE CC.   RETURN OF ATHANASIUS IN 337.   141

Hefele *Councils* § 52 follows Tillemont *Mémoires*, viii. 671, and is himself followed by Bright *Hist. Treatises*, in shifting the letter to 338; and his arguments need examination. He declares it impossible, "considering the imperfect state of the roads and means of communication at that time," for the news of Constantine's death at Nicomedia May 22, 337 to have reached Trier so early as June 17. I venture to think otherwise. The distance is about 1300 English miles in a straight line, with the Bosphorus and the Balkans to cross on the way. As the Rhætian frontier was quiet in 337, the couriers would be able to avoid the Alps by entering Gaul at Arbor Felix on the Bodensee, so that they would have no higher pass than that of Succi, which is hardly 1800 feet above the sea. The necessary speed would therefore average less than 80 Roman miles daily; and Constantine's care of the *cursus publicus* (e.g. *C. Theod.* viii. 5, 2) must have been to very little purpose if it could not carry news of the first importance at this rate.

Passing over instances from earlier times (Friedländer *Sittengesch.* ii. 16—19), Sievers mentions the extraordinary journey of Cæsarius in 387, from Antioch to Constantinople in less than five days. But the best comparison occurs during the revolt of Procopius, whose occupation of the capital September 28, 365 was announced to Valentinian as he entered Paris November 1. Here the direct distance is a trifle shorter, and the time somewhat longer than in 337; but the Alemanni were sweeping over Gaul and Rhætia, so that the news must have come round by Italy and over the Alps. Again, when Constantius died at Mopsucrenæ November 3, 361, the news reached Julian at Naissus (Ammianus xxi. 10, 5. Zosimus iii. 11). The distance is about 850 miles in a straight line—the Bordeaux pilgrim counts 1163 Roman miles by the road—yet he was able to complete an ordinary march of 400 miles to Constantinople by December 11.

Two modern cases may be worth comparison: (1) In 1788 Fox came from Bologna to London (Stanhope *Life of Pitt* i. 317) in nine days—800 miles, with the Alps and the Channel to cross. (2) In 1741 the Indian who bore Don Joseph Pizarro's letter (Anson's *Voyage*, p. 34) crossed the Pampas and the Cordilleras in thirteen days from Buenos Ayres to Santiago in Chili—800 miles in a straight line. This was an extraordinary speed; but it was accomplished in the depth of winter, and the route would cross the Andes southward of Aconcagua by the dangerous Uzpallata pass, at a height of 12,800 feet above the sea. The Portillo is a little lower and a little nearer, but I believe it was not in use in Spanish times.

There is one more argument for the year 337. We have a law *Cod. Theod.* x. 10, 4 *Imp. Constantius A. Celsino Pf. P.*, dated from Viminacium, June 12, 338. If it could be shewn that Celsinus held the Gaulish Prefecture, the law would belong to the younger Constantine, and the letter dated from Trier, June 17, would be positively fixed for 337.

The evidence on this point is nearly conclusive. *Cod. Theod.* xii. 1, 27, also addressed to Celsinus, concerns the *curiales* of Carthage, which usually belonged to the Italian prefecture. Its date however from Trier, January 8, 339, shews that he was Constantine's subject, and therefore held the Gaulish prefecture. Upon the whole it is much more likely that Constantine made the authority of the Gaulish prefect coextensive with his own than that he allowed Africa to be ruled by a subject of Constans. The Illyrian prefecture was united with the Italian by Mamertinus 361—365, and his silence *Gratiarum Actio* 22 shews that he was not the first who enjoyed the double honour. The two prefectures were also held together by Rufinus 365—368, by Probus 368—383 (though not continuously), by a series of five others 387—393, and by Nicomachus Flavianus as late as 431. We may therefore suppose that there were only three prefects during the interval 337—340. This will give one for each emperor, according to Diocletian's original arrangement.

Hefele finds a difficulty in the statement of Athanasius *Hist. Ar.* 8, p. 276, that the exiles were recalled by the *three* emperors. But the edict of recall would bear the names of all three; and in any case we need not defer it till after the meeting in Pannonia, which seems fixed for the summer of 338 by Constantine's presence at Viminacium.

Tillemont raises a more serious objection from the interview of Athanasius (*Apol. ad Ctium* 5 p. 236) with Constantius at Viminacium, which must have been on his return from Trier. But even this is not insuperable. The movements of Constantius are too imperfectly known to exclude the possibility of an earlier meeting in the autumn of 337 between him and Constans at Viminacium.

Epiphanius *Hær.* 69, 10 is quoted by Hefele *Councils* § 52: but the passage is absolutely useless—a confusion worthy of Rufinus between the returns of 337 and 346. There is not even a various reading to justify Hefele's use of it.

NOTE D.

THE LEGISLATION OF CONSTANTIUS.

It may be useful to give a general view of the legislation of Constantius. The references are to the *Codex Theodosianus*, unless otherwise stated.

I. Laws consolidating or extending the machinery of government. *C. Just.* ii. 58, 1 (342) strengthens the hands of provincial governors by doing away such remains of the *formula* system as had escaped the rescript of Diocletian (*C. Just.* iii. 3, 2) in 294. The rest of the laws in this class are more or less financial. xi. 22, 1 (346) forbids the transfer of assessments to districts less heavily taxed. xi. 36, 6—13 comprise five laws (342—358) disallowing appeals contrary to the interest of the *fiscus* or the *res privata*. ix. 42, 2 (356) waives the right of the *fiscus* to claim the property of criminals executed for offences other than treason or magic; but is repealed by ix. 42, 4 (358). In xii. 1, 25—49 we find as many as ten laws (338—361) on the *curiales*, fixing the qualification at 25 *jugera* of land, and refusing exemption to the plea of honours real or pretended, to sham soldiers, and even to the sons of the *veterani* who neglected to follow the calling of their fathers, while the last law of the series regulates the claims of the *curia* on the property of ordained *curiales*. Similarly xi. 24. 1 (360) recalls to their burdens the numerous *coloni* in Egypt who had placed themselves under the protection of officials.

To the same class of laws rather than to the department of religious policy we may refer xvi. 8, 6 (*ad Evagrium* P. O, and therefore best dated in 353), forbidding Jews to marry Christian women from the *gynæcea*. It should be compared with xiv. 3, 10 (355), subjecting sons in law of *pistores* to the burdens of *pistores*, or with the law of Valentinian (x. 20, 5) in 371, reducing the man who married a *murilegula* to the condition of a *murilegulus*.

II. Laws alleviating the public burdens, or aimed at the misconduct of officials. Of these ix. 1, 7 (338) is against delays of trial, and *C. Just.* vii. 37, 1 (*ad Orfitum* P. U, and therefore 353—359) gives up the claims of the *fiscus* to property after four years interval. We may also claim for Constantius xi. 7, 7 (353 Haenel. 346 Godefroy, breaking the order), which forbids the use of torture in collecting the revenue. But the most characteristic of these laws are the five vi.

29, 1—5 (353—359), which forbid the *curiosi* to abuse the *evectiones*, to lay false charges, or to imprison anyone on their own authority. To these add ii. 1, 3 (357), against extortions and gross outrages by the *agentes in rebus*.

But the reign of Constantius is not productive in laws of this kind. His activity will bear no comparison with that of Valentinian; much less with the fifteen months of Julian.

III. Laws enacted in the interest of public morals, or with a more or less distinct religious aim. ix. 3, 3 (340) orders the separation of the sexes in prisons; iii. 12, 1 (342) forbids the marriage of an uncle with his niece; xv. 8, 1 (343) and ix. 25, 1 (354) deal with the rape of consecrated women, whether virgins or not; iii. 12, 2 (355) prohibits marriage with a deceased brother's wife or a deceased wife's sister; and ix. 17, 3 ; 4 (both of 357) denounce the quarrying of stones from tombs for private use; while xv. 12, 2 (357, after leaving Rome) forbids soldiers and *palatini* to hire themselves out as gladiators.

Heathenism is first struck at by xvi. 10, 2, an isolated prohibition of sacrifice (no penalty specified) issued in 341, but not again till after the Magnentian war. In one group of laws we have xvi. 10, 4 (353), which closes the temples and makes sacrifice a capital crime. The latter part is found again in the same title, *l*. 6 (356); while *l*. 5 (353) repeals the permission given by Magnentius for nocturnal sacrifices. The other group is ix. 16, 4—6 (357—8) against the use of magic. The relation of Constantius to heathenism is discussed by Chastel *Destruction du Paganisme* 77—95 ; and a few more points are given by Lasaulx *Untergang des Hellenismus* 52—58, and Wordsworth in *Dict. Chr. Biogr.* Art. *Constantine*.

Two laws are devoted to Jewish affairs. xvi. 8, 7 (357) confiscates the property of renegades, and xvi. 9, 2 (*ad Evagrium:* best dated 353) forbids the Jews to hold slaves of any other sect or nation. The latter law is usually assigned to the year 339. But (*a*) it is indefinitely ascribed to the sons of Constantine by Soz. iii. 17 and Niceph. Call. ix. 20, while Constantius and Constans are specified by Theophanes p. 54 and Cedrenus i. p. 522 (Bonn editions): (*b*) the corrupt inscription points to a joint consulship of Constantius and Constans (or Gallus), which might fall in 339, 342, 346, 352, 353 or 354. The first three dates are excluded by the prefectures of Acindynus, Leontius and Philippus; but there is little choice among the rest. It is however best placed after the Jewish war of 352.

Nine laws (xvi. 2, 8—15) regulate the immunities of the clergy. By *l.* 8 (343) they are freed from extraordinary taxes, from billeting, and (if traders for their living) from trade taxes; by *l.* 9 (349) from all the burdens of the *curia*, the exemption extending to their sons if clerics also. In *l.* 10 (353) is a general exemption, specially including the *parangariæ*, and protected by *l.* 11 (354). The bishops are next exempted by *l.* 12 (355) from the secular courts, while *l.* 13 (*ad Leontium:* hence 356) and *l.* 14 (*Felici episcopo*, 357) confirm the privileges of the Roman clergy. But *l.* 15 (360) refuses the petition of the bishops at Ariminum for personal exemption from the land tax, and subjects their lands to the usual burdens. The last of the series is *l.* 16 (361), which extends the exemptions to the village clergy. The language is obscure, but it can hardly refer to monks.

It will be noticed that the important title xvi. 5—*de hæreticis* is a blank throughout the reign of Constantius. The iniquities of Gregory, Macedonius and George have left no trace in the *Codex Theodosianus*.

CHAPTER V.

THE HOMŒAN VICTORY.

IN the mean time new troubles were gathering in the West. While the Eastern churches were distracted with the crimes or wrongs of Marcellus and Athanasius, Europe remained at peace from the Atlantic to the pass of Succi. The western frontier of Constantius was also the western limit of the storm. Africa had a chronic trouble of its own in the alternate outbursts of Donatist fanaticism and imperial intolerance, but the distant rumours of the Eastern controversies were very faintly heard in Gaul and Spain. The churches of Europe are lost for awhile in tranquil obscurity.

Constans was not ill disposed, but prosperity did not improve him. For a few years his government was just and firm; but afterwards—it might be that his health was failing— he lived in seclusion among his Frankish guards, and left his subjects to the oppression of unworthy favourites[1]. Rumours of nameless orgies crept abroad, and few regretted their weak

---

[1] We are not told much about Constans, but his character seems too favourably drawn by Broglie iii. 58.

Athanasius is the only writer who could have told us anything from personal knowledge; but he gives us little more than vague regrets for his benefactor. Eutropius x. 9 gives Constans credit for good government in his earlier years, but adds that weak health and bad company caused a change for the worse. All authorities are agreed that he had his full share of the Flavian weakness for unworthy favourites. Aurelius Victor pronounces him *ministrorum pravitate exsecrabilis, atque præceps in avaritiam*, the younger Victor complains that he sold promotions, and Libanius I. 426 mentions a specific case of oppression at Corinth by his *magister officiorum* (Sievers *Libanius* 94) Eugenius.

In perfect harmony with these accounts are the allusions which remain to us from the work of Ammianus, to the effect (xxx. 7, 5) that Constans was the terror of the Franks, and (xvi. 7, 5) that he would have committed but venial offences at the worst if he had followed the advice of his virtuous chamberlain Eutherius.

Notwithstanding his weak health, which the younger Victor and Zonaras xiii. 6 tell us was owing to a chronic pain in the joints, Constans was devoted to hunting (so also Zos. ii. 42, 47), and often spent whole days together in the woods with his Frankish

master's fate when the army of Gaul proclaimed Magnentius Augustus (Jan. 350). But the memory of Constantine was still a power which could set up emperors and pull them down. Vetranio at Sirmium received the purple from Constantine's daughter, and Nepotianus claimed it at Rome as Constantine's nephew. The Magnentian generals scattered the gladiators of Nepotianus, and disgraced their easy victory with long-remembered slaughter and proscription. Meanwhile Constantius came up from Syria, won over the legions of Illyricum, reduced Vetranio to a peaceful abdication, and pushed on with augmented forces towards the Julian Alps, there to decide the strife between Magnentius and the house of Constantine.

Magnentius was on one side a Frank by birth, and appears entitled to the credit of a bold and able general[1]. Severely as the historians condemn his government, it does not seem to have been much worse than that of Constans. Oppressive no doubt it was, and full of cruelty. But the Empire was terribly oppressive at its best; and the needs of a great war were not likely to abate the taxgatherer's demands[2]. His cruelty again would weigh less heavily upon him if it had not made Rome his enemy. The ancient Mother of the Nations had no forgiveness for the intruder who had disturbed her queenly rest with civil war, and filled her streets with blood—lest forsooth she should forget his hateful barbarian birth[3]. It may be that even the impartial narrative of Ammianus is tinged with prejudice by Rome's abiding hatred of Magnentius. Towards heathenism he was something more than neutral.

guards. Hence arose grave suspicions, confirmed by Zosimus, Aurelius Victor (*pro certo*), Zonaras his guide and the *Passio S. Artemii*, which seems not entirely contemptible as an authority for this part of the history.

The fate of Constans much resembles that of Gratian; but the choice of Magnentius is enough to shew that the mutiny was not originally due to Roman impatience of his barbarian favourites.

[1] We cannot lay any stress on the account in Julian *Or.* i. p. 38 of his luxury at Aquileia—οὐδὲ ὑπαίθριος ἐτόλμα στρατεύειν. It may however be noticed that *Ep.* 59 twice joins Constans and Magnentius.

[2] His exactions in Julian *Or.* i. p. 34 are authenticated by the remarkable fact that the *citizens* resisted him at Mursa (Zos. ii. 49) and at Trier (Ammianus xv. 6, 4). His cruelty in Julian *Or.* i. 39 may have been on some particular occasion of which we know nothing.

[3] The sarcasm is due to Julian *Or.* i. p. 33 ὥσπερ οἶμαι δεδιὼς μή τις αὐτὸν πολίτην μοχθηρὸν, ἀλλ' οὐχὶ βάρβαρον ὑπολάβῃ φύσει. The slaughter made a deep impression—Ammianus xxviii. 1, 1 counts the sixteenth year from it to the persecution of the Roman nobles by Maximin.

Constans had been so decided a persecutor that his successor naturally leaned the other way. Magnentius however was not himself a heathen; and it cannot be said that he went beyond the limits of a just toleration in repealing the persecuting laws of the last twenty years and returning to the broad religious freedom of the edict of Milan. This was the policy of common sense adopted by Julian and Valentinian, and it was an evil day for Rome when Gratian and Theodosius departed from it. The crimes of Magnentius admit of no defence; yet it was hardly a mere tyranny which commanded the support of old officials like Titianus and Celsinus, and even of Vulcatius Rufinus the uncle of Gallus, a Roman noble whom every emperor from Constans to Valentinian delighted to honour. The government of Magnentius was regretted in the days of Florentius and Paul *Catena*. Julian unwillingly allows its merits, and years afterwards Valentinian found it worth his while to marry the usurper's widow[1].

But for the present all was forgotten in the din of war. Each of the combatants tried the resources of intrigue; but while Constantius won over the Frank Silvanus from the Western camp, the envoys of Magnentius who sounded Athanasius gained nothing from the wary Greek[2]. The armies touched each other near Siscia, and Constantius was driven back upon the scene of his father's victory over Licinius at Cibalæ. Not there however but near the adjoining town of Mursa the decisive battle was fought (Sept. 28, 351). Both armies well sustained the honour of the Roman name, and it was only after a frightful slaughter that the usurper was thrown back on

---

[1] Pagan discontent may have had its share in the overthrow of Constans, but it does not appear upon the whole that the reign of Magnentius was a pagan reaction.

We cannot infer much on one side from the accounts of Athanasius, *Apol. ad Ctium*, 7, p. 237 that Magnentius was given to magic, of Libanius *Or. fun. in Jul.* p. 268 that he kept the old laws of the Empire, or of Philostorgius iii. 21 that his army was full of pagans, and iii. 26 himself was a worshipper of the demons: or on the other from the Christian coins issued by Magnentius and Decentius; and for that matter by Eugenius also, whose reign was undoubtedly a pagan reaction.

More significant are his restoration of the altar of Victory in the *curia* (Symmachus, *Ep.* x. 61; Sievers *Studien*, 470), and his permission even for nocturnal sacrifices (repealed in 353 by *C. Th.* xvi. 10, 5).

[2] The intrigue is discussed by Fialon *Saint Athanase* 170; but he has not shewn that Constantius went round by Alexandria in 350.

Aquileia. Next summer[1] he was forced to evacuate Italy, and in 353 his destruction was completed at Mount Seleucus in the Cottian Alps. Magnentius fell upon his sword, and Constantius remained the master of the world.

The Eusebians were not slow to take advantage of the confusion. The fires of controversy in the East were smouldering through the years of rest, and it was no hard task to make them blaze afresh. Maximus of Jerusalem had welcomed Athanasius on his return in 346; but Acacius and Patrophilus kept aloof, and before long contrived to establish Cyril in his place[2] as their own nominee. And since the recall of the exiles was due to Western influence, the death of Constans in 350 left the field clear for further operations. Already at Sirmium in 347[3] they had accepted the condemnation of Photinus at Milan as involving that of his teacher Marcellus, and by consequence reopening all the questions which had been decided at Sardica. The next step was to hold a new council at Sirmium after the battle of Mursa[4], at which Marcellus and his disciple Photinus were again and finally deposed. Ancyra was restored to Basil, while Germinius of Cyzicus[5], an active friend of Ursacius and Valens, was translated to Sirmium. Of Marcellus we hear no more for many years; but Photinus hazarded an appeal to the emperor, which was decided against him in the spring of 355[6].

---

[1] We may take the appointment of Neratius Cerealis as *præfectus urbi* (Sept. 26, 352) to shew when Rome fell into the hands of Constantius.

[2] Maximus was dead according to Jerome and Theodoret, while Socrates and Sozomen tell us that he was expelled. See Touttée p. xviii. Hort *Two Diss.* 92 leaves the question open; and I have followed his example.

To this period we may also refer the expulsion of the Apollinarii (Soz. vi. 25) by George of Laodicea.

[3] For the date, Zahn *Marcellus* 80.

[4] In the winter of 351—2. So Hefele *Councils* § 73, but without support from Ath. *Hist. Ar.* 30, p. 285 διερχόμενος, ὅτε πρὸς Μαγνέντιον ἔσπευδε, which may suit either date. Broglie iii. 212 places it in 350—1, but without discussion.

The case is not clear, but we may argue for the later date (1) that Constantius deposed Vetranio ten months after March 350, and therefore cannot have held the Sirmian council much before the beginning of the campaign of 351. At Sirmium however we find him as late as March 15. (2) It is better left till the battle of Mursa had cleared the situation.

Hefele's narrative is very careless. There is no trace for example of Constantius at Rome in 352.

[5] Ath. *Hist. Ar.* 74, p. 307.

[6] Socr. ii. 30 and Socr. iv. 16 seem to put the appeal of Photinus after the Sirmian manifesto of 357; but there is nothing in their accounts to prevent us from carrying it as far back as the winter of 351.

Epiphanius *Hær.* 71, 1 tells us that

150   *ECCLESIASTICAL HISTORY.*   [CH.

Other bishops appear to have been expelled in the East before this, but only Paul of Constantinople[1] is known to us by name. Athanasius however was too strong to be disturbed: so he was reserved for the present.

A new creed was also issued, commonly known as the First of Sirmium. It begins by repeating the Fourth of Antioch[2], with the addition of as many as 27 anathemas. Its interest lies partly in its direct attack on Marcellus[3], partly also in its indications of the rise of new questions. Three of the anathemas (20—22) are on the doctrine of the Holy Spirit; while

the disputation with Basil of Ancyra was held, apparently at Sirmium, in the presence of Thalassius, Datianus, Cerealis, Taurus, Leontius and others, and that the notes taken by a clerk of the prefect Rufinus were sealed up and sent to the emperor. These data seem to point to the beginning of 355.

Valesius prefers the winter of 351—2. This date cannot be positively disproved; but it does not seem likely. For (1) Constantius was then at Sirmium, and could not have resisted the attractions of a great theological debate. (2) Thalassius seems to have been sent with Gallus into Syria in March 351, not returning before the appointment of Domitian in 353. In Ammianus xiv. 7, 9 *eum odisse* (Gardthausen) seems the true reading, though *eum obisse*, on which Valesius argues, may be supported by *S. Artemii Passio* 13. But on this see Sievers *Libanius* 227. (3) The appeal must have taken time, and is better not placed so soon after the council of 351.

If the Valesian date is rejected, there is no halting-place till the beginning of 355. Thalassius could not have been present before 353, and Cerealis could hardly have been spared from Rome during the critical time of his prefecture (Sept. 352—Dec. 353). Leontius was sent as quæstor to Syria after the murder of Montius in 353, and accompanied Gallus on his fatal journey westward in the winter of 354, reappearing after July 355 as *præfectus urbi* for nearly two years. In the first months of 355 we have also a gap in the official life of Taurus, who seems to have held the Illyrian prefecture in 353—4, and the Italian from Apr. 355 to his flight in 361. It may be added that Constantius was then at Milan, and that Datianus was with him in the summer of 356 (evidence in Sievers *Libanius* p. 218).

Vulcatius Rufinus appears to have held the Gaulish prefecture from his appointment by Constans in 349 (with perhaps an interval in the Magnentian war) till 355—6, his successor Honoratus being replaced by Florentius before the battle of Argentoratum in 357. Rufinus then retired from official life till 366. These circumstances seem to exclude the date 357—8 for the disputation. It may further be noted that Basil was in Asia for at least a year before the summer of 358, and that the whole year 358 seems negatived (in an official document like this) by the omission to designate Datianus and Cerealis as consuls.

[1] Sozomen iv. 2 may be guilty of confusion between two of Paul's exiles, but there can be no question that Paul was restored after the council of Sardica, and only now finally expelled. His last exile is universally connected with the prefecture of Philippus, and by Ath. *Hist. Ar.* 7, p. 275 with its last year. Now Philippus was prefect about 345—351, and as he accompanied Constantius to Sirmium, Paul's execution will be fixed for 350.

[2] Or rather that of Philippopolis, with which it is twice directly connected by the Semiarians at Ancyra (Epiph. *Hær.* 73, 2). They do not notice the μακρόστιχος.

[3] c. 5—7. Photinus is not touched till c. 9.

two more (12, 13) deny the passibility of the divine element of the Lord's Person, and shew us that the Christological side of the controversy was beginning to attract attention. They at least amount to a direct denial of the Arian theory of the Incarnation[1].

Magnentius had not meddled with the controversy. To him indeed it would rather seem to offer the chance of an ally in the East than as a matter of practical interest in the West. But as soon as Constantius was in possession of Gaul, he determined to force on the Westerns an indirect but effectual condemnation of the Nicene faith in the person of Athanasius. There could be no serious hope of securing any direct approval of Arianism in the West, for conservative feeling was firmly set against it by the councils of Nicea and Sardica. The bishops were almost uniformly[2] resolute against it, and Gaul itself was the centre of the Nicene resistance. Liberius of Rome followed the steps of his predecessor Julius. Hosius of Cordova was still the patriarch of Christendom, while Paulinus of Trier, Rhodanius of Toulouse and Dionysius of Milan proved their faith in exile. Creatures of the palace like Saturninus of Arles and the Cappadocian Auxentius were no counterpoise to men like these.

Doctrine was therefore kept in the background for the present. Constantius began by demanding from the Western bishops a summary condemnation of Athanasius, coming for-

---

[1] A light is thrown on the conservative character of the Sirmian creed by its interpretations of Scripture. Four passages from Genesis are quoted against Marcellus in Anathemas 14—17; —viz. (a) i. 26, (b) xviii. 1, (c) xxxii. 24, (d) xix. 24. In the mere interpretation the other parties were agreed against him. Thus from Athanasius we have for (a) c. Gentes 46, p. 36. Or. iii. 29, p. 459; for (b) Or. i. 38, p. 349, ii. 13, p. 379; for (c) Or. iii. 12, p. 445, iii. 16, p. 448; for (d) Or. ii. 13, p. 380. The point to notice is the selection of the texts. We find (b) (c) (d) in the Antiochene letter of 269, (a) (b) (c) (d) in Eus. H. E. i. 2, and (b) (c) (d) in Eus. Ecl. Proph. i. 3—7: also (a) (d) in Eus. Præp. vii. 12, p. 322, (d) Ecl. Proph. iii. 13. Only (a) is examined in the μακρόστιχος.

[2] On the Arian side we find scarcely any but Ursacius, Germinius and Valens on the Danube, Saturninus of Arles, and the renegade Potamius of Lisbon. A few years later we glean the names of Caius in Illyricum and Paternus of Petrocorii, and Sulpicius Severus Chron. 38 adds that nearly all the bishops of Pannonia (there were only half-a-dozen or so) were Arians. We may also set down the nominees of the court—Auxentius of Milan, Felix of Rome, and Epictetus of Centumcellæ Ath. Hist. Ar. 74, p. 307. Euphrates of Cologne was not an Arian (Hefele Councils, § 69).

ward himself as the accuser at a time when Athanasius was ruling Alexandria in peace upon the faith of his solemn and repeated promises of protection. We may be sceptical as to some of the outrageous declarations put into his mouth by Lucifer and Athanasius[1], but there can be no doubt of his utter lawlessness in resting everything on his own command, without even condescending to repeat the comparatively decent argument used at Sardica, that councils ought to respect each other's decisions.

The first step was to hold a synod at Arles (Oct. 353), as soon as Constantius was settled there for the winter. It soon appeared that the bishops were not unwilling to take the emperor's word for the crimes of Athanasius, provided the court party cleared itself from the suspicion of heresy by anathematizing Arianism. It needed much management and no little violence to get rid of the condition, but in the end the council yielded. The Roman legate Vincent of Capua had been at Sardica, and had signed the original Nicene creed itself; but this time he gave way with the rest. Paulinus of Trier alone stood firm, and was sent into exile among the Phrygian Montanists.

There was a sort of armed truce for the next two years. Liberius of Rome disavowed the weakness of his legates and besought the emperor to hold a new council. But Constantius

---

[1] The language ascribed to Constantius is no unfair account of his conduct from the Nicene point of view; but he cannot have used it himself. We have:—
Athanasius *Hist. Ar.* 33, p. 287 εὐθὺς ἐκεῖνος. 'Ἀλλ' ὅπερ ἐγὼ βούλομαι τοῦτο κανών, ἔλεγε, νομιζέσθω· οὕτω γάρ μου λέγοντος ἀνέχονται οἱ τῆς Συρίας λεγόμενοι ἐπίσκοποι......'Ἀλλ' οὔτε ἤκουεν ἐκείνος, οὔτε τι πλέον αὐτοὺς λέγειν ἐπέτρεπεν, ἀλλὰ καὶ μᾶλλον ἠπείλει, καὶ ξίφος ἐγύμνου κατ' αὐτῶν (will any one take this literally?) καὶ ἀπάγεσθαι δέ τινας ἐξ αὐτῶν ἐκέλευσε· καὶ πάλιν ὡς ὁ Φαραὼ μετεγίνωσκεν.
Lucifer *De regibus apostaticis* p. 798 *Si male, inquis, egissem, si quomodo dicit Lucifer essem hæreticus, jam mihi abstulisset Deus regnum.* p. 807 *Si non bene servirem Deo, si non recte credens fuissem, nunquam regnum Romanorum vidissem in mea potestate collocatum, aut sic diu fuissem vivens in regno.* p. 813 *Bene facimus......constituere eos* [episcopos] *qui confiteantur sicuti confitebatur Arius. De non Conveniendo* p. 776 *Dixisti, Facite pacem cum episcopis sectæ meæ Arianæ, et estote in unum.*

More might be added, but these are clearly hostile renderings of the emperor's words. Athanasius scarcely pretends to report them exactly, and Lucifer is too scurrilous to carry much weight. Even the rich collections of his editors do scanty justice to his unrivalled mastery of abusive language.

The point is important because it has been neglected. Even Rendall *Julian* 32 quotes Lucifer without hint of suspicion.

was occupied with the barbarians in Rhætia and on the Danube, and had to leave the matter till he came to winter at Milan in the autumn of 355. There Julian was invested with the purple and sent as Cæsar to drive the Alemanni out of Gaul, or as intriguers hoped, to perish in the effort. The council however for a long time was quite unmanageable, and only yielded at last to open violence. Dionysius of Milan, Eusebius of Vercellæ and Lucifer of Calaris were the only bishops who had to be exiled.

The appearance of Lucifer is enough to shew that the controversy had entered on a new stage. The lawless despotism of Constantius had roused an aggressive fanaticism which went far beyond the Donatist claim of independence for the church. In dauntless courage and determined orthodoxy Lucifer may rival Athanasius himself; but any cause would have been disgraced by his narrow partizanship and outrageous violence. He had nothing of the Greek's wary self-respect, nothing of the spirit of love which avoids offence even to the fallen brethren. Indignation every now and then supplies the place of eloquence, but more often common sense itself is almost lost in the weary flow of vulgar scolding and interminable abuse. He scarcely condescends to reason, scarcely even to define his own belief[1], but revels in the more congenial occupation of denouncing the fires of damnation against the disobedient emperor. It was well for Christendom that violence worthy of Peter Damiani was not sustained by a genius like that of Hildebrand[2].

The victory was not to be won by an arm of flesh like this. Arianism had a more dangerous enemy than Lucifer. From

---

[1] Lucifer's chief doctrinal statements may be found in (a) pro S. Ath. i. pp. 864, 875. (b) pro S. Ath. ii. p. 898 cum te contra et contra omnes Dei inimicos clamet sanctæ ecclesiæ fides, credere se in Deum verum Patrem innatum, et in unicum Filium ejus natum ex innato et vero Patre, hoc est de substantia Patris, Deum de Deo, lumen de lumine, Deum verum de Deo vero, natum non factum, unius substantiæ cum Patre, quod Græci dicunt omousion, per quem omnia facta sunt, et sine quo factum est nihil, et in Spiritum paracletum verum Dei Spiritum. There seems to be no creed exactly like this; and it may pass for a paraphrase of the Nicene like that of Damasus. (c) de non parcendo p. 973—the Nicene creed in full. (d) ditto p. 987. (e) Moriendum p. 1013. (f) ditto p. 1015—part of the Nicene creed, followed by an allusion to the Sirmian manifesto. Compare also pp. 781, 854, 934, 1032 for further statements.

[2] Lucifer's character is well drawn by Neander Ch. Hist. iv. 54. But the best account of him is in Krüger's Lucifer.

the sunny land of Aquitaine, the firmest conquest of Roman civilization in Atlantic Europe, came Hilary of Poitiers, the noblest representative of Western literature in the Nicene age. Hilary was by birth a heathen, and only turned in ripe manhood from philosophy to Scripture, coming before us in 355 as an old convert, and a bishop of some standing. He was by far the deepest thinker of the West, and equally at home in Scripture and philosophy. In depth of earnestness and massive strength of intellect he is a match for Athanasius himself, and in powers of orderly arrangement decidedly superior. But Hilary was a student rather than an orator, a thinker rather than a statesman like Athanasius. He had not touched the controversy till it was forced upon him, and would much have preferred to keep out of it. But when once he had studied the Nicene Creed and found its correspondence with his own conclusions from Scripture, a clear sense of duty forbade him to shrink from manfully defending its endangered truth[1].

Such was the man whom the brutal policy of Constantius forced to take his place at the head of the Nicene opposition. He was not present at Milan, but the courtiers were determined to get rid of him. He was therefore brought before Saturninus of Arles in the spring of 356. The charge seems to have been one of immorality, but we are not told exactly what it was. However, it served its purpose. Hilary was exiled to Asia.

Meanwhile Hosius of Cordova was ordered to Sirmium and there detained. His protest[2] was disregarded, and the creatures of the palace were left to do their will upon him. After this there was only one power in the West which could not be summarily dealt with. The grandeur of Hosius was merely personal, but Liberius claimed the universal reverence due to the apostolic and imperial[3] see of Rome. It was a great and wealthy church, and during the last two hundred years had

---

[1] As Hilary's works are not of much value for controversial purposes, very few English writers seem to have studied them. The chief monograph is Reinkens *Hilarius von Poitiers*. His doctrine is discussed by Möhler *Athanasius*, 449—483, and with special success by Dorner, ii. 399—421.

[2] His letter to Constantius is given by Ath. *Hist. Ar.* 44, p. 292.

[3] Ath. *Hist. Ar.* 34, p. 288 μέχρι τῶν ἐκεῖ τὴν μανίαν ἐξέτειναν· καὶ οὐχ ὅτι ἀποστολικός ἐστι θρόνος ᾐδέσθησαν, οὔθ' ὅτι μητρόπολις ἡ 'Ρώμη τῆς 'Ρωμανίας ἐστὶν εὐλαβήθησαν.

won a noble fame for world-wide charity. Its orthodoxy was without a stain, for whatever heresies might flow to the great city, no heresy had ever issued thence. The strangers of every nation who found their way to Rome were welcomed from Saint Peter's throne with the majestic blessing of an universal father[1]. "The church of God which sojourneth in Rome" was the immemorial counsellor of all the churches; and now that the voice of counsel was passing into that of command, bishop Julius had made a worthy use of his authority as a judge of Christendom[2].

Such a bishop was a power of the first importance, especially when Arianism was dividing the Empire round the hostile camps of Gaul and Asia. If the Roman church had partly ceased to be a Greek colony in the Latin capital, it was still the connecting link of East and West, the representative of Western Christianity to the Easterns and the interpreter of Eastern to the Latin West. Liberius could therefore treat with the emperor almost on the footing of an independent sovereign. He could not condemn Athanasius unheard, and after so many acquittals. The charges might indeed be re-examined, but only in a free council, and only if the Arians were first expelled. To this demand he steadily adhered. When his legates yielded at Arles, he publicly disavowed their action. The emperor's threats he disregarded, the emperor's gifts he flung out of the church[3]. Such a defiance could have but one result; and it was not long before the world was scandalized by the news that Constantius had arrested and exiled the bishop of Rome.

The way was clear for a final attack on Athanasius. Attempts had already been made[4] to dislodge him from Alexandria,

---

[1] This aspect of the Roman church is as conspicuous as its charity even in Soter's time, about A.D. 170. Dionysius of Corinth in Eus. *Hist. Eccl.* iv. 24.

[2] On the Roman see in the Nicene age Harnack *D.G.* ii. 97—104. Bright *Roman See* 66—111.

[3] Ath. *Hist. Ar.* 37, p. 289. Theodoret ii. 16 has a good deal of rhetoric, which needs no notice.

[4] The sequence of events may be set down as follows, chiefly from the Index and the *Hist. Aceph.*, on which Sozomen depends.

Athanasius became seriously alarmed in May 353, as shewn by the mission of Serapion. To the same period we may refer the letter of the eighty Egyptian bishops to Liberius (Hil. *Fragm.* 5). One alarming sign may have been the removal of Nestorius of Gaza in 352—3, who had been prefect since 344—5, and was therefore apparently friendly, as is further hinted by the strange order of Constantius in Ath. *Hist. Ar.* 51, p. 296. Four days after

but he had defeated them by refusing obedience to anything short of written orders from the emperor. As Constantius had given him a solemn promise of protection in 346 and three times written to repeat it since his brother's death, duty as well as policy forbade him to credit the mere assertions of Montanus or Diogenes. The most pious emperor could not be supposed to mean such treachery; but he must send a plainer message if he did.

But treachery was just what was intended; and the message was plain enough when it came. Soldiers were collected from all parts of the country, and when all was ready Syrianus the *dux Ægypti* surrounded the church of Theonas with a force of more than five thousand men. It was a night of vigil on Thursday, Feb. 8[1], 356. The doors were broken up and the troops pressed up the church, enclosing the whole congregation as in a net. Athanasius fainted in the tumult; yet somehow before they reached the bishop's throne, its occupant had been safely conveyed away.

If the soldiers connived at the escape of Athanasius, they were all the less disposed to spare his flock. The outrages of Philagrius and Gregory were repeated by Syrianus and the prefect Cataphronius; and the evil work went on apace when the new bishop George arrived in Lent 357[2], and was vigorously seconded by the Manichee Sebastian, who had succeeded

Serapion's departure comes Montanus with orders forbidding him to go to the *comitatus*, and also an answer to the forged request of Athanasius to visit the emperor. On this Ath. *Apol. ad Ctium* 19, p. 243. After an interval of more than two years, Diogenes arrived in August 355, and besieged the church of Theonas from Sept. 3 to Dec. 23, but was defeated by the opposition of the people (*populo et judicibus*). Syrianus came Jan. 5, 356, with an overwhelming force, but soon agreed to refer the question to the emperor. The decisive attack on the night of Thursday, Feb. 8, was a direct breach of the arrangement.

[1] The irruption of Syrianus is fixed for the night of Thur.-Fri., Feb. 8—9, 356 (=Mechir 13-14), by the concurrent statements of the Index, the *Hist. Aceph.*, and the Egyptian bishops in Ath. *Hist. Ar.* 80, p. 311, who further date their protest Feb. 12 (=Mechir 17).

Bright *Hist. Treatises* lxix. shifts it to Feb. 7, objecting that (1) Easter falling Apr. 7, Thursday would be Feb. 7. Here he forgets that 356 was a leap year. (2) Mechir 1=Jan. 26, therefore Mechir 14=Feb. 8, not Feb. 9. The arithmetic is correct this time, and I cannot fully clear up the difficulty. But Galle in Larsow *Festbriefe* 51, plainly makes Mechir 1=Jan. 27 in leap years only. And an astronomer can be trusted to know the reckoning.

[2] The arrival of George is deferred to 357 (Feb. 24) in the circumstantial narratives of the Index and the *Hist. Aceph.*, and we may follow them in the absence of anything directly contrary in Ath. *de Fuga* 6, p. 256.

See further Robertson *Ath. Int.* lii.

Syrianus in the command of the army. Indiscriminate oppression of Nicenes and heathens provoked retaliation from the fierce populace of Alexandria. George escaped with difficulty from one riot in August 358, and was fairly driven from the city by another in October. A commission of blood was held by Paul *Catena*, but henceforth it is likely that some check was put on the worst licence of the Arian gang.

Meanwhile Athanasius had disappeared from the eyes of men. A full year after the raid of Syrianus he was hardly convinced of the emperor's treachery. Outrage after outrage might be the work of underlings, and there was room even yet for a personal appeal to their master's piety. Constantine himself had not despised his cry for justice; and if he could but stand within the vail, his presence might even yet confound the gang of eunuchs[1]. Even the weakness of Athanasius is full of grandeur; and it has given us the noble Apology to Constantius[2]. But the bitterness of exile was growing on him. When his old enemies Narcissus and Leontius and George of Laodicea presumed to mock at the fugitive bishop, he turned fiercely on them with his *de Fuga*. Only when the work of outrage had gone on many months did Athanasius return the emperor's challenge in a secret libel[3].

---

[1] Ath. *Hist. Ar.* 38, p. 290 σπαδόν-των αἵρεσιν.

[2] The respectful tone of his *Apol. ad Ctium* sufficiently guarantees its own sincerity. Athanasius surely was not fool enough to sit on two stools. If he had ceased to trust Constantius, there was nothing to be gained by flattering him. Even Athanasius had his day-dream of an appeal unto Cæsar: but he was not one of the men who cling to what they know to be dreams. How he came to cherish it so long is another question, nowhere better traced out than by Bright *Hist. Treatises* lxi.—lxv.

The chronology needs attention. Dating the *Apol. ad Ctium* "in the spring or early summer of 356" and connecting the *de Fuga* with the death of Leontius (not yet known to Athanasius) "about the end of 357," we get a safe interval between them. But (1) both works fall within the period of George's tyranny, Feb. 24, 357—Oct. 2, 358: (2) the death of Leontius must be placed in the summer of 357, if we are to leave room first for the Acacian synod held by his successor Eudoxius and then for the letter of George of Laodicea, before the council of Ancyra in Lent 358.

These changes bring the *de Fuga* much nearer to the *Apol. ad Ctium*. If it was written first, Gibbon's charge of duplicity will be established after all. This however is most unlikely. We cannot convict Athanasius on absolutely open evidence. It may however be noticed that the *de Fuga* seems more allied to the *Apol. ad Ctium* than to the fierce *Hist. Ar.* It generally avoids personal attacks on Constantius; and the single exception (c. 26, p. 266, K. ὁ αἱρετικὸς) is not certainly genuine.

[3] Fialon *Saint Ath.* 193—199, remarks on the frequency of such secret pamphlets.

But then he threw off all restraint. Even George the pork-contractor is not assailed with such a storm of merciless invective as his holiness Constantius Augustus. George might sin "like the beasts who know no better[1]"; but no wickedness of common mortals could attain to that of the new Belshazzar or Maximian, of the Lord's anointed "self-abandoned to eternal fire."

The exile governed Egypt from his hiding in the desert. Alexandria was searched in vain; in vain the malice of Constantius pursued him to the court of Ethiopia. Letter after letter issued from his inaccessible retreat to keep alive the indignation of the faithful, and invisible hands conveyed them to the furthest corners of the land. We may still read his words among the tombs of the Pharaohs in the cave of Abdelkurna[2]. The great archbishop was never greater than when he seemed to stand alone in defence of the great council.

Constantius had his revenge, but it shook the Empire to its base. Even the catastrophe of Hadrianople was hardly more disastrous than the flight of Athanasius. Egypt had not escaped its share of provincial disturbance and confusion. As early as the reign of Marcus, the savage herdsmen of the Delta had daunted even Avidius Cassius by their numbers and desperation[3]. Riots at Alexandria were continual and bloody, and the desolation of Bruchion still recalled the dreadful tumults of the days of Gallienus. Against the Illyrian emperors there had been at least two great national revolts. The first was that of Firmus the merchant-prince—the brigand, as his conqueror Aurelian so carefully describes him, as if to shew that he headed a real Coptic rising[4], not a mutiny of the usual sort.

---

[1] Ath. *de Synodis* 37, p. 601.

[2] Boeckh 8607 (quoted by Fialon *Saint Ath.* 133) is a letter of Athanasius from the ruins of Thebes.

[3] Dio Cassius lxxi. 4. They had cut up and eaten a Roman centurion. They are frequent characters in the novels.

[4] *Latronem Ægyptium, barbaricis motibus æstuantem...latronem impium*, in Vop. *Firmus* 1, 2. It reminds us of the Jewish λῃσταί. Vopiscus himself ranks him among the *tyranni*, on the ground that he assumed the titles of Imperator and Augustus, coined money and wore the purple. But statements of his own confirm Aurelian's words— e.g. *Alexandriam Ægyptiorum incitatus furore pervasit...cum Blemyis societatem maximam tenuit, et cum Saracenis.*

So also Finlay *Greece* i. 116.

The fullest account of these events is given by Preuss, *Kaiser Diocletian* 68—76. From another point of view Priaulx, *Apollonius of Tyana* 165.

The revolt of Achilleus, quelled in 226 by Diocletian, centred in Alexandria, but reached far beyond the Greek city to Busiris and Coptos, was connected with movements of the Blemmyes, and seems much like that of Firmus. But this was the last of the Coptic risings. Africa was full of revolts[1], but there were none in Egypt. It was not that the Empire was less oppressive after Diocletian had based it on the terrorism of a host of predaceous officials, but because the flight of Athanasius revealed the secret that disaffection may have surer weapons than the sword of rebellion. For the first time since the fall of Israel a nation defied the Empire in the name of God; for Christianity was raising a new Coptic nation on the ruins of the various worships which had kept apart the nomes of Egypt[2]. It was a national rising, none the less real for not breaking out in formal war. This time Greeks and Copts were united by a common love of the Nicene faith; so that the contest was at an end when the Empire surrendered Arianism. But Athanasius had shewn the way for meaner men like Cyril and Mokaukas to play their part in the decline and fall of Rome. In the next century the councils of the church became the battlefield of nations, and the victory of Hellenic orthodoxy implied sooner or later the separation of Monophysite Egypt and Nestorian Syria. Their disaffection was a recognized and standing danger to the Empire from the Council of Chalcedon onward. Effort after effort of the ablest emperors failed to avert it—Marcian and Anastasius, Justinian and Heraclius failed alike, and the Roman power beyond Mount Taurus fell because the provincials refused to lift a hand against the Saracens[3].

[1] In one century we find those of Alexander, Firmus, Gildo and Heraclian. The first however was rather a mutiny. Meanwhile in Egypt, there is a charge Socr. i. 27 against Athanasius in 335 of sending money to one Philumenus for seditious purposes; but we hear no more of him. He has been identified with Calocerus in Cyprus.

[2] On the variety of gods in Egypt, see Kuhn *Verfassung* i. 455 &c., also Mayor on Juv. xv. 36. Ath. *c. Gentes* 23, p. 18—one of the few passages where he has Egypt in view.

[3] The general fact is not seriously qualified by the resistance of the Monothelete Mardaïtes of the Lebanon, or of the Greek city of Alexandria; or even by the difficulties experienced by Mokaukas amongst the Copts themselves.

On this subject cf. Freeman *Hist. Essays* (*Third Series*) p. 253—256: also a striking series of articles on Algeria in *La République Française* for Sept. 1875. I cannot learn that they have been republished.

The flight of Athanasius rather than the death of Constantius marks the lowest depression of the Nicene cause. But it was far from hopeless even then. Its position was not unlike that of the French republic after 1873. It seemed quite in the hands of its enemies, and was really surrounded with dangers which only the most cautious moderation could escape; yet its enemies with all their seeming power could do nothing to prevent its final victory. Three groups of conspirators agreed to profane the honourable name of conservatism, but could agree in nothing else, and could hardly even adjourn their mutual quarrels till the victory was safe. As with the French republic, it might have been foreseen that the prize would fall to the genuine conservatives. The danger to the Nicene side was not in the mere tyranny of the court, which only worked against its authors[1], but in the excesses of *irreconcilables* like Marcellus or Lucifer, which gave a colour of truth to the systematic slanders spread by the moral order adventurers in power.

It was not the Nicene cause but the conservative coalition which the flight of Athanasius destroyed. The victory seemed won when the last great enemy was driven into the desert; and the intriguers hasted to the spoil. They forgot that the West was merely terrorized for the moment, that Egypt was devoted to its patriarch, that there was a strong opposition in the East, and that even the conservatives who had won the battle for them were certain to desert their unworthy leaders the moment they declared for Arianism. Of that however there was little danger. It was not for Arianism that Ursacius and Valens, Eudoxius and George of Alexandria were fighting, but simply for themselves. There is much to be said for some of their allies, possibly something even for Acacius of Cæsarea; but if these four men had any nobler purpose in their lives, no trace of it is left in history. Nor do we judge them merely by the denunciations of their enemies. They are sufficiently condemned by their own words, and by the broad outlines of their policy. And in the case of George, to whose learning Athanasius does clear injustice, we have the decisive evidence of "the cool and impartial heathen" Ammianus[2].

[1] Thus Ath. *Hist. Ar.* 34, p. 288.   [2] Ammianus xxii. 11, 3—7.

THE SIRMIAN MANIFESTO.

All bade fair for the intriguers. The visit of Constantius to Rome in the summer of 357 fairly marks the culmination of his prosperity. It was a happier visit than his father's tragic *Vicennalia*. He was assailed indeed with cries for the recall of Liberius; but the heathen populace was well pleased with a sovereign who admired the majesty of Rome and could respect her ancient faith, albeit not his own[1]. He viewed the temples with placid curiosity, gratified the senators by distributing the vacant priesthoods, and forbore to scoff[2] at the immemorial procession of the knights. No marvel if he left a pleasant memory behind him in his heathen capital.

During the summer Ursacius and Valens held a conference of Western bishops at Sirmium. It was only a small synod, and we are not even told whether Constantius himself was present[3]. A manifesto was drawn up, perhaps by Potamius of Lisbon, to the following effect. "We acknowledge with the whole church one God almighty, the Father: also his only (unicum) Son Jesus Christ, the Lord our Saviour. But two Gods cannot and must not be preached (Jno. xx. 17, Rom. iii. 29, &c.). Of the word $οὐσία$ and its compounds $ὁμοούσιον$ and $ὁμοιούσιον$, which have disturbed the minds of some, no mention shall henceforth be made, for (1) the word is not found in Scripture: (2) the subject is beyond our understanding (Isa. liii. 8). No doubt the Father is greater than the Son in honour, rank, glory, majesty[4] and the very name[5], as the Son himself declares (Jno. xiv. 28)[6]. There are two Persons of the Father and the Son; of which the Father is the greater, the Son subject, together with all that the Father has subjected to him. The Father is without beginning, invisible, immortal, impassible. The Son is born of the Father, God of God, light

---

[1] Symmachus *Ep.* x. 61.
[2] This was the special offence given by Constantine in 326 (Zos. ii. 29).
[3] Constantius was at Milan in June and July, and proceeded over the Brenner (Ammianus xvi. 11, 20) into Illyricum. Thence he sent Severus into Gaul, and ordered Ursicinus to court, who at once repaired to Sirmium. Thus Constantius was pretty certainly at Sirmium in August; and is not likely to have missed a theological debate. We find him again at Milan in Nov. and Dec., and at Sirmium Dec. 18. The question is discussed by Tillemont *Empereurs*, iv. 685.
[4] Athanasius *de Syn.* 28, p. 595 translates these two words by $θεότητι$.
[5] This may allude to the spurious Sardican confession in Theodoret ii. 8.
[6] To this clause Marius Victorinus *adv. Ar.* i. 9 opposes Phil. ii. 6.

of light, by an inscrutable generation, and took flesh or body, that is man, of the Virgin Mary, and through this man he suffered with him (*compassum*). The Holy Spirit is through the Son, and came according to his promise to teach and sanctify all believers."

The Sirmian manifesto is the turning-point of the whole contest. Arius had been so utterly defeated at Nicæa that the leaders of his party were forced to throw him over and keep his doctrines in the background for a whole generation; and even when the cause of the great council seemed hopelessly lost, not one of them ventured to confess himself an Arian. But the Anomœans disdained to hide their belief in holes and corners; and now that they had succeeded in challenging the light of day with an imperial proclamation[1], the Eastern conservatives were obliged in self-defence to look for a Nicene alliance. Suspicions and misunderstandings, and at last mere force delayed its consolidation till the reign of Theodosius; but the Eusebian coalition fell to pieces the moment Arianism ventured to have a policy of its own.

Ursacius and Valens had blown a trumpet which was heard from one end of the Empire to the other. The Sirmian manifesto unveiled the heresy as it had never been unveiled before. Its avowal of Anomœan doctrine caused a stir even in the West, where Arians were only a handful of intruders. Unlike the creeds of Antioch, it was a Western document, drawn up in Latin by Western bishops. Besides this, the high-handed violence of Constantius had made it clear that the battle was no longer for the personal case of Athanasius, but for the faith itself. The spirit of the West was fairly roused; and the Gaulish bishops, now partly shielded from persecution by the varying fortunes of Julian's Alemannic war[2],

---

[1] Hilary *de Syn.* 78 *Antea enim in obscuro atque in angulis Dominus Christus Dei esse secundum naturam filium negabatur...At vero nunc publicæ auctoritatis professione hæresis prorumpens, id quod antea furtim mussitabat, nunc non clam victrix gloriabatur.*

[2] Julian's first campaign in 356 was not very successful. He was even besieged for a month in his winter-quarters with the Senones. Even his second campaign in 357 was seriously hampered by the misconduct of Barbatio, and the decisive battle of Argentoratum was not fought till about August. There is a monograph on it by Felix Dahn, *Die Alamannenschlacht bei Strassburg*, Braunschweig 1880.

were watching in moody anger[1] for the next steps of the gang of court intriguers. Thus everything increased the ferment. Phœbadius of Agen took the lead, and a Gaulish synod at once condemned the Sirmian manifesto.

The pamphlet of Phœbadius deserves attention as giving a purely Western view of the Sirmian manifesto, free from the Semiarian influence so visible in the *de Synodis* of Hilary, and even in his own later work[2]. He begins with a complaint of Arian subtlety—"there is nothing straightforward in it, nothing but diabolical fraud." Next he lays down his positions. Even the unity of God is maintained only in order to deny the Lord's divinity, and reduce the Saviour to the level of a creature[3]. The word essence is denounced in order to establish a difference of essence. He is said to have a beginning; yet his generation is declared unknown in spite of his own and other plain statements that it is from the Father. All they care for is to limit it to time, as we see from their impudent omission of the final clause of Mt. xi. 27, "no man knoweth the Son save the Father, and he to whomsoever the Son willeth to reveal him[4]." Next the Son's inferiority and subjection are not filial only, but that of a creature absolutely separate from God. Beginning is denied of the Father merely that it may be ascribed to the Son; from which it follows that he may also have an end. Finally the Father's superiority in the attributes of deity is insisted on merely in order to insinuate the absence of them in the Son[5]. Now all these doctrines are flatly contrary to Scripture. Half the error comes from the Arian habit of ascribing to the Logos what is spoken *de homine ejus,* and in every way confusing the two[6]. After a passionate appeal to the Nicene fathers, he explains *sub-*

---

[1] Not less dangerous for the loss of their natural leaders. The bishops of Rome (Liberius returned only in Aug. 358), Cordova, Trier, Toulouse and Milan were in exile, also Lucifer, Hilary and Eusebius of Vercellæ: Arles was held by the Arian Saturninus, and Fortunatian of Aquileia had yielded with African levity to the tempters of the palace.

There are traces of obscurer confessors in Anatolius of Eubœa (Ath. *ad Antiochenos* 10, p. 619), and the four African bishops who sign the Sirmian creed with Liberius (Soz. iv. 15).

[2] Phœbadius *de Filii divinitate Tractatus,* esp. *Proœm—non aliunde natum quam proprie de Patre, totum de toto, integrum de integro, perfectum de perfecto, consummatamque virtutem.*

[3] Phœbadius *c. Ar.* 4, 15.

[4] *c. Ar.* 9—11.

[5] *c. Ar.* 12—14.

[6] *c. Ar.* 19.

stantia of a self-existent being,—which is God alone[1]. The word is scriptural, its meaning well known; and there can be no reasonable objection to it. He ends with an allusion to Hosius, "whose name they use against us like a battering-ram[2]." If he has been wrong for ninety years, he is not likely to be right now.

If the Sirmian manifesto caused a stir even in the West, it spread dismay through the ranks of the Eastern conservatives. Plain men were weary of the strife, and only the fishers in troubled waters cared for more of it. They had hoped, say the bishops at Ancyra[3], that after the fiery trials of the faith, after the repeated councils of Antioch, Sardica (they mean Philippopolis) and Sirmium, now that Marcellus and Photinus (they do not add Athanasius and Liberius) were at last expelled, the weary church would have the rest it needed, and leisure for more peaceful work. But the Sirmian manifesto opened an abyss at their feet. They had put down Sabellianism after more than twenty years of contest; but the fruits of their hard-won victories were falling to the Anomœans. It was time to defend themselves, for Ursacius and Valens had the emperor's ear. And as if to bring the danger nearer home, a Syrian synod was convened by Eudoxius the new bishop of Antioch, and his friends Acacius of Cæsarea and Uranius of Tyre, and a letter of thanks addressed to the authors of the manifesto.

No time was to be lost, so the conservative counterblow was struck at once. The first move was a letter[4] from George of Laodicea to Basil of Ancyra, Macedonius of Constantinople, Eugenius of Nicæa and the rest. So in Lent 358, Basil summoned a small synod for the dedication of a church at Ancyra. Only twelve bishops were present. Even George was absent (no great loss), and his place was taken by Eustathius of

---

[1] Compare *Tractatus* 4, *Quæ est enim substantia Dei? Ipsum quod Deus est simplex, singulare, purum, nulla concretione permixtum, limpidum, bonum, perfectum, beatum, integrum, sanctum-totum.*
Among the passages quoted in *c. Ar.* 7, notice Ps. lxviii. (=lxix. Hebr.) 3 *infixus sum in limo profundi, et non est substantia* (מָעֳמָד), and Jer. xxiii. 22 *si stetissent in substantia mea* (בְּסוֹדִי).

[2] *c. Ar.* 23.
[3] Epiph. *Hær.* 72, 2.
[4] Soz. iv. 13.

Sebastia[1]. But its weight was far beyond its numbers. Basil's name stood high for learning; and he more than any man could sway the vacillating emperor. Eustathius also was a man of mark, and his ascetic eccentricities long ago condemned at Gangra seem by this time to have been forgotten[2]. Above all, the council was known to state the opinions of a large majority of the Eastern bishops. Pontus was devoted to conservatism, and the more decided Arianizers were hardly more than a busy clique even in Asia and Syria. They had everything in their favour in 359 at Seleucia, yet they were outnumbered by three to one. The council of Ancyra might therefore be understood to speak for the East in general.

Its decisions are clumsily expressed, and shew the embarrassment of men whom the appearance of a new enemy has forced to execute a complete and hasty change of front. First comes a long synodical letter to the following effect[3]. "We had hoped for peace after the fiery trials of the church; but since the devil has invented fresh heresies, we must make fresh declarations of our faith. We were baptized then according to the Lord's command into the name of the Father, the Son and the Holy Spirit, not of an ἄσαρκος and a σαρκωθείς, an ἀγέννητος and a γεννητός, or a κτίστης and a κτίσμα[4]. These names imply a difference of essence, whereas the very purpose for which we speak of Father and Son is to enforce the likeness. Rejecting materializing views of the divine Sonship (πάθος, ἀπόρροια, μερισμός), and rejecting also the Marcellian ἐνέργεια, there remains only similarity, ἐπειδὴ πᾶς πατὴρ ὁμοίας αὐτοῦ οὐσίας νοεῖται πατήρ: and if this be rejected too, the Sonship becomes an idle name. On the contrary, the divine is (κυρίως) the true paternity, and its confession is the distinction of the church from Jews and heathen, who know only of a Creator[5]. It is

---

[1] The names are given by Epiph. *Hær.* 73, 11, but without their sees. We can certainly recognize only Basil and Eustathius; but Eutyches and Eutychianus (but more likely the Homœan of Eleutheropolis) recur at Constantinople *Chron. Pasch.* 360, and Hyperechius and Alexander in the letter of Liberius to the Semiarians Socr. iv. 12.

[2] Note E. *The date of the Council of Gangra.*

[3] Hefele *Councils* § 80 gives a short analysis of it.

[4] So Ath. *de decr.* 31, p. 186.

[5] This is a commonplace, but Eus. *Eccl. Theol.* i. 8, p. 65 is worth comparison.

the ideal of the human, as we read[1] ἐξ οὗ πᾶσα πατριὰ ἐν οὐρανῷ καὶ ἐπὶ γῆς ὀνομάζεται, and κυρίως implies μόνον ἐκ μόνου ὅμοιον κατ' οὐσίαν τέλειον ἐκ τελείου. An impossible generation is a mystery, but not to be rejected on that account any more than the scandal of the cross. The Son is no mere quality or creature but Wisdom personal, and like in essence to the wise Father. The Lord's divinity is on the same footing with his manhood, implying the same essential likeness and similar limitations[2]."

Then follow eighteen anathemas, aimed alternately at Marcellus and Aetius. Here again we see the transition from Eusebian to Semiarian conservatism. They start from the protest of the Lucianic creed that the divine sonship is no idle phrase, and amount to a declaration that the Son is no creature, and that "wisdom" or "image" to whom it was given to have life in himself, is not on that account unlike in essence to the Father. The divine generation is also put outside time, and referred not to the power, but to the power and essence together (ἐξουσίᾳ ὁμοῦ καὶ οὐσίᾳ) of the Father. On the other hand, ὁμοούσιον is included with ταυτοούσιον in one denunciation, which implies that it is Sabellian.

The synod broke up. Basil and Eustathius proceeded to the court at Sirmium, taking with them Eleusius of Cyzicus. It must have been to conciliate the Nicenes that they suppressed six of the anathemas of Ancyra. They were just in time to prevent Constantius from declaring for Eudoxius and the Anomœans. After some more intrigues, a new council was called, and peace made on the Semiarian terms. A collection was made of the decisions against Paul of Samosata and Photinus of Sirmium, together with the Lucianic[3] creed. This was signed by Liberius of Rome and four African bishops, by Ursacius and Valens, and by all the Easterns present.

---

[1] Eph. iii. 15: found in creeds only in the fourth of Antioch and its reissues. Athanasius quotes it only *Or.* i. 23, p. 337, a passage where he is laying down the same principles.

[2] The parallel is repeated in the minute of Basil and George, Epiph. *Hær.* 73, 18.

[3] Soz. iv. 15, τὴν ἐν τοῖς ἐγκαινίοις τῆς Ἀντιοχέων ἐκκλησίας ought in accordance with Semiarian opinions to be the Lucianic creed. Hefele *Councils* § 81 prefers the fourth creed as having been repeated at Philippopolis and Sirmium.

The Semiarians had won a complete victory, and were strong enough to let Liberius return to Rome in August[1]. Their next step was a fatal error. Eudoxius, Aetius, and (so we are told) no less than seventy others were sent into exile[2]. After all, the Semiarians only aimed at replacing one tyranny by another. The exiles were soon recalled, and the strife began again with increased bitterness.

Here was an opening for a new party. Neither Semiarians nor Nicenes nor Anomœans seemed able to bring this interminable controversy to a decision. The Anomœans indeed almost deserved success for their boldness and activity, but pure Arianism was hopelessly discredited throughout the Empire. Egypt and the West were devoted to the Nicene cause, but they could not expect for the present to overcome the opposition of Asia and the camarilla. The Eastern Semiarians might have played the part of mediators; but men who began with wholesale deportations were not likely to secure a lasting domination. No man was safe if zealots like Eleusius or Marathonius were to have their own way. In this deadlock better men than

---

[1] Note F. *The Fall of Liberius.*
[2] The number is given by Philost. iv. 8. It must be much exaggerated, but we can well believe that the exiles were not a few.

Few of the Semiarian leaders can escape the charge of persecution. The exile of the Arians in 358 fixes it on Basil and Eustathius. The cruelties of Macedonius against the Nicenes and Novatians of Constantinople are recorded by Socrates ii. 38, and were blamed even by Constantius (Soz. iv. 2). The demolition of a Novatian church (Socr. iii. 11) shews that Eleusius was as busy at Cyzicus, and a similar outrage against the pagans is recorded (Soz. v. 10) of Mark at Arethusa. Julian *Ep.* 52 speaks of multitudes of heretics slaughtered, as at Samosata and Cyzicus, in Paphlagonia, Bithynia and Galatia. The references will be to Eleusius of Cyzicus, possibly to Eusebius of Samosata and Sophronius of Pompeiopolis, and pretty certainly to Marathonius of Nicomedia (Socr. ii. 38) and Basil of Ancyra. He may be overstating their misdeeds, but his account is fairly confirmed by Socr. ii. 38. He also speaks *Ep.* 43 of Arian outrages against the Valentinians at Edessa; but the bishop's name is unknown. To this list we may perhaps add the expulsion of the Apollinarii by George of Laodicea.

The Nicenes upon the whole can shew a better record, though persecution began on their side in the exile of Arius. The only charges against them are in the cases (*a*) of the Meletians, denied by the Egyptian bishops (Ath. *Apol. c. Ar.* 5, p. 100), and (*b*) of Ursacius and Valens, denied by Hosius, and also by Athanasius (Ath. *Hist. Ar.* 44, 27, pp. 292, 285). Athanasius himself not only objects to persecution in the writings of his exile (*de Fuga* 23, p. 265, *Hist. Ar.* 33, 67; pp. 287, 301), but shews a spirit of comprehensive charity in his *de Synodis* and at the council of Alexandria. The great persecutor was Theodosius, and even he scarcely attempted to carry out some of his worst laws. There was not much vigorous persecution of individuals (except of Priscillianists and Donatists) before the fall of Stilicho.

Ursacius and Valens might have been tempted to devise some scheme of compromise. But if all the existing parties were to be disavowed, there was nothing left but specious charity and colourless indefiniteness. And this was the plan of the new Homœan party formed by Acacius in the East, Ursacius and Valens in the West.

Now that the Semiarians were forced to treat with their late victims on equal terms, it became necessary to hold a general council. All parties agreed to the scheme, for all had hopes of success. If the Homœan influence was increasing at court, the Semiarians were strong in the East, and might count on more or less help from the Western Nicenes. But the court was resolved to secure a decision to its own mind. A single council would have represented the whole Empire and might have been too independent. It was therefore divided. After a few changes of plan, it was settled that the Westerns were to meet at Ariminum, the Easterns at Seleucia in Cilicia. As the councils might be expected to disagree, it was ordered that in that case ten deputies from each should report at court and hold a conference before the emperor.

Parties began to group themselves afresh. The Anomœans naturally leaned to the Acacian side. They could expect no favour from Nicenes or Semiarians; but to the Homœans they might look for at least connivance. The Semiarians therefore were obliged to draw still closer to the Nicenes.

The chief mediator of the new alliance was Hilary of Poitiers. If his exile had shewn him the practical worldliness of the Asiatic bishops, he had found among them men of character and learning who were in earnest against Arianism, and not so far from the Nicene faith as was supposed. Heresy was often the result of ignorance or misunderstanding rather than of genuine ill-will. It was in order to remove the mutual suspicions of East and West that he addressed the treatise *de Synodis*[1] to his friends in Gaul about the end of 358. After some high praise of their firm resistance to the violence of Saturninus, he tells them that the example of Gaulish orthodoxy

[1] The work is discussed by Reinkens *Hilarius* 171—184. I modify his date a little: it seems to make a needless allowance of time for the negotiations after the earthquake at Nicomedia.

had brought some of the Eastern bishops to a better mind. Some forms had been drawn up which if not altogether satisfactory, at all events clearly repudiated the Sirmian manifesto. Next, after asking his readers to reserve their judgment for awhile, he gives the *Blasphemia* in full, and explains twelve of the anathemas issued in reply from Ancyra. But since these were the work of a few bishops only, the general drift of opinion in the East would be made clearer by a review of some other creeds which had been drawn up at various times. He therefore submits for consideration the Lucianic formula, the creed of Philippopolis and the First of Sirmium "against Photinus"— he says nothing of Marcellus. Each of these he discusses to the general effect that its doctrine is not unsound, if only its questionable clauses are interpreted with a due regard to their original purpose. Thus the Lucianic *per substantiam tria, per consonantiam vero unum* was only aimed at Sabellian confusion; and even the Sirmian *non enim exaequamus vel comparamus Filium Patri, sed subjectum intelligimus* does not imply any difference of essence. This multitude of written creeds was unknown in the West; but the less fortunate Easterns were more troubled with heresies, and could not avoid the necessity. This closes the first part of the *de Synodis*.

The next step is to clear the way by a statement of his own belief. This made, he repeats his caution to the reader, and proceeds to examine (*a*) the word ὁμοούσιον. Without formally admitting the validity of the conservative objections, he shews that it is capable of misuse in either a Sabellian or a Manichean sense, or again as implying a prior essence. It is not the sole and necessary talisman of sound belief, as if there could be no true faith without it. There are many questions to be settled and many cautions to be attended to before its use becomes of any value as a test of orthodoxy. It may be rightly used, and it may be rightly forborne. Next (*b*) ὁμοιούσιον is shewn to be similarly capable of a right and a wrong use. The former is partly equivalent to ὁμοούσιον, for complete likeness undoubtedly implies equality, and indeed is based on it. What the word fails to express is the numerical unity and as it were organic cohesion of the divine nature.

Lastly he turns to the Semiarians themselves with warm praise for their noble resistance at Ancyra to the Anomœan outbreak. It was as a light in the darkness, and gave a good hope of recovering the true faith. After running over some of the absurdities of the Sirmian manifesto, "which Valens and Ursacius are old enough to comprehend," he examines the Semiarian objections to the word ὁμοούσιον. Sabellius and Paul of Samosata are no doubt heretics; but if things are to be rejected merely for their abuse, we shall need a penknife to criticize the Gospels[1]. A third argument, that the word is not found in Scripture, is really surprising, for it will bear hard on their own ὁμοιούσιον. If it was condemned at Antioch by eighty bishops, it was sanctioned at Nicæa by the holy number of three hundred and eighteen. The conservatives are not Arians, but they will be counted for Arians as long as they refuse the Nicene watchword. Their own ὁμοιούσιον is just as dangerous a word to use alone, and is moreover defective and ambiguous. The missing anathemas of Ancyra he is willing to believe were removed in order to avoid offence: but in that case care must be taken that they did not reappear. The rival watchwords were identical if rightly used; for there is no likeness but that of unity, and no use in the idea of likeness except to exclude Sabellian confusion. Only the one word guards against evasion and the other does not. It was therefore time frankly to accept the unequivocal one; and then they could all consult in common on the faith.

Meanwhile the intriguers were busy at the court. In order to complete the subjection of the councils, it was decided to compose a creed before their meeting and lay it before them for acceptance. The "dated creed" or fourth of Sirmium was drawn up in Latin[2] on Pentecost Eve, May 22, 359, by Mark of Arethusa, on behalf of a convention of Acacian and Semiarian leaders[3]

---

[1] Here (c. 85) he gives a most interesting collection of Scripture difficulties.

[2] Socr., Soz. The silence of Athanasius is of no weight here.

[3] On the Semiarian side we can name Basil and Mark, Hypatianus of Heraclea, and (if present) George of Laodicea. That Hypatianus was on this side may be presumed from his mission to Valentinian in Soz. vi. 7: also by his deposition (*Hist. Aceph.* § 9, p. 157) in company with Seleucius (Eleusius?) and Macedonius.

On the Acacian side were George of Alexandria, Pancratius of Pelusium (signs at Seleucia too, Epiph. *Hær.* 73, 26) and οἱ πλεῖστοι ἐπίσκοποι τῆς δύσεως (Epiph.), meaning Ursacius, Valens, Germinius and a few more.

held before the emperor. The only various reading of importance concerns the words κατὰ πάντα in the last clause. They do not appear in the revisions of the dated creed at Nicé and Constantinople[1]; and a few years later Valens and Ursacius denied their existence in the original document at Sirmium. Their presence however is proved by the minute of Basil and George, and by the direct testimony of Germinius[2].

Its language is upon the whole conservative. If a few of its expressions[3] indicate the inferiority of the Son, they do not pass the bounds of conservative comprehension. It has been already noticed[4] that nearly every phrase not found in the Lucianic creed has close parallels in the work of Cyril. Western influence may have contributed to the insertion of εἰς τὰ καταχθόνια κατελθόντα, a clause on which stress was laid in the West in order clearly to state the truth of our Lord's death, but which is found in no other Eastern creed but those of Nicé and Constantinople. It disappears even from that of Seleucia. But the prevailing character of the dated creed is conservative, as we see from its repeated appeals to Scripture, its solemn tone of reverence for the Person of the Lord, its rejection of οὐσία on the old conservative ground that it is not found in Scripture, and above all from the unexampled emphasis it lays on the mystery of the eternal generation[5]. Surely no Anomœan would have the impudence to sign ὅμοιον κατὰ πάντα. It seemed as if the conservatives had won another victory.

So Valens also thought, when he attempted to omit κατὰ πάντα from his subscription[6]. This however was too much for

---

[1] At Seleucia the whole passage was cast in a different form.

[2] The correspondence is given by Hilary *Fragm.* xiii.—xv. Ursacius and Valens must have lied.

[3] As τὸν μόνον καὶ ἀληθινὸν Θεὸν of the Father—νεύματι πατρικῷ—κατὰ τὴν πατρικὴν βούλησιν—τῇ δόξῃ τῇ πατρικῇ —all of them new in the conservative series of creeds, though the first is found in the Antiochene creed of Cassian, and was used by Asterius and defended by Eusebius.

On the other hand μόνον ἐκ μόνου is shifted from its place in the Lucianic creed and used to explain μονογενῆ in accordance with the new views of Eunomius, so that the Sirmian μονογενῆ μόνον ἐκ μόνου τοῦ Πατρὸς Θεὸν ἐκ θεοῦ corresponds to the Nicene μονογενῆ τοῦτ' ἐστὶν ἐκ τῆς οὐσίας τοῦ Πατρὸς θεὸν ἐκ θεοῦ. The clause is dropped at Seleucia, but reappears at Nicé and Constantinople.

[4] *Supra*, p. 132.

[5] Its language on this subject seems suggested by C. Ancyra, *Can.* 15, with possibly a less direct allusion to Cyril, *Cat.* vii. 5. Compare also Eusebius *c. Marc.* i. 12, p. 71.

[6] Epiphanius (or possibly Basil) *Hær.* 73, 22.

Constantius, who forced (ἀναγκάσαντος) him to restore the clause. In order to guard against any evasion of its meaning, Basil added to his own signature the strong words κατὰ πάντα δὲ οὐ μόνον κατὰ τὴν βούλησιν ἀλλὰ κατὰ τὴν ὑπόστασιν καὶ κατὰ τὴν ὕπαρξιν καὶ κατὰ τὸ εἶναι. In this form the document was given to Valens to be read before the Western council.

In order to remove all ambiguity, Basil and George of Laodicea[1] issued a minute[2] of their own on the subject. "The word οὐσία," they say, "is not found in Scripture, but is everywhere implied, as for example in the sacred name ὁ ὤν. It was also used by the Fathers against Paul of Samosata to shew that the Son has a separate personal existence[3], and is not a mere ῥῆμα or ἐνέργεια λεκτική. The new heresy confesses his likeness to the Father in will and operation only, and maintains him to be in himself (αὐτός) unlike God, being a mere creature differing from others only in that he is the immediate instrument of their creation. We catholics however have learned from Scripture that the Father and the Son are like each other except as regards the incarnation, which does not affect the deity, for ἀγεννησία is not its essence. The heretics at Sirmium thought they could advance their views by getting rid of οὐσία; but they have gained nothing, for ὅμοιον κατὰ πάντα includes everything, if only it be honestly accepted. Neither let the Westerns be troubled by our Eastern use of ὑποστάσεις to denote not three first principles (ἀρχάς), but the permanence and reality of the Personal distinctions (τὰς ἰδιότητας τῶν προσώπων ὑφεστώσας καὶ ὑπαρχούσας), which does not controvert either the unity or the distinct personality (τέλειον ἐκ τελείου) implied in the Lord's Baptismal Formula. As his coming 'in the likeness' of flesh of sin does not destroy his humanity, so neither does his 'likeness' to the Father negative his deity. As he assumed true human flesh, differing from men only in his miraculous birth

---

[1] He is nowhere mentioned as present at the conference, but may have been one of the unnamed bishops (Epiph. *supra*). George of Alexandria was there but he belonged to the other party.

[2] It is given by Epiphanius *Hær.* 72, c. 12—22, and was formerly supposed to be his own work. Its true authorship was determined by Petavius *ad loc.* Baur *Dreieinigkeit* i. 487 has strangely overlooked this, quoting it as "Epiphanius," and complaining of *seine verworrene Polemik gegen die Semiarianer.*

[3] Their words are οὐσίᾳ καὶ ὑποστάσει θεόν. Notice the reference to the old enemy Paul of Samosata.

and sinless action, so also he is true divine spirit, differing from the Father only in his ineffable generation and ministerial working. Their favourite word τὸ ἀγέννητον is not found in Scripture any more than οὐσία, for his proper relation to the Son is denoted by Father[1], and the two words are strictly correlative. It was they who introduced the word οὐσία in order to say ἀνόμοιον κατ' οὐσίαν; but if they wish to drop it, we shall be content, provided they are willing to accept ὅμοιον κατὰ πάντα in the inclusive sense required to constitute a genuine sonship."

The Nicene exiles might well hail Basil's manifesto with delight, for it was a surrender at discretion. The stubborn fight of thirty years had collapsed in a moment. So completely was the old conservative position given up, that even the Lucianic τέλειον ἐκ τελείου was turned round against the common enemy. Basil had not only borrowed Nicene arguments in all directions, but shewn that even he could do nothing without them. His rejection of the Arian use of ἀγέννητον implied a revision of the very idea of deity. His defence of the word οὐσία in spite of its absence from Scripture gave up the right to object on *that* ground to ὁμοούσιον. Even his abandonment of it served the Nicene cause by bringing forward with clear emphasis the common doctrine of the strict and primary sense of the divine Sonship, and reducing the difference to the question whether ἐκ τῆς οὐσίας would guard it any better than the equally non-scriptural[2] ὅμοιον κατὰ πάντα. Athanasius need not have gone back[3] to the Lucianic οὐσίας ἀπαράλλακτον εἰκόνα to shew the inconsistency of the conservative objection to ὁμοούσιον as foreign to the letter of Scripture.

The dated creed seemed conservative enough; but the Anomœans soon found plenty of loopholes in it. For example, the careful reference to Scripture might be taken as limiting κατὰ πάντα, so as merely to forbid any extension of the likeness beyond what Scripture allows. Again it might be said, as by the Arian at Seleucia[4], "like the Father if you will, but not

---

[1] So Athanasius *de Decr.* 31, p. 186; *Or.* i. 34, p. 345.
[2] Hilary *c. Ctium* 17—22.
[3] Ath. *de Syn.* 36, p. 600.
[4] Hilary *c. Ctium* 14. It was the old argument of Arius himself, as given by Ath. *Or.* i. 6, p. 323 καὶ πάντων ξένων καὶ ἀνομοίων ὄντων τοῦ

like God, for no creature can be." But the chief evasion was that by the force of language ὅμοιον κατὰ πάντα cannot refer to essence, for all likeness which is not identity implies difference, if the comparison is only pushed far enough. Here, at any rate, as Athanasius points out[1], the Anomœans had sound logic on their side, so that they were fully justified in their acceptance of the Sirmian formula.

The Semiarian leaders had ruined their position. By consenting to treat with the Anomœans, they lowered the contest to a mere court intrigue, in which the victory was sure to rest with the least scrupulous competitor. There is grandeur in the flight of Athanasius, and dignity in the exile of Eunomius; but the conservatives fell ignobly and unregretted, the victims of their own violence and unprincipled intrigue.

The conference broke up, and Ursacius and Valens proceeded to Ariminum. With them they took the new creed, and also the emperor's letter, which directed that doctrinal questions were to be settled first, and that the bishops were not to meddle with Eastern affairs.

Ursacius and Valens found the Westerns waiting[2] for them, to the number of more than two hundred[3]. They were in no courtly temper, and it was already clear that the intimidation would prove no easy task. They had even refused the usual imperial help for the expenses of their journey[4]. The new creed was very ill received; and when the Homœan leaders refused to anathematize Arianism, they were deposed (July 21) "as well for their present conspiracy to introduce heresy as for the con-

Θεοῦ κατ᾽ οὐσίαν, οὕτω καὶ ὁ Λόγος ἀλλότριος καὶ ἀνόμοιος, κ.τ.λ.
[1] Ath. de Syn. 53, p. 612.
[2] Somewhere between Oct. 10 and Dec. 31, Taurus says *jam septimum mensem* (Sulp. Sev. *Hist.* ii. 44). We need not suppose that they had all been there since April.
[3] Athanasius *de Syn.* 8, p. 576; 33, p. 598 says "more than 400"; but *ad Afros* 3, p. 713 he reckons a Nicene majority of about 200. Damasus *Ep.* ap. Thdt. ii. 22 implies a larger council than that of Nicæa. Auxentius ap. Hil. *ctra Aux.* 13 says 600; but it was his interest to exaggerate. Sulpicius

Severus *Chron.* ii. 41 counts "rather more than 400" in all; but his minority of 80 Arians is quite incredible. The Arian Maximin ap. Aug. vii. 1001 claims only 330, while Julian of Eclanum ap. Aug. *Opus imperf.* i. 75 seems to imply 650. Most of these numbers must be exaggerated, especially if the plan was carried out of summoning only one or two bishops from each province of Gaul. Hil. *de Syn.* 8.
[4] Three British bishops accepted it on the ground of poverty, but only in order that they might not be burdensome to the rest.

fusion they had caused in all the churches by their repeated changes of faith." Ursacius and Valens would appreciate the last clause. The Nicene definition was next confirmed, and a statement added to defend the use of οὐσία and anathematize the doctrines of Arius. This done, envoys were sent to report at court and ask the emperor to dismiss them to their dioceses, from which they could ill be spared. The Homœans also sent a deputation in their own behalf. Meanwhile the bishops at Ariminum occupied themselves with questions of clerical privilege, vainly endeavouring to obtain exemption from the crushing land-tax which Constantius had imposed on the exhausted Gaulish provinces[1].

The emperor's presence was urgently needed in Syria, for the Persians had broken out afresh in 358, and Sapor's host was now besieging Amida. He seems to have left Sirmium in June[2], but other cares detained him through the winter at Constantinople. The fall of Amida in October was the greatest disaster which the Empire had met with on the Euphrates since Valerian's time; but it was not before the spring of 360 that Constantius took the field in Syria.

The emperor "was busy with his preparations," and refused to see the envoys of the council. They were sent to wait his leisure, first at Hadrianople, then at the neighbouring town of Nicé, where Ursacius and Valens induced them to sign (Oct. 10) a revised translation of the dated creed. We are told[3] that Nicé was chosen in order to cause confusion with Nicæa. The changes made were not extensive. The unlucky date was

[1] This is not mentioned by the historians, but comes out incidentally in *C. Th.* xvi. 2, 15, where Constantius replies by abolishing the exemption from the *parangariæ* granted in 353. Some idea of the taxation may be formed from the statement of Ammianus xvi. 5, 14, that Julian found a tax of twenty-five *aurei* to the *caput*, and reduced it to seven.

[2] Ammianus xix. 11, 17 seems to say that Constantius left Sirmium on the news of the fall of Amida, which would be late in October. But we find him at Singidunum June 18, and he may have gone on to Constantinople. It is also more natural to suppose

(a) that the deputies nearing the capital in August were ordered to halt at Hadrianople, than (b) that they were refused an audience at Sirmium and ordered right away to Hadrianople. The one course would be evasive like the emperor's letter, the other would be needlessly discourteous, which the emperor's letter is not.

[3] Socr. ii. 37, Soz. iv. 19. It is a hostile account; but Ursacius and Valens were quite equal to the fraud. It also explains why it was thought worth while to remove the deputies for so short a distance from Hadrianople.

omitted, the clauses on the eternal generation much shortened, those on the Holy Spirit extended, ὑπόστασις forbidden as well as οὐσία, κατὰ πάντα left out, and a few verbal changes made to adapt the creed for Western use.

Meanwhile the Easterns assembled at Seleucia near the Cilician coast, a fairly central place, and accessible enough from Egypt and Syria by sea, but otherwise most unsuitable for such a meeting. It was a mere fortress, not lying in the level plain of Tarsus, but in the rugged country further west, where the spurs of Mount Taurus reach the sea; and the inland road from Laranda was infested by the ever-restless marauders of Isauria. They had attacked Seleucia itself that spring, and it was still the head-quarters of the count Lauricius, who had been sent against them. Tarsus would have been every way a better meeting-place; and the access to it was safe, for the Isaurians do not seem this time to have reached the eastern pass from Tyana through the Cilician Gates. However, the court party[1] preferred to have plenty of troops at hand[2].

To this wild mountain fortress only 150 or 160 bishops came—a small fraction of the eastern episcopate. Of these about 110 were conservatives, or Semiarians as we must henceforth call them; and there may have been a few Nicenes from Egypt. The Acacians and Anomœans were about forty, and a good many of these were mere intruders[3]. But they had a clear policy, and the court in their favour, while the Semiarian chiefs had put themselves in a false position by signing the dated creed, so that the conservative defence had to be left to leaders of the second rank like Silvanus of Tarsus, Eleusius of Cyzicus and Sophronius of Pompeiopolis. With them however came a greater than any of the Semiarians, for Hilary of

---

[1] Philost. iv. 11 names Eudoxius and Aetius.

[2] On the Isaurians, Finlay i. 199, Reinkens *Hilarius* 185—188, and especially Sievers *Studien* 489—502. On the passes of Mount Taurus, Lewin *Life of St Paul* i. 165.

The original authorities for the Isaurian risings within our period are as follows—(a) Rising in 353 and destruction of Isaura, Ammianus xiv. 2, 1; 8, 2. (b) Rising of 359, Ammianus xix. 13, 1. (c) Rising of 368 and defeat of Musonius the *Vicarius Asiæ*, Ammianus xxvii. 9, 6, Eunapius p. 77, Bonn. (d) Rising about 376, Zosimus iv. 20. Sievers, p. 494, refers this to (c); but it is fixed for a later date by the mention of Valens at Antioch. None of these risings seem to have been so destructive as that of 405.

[3] Note G. *The Bishops at Seleucia*.

Poitiers had somehow received orders to attend the council with the rest. He found there "as many blasphemers as it pleased Constantius[1]" to assemble; but the Semiarians welcomed him, and he skilfully used his opportunity of cementing their new alliance with the Nicenes. After clearing the Gaulish bishops from the current charge of Sabellianism[2], he was received by the majority to full communion—no doubt on Sunday, Sept. 26.

Next morning the first sitting was held, in the presence of the counts Leonas and Lauricius. The emperor's uncertain directions caused a good deal of trouble in settling the order of proceedings; but in the end the Acacians carried their point, that questions of faith should be taken first. They therefore began by proposing the abolition of the Nicene definition in favour of one to be drawn up in scriptural language. But the courtiers impatiently threw off the restraints of consistency, arguing in defiance of their own Sirmian creed, that "nothing can be like the divine essence, and that generation is quite unworthy of the Father. The Lord is creature, not Son, and his generation is nothing but creation[3]." The Semiarians however had no objection to the Nicene creed, beyond the obscurity of the word $\delta\mu oo\dot{\upsilon}\sigma\iota o\nu$[4]: the still more important $\dot{\epsilon}\kappa\ \tau\hat{\eta}s\ o\dot{\upsilon}\sigma\dot{\iota}as\ \tau o\hat{\upsilon}\ \Pi a\tau\rho\dot{o}s$ they seem to have accepted without any scruples. Towards evening Silvanus of Tarsus proposed to confirm the Lucianic[5] creed. The Acacians left the church by way of protest. Next morning, when the Semiarians signed it with closed doors, Acacius could only remind them that "deeds of darkness were of no validity." On Wednesday Basil of Ancyra and Macedonius of Constantinople arrived. The Acacians refused to take their seats till the accused bishops[6] had withdrawn; and after much discussion this was agreed to. Leonas then read before the council a document he had received from Acacius, which proved to be a new creed. After some complaints of

---

[1] Hilary, c. *Ctium*, 12.
[2] No doubt resting on the Western use of $\mu\iota a\ \dot{\upsilon}\pi\dot{o}\sigma\tau a\sigma\iota s$.
[3] Hilary, *supra*.
[4] Ath. *de Syn.* 12, p. 580 ὡς ἐκ τῆς ἀσαφείας ὕποπτον. We hear of no objection to it as not found in Scripture.
[5] *Supra*, p. 119. It was also ratified at Lampsacus.
[6] Cyril, Hilary and Eustathius for certain: perhaps also Basil and Macedonius.

Cyril's appeal is discussed by Couret *Palestine sous les Empereurs grecs* 55. He refers it to *Cod. Just.* vii. 62, 20, issued by Constantius in 341.

Monday's violence, the Acacians say that they are far from despising the Lucianic formula, though it was composed with reference to other controversies. The disputed words ὁμοούσιον and ὁμοιούσιον are next rejected as non-scriptural[1], and the newly-invented ἀνόμοιον anathematized—"but we clearly confess the likeness of the Son to the Father according to the apostle's words, Who is the image of the invisible God." Then follows the dated creed revised for Eastern acceptance. The eternal generation is more shortly though still distinctly stated, the descent into Hades left out, and many minor omissions made. The most important further changes are the substitution of σάρκα ἀνειληφέναι for γεννηθέντα, no doubt in a purely Arian interest[2], and the insertion of φῶς, ζωήν, ἀλήθειαν, σοφίαν, δύναμιν, after the fourth creed of Antioch, where we find λόγον ὄντα καὶ σοφίαν καὶ δύναμιν καὶ φῶς ἀληθινόν. They finish with a statement that the above creed is equivalent to that lately put forth at Sirmium.

Next morning (Thursday, Sept. 30) Acacius defended himself by arguing that the Nicene creed had often been altered before, so that there was no reason why it should not be altered again now. To this Eleusius could only reply that the faith of the fathers had already been sufficiently set forth at Antioch. The next step was to ask the court party how they reconciled the likeness of the Son to the Father as laid down in their creed with their declarations at the first session of his absolute unlikeness. Acacius answered that the likeness is only one of will, and does not extend to essence. It was strange language from the eager defender of the Lucianic creed against Marcellus[3];

---

[1] The Nicene creed is, however, treated with more respect than at Sirmium and Nicé, by the omission of the clause διὰ τὸ ἁπλούστερον ὑπὸ τῶν πατέρων τεθεῖσθαι.

[2] The expression is found elsewhere only in the first creed of Antioch, and perhaps (the reading is uncertain) in the confession of Arius and Euzoius. Other creeds keep inside the orthodox circle of σαρκωθέντα, ἐνανθρωπήσαντα, γεννηθέντα though (τὸ) κατὰ σάρκα is added to the last in the creeds of Nicé and Constantinople, and by Auxentius.

[3] Even the fragments preserved by

Epiph.(Hær.72,6—10) are clear enough. Acacius explains οὐσίας ἀπαράλλακτον εἰκόνα by τὸ ἔκτυπον καὶ τρανὲς ἐκμαγεῖον τοῦ Θεοῦ τῆς οὐσίας......ἐκτυπῶς καὶ ἀκριβῶς ὡμοιωμένην πρὸς πατρικὴν ἀγαθότητα καὶ θεότητα καὶ πᾶσαν ἐνέργειαν ......οὐ γὰρ ἔξωθεν τὸ ἀξίωμα, εἰς οὐσίαν δὲ αὐτῷ συντελεῖ, ὁμοίως πατρὶ γεννήσαντι......οὐσίας εἰκόνα λέγομεν, οὐκ ἄψυχον καὶ νεκράν, ἀλλ' οὐσιώδη...οὐσίας αὐτοουσίαν εἰκόνα...οὐσίας οὖν κ.τ.λ. ἀπαράλλακτον λέγων 'Αστέριος εἰκόνα τὸν υἱὸν τοῦ πατρός, πάντως οἰονεὶ τοὺς πατρικοὺς χαρακτῆρας ἐνεῖναι λέγει τῷ υἱῷ...ἐν τῷ εἶναι αὐτοῦ οἱ χαρακτῆρές εἰσι, καὶ ἐν τοῖς

but Acacius replied that "men were not to be judged by their writings." So indeed it would seem. A stormy controversy followed, in the course of which conservative horror was raised to the utmost by an obscene extract which was read from a sermon of Eudoxius at Antioch[1]. At last Eleusius broke in with soldierly bluntness on the sophistries of Acacius—"It is no concern of ours if Mark or Basil have made agreements with you in holes and corners, or whether it was you or they who broke them. We need not even take the trouble to discuss your creed, for whoso teaches any other than the Lucianic is an enemy of the church."

Next morning Acacius and George refused to appear; and when Leonas was sent for, he too declined to come. The majority therefore assembled without them and deposed Acacius, Eudoxius, George and six other contumacious Arians, at the same time suspending nine more from communion. It is worth notice that none of the eighteen came from Egypt except George[2]. Leonas seems to have regarded the proceedings as altogether irregular. "They might go and chatter in the church if they pleased, but he was not sent to preside at a council which could not agree." When however they ventured to appoint the Antiochene presbyter Anianus in the place of Eudoxius, the Homœans had him sent into exile, so that we hear no more of him for the present.

The exiled patriarch of Alexandria was watching from his refuge in the desert; and this was the time he chose for an overture of friendship to his old conservative enemies. Though

χαρακτῆρσι τὸ εἶναι αὐτοῦ. Eudoxius had also followed Asterius in holding these views, according to Philost. iv. 4.

Acacius had also written (Soz. iv. 22) to Macedonius κατὰ πάντα ὅμοιον... τῆς αὐτῆς οὐσίας.

[1] The fragment may be found in Hilary c. Ctium 13: fortunately it need not defile these pages. It may however have been read at the first sitting.

Eudoxius is perhaps the worst of the whole gang, adding his own profanity to the untruthfulness of the others. His well-known jest at the consecration of the great church at Constantinople (Socr. ii. 43, Soz. iv. 26 ὁ Πατὴρ ἀσεβής, ὅτι οὐδένα σέβει· ὁ δὲ Υἱὸς εὐσεβής, ὅτι σέβει τὸν Πατέρα) is authenticated as to doctrine by the peculiar turn of his own confession (ap. Caspari *Alte u. neue Quellen* p. 179 εἰς ἕνα τὸν μόνον ἀληθινὸν θεὸν καὶ πατέρα, τὴν μόνην φύσιν ἀγέννητον καὶ ἀπάτορα, ὅτι μηδένα σέβειν πέφυκεν ὡς ἐπαναβεβηκυῖα, καὶ εἰς ἕνα κύριον τὸν υἱόν, εὐσεβῆ ἐκ τοῦ σέβειν τὸν πατέρα) and with regard to irreverence by other cases, like his profane use of 1 Cor. ix. 3 (Philost. vi. 1), and the obscene sermon at Antioch.

[2] *Supra*, p. 33 n.

Basil's manifesto had not reached his hiding-place, he knew its
purport and had full accounts of the hopeful opening of the
councils. If he was slow to see his opportunity, at least he used
it nobly. The Eastern church has no more honoured name
than that of Athanasius; yet even Athanasius rises above himself in his *de Synodis*. He had been a champion of controversy
since his youth, and spent his manhood in the forefront of its
hottest battle. The care of many churches rested on him, the
pertinacity of many enemies wore out his life. Twice he had
been driven from his see and twice come back in triumph, and
now far on in life he saw his work again destroyed, himself once
more a fugitive. We do not look for calm impartiality in a
Demosthenes or a Mazzini, and cannot wonder if even Athanasius
grows more and more bitter and unjust to the authors of his
exile. Yet no sooner is he cheered with the news of hope than
the importunate jealousies of forty years are hushed in a
moment, as though the Lord had spoken peace to the tumult
of the grey old exile's troubled soul. To the impenitent Arians
he is the same as ever, but for old enemies returning to a
better mind he has nothing but brotherly consideration and
respectful sympathy.

The *de Synodis*[1] begins with an exposure of court intrigues.
There was no good reason for holding a council at all, much less
for suddenly dividing it into two. All that the schemers cared
for was to upset the condemnation of their own heresies at
Nicæa. Next he quotes the dated creed and holds it up to
ridicule, adding an account of its ignominious rejection by both
councils in their earlier sittings. After this he reviews eleven
successive Arian documents in chronological order, from the
Thalia of Arius as far as the creed of Seleucia[2]. He is not however selecting documents like Hilary to shew the real drift of
opinion in the East, but merely throwing them together as a
satire on Arian vacillation, and commenting on them like an old
disputer who knows the early history of the controversy much

---

[1] Only a short account is needed here of the *de Synodis*. Bright *Hist. Treatises*, lxxix.—xcvi., has given an excellent analysis of it.

[2] In a postscript (c. 30, 31), inserted some years later, he adds to the series the Homœan creeds of Nicé and Constantinople, and alludes to an Anomœan formula put forth at Antioch.

better than its later phases. Next he discusses the current objections to the Nicene doctrine.

Passing over his reply to the Homœans (c. 33—40), we have to note his treatment of the Semiarians who accepted the Nicene anathemas and the decisive ἐκ τῆς οὐσίας, and doubted only of the word ὁμοούσιον. Men like Basil of Ancyra are not to be set down as Arians or treated as enemies, but to be reasoned with as brethren who differ from us only about the use of a word which will be found to sum up their own teaching as well as ours. When they confess that the Lord is a true Son of God and not a creature, they grant all that we care to contend for. Their own ὁμοιούσιον without the addition of ἐκ τῆς οὐσίας does not effectually exclude the idea of a creature; but the two together are precisely equivalent to ὁμοούσιον. And if they accept our doctrine, they cannot in consistency refuse the word which best expresses it. Do they fear that the term subjects the divine generation to human conditions? Basil himself has not hesitated to compare the divine relation with the human. He has pointed out the limits of the illustration; and if the metaphor of Sonship still suggests any materializing views, it must be checked by the complementary metaphors of the Word and the Wisdom. Our brethren mean just what we mean: do they hesitate because the word sanctioned at Nicæa had been condemned before at Antioch in 269? Well, the Dionysii were still earlier. But let that pass: they were all fathers and all fell asleep in Christ, so we must not make them contradict each other. The fathers at Antioch set aside the word because Paul of Samosata threatened a materializing inference from it, whereas those of Nicæa adopted it in order to condemn the Arian denial of the Sonship. We however are not bound by Paul's sophistries; though even in that case, we may fairly contend that if two essences are derived from a prior essence, each of them is necessarily co-essential with its parent. Neither does the word imply any dualism; for here again it is checked by the metaphors of the Logos and Wisdom. The Semiarian ὁμοιούσιον is moreover misleading, for likeness and unlikeness refer to properties and qualities[1], and not to essence. The

---

[1] For the same reason Basil *Ep.* 8 § 63 rejects both, preferring κατ' οὐσίαν θεός.

word therefore rather suggests than excludes the idea of a Sonship which means no more than a share of grace; whereas our ὁμοούσιον shuts it out effectually. Sooner or later they will see their way to accept a term which is after all no more than a necessary safeguard of the belief they hold in common with ourselves.

Athanasius wrote at a crisis when affairs seemed more hopeful than they really were. The councils had both refused the dated creed, but the Homœan intriguers had not exhausted their resources. The Western deputies were sent back to Ariminum; and the bishops, already reduced to great distress by their continued detention, were plied with threats and cajolery till most of them yielded. Phœbadius and a score of others remained firm, and their resistance had to be overcome by a piece of villainy almost without a parallel in history. Valens came forward and declared that he was not one of the Arians, but detested their blasphemies from the bottom of his heart. There need be no objection to the creed as it stood, especially as (so he said) the Easterns had accepted it already. However, if any of them were not satisfied, they were welcome to propose additions. Phœbadius accordingly drew up a stringent series of anathemas against Arius and all his misbelief, Valens himself contributing one against "those who say that the Son of God is a creature like other creatures." The court party accepted everything, and the council assembled for a final reading of the amended creed. Shout after shout of joy rang through the church as Valens protested that the heresies were none of his, and with his own lips pronounced the whole series of anathemas. And when Claudius of Picenum produced a few more rumours of heresy against him "which my lord and brother Valens has forgotten," they were disavowed with equal readiness. The hearts of all men melted towards the veteran dissembler, and the bishops dispersed in the full belief that the council of Ariminum would take its place in history among the bulwarks of the faith[1].

[1] The above account is fully given only by Jerome *adv. Lucif.* p. 189, who appeals to the records of the churches and the notoriety of the events. He is not the most accurate of historians; but in this case his narrative is confirmed by Sulpicius Severus *Chron.* ii. 44, and by the allusions of Hilary *Fragm.* x. to the anathemas of Phœbadius, for it is only in them that we

The Western council was dissolved in seeming harmony, but a strong minority disputed the conclusions of the Easterns at Seleucia. Both parties therefore hurried to Constantinople to decide the strife. There Acacius was in his element. He held a splendid position as the bishop of a venerated church, the disciple and successor of Eusebius, and himself a patron of learning and a writer of high repute. His fine gifts of subtle thought and ready energy, his commanding influence and skilful policy, marked him out for a glorious work in history, and nothing but his own falseness degraded him to be the greatest living master of backstairs intrigue. If Athanasius is the Demosthenes of the Nicene age, Acacius will be its Æschines. He had found his account in abandoning conservatism for pure Arianism, and was now preparing to complete his victory by a new treachery to the Anomœans.

If Basil and Eustathius were to be overthrown, the prohibition of ὁμοιούσιον would have to be enforced: but since Constantius objected to the Anomœans, nothing could be done without also disavowing ἀνόμοιον. The Homœans had denounced it at Seleucia, and repeated their rejection of it at Constantinople, sacrificing Aetius also to prove their sincerity. After this it became possible to expel the obstinate defenders of ὁμοιούσιον.

Meanwhile the final report arrived from the council of Ariminum. Valens at once interpreted the anathemas of Phœbadius in an Arian sense. "Not a creature like other creatures." Then creature he is. "Not from nothing." Quite

find the clauses *non esse creatum velut cæteras facturas, de nullis exstantibus sed ex Deo*, and *æternum cum Patre*. The silence of other writers is of less consequence or so unpleasant a subject. Hilary *ctra Auxentium* 8 dismisses it with *de Ariminensi synodo, quæ ab omnibus est religiose dissoluta, nihil dicamus: tantum diaboli commenta pandenda sunt*.

As the words *velut cæteras facturas* are wanting in the anathemas of the council as given by Hilary *Fragm.* vii., we have the alternative of supposing them a fraudulent insertion of Valens. This is no unlikely charge against the man who fraudulently omitted κατὰ πάντα from the dated creed. Nor does Jerome's account of Claudius of Picenum give us the idea that he was one of the *homines adulescentes, parum docti et parum cauti* (Sulp. Sev.), the *plumbei animi* (Aug.) who could not be expected to recognize the old evasion κτίσμα τοῦ θεοῦ τέλειον. ἀλλ' οὐχ ὡς ἓν τῶν κτισμάτων.

I have not thought it necessary to work through the controversies connected with the name of Gregorius Bæticus. They are summed up in Mr Daniel's article on him in the *Dict. Chr. Biogr.*

so: from the will of the Father, not from his essence. "Eternal." Of course, as regards the future. However, the Homœans repeated the process of swearing that they were not Arians, the emperor was threatening, and at last the Seleucian deputies signed the decisions of Ariminum late on the night of Dec. 31, 359.

Acacian policy had triumphed, and a single decisive manœuvre was needed to complete the victory. As the dedication of Constantine's great church was approaching, the bishops mostly stayed for the occasion. But first (Jan. 360) a council was held. As the Semiarians of the Hellespont prudently declined to attend it[1], the Homœans were completely dominant. Only seventy-two bishops were present[2]. Its first care was to reissue the creed of Nicé, of course omitting the anathemas of Phœbadius, which had served their purpose. We find as many as twenty-nine variations from its original text, but they are mostly verbal, sometimes improving the sense but upon the whole shewing no clear doctrinal aim. Only a few of them are borrowed from the creed of Seleucia.

The next step was to degrade and anathematize Aetius for his impious and heretical writings, and as "the author of all the scandals, troubles and divisions." This was needed to satisfy Constantius; but nothing more clearly shews the Anomœan leanings of the council than the fact that as many as nine[3]

[1] Soz. iv. 24.

[2] Socrates and Sozomen speak of fifty. The number in the text is from the *Chronicon Paschale*, where a list of fifty-four bishops is given, but without their sees. Among these we may safely identify most of the Eastern Acacians, including Maris of Chalcedon, Theodore of Heraclea, Demophilus of Berœa, and George (of Laodicea,—the Alexandrian George was not present, Theodoret ii. 28), besides some twenty who had signed at Seleucia. To these we may add Theophilus of Libya (Theodoret ii. 23, Philost. vii. 6), Ulphilas the Goth (Soz. iv. 24), Euippius from Galatia (Basil *Ep.* 251), and most likely a few of the Westerns. Saturninus of Arles was in the city (Hilary *ad Ctium* ii. 2) about this time, and we may presume that Valens and Ursacius would be shrewd enough not to miss so important a meeting. The account in the *Chronicon Paschale* is mostly concerned with the dedication of the great church, and therefore only mentions the deposition of Macedonius. Of the Anomœan schism nothing is said, though the list seems to include five of the malcontents.

[3] Sozomen iv. 25 carelessly relates the story as if the depositions objected to were those of the Semiarians. Fortunately Theodoret ii. 28 has preserved the letter in which the council notifies to George of Alexandria (then perhaps at Antioch—his movements are traced by Sievers *Einl.* § 25) its decision with regard to the four Egyptians, Seras, Stephen, Heliodorus and Theophilus. To these we may add from Philostorgius vii. 6 Leontius and Theodulus, viii. 4 Phœbus, viii. 3 Theodosius (? of Philadelphia).

bishops were found to protest against it. They were allowed six months to reconsider the matter, and soon began to form communities of their own.

Having cleared themselves from the charge of heresy by laying the foundation of a permanent schism, the Homœans were able to undertake the expulsion of the Semiarian leaders. As men who had signed the creed of Nicé could not well be accused of heresy, they were deposed for various irregularities. Macedonius, Basil, Eleusius, Eustathius, Cyril, Sophronius, Silvanus and three others were displaced[1]. Mark of Arethusa is not mentioned, while George of Laodicea had gone over in good time to the winning side, and is next found forcing the creed of Nicé on Dianius of Cæsarea.

The Homœan supremacy established at Constantinople was limited to the East. Violence was its only hope beyond the Alps; and violence was out of the question after the mutiny at Paris. Now that Julian was free to act for himself, common sense as well as inclination forbade him to continue the mischievous policy of Constantius. It must have been almost under the protection of his army that the Gaulish bishops met at Paris to ratify the Nicene faith and excommunicate the Western Arians[2]. After this there was no further question of Arian domination. Very few[3] bishops were committed to the losing side, and those few soon disappeared in the course of nature. Auxentius the Cappadocian, who held the see of Milan till his death in 374, must have been one of the last survivors of the victors of Ariminum.

But in the East the Homœan supremacy lasted for nearly twenty years. It was interrupted for a short time by Julian and Jovian, but Eudoxius and Demophilus maintained it

---

[1] Some of these however were not removed till a later synod. On the depositions at Constantinople there is an invective in Basil *c. Eunom.* i. p. 210.

[2] Their letter to the Easterns is given by Hilary *Fragm.* 11. They specially complain of the *fraus diaboli* which had divided the council and falsely used the authority of the Easterns to secure the rejection of οὐσία by the deputies of Ariminum.

Broglie iv. 93 dates the council in 361, and points out that it was part of Julian's conciliatory policy to allow it. See Reinkens *Hilarius* 246—251.

[3] We hear only of Saturninus of Arles and Paternus of Petrocorii. Epictetus of Centumcellæ was with Constantius, if we read with Petavius in Julian *ad Ath.* 286 Κεντουμκελ-λῶν for τινὰ τῶν Γαλλιῶν. Sulpicius Severus *Chron.* ii. 41 brings no less than eighty Arians to Ariminum: but this must be a gross exaggeration.

throughout the reign of Valens. It seems at first sight a purely artificial power, resting partly on court intrigues, and partly on the divisions of its enemies. Upon the whole this may be the fact: yet even the Homœans had some support for their long dominion. Eusebian conservatism was fairly worn out, but the Nicene doctrine had not yet replaced it. Men were tired of the philosophical word-battles[1], and ready to ask whether the difference between Nicé and Nicæa was worth fighting about. The Homœan formula seemed reverent and safe, and its bitterest enemies hardly ventured to dispute its abstract truth. When even the court preached peace and charity, the sermon was not likely to want an audience.

The Homœans were at first less hostile to the Nicene faith than the Eusebians had been. After casting off the Anomœans and declaring war on the Semiarians, they were obliged to bid for Nicene support. In this they succeeded quite as well as they deserved; for they had a creed worthy of better men than Valens or Eudoxius. Thus the appointments of Acacius, as Philostorgius complains[2], were mostly Nicene, like those of Athanasius at Ancyra and of the ascetic Pelagius at Laodicea. Some will draw another inference from the enthronement of Eudoxius at Constantinople and the consecration of Eunomius the Anomœan in the see of Cyzicus: but these appointments would seem to represent a different section of the Homœan party.

The most important nomination directly ascribed to Acacius is that of Meletius at Antioch. The election was a stormy one, for party quarrels were raging with increased fury after their long repression by Leontius. The new bishop was a man of distinguished eloquence and undoubted piety, and further suited for a dangerous elevation by his peaceful temper and winning manners. He was counted among the Homœans[3], and they had

---

[1] Their weariness of controversy finds expression in the writings of Cyril, and remarkably in the *de fide adv. Sabellium* ii. (p. 1070 of Migne's Eusebius vi.)—a work against Marcellus ascribed by Thilo *Ueber die Schriften des Eus. von Alexandrien u. Eus. von Emisa* 64 to Eusebius of Emesa.

[2] Philost. v. 1. He adds the names of Onesimus of Nicomedia and Acacius of Tarsus, but we do not find them elsewhere. Zahn *Marcellus* 89 has a theory that Ancyra was divided into three parties like Antioch, Athanasius being the Nicene bishop, Basil the Semiarian, and the Arian unknown. In this case Marcellus ought to be a fourth.

[3] Philost. v. 1 τὸ ἑτεροούσιον ὑπεκρίνετο: but we need not believe this.

chosen him a year before to replace Eustathius at Sebastia in Armenia; and his uncanonical translation to the apostolic see of Antioch engaged him all the more to remain on friendly terms with them[1]. Such a man—and no doubt Acacius was shrewd enough to see it—would have been a tower of strength to them. Unfortunately for once, Acacius was not all-powerful[2]. Somebody put Constantius on demanding from the new bishop a sermon on the crucial passage—Prov. viii. 22, κύριος ἔκτισέ με, κ.τ.λ. Acacius might evade the test, but Meletius as a man of honour could not refuse to declare himself, especially when George of Laodicea had just openly preached Arianism[3]. To the delight of the populace, the sermon proved substantially Nicene[4]. It was a test for his hearers as well as for himself. It carefully avoided technical terms, repudiated Marcellus, and repeatedly deprecated controversy on the ineffable mystery of the divine generation[5]. It closely followed the lines of the Sirmian creed, and the reception given to it by the Homœans is a decisive proof of their insincerity.

The people applauded, but the courtiers were covered with shame. There was nothing for it but to exile Meletius at once and proceed to a fresh election. This time they made sure of their man by choosing Euzoius the old companion of Arius. But the mischief was already done. The old congregation of Leontius was broken up, and a new schism more dangerous than the Eustathian formed round Meletius. Many jealousies still divided him from the Nicenes, but his bold confession

---

[1] Its inconsistency was flagrant, for the Homœans had deposed Dracontius of Pergamus a year before on the ground that he had formerly held a see in Galatia.

[2] As the nomination of Meletius is ascribed to Acacius by Epiphanius, Jerome and Philostorgius, we may presume that his sudden removal was the work of another party. Acacius must have been more or less aware of his leanings before the election, and is found on friendly terms with him for some years after his expulsion, which we may therefore ascribe to Homœan divisions rather than to the duplicity of Acacius.

[3] The expression of Theodoret ii. 31 τὴν αἱρετικὴν ἐξήμεσε δυσοσμίαν is more abusive than definite, but this may be its meaning. If so, it was the last of the long series of George's misdeeds. He was succeeded within a few months by Pelagius.

[4] It is preserved by Epiphanius *Hær.* 73, 29—33.

[5] A few of its leading phrases may be noted here. We have θεὸς ἐκ θεοῦ, εἷς ἐξ ἑνός, ἐξ ἀγεννήτου μονογενής, ἐξαίρετον γέννημα τοῦ γεγεννηκότος...γέννημα τέλειόν τε καὶ μένον...ἀπαθῶς καὶ ὁλοκλήρως προελθὸν...οὐδὲ κίνησις τοῦ ἡγεμονικοῦ καὶ ἐνέργεια (against Marcellus)... διὰ μὲν τοῦ ἔκτισε τὸ ἐνυπόστατον καὶ μόνιμον, διὰ δὲ τοῦ ἐγέννησε τὸ ἐξαίρετον τοῦ μονογενοῦς καὶ ἰδιάζον παριστᾷ.

proved to be the first effective blow at the Homœan supremacy.

The idea of conciliating Nicene support was not entirely given up. Acacius remained on friendly terms with Meletius, and was still able to name Pelagius for the see of Laodicea. But Euzoius was an avowed Arian, Eudoxius differed little from him, and only the remaining scruples of Constantius delayed the final victory of Anomœan Arianism.

NOTE E.

DATE OF THE COUNCIL OF GANGRA.

Socrates ii. 43 and Sozomen iii. 14, iv. 24 are fully agreed that the Eustathius whose followers were condemned by the council of Gangra was no other than the well-known Semiarian leader, the ascetic bishop of Sebastia in Armenia. The identification has been doubted by Baronius and others, but seems fully established by Neander (E Tr. iii. 346), and the Benedictines in their life of Basil (p. lviii. of Gaume's Basil).

On the date however of the council the two historians differ by more than twenty years. Socrates twice expressly puts it after that of Constantinople in 360, while Sozomen seems to date it before that of Antioch, meaning probably that of the Dedication in 341. In this case the evidence is in favour of the earlier date. Sozomen indeed seems everywhere much better acquainted with Semiarian movements than Socrates.

Thirteen bishops met at Gangra under the presidency of a Eusebius; but the sees not being given, we cannot identify a single name with positive certainty. In the absence however of the usual clause ἐκ διαφόρων ἐπαρχιῶν, found even at the small gathering of Ancyra, we may take for granted that they all came from the great Pontic diocese. If it be possible then let us assume with Tillemont as a first hypothesis that Sozomen's date is the true one. In this case we find a natural president for the council in Eusebius of Nicomedia. We also have Gregory, bishop of Nazianzus since 329 or (Montaut *Quest. hist.* 10) 334, and may perhaps identify Eulalius with the bishop of Sebastia. Only ten Pontic bishops (including Maris of Chalcedon) are distinctly named at Philippopolis; but adding two or three more as a reasonable proportion of the fourteen signatures we cannot trace, we get 12 or 13 for the total number present. Of these we may reasonably identify Basil of Ancyra, Proæresius of Sinope, Philetus of Juliopolis or of Cratia, Bithynicus of Zela, and perhaps an unknown Eugenius. To these the admirers of legend might add Hypatius of Gangra, on whom see Tillemont, *Mém.* vi. 642. On the other hand, "Bassus a Car" is more likely from Carrhæ in Osrhoene, Eugenius of Eucarpia (signs at Nicæa) is just outside our limits, and Olympius of Ænos was moreover at Sardica. Thus we get from six to eight coincidences, of which three involve names (Proæresius, Bithynicus, Philetus) which scarcely recur in the episcopate of Christendom—at least I have not noticed them elsewhere in running over the pages of Le Quien's *Oriens Christianus*.

The force of this argument is best seen by applying it to other dates. Assuming then with the Ballerini as a second hypothesis that Socrates is right, we get a natural president again in Eusebius of Cæsarea Mazaca (362—370). We also have for comparison as many as 250 names (repetitions included) connected with the councils of Ancyra, Seleucia and Constantinople (360), the petitions to Jovian Socr. iii. 25, the letter of the Semiarians to Liberius Socr. iv. 12, and (if we date it about 371) the encyclical to the Italians in Basil *Ep.* 92. Of these fully seventy must have come from Pontus. Yet the only possible identifications are Eugenius of Nicæa, Eulalius of Amasea, an unknown Bassus, and Gregory,—either Basil's uncle or the bishop of Nazianzus. Only four or five coincidences, and these far from cogent.

Next we have for consideration the tempting theory of Dr Reynolds *Dict. of Chr. Biogr.* Art. *Eusebius of Samosata*. He dates the council in the year 372 or 373, making Eusebius of Samosata its president, and identifying amongst its members Basil of Cæsarea, with Hypatius (*Ep.* 31; hardly the Hypatius of Nicæa mentioned by Philost. ix. 19, who was most likely a disciple of Aetius—Epiph. *Hær.* 73, 38) " and others of his friends." But these others are not easily traced. His brother Gregory (of Nyssa 372) may be one of them; or his uncle Gregory, though the estrangement must have been about this time: but the bishop of Nazianzus was now too infirm to appear at Gangra. Bassus is also named next to Basil in *Ep.* 92 (though the Benedictines prefer to identify him with Barses of Edessa), and Olympius of Neocæsarea in Bithynia signs at Constantinople. On the other hand, Eugenius of Nicæa was dead in 370 (Philost. ix. 8), Eulalius of Amasea probably in exile, Eulalius of Doara (Greg. Naz. *Or.* xii.) and Olympius of Pernasus not yet v.]   NOTE E. THE COUNCIL OF GANGRA.   191

appointed. The last signs at Constantinople, but in Basil's time (comparing *Epp.* 237, 239) we find first Hypsia, then Ecdicius in possession of the see. Thus we have four or five coincidences, but none of them very clear—nothing like the triple knot of names at Philippopolis.

The next date proposed is 376, by Remi Ceillier, but the only reasonable identifications are of Basil, Hypatius and Olympius. Eusebius of Samosata, the two Eulalii, and Gregory of Nyssa were in exile.

Comparing then the four dates proposed, which may be approximately given as 340 (Tillemont), 365 (the Ballerini), 372 (Reynolds), and 376 (Ceillier), we find the evidence of names decidedly in Tillemont's favour, though there is also a fair case for Dr Reynolds. Ceillier's theory is almost hopeless. Now for wider considerations.

Dr Reynolds' theory seems to force the chronology. Basil became bishop of Cæsarea in the autumn of 370, and was then on good terms with Eustathius. The quarrel broke out later, and must have lasted some time before the council met. Eusebius was exiled after this; and we have still to find room for the episcopates of Eunomius and Lucius before the death of Athanasius in May 373, when Euzoius installed Lucius of Samosata (Theodoret iv. 21) at Alexandria.

We are not dependent on Theodoret's questionable identification of Lucius with the Alexandrian intruder. The Benedictines shift the exile of Eusebius to the summer of 374, but their own chronology leaves no room for a previous journey to Gangra. He was present indeed at Basil's election in the autumn of 370, but was never able to repeat his visit to Cæsarea, so that Basil (*Ep.* 138) had to seek him out at Samosata in 372. And if he did not even reach Cæsarea, we cannot suppose that he found his way as far as Gangra. In that case Dr Reynolds' date must be given up.

It may further be noted as against both Dr Reynolds and the Ballerini that we miss the signature of Basilides, who (Basil *Ep.* 226) held the bishopric of Gangra from 362 at least as late as 375.

Basil never mentions the council of Gangra in the course of his disputes with Eustathius. His silence must be deliberate on any theory but Ceillier's: yet I venture to think it accords best with the earliest date. The stigma of heresy, if that was his reason, would attach better to Eusebius of Constantinople (*Ep.* 244 ἄνδρα κορυφαῖαν τοῦ κατὰ Ἄρειον κύκλου, ὡς οἱ πειραθέντες φασίν: also *Ep.* 263, *infra*) and Basil of Ancyra, than to Eusebius of Cæsarea, Eulalius of

Amasea and the saintly Gregory. Mere lapse of time might throw into the shade a council held more than thirty years before, when Basil was quite young; but it is hard to understand his silence on the theory of the Ballerini, impossible on that of Dr Reynolds, especially as *Epp.* 237, 239 were written to Eusebius of Samosata in his exile. And if the ascetic Basil was half inclined on some points to sympathize with Eustathius as against the council, we may perhaps find an allusion to it in *Ep.* 263, where he tells us that Eustathius after the death of Hermogenes εὐθὺς ἔδραμεν πρὸς τὸν ἐπὶ τῆς Κωνσταντινουπόλεως Εὐσέβιον, οὐδενὸς ἔλαττον καὶ αὐτὸν τὸ δυσσεβὲς δόγμα τοῦ Ἀρείου πρεσβεύοντα· εἶτα ἐκεῖθεν διὰ οἵας δήποτε αἰτίας ἀπελαθείς, ἐλθὼν τοῖς ἐπὶ τῆς πατρίδος αὐτοῦ ἀπελογήσατο πάλιν, and afterwards obtained a bishopric. Accordingly the council never speaks of him as a bishop; and the charge *Can.* 5, 6, of encouraging conventicles, is more suitable to a presbyter. On the other hand, Sozomen iv. 24 seems to distinguish the deposition of Eustathius by Eusebius of Nicomedia from that by the council of Gangra.

In any case the career of Eustathius was a long one, for Athanasius *Hist. Ar.* 5, p. 274 names him as one of the heretics whom Eustathius of Antioch refused to ordain. This must have been before 330.

The Syriac list in Cowper *Syr. Miscell.* 42 increases the number of bishops to 15 by repeating the name of Eugenius and adding that of Heraclius. Similarly an inscription (Boeckh 8955) from Helena's church at Bethlehem, dating certainly (Boeckh 8964) after 680, but perhaps before the repair of the church (Boeckh 8736) in 1167. Cowper notices seven coincidences with the Nicene signatures; but only two of these come from Pontus.

NOTE F.

The Fall of Liberius.

I have not worked through the immense literature of the Liberian controversy; nor is it necessary to do so for the present subject. The general bearing of the evidence is easily stated.

It is clear from the language of Athanasius and Hilary that Liberius signed some more or less compromising document or other, and that if it was not the second Sirmian formula, it was the first or third. Sozomen distinctly says it was the third; and this (if drawn up before his release) he would most likely be required to subscribe in any case. But is this enough to account for the strong words of Athanasius, Hilary, Faustinus and Jerome?

Now we have to take into account the three letters of Liberius preserved and commented on by Hilary *Fragm.* 6. Hefele *Councils* § 81 rejects them as spurious, but without making out any strong case against them. (1) Their poverty of style is *not* unnatural after two years of exile, perhaps also of ill health. Neither have we much undoubted Liberian matter to compare them with; for "the eloquent dialogue with the emperor" is mostly due to Theodoret. Besides, as one writer remarks, popes do not always write the letters for which they are responsible. (2) There is no difficulty in Fortunatian's presence at Berœa, for we cannot prove that he was elsewhere. He may have been there either accidentally or on a mission to Liberius: and in any case he was a natural mediator even if the letter had to go round to Aquileia in search of him. (3) It is said to be strange that Liberius was not released at once if he really signed the *Blasphemia*, especially as the Roman populace was so threatening. Yet it must be remembered that a bishop of Rome was no ordinary offender; and that the disturbance of the capital might seem all the more reason for keeping him away from his diocese. (4) The letters are no credit to Liberius, but they are not on that account doubtful. Two years of exile might have bent even the speaker of Theodoret's dialogue. And if there is nothing specially discreditable about the later years of Liberius, there is also nothing specially heroic about them. He was not in the front of danger at Ariminum; and afterwards he appears rather as a peacemaker than a hero of the faith. (5) The comments of the Fragmentist may be "unworthy of Hilary," and are certainly violent enough. But they are quite in the spirit of Hilary's attack on Constantius. (6) The statement that Athanasius had already been removed from the communion of the Roman church is easily understood. Even if we adopt the reading of Baronius, which implies that it had been done "before Liberius reached the court," it may very well refer (as the Benedictines notice) to his arrival at Sirmium in 357 or 358. (7) The list of bishops only suits the first Sirmian formula, though the *perfidia Ariana* can only be the second: and this is a difficulty. Easterns may have been present in 357; but Theodore of Heraclea was dead, Basil of Ancyra quite opposed to the *Blasphemia Potamii*. On the other hand, Hilary (in the *de Synodis*, be it remembered) judges the first Sirmian formula so mildly that Hefele is quite justified in refusing to believe that Liberius signed this document alone, which was moreover obsolete in 357. But his arguments are just as valid against his own theory, which limits the signature of Liberius to the third Sirmian formula. It is more likely that the subscriptions are misplaced than that Hilary had stultified himself.

But the case would be clear even if these letters were spurious. Four writers independently mention the fall of Liberius; and there is nothing to set against them but the silence of Socrates and Theodoret. Believers in papal infallibility may hesitate, but the historian cannot.

NOTE G.

The Bishops at Seleucia.

All authorities agree that the council consisted of from 150 to 160 bishops, and that the Semiarians were in a large majority. But what were the actual numbers on each side? Hilary *c. Ctium* 12 gives 105 Semiarians, nineteen Anomœans, and the Egyptians (number not stated) orthodox except George of Alexandria. Socrates ii. 39 and Sozomen iv. 22 estimate the Anomœans at thirty-six, and Epiphanius *Hær.* 72, 26 gives a list of thirty-eight signatures (not forty-three: see Petavius *ad loc.* whom Hefele and others have neglected) to the Acacian creed, including ten from Egypt as far up the Nile as Oxyrhynchus. Athanasius *de Syn.* 13, p. 580 merely says that the malcontents were ὀλίγοι παντελῶς.

Hilary was an eyewitness of the council, and most writers follow him. Thus Reinkens *Hilarius* 190 computes 105 Semiarians, nineteen Anomœans and thirty-six orthodox Nicenes to make up a total of 160 bishops, and Bright *Hist. Treatises* lxxxvi. supposes him to ignore the Acacians.

Yet at least two out of Hilary's three statements are certainly incorrect. The list in Epiphanius bears every mark of truth. Five of the ten Egyptian bishops (Seras, Stephen, Pollux, Pancratius and the Meletian Ptolemy) are named as present by Athanasius *supra:* and Seras was an old enemy of his. A few months later (Theodoret ii. 28) Stephen, Seras and Heliodorus refuse to concur in the condemnation of Aetius. A little later still we find them (Philost. viii. 2) set over Libya and Egypt by the Anomœans. Stephen and Heliodorus are also connected with the Anomœan creed in the *Hist. Aceph.* § 9, p. 157 Sievers; and Apollonius of Oxyrhynchus is named by the Luciferians Marcellus and Faustinus *Libell.* 27 as a Meletian adherent of George. So much for Hilary's story that the rest of the Egyptians were Nicenes.

The only escape is to suppose that the Epiphanian list is half made up of unwilling Semiarian signatures. But this too is inadmissible. For (1) There was no serious intimidation at Seleucia. Leonas hardly seems even to have attempted it; and if there was any, it came from quite the other direction. (2) The distribution of the bishops is natural, nineteen coming from the Oriental diocese, ten from Lower Egypt, eight from Asia, and one (Elissæus of Diocletianopolis) from Thrace. It will be noticed that there are none from Pontus or even from Cilicia itself. Eustathius seems settled for the Syrian Epiphania by the story in the *Chronicon Paschale* 362, and we hear nothing of Narcissus of Neronias, or even of the old confessor Auxentius of Mopsuestia. (3) Scarcely any of them can be traced as bearing a hand in later moderate movements. Only four of the names recur in the letter of Liberius to the Macedonian bishops (Socr. iv. 12) where the sees are unfortunately not mentioned. Of these Eusebius is too common a name to be identified, and Leontius of Tripolis in Lydia was at this time an active Anomœan. Uranius was the bishop of Apamea, or even of Adraa, for the old Arians of Tyre and Melitene were now replaced by moderates: we find Zeno and Otreius at Tyana in 367, Soz. vi. 12. Charisius is left as the only identification possible. (4) As many as twenty-three can be more or less certainly recognized in later Arianizing movements. Of the remainder, old Patrophilus of Scythopolis was in bad health at Seleucia (Soz. iv. 22), absent from Constantinople (Socr. ii. 43), and dead before 362 (*Chron. Pasch.*); while the others mostly came from distant parts.

The Semiarian list is in a much less satisfactory state. It has to be pieced out chiefly from Sozomen iii. 22 and the letter in Hilary *Fragm.* x. where we cannot be sure that all who signed were present at Seleucia. However, the contrast is instructive. Assuming a few probable identifications, we find twenty-four bishops mentioned by name, of whom seven can be traced to the Oriental diocese, five to Pontus and only two to Asia, while Macedonius alone represents Europe. Thirteen of the names recur in the letter of Liberius: and of the other eleven, Macedonius, Eleusius and Sophronius appear to have kept aloof from the reunion schemes, while George of Laodicea, Basil of Ancyra and Dracontius of Pergamus were no longer in possession of those sees.

Upon the whole we may estimate the Semiarians from 110 to 120, and the minority thirty-eight. Hilary seems to have been misled by the official documents of the council, which must indeed have been his only definite source of information. If a few of the Semiarians evaded the responsibility of signing the Lucianic creed at the second sitting—we may safely name George of Laodicea for one—their numbers might fall to 105. Again, his estimate of nineteen Anomœans would seem to represent the list given by Athanasius and Socrates of nine deposed and nine excommunicated; and in this case his statement that the Egyptians were all orthodox but George of Alexandria will be an inference from the fact that none of the others were included in the censures of the council.

CHAPTER VI.

THE REIGN OF JULIAN.

BUT the misgovernment of Constantius was coming to its end. Nearly two years had been spent in vain negotiations with the Gaulish Cæsar since the mutiny at Paris. Julian had no mind to share the fate of Gallus, and there was no other escape from civil war. During the campaign of 360 the rival emperors were occupied with the enemies of Rome on the Euphrates and the Rhine, so that it was not till the summer of 361 that Julian pushed down the Danube. His march was a triumphal progress. The prefects of Italy and Illyricum fled before him, the count Lucilianus was surprised at Sirmium, and one more daring blow secured the pass of Succi. He was master of three prefectures when he halted at Naissus. But the victory was not yet secure. Two legions in his rear had seized Aquileia for Constantius; before him lay the Eastern cavalry commanded by the veteran Arbetio, and the main army of Syria under Agilo the Frank was coming up from Hierapolis and Antioch. Yet the strife was not decided by the chance of war. While Julian was anxiously taking omens and inspecting entrails at Naissus, two barbarian counts rode into his camp with the news that Constantius was dead. A sudden fever had carried him off at Mopsucrenæ beneath Mount Taurus, and the Eastern army presented its allegiance to Julian Augustus.

It is no part of our purpose to write a history of Julian's reign, or even fully to discuss his policy towards the Christians as a body. Our special concern is with the bearings of his reign upon the Arian reaction.

The life of Julian is one of the noblest wrecks in history. The years of painful self-repression and forced dissimulation which had turned his bright youth to bitterness and filled his mind with angry prejudice had only consolidated his self-reliant pride and firm determination to walk worthily before the gods. Small chance was his of escaping the "purple death" of Gallus and Silvanus when Constantius took him from the schools of Athens and sent him, more like a prisoner of state than an emperor, to clear the Germans out of Gaul. Success against the barbarian would only expose him to the informer, or (a better fate) to the assassin. But Julian brought to his task versatility worthy of Hadrian himself. His splendid energy commanded victory in spite of the intrigues of the ring of traitors whom Constantius allowed to thwart him[1]. Within four years all Gaul was at his feet. The army was devoted to its brilliant general, and the overburdened provincials were won by the unaffected sympathy of the young Cæsar who had ventured to check the exactions of Florentius. And Julian relaxed nothing of his faithful self-devotion to the empire when he found himself master of the world at the age of thirty. Kindly to others and rigid to himself, he needed no more

---

[1] Though the apologist of Constantius will hardly venture to defend his treatment of Julian, he may fairly point out a few extenuating circumstances.

In the first place, our accounts of it come mostly from Julian himself and his admirer Ammianus, who are not likely to be entirely impartial. It must also be noted that if any confidence between Constantius and Julian survived the massacre of 337, it must have been destroyed by the execution of Gallus.

This being premised, the emperor's action will not be quite so bad as we should suppose from Julian's complaints. He allowed him a decent state at Macellum, and placed him in possession of Basilina's Asiatic property before the legal age at which the duties of a *curator* ended. As for the charge of surrounding him with spies, Constantius was honestly incapable of finding men who were not spies. He gave him the best education of the time; and though he was forbidden to attend Libanius, his intercourse with the philosophers at Nicomedia, Pergamus and Athens does not seem to have been much hampered with spies.

With regard to the Gaulish Cæsarship, Julian's escort was a small one, but perhaps it was never intended for an army. He was also put under close restrictions; but a more generous master than Constantius might have imposed them on so inexperienced a youth as Julian was in 355. At any rate they were relaxed after his first campaign, when Marcellus was replaced by a capable general.

Nor can we blame Constantius for the demand of reinforcements which led to the mutiny. Julian had quieted the Rhine, whereas troops were urgently required in Syria after the fall of Amida.

warnings against Asiatic levity. The impatience of youth was only seen in his restless fussiness, for nothing could exceed the assiduity of his attention to an endless round of business. If his legislation shews little of the farsighted patience which marks the highest statesmanship, it is at least vigilant and strong, public-spirited and far from undiscriminating[1]. We cannot doubt that he began his reign in the full determination to do right and justice to all his subjects.

But here came in that fatal heathen prejudice which put him in a false relation to all the living powers of his time, and was the direct cause even of his military disaster in Assyria. Heathen pride came to him with Basilina's Anician blood, and the dream-world of his lonely youth was a world of heathen literature[2]. Meanwhile Christianity was nothing to him but "the slavery of a Persian prison[3]." Fine preachers of the kingdom of heaven were those fawning eunuchs and episcopal sycophants, and the arch-murderer Constantius behind them. Even Arianism had worthier representatives than these, but Julian seems never to have met with better men till it was too late. As it was, every force about him worked for heathenism. The influence of his old pedagogue Mardonius was practically heathen; and the rest were as heathen as utter worldliness could make them[4]. Julian was not deceived by their hypocrisy. He may have been too young to appreciate Eusebius of Constantinople, but he formed even at Macellum a very clear idea of George the pork-contractor, and cannot have found much difficulty in understanding Hecebolius a few years later.

Full of thoughts like these, which corroded his mind all the more for the danger of expressing them, Julian was easily and permanently won to the cause of heathenism by the fatherly

---

[1] Note H. *The Legislation of Julian.*
[2] Rendall *Julian* 240—243.
[3] Julian *ad S. P. Q. Athen.* p. 271.
[4] Rode *Julian* 32 notes the bad character of the Arian bishops known to Julian.

Dianius of Cæsarea was another sort of man, but not one likely to do Julian much good if they met at Macellum. Was he the bishop whom Julian (*c. Chr.* p. 347) puzzled over Gen. iv. 7 (LXX) οὐκ ἐὰν ὀρθῶς προσενέγκῃς, ὀρθῶς δὲ μὴ διέλῃς, ἥμαρτες?

Among the eunuchs an exception may have to be made in favour of the virtuous Eutherius (Ammianus xvi. 7, 5), who being an Armenian by birth and educated in Constantine's palace was probably a Christian. But his intercourse with Julian belongs to a later period.

welcome he received from the philosophers at Nicomedia. Like a voice of love from heaven came the teaching of Chrysanthius and Maximus; and Julian gave himself up heart and soul to the mysterious fascination of their lying theurgy. For ten more years of painful dissimulation he "walked with the gods" in secret; and it was not till the spring of 361 that the young lion of heathenism could venture openly to throw off the "donkey's skin" of Christianity.

Once undisputed master of the world, Julian could take his own view of its needs, without seeing through the eyes of the Asiatic camarilla. Informers and bishops had fattened on the spoils of the temples, and not a department of the government was free from jobbery and malversation. And Constantius was utterly callous to the universal oppression, to spoliations and wrong which cried to the immortal gods for vengeance. It was high time to put an end to this Christian tyranny, which had brought the Empire to the verge of ruin.

But Julian had no desire to raise a savage persecution. He was no Galerius to sup on human blood, but a philosopher who professed to commiserate[1] even the misguided Christians. Cruelty had failed on ample trial; and after all it would be a poor success to stamp out the Galilean imposture without putting something better in its place. As the Christians had filled the world with their "tombs[2]," so must it be filled with the knowledge of the living gods. The aim therefore of Julian's policy was the reformation of heathenism rather than the suppression of Christianity. Freedom of worship was proclaimed for all, but the emperor's favour was reserved for the servants of the gods[3]. Sacrifices were encouraged, the good things of Christianity borrowed in all directions, and a pagan hierarchy with a regular system of canonical discipline established in opposition to the

---

[1] Julian *Epp.* 7, 42 (end).
[2] Julian *c. Chr.* p. 335 πάντα ἐπληρώσατε τάφων καὶ μνημάτων.
[3] Julian lays down his policy clearly enough in *Ep.* 7 ἐγὼ μὰ τοὺς θεοὺς οὔτε κτείνεσθαι τοὺς Γαλιλαίους οὔτε τύπτεσθαι παρὰ τὸ δίκαιον οὔτε ἄλλο τι πάσχειν κακὸν βούλομαι, προτιμᾶσθαι μέντοι τοὺς θεοσεβεῖς πάνυ φημὶ δεῖν· διὰ μὲν τὴν Γαλιλαίων μωρίαν ὀλίγου δεῖν ἅπαντα ἀνετράπη, διὰ δὲ τὴν τῶν θεῶν εὐμένειαν σῳζόμεθα πάντες. Similarly *Ep.* 43, though he cannot repress a sneer at the "most admirable law" of poverty. He repudiates persecution even in his disgraceful *Epp.* 42 (on education) and 52 (on Titus of Bostra). No fault can be found with his language so far; nor can we doubt its sincerity.

Christian. Heathen schools were to confront the churches in every town, and heathen almshouses to grow up round them. Heathen sermons were to refute the Christian, and a daily ritual of prayers and hymns was to enshrine the mysteries (whatever they might be) of a purified heathen worship. Above all, the priests were to cultivate temperance and hospitality, and to devote themselves to grave and pious studies[1]. The good cause must no longer be disgraced by the evil lives of its defenders. Julian was following the policy of Maximin Daza's last year, both in coupling a general toleration with a strenuous endeavour to organize the chaos of heathen worships into something like a rival church[2], and in turning education into a means of attack on Christianity[3]. But Daza would have much preferred to persecute openly; whereas Julian returned of his own free will to the edict of Milan, and had no deliberate purpose of evading it. The spirit of his policy was very different from Daza's.

His personal character differed still more. Julian was a model of heathen piety and purity[4], and spared no pains to infect his wondering subjects with his own enthusiasm for the cause of the immortal gods. The emperor sacrificed like a devotee, and inspected entrails with unwearied assiduity. Not a temple missed its visit, not a high place near his line of march was left unclimbed. But it was all in vain. Crowds of course applauded Cæsar; but only with the empty cheers they gave the jockeys and the preachers. Multitudes came to see

---

[1] Chastel *Destr. du Paganisme* 132, Rendall *Julian* 251—254. Duculot *Rest. Neopl.* 128—137. Lasaulx *Unterg. des Hellenismus* 66—70.

Significant is the agreement (noted by Ullmann *Gregorius* 368) of Julian with his Christian enemies in the idea of the priestly office. Some will trace it to the unconscious influence of his Christian education; others with more reason to the prevalence of heathen thought within the churches. Julian's idea is beyond doubt good heathenism, whatever be said of its Christianity.

The demands he makes of his priests (*Ep.* 49 and *Fragm.*) are mostly common in the councils, though reversely *Canon* 18 of Carthage (none to be ordained till they have converted their own families) might have been copied from Julian.

[2] Maximin's policy is well appreciated by Mason *Persecution of Diocletian* 308—320.

[3] Rendall *Julian* 214 has overlooked the operations of Maximin and Theotecnus in Eusebius *H. E.* ix. 5.

[4] The case is reviewed by Rendall *Julian* 132. Even de Broglie iv. 51 admits it, after a vain attempt to weaken the evidence of Ammianus. If the old soldier's censure of vice would have been milder than a Christian bishop's, his eye would have been just as keen to note a failure in the *imperialis verecundia*. With one exception, nine successive emperors from Constantine to Marcian seem so far

an emperor's devotions; but they only quizzed his shaggy beard or tittered at the antiquated ceremonies[1]. The army was devout enough—while the sacrificial dinners lasted. Renegades came in too, and some of them very promptly. Some were already heathens at heart like Pegasius of Ilium[2], while Elpidius and others needed Julian's pardon for their intrigues against him; but the larger number were mere timeservers like Modestus or Hecebolius. Men of this sort returned to the church as soon as Julian was dead. The cause of the gods was hopeless, by the confession of its own adherents. Leaders like Chrysanthius and Libanius held cautiously aloof from Julian's reforms; and if meaner men paused in their giddy round of pleasure, it was only to amuse themselves with the strange spectacle of imperial earnestness.

Christianity then was rather discouraged than persecuted by Julian. The authentic outrages of his reign are limited to the East, and seldom implicate him personally[3]. Allowance must be made for local savagery, for Christian provocation and for the increasing bitterness of Julian as he saw the failure of his plans. But after all allowance is made, we shall find that Julian went much further on one side than Constantine had done on the other. So far as concerns the use of court favour and every sort of worldly influence to obtain proselytes, there is little to choose between them. Julian's bribes attracted just as odious a set of flatterers as Constantine's; and if "the hypocrisy was indescribable[4]," the historian will care as little as themselves whether the hypocrites were philosophers or bishops. But while Constantine despised idolatry, Julian hated Christianity too much to be impartial. Other worships were the gifts of heaven, that all the nations might serve the gods according to their ancestral traditions: Christianity alone

blameless. Can any state of modern Europe shew the like?

Julian's detractors might have made something more of Ammianus xvi. 7, 8 *Asiaticis coalitum moribus, ideoque levem.*

[1] Rendall *Julian* 225 for a lively picture of his annoyances at Christian Antioch.

His zeal is condemned even by Ammianus xxv. 4, 16 *superstitiosus magis quam sacrorum legitimus observator.* It may have been a "pitiful superstition," but we have seen something worse at Lourdes.

[2] Julian *Ep.* 78.

[3] Note I. *Our Authorities for Julian's Persecution.*

[4] Eusebius *V. C.* iv. 54, ἄλεκτος εἰρωνεία, of Constantine's court.

was not divine at all, but a base imposture which combined the perversity of Jewish barbarism with the lowest degeneracy of Greek vulgarity[1]. An emperor's public and repeated denunciations of the impious Galileans were sure to lead to violence against them[2]; and Julian cared little to prevent it. If he never failed to disapprove of lawless outrages, his frequent remissness in punishing them must have been very like a proclamation of impunity. If he did not formally dismiss his Christian generals, he imposed on his household troops a heathen[3] offering of incense. Sometimes his animosity takes the form of downright malice, as when he gives the people of Bostra a plain hint to drive out their bishop Titus. Above all, his education edict forbidding Christians to teach the classics was condemned by the heathens themselves. It was a barbarous deed, says Ammianus, and worthy to be buried in perpetual silence[4].

The truth is that there was even more fanaticism than spite in the matter: and heathen fanaticism was a mystery even to the heathen Ammianus. Mere literature is doubtless the common property of mankind; but on Julian's ground that Homer and Plato were also prophets of the gods, there is no denying that a Christian rhetorician is as great a scandal as a heathen bishop. This may clear Julian so far as the edict refers to the state professors, though its relaxation in favour of Proæresius was illogical; but its further extension was pure malice and intolerance. We may ourselves be thankful to him for giving a much needed notice to the world that Christianity is something more than an offshoot of philosophy. In this way he struck a heavy blow at Arianism, which was nothing else than

---

[1] This is a favourite thought of Julian, c. Chr. pp. 39, 43, 238.

[2] Chastel Destr. du Paganisme 140: but his picture is too darkly drawn.

[3] I cannot follow Rendall Julian 173 in his view of the matter. It may be true that "the ceremony was made easy to the most scrupulous. No Pagan image was there, no Pagan God invoked. There was mere compliance with a piece of military etiquette." So Julian himself might have said: but the fact remains that this piece of military etiquette was usually understood to imply a denial of Christianity, and therefore did imply it.

That the ceremony was imposed only on the *domestici* is shewn by Rode *Julian* 63 n. Sozomen v. 17 τοῖς ἐν τοῖς βασιλείοις στρατευομένων may possibly include officials, but cannot be extended to the army in general.

[4] Ammianus xxii. 10, 7 *Illud autem erat inclemens, obruendum perenni silentio;* and again xxv. 4, 20 in nearly the same words.

philosophic heathenism inside the church. Eunomius threw away his eloquence on men who began to see how little ground is really common to Christianity and Neoplatonism. Greek culture was far too weak to sustain the burden of a sinking world; and its guardians could have devised no more fatal policy than that of setting it in direct antagonism to the living power of Christianity..

Could Julian have leaned on Rome instead of Greece? He seemed to court defeat at Constantinople and Christian Antioch, where even the professional defenders of heathenism hardly took the trouble to support him. The contest was still doubtful in the West, whereas his Eastern enemies could already take the conservative ground, that an attack on Christianity threatened nothing less than confusion to the world, and destruction to the Roman power[1]. All this we may grant; yet the answer is easy. In the first place, it was more than Julian could do. Whatever he might owe to his mother's Roman blood, he was by taste and education a genuine enthusiast of Hellenic culture[2]. His studies were Greek, his writings are Greek[3], and the very soldiers called him *Græculus* and *Asianus*[4]. His religion too was not Roman, but Greek and Neoplatonic. King Sun was his guardian deity and Greece his Holy Land, and the philosopher's mantle dearer to him than the diadem of empire. In other words, Julian's character forbade him to lean on Rome. We may also doubt whether the contest was really undecided even in the West. Heathenism was still enthroned in lordly state at Rome; but it was like some ancient warrior seated in his tomb, who crumbles

---

[1] Lasaulx *Untergang des Hellenismus* 77 quotes Julian *Misop.* 360 παρ' ἐμὲ τὰ τοῦ κόσμου πράγματα ἀνατέτραπται [add *Misop.* 370 ὃς δὴ τοὺς πανούργους καὶ κλέπτας οὕτω κολάζων εἰκότως ὑμῖν φαίνομαι τὸν κόσμον ἀνατρέπειν], also Greg. Naz. *Or.* iv. 74 τὸ πειρᾶσθαι τὰ Χριστιανῶν μετατιθέναι καὶ παρακινεῖν, οὐδὲν ἕτερον ἦν ἢ τὴν 'Ρωμαίων παρασαλεύειν ἀρχήν, καὶ τῷ κοινῷ παντὶ κινδυνεύειν.

These passages may be balanced by others from Libanius, but they shew how solidly Constantine's work was done.

[2] So Chastel *Destr. du Paganisme* 152.

[3] Julian's laws may sometimes be his own composition (though *C. Th.* xiii. 3, 4 seems a draft of Jovius from *Ep.* 25), and are our only specimen of his Latin style. We notice the intrusion of Greek words even in these. Thus *C. Th.* vi. 24, 1 *ad pleromos* (Godefroy explains πληρώματα for *numeros*) *suos ac terminos redire;* xii. 7, 2 *quem sermo Græcus appellat zygostaten;* and xi. 39, 5 is the only law of the whole *Codex* which is written in Greek.

[4] Ammianus xvii. 9, 3.

into dust at the touch of living men. Julian could not have fared much better than Maxentius. At any rate, his success would have been the total ruin of the Empire. Apart from the proved incapacity of heathenism to regenerate a corrupt society, it is clear that for better or for worse the East was already committed to Christianity, so that no real victory could have been won for paganism in the West but at the cost of a civil war of religion. Western heathenism in the hand of Arbogast was strong enough to do irreparable mischief to the Empire; and if it had caught one spark of Julian's enthusiasm, it would have involved both East and West in common ruin. Christianity was still as closely leagued with Greek civilization as with the Roman Empire, and Julian struck equally at both of these alliances. Hellenic culture was destroyed by its identification with the cause of heathenism, but the Christian Empire was able to survive the downfall of the ancient world.

Every blow struck by Julian at Christianity fell first on the Arianizers whom Constantius had left in power; and the reaction he provoked against Hellenic culture directly threatened the philosophic postulates of Arianism within the church. In both ways he powerfully helped the Nicene cause. Yet he cared little for the quarrels of the Christians among themselves. His personal acquaintance with Aetius and George of Alexandria on one side, Basil and Gregory of Nazianzus on the other[1], had no influence on his public policy[2]. Instead of condescending to take a side, he told them that they would not be allowed to bite and devour one another any longer, so that

---

[1] Julian *Ep.* 9 knows most of George's library from the loan of books to copy when he was in Cappadocia (344—350). Aetius was an old friend of Julian (*Ep.* 31 παλαιᾶς γνώσεώς τε καὶ συνηθείας μεμνημένος), and of Gallus (Soz. v. 5), whose wrongs Julian never forgot. Aetius received from Julian an estate in Lesbos Philost. ix. 4; but the letter of Gallus (p. 454, Spanheim) seems spurious. Julian was also on friendly terms with Photinus, to judge from his letter quoted by Facundus of Hermiane (p. 605, Hertlein). This, from the mention of *Diodorus Nazaræi magus*, we may date during Julian's stay at Antioch.

His intimacy with Basil and Gregory is well known. Amongst his fellow-pupils under Maximus was also (Soz. v. 21) the learned Novatian Sisinnius, bishop of Constantinople 395—407.

[2] Rendall *Julian* 229 seems to take another view. But in the first place, Aetius was not yet a bishop even of his own party, and seems never to have held any particular see: in the second, we need not believe all the scandals told of him by Athanasius of Ancyra. It may also be added that there is no sign of any intention on Julian's part to play the Arians against the Nicenes.

they had better keep the peace[1]. His rule of contemptuous impartiality was only broken when he instinctively recognized a greater than himself in "the detestable[2]" Athanasius.

His first move[3] was to proclaim full toleration for all sorts and sects of men. This was in itself no more than a return to the edict of Milan; but it was enough to cause a serious fear that his ultimate purpose was to recede one step further, to the persecution of Galerius. State support and immunities were also withdrawn from the impious Galileans, so that heathenism was left the only endowed religion of the Empire. There was good financial reason for making the clergy take their share of the public burdens; but it was hardly Julian's reason, as he shewed by his liberal gifts to the priests[4]. At the same time came out a restitution edict, throwing open the temples and ordering the restoration of their confiscated property. It was often enforced on innocent and friendly purchasers with a pedantic harshness which shocked the better class of heathens[5]. But nothing embitters religious hatred like the alternate seizure and restoration of sacred things. The reformers found this out to their cost when moderate men like Heath and Tonstal joined the Marian reaction as the only hope of checking the systematic pillage of the church by King Edward's nobles. The situation was not so very different in Julian's time. Only Constantius had not organized the plunder so successfully as Northumberland.

It was only too easy to strike at the church by doing common justice to the sects[6]. A few days later[7] came another law, by which all the exiled bishops were recalled, and their

---

[1] Julian *Ep.* 52, c. *Chr.* p. 206. Ammianus xxii. 5, 3.

[2] Julian *Epp.* 6, 26, 51 calls Athanasius as many bad names as he can well find room for.

[3] Sievers *Libanius* 103 points out from the *Hist. Aceph.* that it was made before the designation of consuls for 362, so that it must have been one of Julian's first acts at Constantinople.

[4] In this respect it makes little difference whether these gifts were intended for the priests themselves or for charitable uses. The burden on the exchequer was the same in either case.

[5] Instances are given by Rendall *Julian* 166.

[6] Thus Socr. ii. 38, iii. 11 he compels the Semiarian Eleusius to rebuild the Novatian church at Cyzicus, and *Ep.* 43 confiscates Arian property at Edessa, in punishment of lawless attacks on the Valentinians. Similarly he restores churches to the African Donatists.

[7] It was known at Alexandria (*Hist. Aceph.*) four days after the other. Socrates iii. 1 assigns it to its place as part of an extensive policy of conciliation.

confiscated property restored to them. They were not however replaced in their churches. Others were usually in possession, and it was no business of Julian's to turn them out. The Galileans might look after their own squabbles[1]. This sounds fairly well, and suits Julian's professions of toleration; but even Ammianus tells us that his exhortations to peace were given with a malicious hope of still further embroiling the ecclesiastical confusion. If the Christians were only left to themselves, they were sure to "quarrel like beasts[2]."

Julian was gratified with a few unseemly wrangles; but the general effect of his policy was something very unexpected. It took the Christians by surprise[3], and fairly shamed them into a sort of truce. Julian could not see that the very divisions of the churches were in one sense a sign of life. If men do not care for religion, they will find something else to quarrel over. "Nations redeem each other," and so do parties; so that the dignified slumber of a catholic uniformity may be more fatal to spiritual life than the vulgar wranglings of a thousand sects. Nicenes and Arians closed their ranks before the common enemy. However they might hate each other, they hated the renegade emperor still more. Julian was encountered with fanaticism equal to his own. A yell of execration ran all along the Christian line, from the extreme Apollinarian right to the furthest Anomœan left. Basil of Cæsarea renounced the apostate's friendship, and the populace of Antioch assailed him with scurrilous lampoons[4] and antipagan riots. Nor were the Arians behind in hate—blind old Maris of Chalcedon cursed him to his face. Nor has literature been kinder to his memory. Heathens like Libanius or Ammianus might regret his fate, but the Christians are utterly merciless. Gregory of Nazianzus forgets his gentleness, Theodoret

---

[1] So Julian *Ep.* 26 τοῖς Γαλιλαίοις τοῖς φυγαδευθεῖσιν ὑπὸ τοῦ μακαρίτου Κωνσταντίου οὐ κάθοδον εἰς τὰς ἐκκλησίας αὐτοῖς, ἀλλὰ τὴν εἰς τὰς πατρίδας συνεχωρήσαμεν. So *Ep.* 52. The point has not always been understood.

[2] The irreverent comparison is due to Ammianus xxii. 5, 3, or perhaps to Julian himself.

[3] Rendall *Julian* 184.

[4] One of their devices is worth notice for its malicious ingenuity. "*Felix Julianus Augustus*" looks innocent enough. But Felix was dead, Count Julian was dead, and they hoped the emperor would follow (Ammianus xxiii. 1, 4).

his Christian charity. One writer collects uncertain stories, another decks them out with rhetoric, and the Anomœan Philostorgius gives his ready help in adding to the heap of slanders. The heathens mocked, the Christians cursed, and Israel alone remembered Julian for good. Nor has Julian escaped a share of Israel's doom, to be an astonishment, a proverb and a byword among the nations. It was in no spirit of unworthy timeserving that the mediæval churches dealt so tenderly with the imperial dead, but in the solemn faith that a power ordained of God is holier than the erring men to whom it is committed. The Lord himself shall judge the Lord's anointed. Sin may be borne with in the living, and even heresy forgiven to the dead; but an apostate emperor is a defiance to mankind, a more unnatural monster than Nero or Domitian. Constantine Copronymus is a name of horror to the Eastern Church, Sicilian Frederick to the Western[1]; and the curse of the Iconoclast meets that of the Hohenstaufen on the head of Julian.

Back to their dioceses came the survivors of the exiled bishops, no longer travelling to their noisy councils with the pomp and circumstance of the *cursus publicus*, but bound on the nobler errand of seeking out their lost or scattered flocks. Eusebius and Lucifer left upper Egypt, Marcellus and Basil returned to Ancyra, while Athanasius reappeared at Alexandria (Feb. 22, 362[2]). The unfortunate George had led a wandering life since his expulsion by the mob in the autumn of 358. We find him first at the Sirmian conference, then at the council of Seleucia, and it was not till late in 361 that he ventured to leave the shelter of the court. It was a rash move, for his flock had not forgotten him. Three days he spent in safety, but on the fourth came news that Constantius was dead and Julian master of the Empire. The heathen populace was wild with delight, and threw George straight into prison. Three weeks later they dragged him out and lynched him. Thus when Julian's edict for the return of the exiles was pub-

---

[1] Constantine V. is the only outcast from the Apostles' Church, Frederick II. the only emperor placed in hell by Dante.

[2] Note J. *The Return of Athanasius in 362.*

lished (Feb. 9, 362), Athanasius was doubly prepared to take advantage of it.

It was time to resume the interrupted work of the council of Ancyra. The Semiarian misuse of victory in 358 had discredited in advance the new conservatism on which Hilary had attempted to lean at Seleucia. Athanasius had circumstances more in his favour, for Julian's reign had sobered Christian partizanship. The apostate was not more hostile to the Nicene cause than Constantius had been; and if he wished the Galileans to quarrel, he also left them free to combine. Twenty-one bishops met at Alexandria in the summer of 362. They were most of them returned exiles[1], and the most conspicuous of them after Athanasius himself are Eusebius of Vercelli and Asterius of Petra, the old deserter from the Eusebian camp at Philippopolis. Lucifer was better occupied at Antioch, and only sent a couple of deacons to the meeting. We shall presently see what he was doing.

Four subjects claimed the council's attention. The first was the reception of Arians who came over to the Nicene side. The stricter party was for making it an ordinary case of penance, which would for ever exclude them from the clerical office. Ultimately however it was agreed that they might retain their rank on the single condition of accepting the Nicene council. On this condition all comers were to be gladly received, and none but the chiefs and active defenders of Arianism were to be reduced to lay communion[2].

This reference to the Holy Spirit marks a new turn of the controversy. Hitherto the question had been on the Person of the Lord, while that of the Holy Spirit had scarcely yet come into the dispute. Significant as is the tone of Scripture on the subject, the proof from Scripture does not lie on the surface.

---

[1] Athanasius, Eusebius and Asterius for certain. Seven other names recur in the list of Egyptian exiles Ath. *Hist. Ar.* 72, p. 305—6.
The decisions were sent to Eusebius, Lucifer, Asterius, Cymatius of Paltus (an exile—Ath. *de Fuga* 3, p. 255—Patricius in Socr. iii. 25, must have been an intruder), and Anatolius of Eubœa. They were afterwards signed by Paulinus of Antioch (an exile, if we may trust Philost. iii. 18) and Carterius (another exile, if of Antaradus Ath. *supra*).

[2] The last detail is expressly given only by Rufinus i. 28. See Krüger *Lucif.* 46.

The divinity of the Holy Spirit is shewn by many convergent lines of evidence; but whether it amounts to coessential and coequal deity was still an open question. Thus Origen leaned to some theory of subordination, while Hilary limits himself[1] with the utmost caution to the words of Scripture. If neither of them lays down in so many words that the Holy Spirit is God, much less does either of them class him with the creatures. The difficulty was the same as with the Person of the Lord—that while the Scriptural data clearly pointed to his deity, its admission involved the dilemma of either Sabellian confusion or polytheistic separation. As soon as attention was fully directed to the subject, it became clear that the theory of hypostatic distinctions must either be extended to the Holy Spirit or entirely abandoned. Athanasius took one course, the Anomœans the other; but the Semiarians endeavoured to draw a distinction between the Lord's deity and that of the Holy Spirit. With them for the moment went Acacius, who had formerly[2] taken a clearly Arian position on the subject, and still thought fit to qualify his acceptance of the Nicene faith by a denial of the deity of the Holy Spirit. We cannot therefore doubt that the decision of the bishops at Alexandria was specially aimed at Acacius rather than against the Semiarians.

A second subject of debate was the rise of Apollinarianism. Against the nascent system it was declared that the Incarnation implied the assumption of a human soul as well as a human body. The bishops would seem to have been thinking quite as much of Arianism, and to have overlooked the triple division of man adopted by the Apollinarians from 1 Thess. v. 23, which enabled them to concede a human $\psi v \chi \dot{\eta}$ while still denying a human $\pi v \epsilon \hat{v} \mu a$.

The third subject before the council was the old misunder-

---

[1] Hilary's chief statements on the subject will be found in his *de Trin.* ii. 29—35, viii. 25, ix. 73, *neque enim de creaturis sumebat Spiritus sanctus, quia Spiritus Dei est*, xii. 55, where he rejects the word *creatura*. Hilary's belief in the deity of the Holy Spirit is hardly more doubtful than St John's: yet he nowhere states it in so many words.

The remaining step is taken in the *de fide orthodoxa* ascribed to Phœbadius, where the coessential deity of the Holy Spirit is distinctly stated. So also Lucifer *de non conveniendo*, p. 781, *de regibus apostaticis*, p. 807, and elsewhere.

[2] Ath. *ad Serap.* iv. 7, p. 560 couples Acacius and Patrophilus as $\pi v \epsilon v \mu a \tau \acute{o}\mu a \chi o \iota$.

standing of the word ὑπόστασις. The Easterns usually followed Origen's use of it in the sense of the Latin *Persona*, of the deity of the Persons of the Trinity in contrast to each other; whereas the Latins employed it as the etymological representative of *substantia*, to express what the Greeks called οὐσία— the common deity of all the Persons of the Trinity. Thus the Westerns who spoke of μία ὑπόστασις regarded the Eastern τρεῖς ὑποστάσεις as tritheist, while the Easterns in their turn suspected μία ὑπόστασις of Sabellianism. In this difficulty Athanasius was the natural mediator. He had connexions with both parties, and agreed with the Westerns in using οὐσία and ὑπόστασις as synonymous terms. As soon as both parties had stated their views before the council, it appeared that both were perfectly orthodox. Since neither was μία ὑπόστασις meant to be Sabellian nor τρεῖς ὑποστάσεις Arian, it was decided that each party might retain its own usage.

The fourth subject which claimed attention was the schism at Antioch. Now that Meletius was free to return, some decision had to be made. The Eustathians had been faithful through thirty years of trouble, and Athanasius was specially bound to his old friends; yet on the other hand some recognition was due to the honourable confession of Meletius. As the Eustathians had no bishop, the simplest course was for them to accept Meletius. This was the desire of the council, and might have been carried out, if Lucifer of Calaris had not taken advantage of his stay at Antioch to denounce Meletius as an associate of Arians, and to consecrate the presbyter Paulinus as bishop for the Eustathians. When the mischief was done it could not be undone. Paulinus added his signature to the decisions of Alexandria, and Meletius was thrown back upon his old alliance with Acacius. Henceforth the rising Nicene party of Pontus and Asia was divided from the older Nicenes of Rome and Egypt by this unfortunate personal question.

Julian could not but see that Athanasius was virtually the king of Egypt. He may not have cared about the council, but the baptism of some heathen ladies at Alexandria was enough to rouse his fiercest anger. Athanasius was an exile again before the summer was over. But his work remained. The lenient policy of the council was most successful, notwithstanding the calamity at Antioch. It gave offence indeed to zealots like Lucifer, and may have admitted more than one unworthy Arianizer[1]; but upon the whole it was a great success. Bishop after bishop gave in his adhesion to the Nicene faith, till Athanasius could boast to Jovian that it was the belief of nearly all the churches. Friendly Semiarians came in like Cyril of Jerusalem, old conservatives followed like Dianius of Cæsarea, and at last the arch-heretic Acacius himself gave in his signature. Even the creeds of the churches were remodelled in all directions. To this period we may refer the revision in a Nicene interest of the local forms in use at Jerusalem and Antioch, in Cappadocia and Mesopotamia[2].

Nor were the other parties idle. The Homœan coalition was even more unstable than the Eusebian. Already before the death of Constantius there had been quarrels over the consecration of Meletius by one section of the party, of Eunomius by the other. Neither was any agreement to be expected on the deposition of Aetius. Hence the league broke up of itself as soon as opinion was free. Acacius and his friends drew nearer to Meletius, while Eudoxius and Euzoius annulled the deposition of the Anomœan bishops. But Aetius and Eunomius do not seem to have organized their schism before the time of Jovian.

The Semiarians for their part were busy also. Guided by Macedonius and Eleusius, they took a middle course between Nicenes and Anomœans, confessing the Lord's deity with the former, and denying that of the Holy Spirit with the latter. But they were far from accepting the Nicene formula or revising their local creeds to suit it. Like true legitimists who had learned nothing and forgotten nothing, they were satisfied with confirming the Seleucian decisions and reissuing their old Lucianic creed. Had they ceased to care for the Nicene alliance, or did they fancy the world had stood still since the council of the Dedication?

[1] This is the characteristic objection of Montaut *Questions historiques* 135, who makes it largely answerable for the low tone of the Eastern bishops of the next generation.
[2] Hort *Two Dissertations* 108—111
—a suggestive review of the controversy under Valens. He adds as a fifth revised creed that read by Charisius at Ephesus; and others may have perished.

Meanwhile Julian had left Constantinople in May 362, and reached Antioch about the middle of July[1]. His stay was not a pleasant one. Julian was heathen and serious, Antioch was Christian and frivolous. Nicenes and Arians forgot their enmity in the pleasant task of reviling the gods and cursing Julian; and even the heathens jeered at his ridiculous earnestness, or grumbled more seriously at the rise of prices caused by the presence of so large an army as he brought with him. All his philosophy was needed to contend against the multiplied vexations of his residence at Antioch[2].

But the Persian war demanded Julian's attention. An emperor so full of heathen enthusiasm was not likely to forgo the dreams of conquest which had brought so many of his predecessors on the path of glory in the East[3]. Nor was it mere enthusiasm, for the disasters of the last few years had laid open the Euphrates frontier, and seemed to call for the invader's immediate punishment. And now that the Goths were quiet (they were not likely always to be quiet[4]), Julian thought it a good opportunity to strike a decisive blow at Persia.

So it was: yet something also may be said for a less ambitious policy. The immediate and crying need of the Empire was a reform of the administration; and though he had done good work at Constantinople, even Julian could hardly clean the Augean stables in a day. He had raised the dust, but he had not given himself time to do much more. Perhaps he could not have done much more, for the work needed the plodding industry of Anastasius rather than the impatient

---

[1] Note K. *Julian's arrival at Antioch.*
[2] Rendall *Julian* 225 has an appreciative account of them, and notes the emperor's increasing bitterness during his stay.
[3] Ammianus xxii. 12, 1 *impatiens otii lituos somniabat et prælia...ornamentis illustrium gloriarum inserere Parthici cognomentum ardebat.*
[4] So Julian himself in Eunapius p. 68, Bonn, though we need not see in it a prophecy of Hadrianople, for the emperor (like a true heathen) had a very ignorant contempt of the Goths (Ammianus xxii. 7, 8). When he wants an example of barbarian valour (c. Chr. pp. 116, 138 Cyril) he prefers to name the Germans. Yet he well knew the merits of his Gothic generals, and had just escorted the first barbarian consul to the *curia*.

Ammianus is worth comparison. The Franks in Amida sadly cumbered the defence; yet he does full justice to the daring valour with which they very nearly killed Sapor in the midst of his host. On the other hand, he grumbles not a little at Nevitta's consulship.

energy of Julian. On the other hand, the danger from Persia was less pressing than it seemed. The legions had not degenerated, and under a decent leader were still invincible[1]. Whatever Ursulus might say, the fall of Amida was no more than an accident of Sabinian's incompetence. And after all his defeats, Constantius had lost neither of the real bulwarks of the Roman power. With one flank guarded by the fortress of Nisibis and the other covered by the mountains of Armenia, any tolerable general should have been able to hold the rugged district of Arzanene against the Persian cavalry. Unfortunately these bulwarks were no longer intact. The Roman eagles still gleamed on the unconquered wall of Nisibis; but Julian's apostasy shook the Armenian alliance to its base, and his failure was mainly caused by the disaffection of Tiranus. The Christians of Armenia were not wanting in bravery to defend their own frontier—only in good will for a heathen emperor starting on a war of conquest. The alliance formed by Constantine was necessarily lost by Julian.

All preparations completed, the emperor left ungrateful Antioch (Mar. 5, 363) for the scene of war. The main army of 65,000 men was to march through the desert, supported by a fleet on the Euphrates; while 30,000 more under Procopius and Sebastian were to operate from Nisibis with the help of 20,000 Armenians. It is dangerous to criticize the operations of so good a general, but the march through the desert seems to have been a military error. It is clear that the Empire hardly ever struck an effective blow at Persia except through Armenia. Trajan, Avidius Cassius, Galerius in 297 and Heraclius all secured Armenia before descending on the Tigris; Crassus and Julian, and Galerius in 296, all struck across the desert. Julian indeed was not ignorant of his danger from Armenian disaffection; but with his usual contempt of barbarians, he seems to have thought a haughty message enough to secure the obedience of Tiranus. Here was another characteristic error of his heathen pride. Constantine might have fallen into

---

[1] Some writers are ready to explain everything by "the degeneracy of the army"; but there cannot have been much degeneracy in the armies which fought at Mursa and Argentoratum. The truth is nowhere better put than by Professor Seeley, *Lectures and Essays*, p. 47.

it, but Julian could scarcely have escaped it. The Armenian contingent deserted; and without it the army of Nisibis could hardly venture through Assyria. Julian's own part of the campaign was a splendid success. But when he had fought his way to the Tigris, he looked in vain for succours from the north. Repulsed from the walls of Ctesiphon and foiled in his effort to penetrate eastward, there was nothing left but a hasty retreat on Carduene. His march lay through a wasted country, and the Persian cavalry hovered round. Even Saracens attacked his rear[1]. Every day the distress increased; but the army made steady progress, and Roman discipline beat off every attack. Julian redoubled his efforts, and nobly redeemed his promise to the legions, to be their general, their leader and their comrade[2]. If he had lived, we cannot doubt that he would have brought back a remnant safe to Nisibis. The campaign would have been at best a brilliant failure; but it was only converted into absolute disaster by the chance arrow (June 26, 363) which cut short his busy life. After all, he was only in his thirty-second year.

Christian charity will not delight in counting up the outbreaks of petty spite and childish vanity[3] which disfigure a noble character of purity and self-devotion. Still less need the historian presume to speculate what Julian would have done if he had returned in triumph from the Persian war. We can only say that he would have had to take a more decided policy—that if he had not bowed his neck to the yoke of Christ, he would have been driven on to persecute like Decius. His bitterness at Antioch might have hardened into a renegade's malice, or it might have melted at our Master's touch. But apart from what he might have done, there is matter enough for the gravest blame in what he did. The scorner must not pass unchallenged to the banquet of the just. Yet when Silenus has done his

---

[1] It is characteristic of Julian that he made these Saracens his enemies by stopping their pensions, and answering their complaints with the remark that he had iron for them, but not gold (Ammianus xxv. 6, 10).

[2] Ammianus xxiii. 5, 19 *adero ubique vobis adjumentum numinis sempiterni imperator et antesignanus et conturmalis.*

[3] Ammianus xxv. 5, 18 *laudum etiam ex minimis rebus intemperans adpetitor.* Yet we must make some allowance for the awful loneliness of his imperial position. Julian needed human sympathy more than a philosopher should.

worst and all is said against him, the clear fact remains that Julian lived a hero's life. He might be blinded by his impatience and sometimes hurried into clear injustice by his heathen prejudice, but we cannot mistake a spirit of self-sacrifice and earnest piety as strange to worldling bishops as to the pleasure-loving heathen populace. Mysterious and full of tragic pathos is the irony of God in history, which allowed one of the very noblest of the emperors to act the part of Jeroboam, and brought the false intriguer Maris of Chalcedon to cry against the altar like the man of God from Judah. But Maris was right, for Julian was the blinder of the two.

The corpse of Julian was hastily embalmed, and in due time brought by Procopius from Nisibis to be deposited in the resting-place of emperors, the church of the Twelve Apostles at Constantinople. There in his tomb of porphyry the great Constantine was already laid; and there, conspicuous above the crowd of meaner emperors afterwards assembled round him—there for long centuries slept Theodosius and Anastasius at Constantine's feet, with Justinian on the other side, and near him Heraclius and the Isaurian Leo. In the shady northern aisle of this imperial mausoleum the Apostate found that rest which the call of duty had denied him in his life on earth.

NOTE H.

THE LEGISLATION OF JULIAN.

The following may serve as a conspectus of Julian's legislation: a fuller discussion will be found in Rendall *Julian* 150—175. The references are to the *Codex Theodosianus*, unless otherwise stated.

I. Laws facilitating the course of justice. i. 16, 8 (also inscription at Amorgos quoted by Haenel *Corpus Legum*) gives fuller powers to the *judices pedanei*. xii. 7, 2 establishes *zygostatæ* in every city to settle coinage disputes. ii. 5, 1 also ii. 12, 1 and *C. Just.* viii. 36, 2 strike at various legal delays. xi. 30, 30 allows appeals only within a reasonable time, while (*l.* 29) those made to the *vicarius urbis* or (*l.* 31) to other officials are to be sent to the *comitatus* within thirty days, under a heavy penalty.

II. Laws directly aimed at the misconduct of officials. v. 12, 1 orders long custom to be followed—perhaps as against the meddling of men in power. xi. 16, 10 forbids the imposition or remission of taxes without the emperor's knowledge, while vii. 1, 6—8 orders *numerarii* to make true returns of the taxes (an old difficulty of Constantine's) on penalty of torture, and puts them out of office every sixth year in order to give room for complaints against them. ii. 29, 1 refuses to recognize corrupt purchases of office, and ix. 42, 5 denounces embezzlement of the property of *proscripti*—such no doubt as Eusebius or Florentius.

viii. 5, 12—15 check the abuse of the *cursus publicus* by "prefects, governors and consulars," by abolishing (Socr. iii. 1) the service of mules, oxen and donkeys, and limiting the use of horses (except under the emperor's own hand) to certain officials on serious occasions. The prætorian prefects might use it at their discretion, and were to give a couple of passes yearly to the *præsides*, while Julian himself would grant ten or a dozen to each of the *vicarii*, and allow the *præsides* to refer to the *comitatus* in case of need. *l.* 16 abolishes the *cursus* in Sardinia as needless.

By ix. 2, 1 accused senators are not to be molested before conviction.

III. Alleviations of public burdens. xii. 13, 1 gives up the *benevolence* of *aurum coronarium*. So Ammianus xxv. 4, 15, adding *remissa debita longa diuturnitate congesta*. We find no general abatement of taxation such as Valens made, but there were many local remissions. Thus xi. 28, 1 (where see Godefroy's notes) remits the arrears of Africa, except gold and silver; *Ep.* 47 half the arrears of Thrace. At Antioch he gave up (*Misop.* p. 365) one fifth of the taxes, besides the whole of the arrears.

In this connexion we may note his clearance of the palace, his attempt to establish a maximum at Antioch, and his regulation (xiv. 4, 3) of the supply of swine's flesh at Rome. He was not very successful in these matters; but the case of Cæsarius is enough to shew that his summary reformation of the palace was not absolutely undiscriminating.

IV. Endeavours to put the municipalities on a sounder footing, especially by doing away with exemptions. xii. 1, 50 and xiii. 1, 4 abolish the immunities of the clergy, xv. 1, 10 the personal privileges granted by preceding emperors. Here again hasty legislation may well (Ammianus xxv. 4, 21) have caused much hardship. xi. 19, 2 subjects *patrimoniales fundi* to the extraordinary taxes levied on those held by *emphyteusis*. xi. 3, 3 and 4 order the taxes on land to be paid by the person in possession. xii. 1, 54 regulates the debts of the new *curiales*, and l. 51 (so Zos. iii. 11) confirms the old privilege by which Antioch added to its *album* anyone not already inscribed elsewhere, whose grandfather was a citizen. By vi. 26, 1 he frees the imperial clerks from liability to the *curia* after fifteen years' service, while vi. 27, 2 gives the same immunity to *agentes in rebus* after three years, xii. 1, 56 to soldiers of curial descent after ten, xiii. 3, 4 confirms the exemption of medical men, and xii. 1, 56 frees even from assessment the fathers of thirteen children.

V. Religious Legislation. We may begin with his marriage laws. Augustine *quæstt. ex utr. Test.* 115 complains that Julian allowed women liberty of divorce. The allusion may be to iii. 13, 2, which Godefroy explains as intended to facilitate divorce. ii. 5, 6 and iv. 11, 6 are also marriage laws; but Julian's aims on this subject are more legal than moral.

We need only allude to his reopening of the temples and restoration of the idols, his clearance of the palace and his expulsion of the Christians from his household, his recall (*Epp.* 26, 31) of the exiles and his restitution of churches to Novatians and Donatists. We have (Soz. v. 1, also *Ep.* 49) his restoration of privileges to the priests, especially their corn allowances. x. 19, 2 seems to belong to Julian, and to be intended to facilitate the rebuilding of the temples. ix. 17, 5 (compare *Ep.* 77) forbids the desecration of tombs, and also the inauspicious habit of conducting funerals by day. It may glance at the Babylas riot three or four months before.

xiii. 3, 5 orders the teachers of rhetoric to be chosen by the *curia* subject to an imperial veto : but *Ep.* 42 absolutely forbids Christians to teach the classics. The former law bears date June 17, 362; and might be issued from somewhere near Pessinus. Rendall *Julian* 209 seems to doubt whether the second was a law for the Empire, on the ground that we have it only among his letters. But though *Ep.* 25 is repeated in *C. Th.* xiii. 3, 4, we cannot be surprised at the omission of an edict corresponding to *Ep.* 42.

NOTE I.

OUR AUTHORITIES FOR JULIAN'S PERSECUTION.

The charges of persecution made by various writers against Julian may be conveniently grouped in four classes, thus :—

I. Local outrages, apparently connected with the restoration of heathenism ; and if so, mostly to be placed early in his reign.

II. Events at Antioch.

III. Attempts to heathenize the army; where the charge of persecution is complicated with questions of military discipline.

IV. Affairs of civil administration and policy, including the clearance of the palace, the execution of Artemius, the Maiuma award, the disgrace of Cæsarea Mazaca, the settlement of religious disputes at Bostra, Cyzicus, Tarsus and Edessa, affairs at Alexandria, the withdrawal of state support from Christianity, the recall of the exiles, the education edicts, and general charges of oppression and partiality. A few monstrous rumours we may safely neglect.

220   *ECCLESIASTICAL HISTORY.*   [CH.

This is a long catalogue; but large deductions must be made from it. Some of the charges rest on errors of fact, others need not imply persecution, and others again cannot be connected with Julian personally. On these points it will be enough to refer to the discussion of Rendall *Julian* esp. 176—216, whose lively sympathy with the heathen emperor seldom seems productive of injustice towards the other side. Here we may notice a few points with regard to the original authorities for the facts.

I. Many of our first class seem derived from an unknown Homœan writer used by Theodoret, whose work extended at least over several years ending with the death of Julian. His traces are clearest in the *Chronicon Paschale*, and will be shewn best by a few extracts.

337. Courtly tone towards Constantius. 350 his great care for the churches. 360 his munificence.

350. ὁ μακάριος Λεόντιος ὁ ἐπίσκοπος Ἀντιοχείας τῆς Συρίας, ἀνὴρ κατὰ πάντα πιστός τε καὶ εὐλαβὴς καὶ ζηλωτὴς ὑπάρχων τῆς ἀληθοῦς πίστεως, introducing a silly miracle. No orthodox writer has a good word for Leontius, unless we accept the equivocal praise of Soz. iii. 20. The *Chronicon* elsewhere (254) quotes Leontius for a legendary account of his predecessor Babylas.

360. Careful account of the deposition of Macedonius and enthronement of Eudoxius. Not a word of the Anomœan schism which figures so largely in Philostorgius.

362. After Julian entered Constantinople (Dec. 361) the peace of the churches was broken up, καὶ ἔστιν τὰ παρακολουθήσαντα ταῦτα. Here then begins a long extract from the Homœan writer, extending at least as far as the mention of Meletius. Theodoret has omissions and additions, but with one exception his order exactly coincides.

We find then in the *Chronicon Paschale*,

(*a*)   Edict for restoration of idols. So Theodoret.

(*b*)   Murder of George of Alexandria. Omitted by Theodoret.

(*c*)   At Sebaste—John the Baptist dug up. Theodoret puts it after (*e*), Rufinus ii. 28 gives it in a different connexion. Philostorgius adds the relics of Elisha. He also tells us that the heathens sometimes offered Christian victims on their altars, and that Julian was much delighted with these sacrifices.

(*d*)   At Scythopolis—"the holy Patrophilus" dug up. Theodoret omits this, knowing better who Patrophilus was.

(*e*)   At Ascalon and Gaza—the virgins. So Theodoret. Sozomen

v. 9, who had family connexions with Gaza, substitutes a story of Eusebius, Zeno, &c., reserving that of the virgins for Heliopolis, and adding his belief that the outrage was in revenge for Constantine's endeavour (Eus. *V.C.* iii. 58 ; *L.C.* 13 § 7 ; *Theophania* ii. 14) to suppress the licentious worships practised in the city. So too, perhaps independently, Nicephorus Callistus. Peter of Alexandria (Theodoret iv. 22) names Heliopolis as a stronghold of heathenism, though with evident exaggeration. Gregory of Nazianzus *Or.* iv. 87 seems to mix up this story with the next. Upon the whole Heliopolis would seem more likely than Gaza. Compare Rendall *Julian* 178. The general picture of outrages and exhumations in Syria is fully confirmed by the faint disapproval of Julian *Misopogon* 361.

(*f*) At Heliopolis—murder &c. of Cyril the deacon. So Theodoret, retouching the narrative at every point, and especially replacing ὁ δὲ ἀνατεμὼν κ.τ.λ. by ὅσοι γὰρ δὴ ἐκείνου τοῦ μύσους μετέλαχον.

(*g*) At Emesa—image of Dionysus set up in the church. So Theodoret, retouching again. Δ. τῷ γύννιδι τὴν νεόδμητον ἀφιέρωσαν ἐκκλησίαν κ.τ.λ. Julian *Misop.* 355 tells us that they burnt the Christian "tombs," i.e. the splendid church mentioned by Soz. iii. 17.

At this point the narratives diverge. Theodoret gives first the story of Æmilianus at Dorostolum, then that of Mark of Arethusa. Meanwhile in the *Chronicon Paschale*,

(*h*) At Epiphania in Syria—an obscene idol brought with much pomp into the church ; the blessed bishop Eustathius, ἀνὴρ εὐλαβὴς καὶ εὐσεβής,...ζῆλον ἔχων ἐν εὐσεβείᾳ, dies of horror at the news. This must be the Eustathius of Epiphania who signed the encyclical of Philippopolis (Hil. *Fragm.* 3), and afterwards the Homœan creed at Seleucia (Epiph. *Hær.* 73, 26).

(*i*) Julian lets loose upon the churches ἅπαντας τοὺς καθαιρεθέντας πρὸ τούτου ἐπὶ διαφόροις ἀτόποις κακοδοξίαις, in order to cause confusion. Meletius in particular who was deposed for heresy (ἐπὶ ἀσεβείᾳ) and other misdeeds returned to Antioch and seized the Old Church by violence, with the help of clerics who had been regularly deposed by the holy synod...and of the layman Vitalis who afterwards formed a schism, and was joined by Apollinarius of Laodicea.

(*j*) Fate of the apostates Theotecnus and Hero. So Philost. vii. 13. The stories may belong to Maximin's time.

(*k*) Case of Valentinian. So Socr. iv. 1 (adding Valens), Soz., Theodt., and Philost. Rendall *Julian* 198 follows Mücke *Julian*

249, 282 in doubting the whole story. Rode *Julian* 69 is willing to suppose that Valentinian was too decided a Christian to be allowed near Julian's person, and was therefore removed to another station.

(*l*) Case of Artemius. So Theodoret and Philostorgius (romance in Joann. Damasc.): and for the fact of his execution, Ammianus xxii. 11, 2.

(*m*) Æmilianus of Dorostolum and the fate of the infamous Thalassius, also called Magnus. Peter of Alexandria (Theodt. iv. 22) mentions Magnus *comes largitionum* in Egypt in 373, who burnt the church at Berytus in Julian's time, and was compelled by Jovian to rebuild it.

(*n*) The hermit Dometius; an incident of Julian's march in 363. From a separate account, and previously given only by Malalas.

From this point the *Chronicon* becomes meagre and seems to follow Nicene authorities, as in the vision (given also by Malalas, traced by John of Damascus *de Imaginibus* i. p. 327 to Helladius of Cæsarea, and said by Glycas to come from a panegyric ascribed to Amphilochius of Iconium) where "the most holy Basil of Cæsarea" sees the Lord commanding Mercurius to slay Julian. Mercurius the *comes somniorum* is coupled by Ammianus xv. 3 with Paul *Catena* as an informer, by Niceph. Call. x. 35 with Artemius as a saint. He may have been executed with him by Julian. Even the chamberlain Eusebius has been turned into a martyr by (Leo Grammaticus) p. 94: but modern credulity has fortunately stopped just short of "S. Eusebius."

These stories are not of Nicene origin. Neither are they Macedonian. Sabinus of Heraclea seems to have written only on the councils; and no Macedonian writer would have stigmatized the exiles as deposed ἐπὶ διαφόροις ἀτόποις κακοδοξίαις. Neither do they seem to come from Anomœan sources. We cannot argue from the silence of Philostorgius: but besides differences of detail and arrangement, there is no effort to glorify the Anomœans, no sign of the bitterness caused by the Theodosian persecution. The writer then was a Homœan, and therefore of the reign of Valens, or very little later, before Homœans ceased to be. Theodoret seems to have followed him for some distance, omitting the Arian Patrophilus, and diverging when he reached the Arian Eustathius.

Valesius (on Theodoret iii. 4) has noticed the generic Arian character of the account in the case of Meletius, Ducange in that of Leontius, but the specific Homœan turn of the narrative has escaped them.

II. Events at Antioch (entirely omitted by the *Chronicon Paschale*) fall into four series:—

(a) Profanation of the great church and evil end of Julian, *comes Orientis* and the emperor's uncle. Most simply told by Sozomen. Theodoret adds the remonstrances of Euzoius and of Julian's wife, relates the horrible death of Felix, and connects Elpidius with the desecration. Philostorgius is silent on the first point, but records the death of Felix, and adds how the divine vengeance overtook Elpidius a few years later. The story may be a little overcoloured, but of its substantial truth there is no reason to doubt. The transaction is fixed for some time during Julian's stay at Antioch by the mention of Felix the *comes S.L.* who was at Constantinople (*Cod. Theod.* xi. 39, 5) March 23. It is specially connected with the Babylas riot in October by Julian's closure (Ammianus) of the church, as well as by the consideration that he could not under ordinary circumstances connive at outrages committed under his eyes by some of his highest officers; also perhaps by the attempt to restore Stephen ascribed to the emperor by Chrysostom *de S. Babyla* 22 (ii. 568 Migne). In this case Count Julian's death before the end of the year, and that of Felix *profluvio sanguinis* a few weeks later, might well have seemed a blow from heaven. See Ammianus xxiii. 1, §§ 4, 5, where the two Julians must be distinguished, Julian *Misop.* 365, and the allusion of Chrysostom *supra*. It must have been another Felix who was also *comes S.L.* under Valens (*C. Th.* x. 17, 2) in 365, or rather in 368 or 370. The fate of Elpidius is nowhere confirmed; but the fall of Procopius was an evil day for Julian's renegades.

Theodoret iii. 12 has the curious error of making Count Julian prætorian prefect, though in the previous chapter he has rightly named Sallust as the holder of that office. Rode *Julian* 69 has similarly misunderstood ὁ τῆς ἑῴας ἄρχων in Philost. vii. 10. So also Rendall *Julian* 269.

(b) Theodore. The use of torture is recorded by Ammianus xxii. 13, 2, but the story of Theodore rests on the authority of Rufinus, and is therefore suspicious. Socrates, Sozomen, Theodoret and Augustine merely copy him; and the inscription at Gerasa (Boeckh 8654) is somewhat later. The miraculous part is vouched for by the *ipsi nos vidimus* of Rufinus, which usually prefaces his own inventions. We need not saddle it on Theodore, as is done by Rode *Julian* 74.

(c) Juventinus and Maximinus. Fairly established by the concurrent evidence of Chrysostom and Theodoret.

(d) Meletius and the youth. Personally vouched for by Theodoret (ἐγὼ ἀκήκοα), and may be accepted.

III. IV. The third class of charges has been discussed elsewhere; nor will the fourth detain us long. The only case deserving of notice (if only for its impudence) is the account of Dorotheus of Tyre in Theophanes *Chron.* p. 74. It appears that Dorotheus was a confessor under Diocletian, and returned to rule the church of Tyre in peace till his execution at Lisbon under Julian, at the age of 107. We can trace six historical bishops of Tyre during the interval—Methodius † 312, Paulinus about 323, Zeno 325 (signs at Nicæa), Paul (at Tyre) 335, Vitalis 343 (signs at Philippopolis), and Uranius 357—359. The tale is worthy of Dexter the Jesuit.

NOTE J.

THE RETURN OF ATHANASIUS IN 362.

There are some difficulties about this date. Ammianus xxii. 11 §§ 2—8 relates first the execution of Artemius in connexion with Julian's arrival at Antioch in July 362, then the murder of his associate George as soon as the news reached Alexandria. The return therefore of Athanasius cannot be placed earlier than August 362.

On the other hand the following series of dates is given in Maffei's *Historia acephala* (Athanasius ii. 1443—1450 Migne: or a better and completer text by Sievers *Athanasii vita acephala* in *Zeitschr. f. die hist. Theol.* xxxviii. p. 89—164)—a document dating from the episcopate of Theophilus (385—412):

361 Nov. 30 (*Cyac* 4). Accession of Julian proclaimed at Alexandria. [News in twenty-seven days from Mopsucrenæ.] Arrest of George.

Dec. 24 (*Cyac* 28). Murder of George.

362 Feb. 4 (*Mechir* 10). Edict published for restoration of idols, &c.

„ 9 (*Mechir* 15). Edict published for return of the exiles.

„ 21 (*Mechir* 27). Return of Athanasius.

NOTE J. THE RETURN OF ATHANASIUS IN 362.

362 Oct. 24 (*Phaophi* 27). Flight of Athanasius after eight full months at Alexandria.
363 Aug. 20 (*Mensore* 26). Death of Julian and accession of Jovian proclaimed at Alexandria. [News in fifty-five days from Persia, or more likely in thirty-nine days, counting from the peace of July 12.]

The news of Julian's accession must have been delayed or come further than from Mopsucrenæ. Otherwise this is a compact and consistent account, and is further supported by (1) The computation *Vita Aceph.* p. 161 that Athanasius was in hiding seventy-two months and fourteen days:—viz. from Feb. 7 (*Mechir* 13) 356. (2) The Index to the *Festal Letters* of Athanasius places his flight *Phaophi* 27, while Epiph. *Hær.* 76. 1, Soz. v. 7 and Niceph. Call. x. 6 agree that George was seized as soon as the death of Constantius was known at Alexandria. Sievers (*supra*) has shewn that Sozomen and the writer of the Index frequently use the *Hist. Aceph.*, and they may have done so in this case; but Epiphanius is certainly independent, and indeed our earliest authority. (3) The *Chronicon Paschale*, copying from an old Homœan writer of the time of Valens (see Note I), places the murder of George among the heathen atrocities immediately connected with Julian's restoration of the idols. On the other hand, in the *S. Artemii Passio* included in the works of John of Damascus (iii. 1251—1320 Migne and discussed by Langen *Johannes von Damaskus* 255—263), but mostly derived from Philostorgius, the scene is laid at Antioch, and the proceedings extend from Julian's arrival to the fire at Daphne in October.

Internal probability is divided. Mr Rendall (*Julian* 289) urges that we should not expect Julian to let Athanasius remain eight months in Alexandria. On the other side, we should not expect the mob to wait for the execution of Artemius in July. His recall or the mere succession of a hostile emperor would have been signal enough for the attack on George.

The evidence of Ammianus is not hastily to be set aside; though there is no reason for Mücke's theory (*Julian* ii. 326), that he was in Egypt at the time. His geographical digressions are the least original part of his work. Ammianus however is not always careful of the exact sequence of events; and in this case there cannot be much doubt that he is wrong in dating the murder of George after the execution of Artemius. On the side of Ammianus there is at worst an oversight: whereas the *Hist. Aceph.* would need to be rewritten.

NOTE K.

Julian's Arrival at Antioch.

CLINTON *F. R.*, Rode *Julian* 68, Rendall *Julian* 289 and others place his arrival some three weeks earlier, "at the end of June or the very beginning of July." But there are a few minor difficulties here, which even the indefatigable Sievers *Libanius* 247 has hardly settled.

First let us clear the ground. We have (1) the stay of ten months at Constantinople ascribed to Julian by Zoz. iii. 11. Mücke *Julian* 106 has accepted this, but it hardly needs discussion. (2) *C. Th.* viii. 4, 7 is dated from Nicomedia,...*Kal. Aug.;* but Godefroy rightly sets aside the date as corrupt. (3) *C. Th.* i. 16, 8 is dated from Antioch July 28. Haenel rejects it, but it matters little.

Setting these aside, our last trace of Julian at Constantinople is *C. Th.* xiii. 3, 4, which is dated May 12. Thence he came (Ammianus xxii. 9) past Nicomedia and Nicæa, turned aside to the temple of Cybele at Pessinus, and circuited back (*redit*) to Ancyra. He resumed his journey June 29 according to the *Acts* of Basil of Ancyra (quoted by Tillemont *Empereurs* iv. 519, 698), and went on by way of Cæsarea (Soz. v. 4 and others, rejecting Julian *Ep.* 75 with Rendall, though the suspicious ending seems spurious), Tyana (*Ep.* 4), and Tarsus. This part of the journey was done quickly (*properans*), though Libanius says σχολῇ beyond Cilicia. He reached Antioch during the mourning for Adonis, and there we find him Aug. 1 (*Ep.* 52 *ad Bostrenos*). He was also present (*Misop.* 361) at a feast during Lous; and Libanius tells us that he was at Antioch "nine months" or "the whole summer and winter." This however is clearly inaccurate, for he cannot have arrived for some weeks after June 5.

Now the Adonis feast or weeping for Tammuz cannot well be placed before the middle of July. Ammianus xix. 1, 11 and xxii. 9, 15 seems to connect it with the harvest, Julian *Or.* iv. p. 155 with the vintage. The one indication would point to June, the other to July. Elsewhere Julian *Misop.* 361 seems to fix it a little before the month of *Lous*, which means August in the *Chron. Pasch*, Malalas (e.g. p. 284 Bonn) and Suidas. Jerome on Ez. viii. 14 puts the weeping in June; but Tammuz being the tenth month extended over most of July, so that Godefroy *Chronol.* lxiv. reads *Julio* for *Junio*.

There remains Macrobius *Sat.* i. 21, 2, whose words seem at first sight to fix it after the autumnal equinox. This however is so clear a mistake that we shall do better if we understand him as referring to the time after the summer solstice, "when the days begin to shorten." And this period may very well cover the whole of July, for at Antioch (Lat. 36° 11′) sunset recedes only from 7 h. 15 min. to 6 h. 59 min. after apparent noon between the solstice and July 30, so that the shortening of the days would be very little noticed before August.

Upon the whole the data before us are best harmonized by placing the Adonis feast, and Julian's arrival with it, about the middle of July.

CHAPTER VII.

THE RESTORED HOMŒAN SUPREMACY.

THE reign of Julian seems at first sight no more than a sudden storm which clears up and leaves everything much as it was before. Far from restoring heathenism, he could not even seriously shake the power of Christianity. No sooner was he dead than the philosophers disappeared, the renegades did penance, and even the reptiles of the palace came back to their accustomed haunts. There was not much gained when Demosthenes the cook succeeded Eusebius the chamberlain, and Modestus reigned at Antioch instead of his fellow-renegade Elpidius. Yet Julian's work was not in vain, for it tested both heathenism and Christianity, and in their strength as well as in their weakness. All that Constantine had given to the churches Julian could take away, but the living power of faith was not at Cæsar's beck and call. Heathenism was really strong in its associations with Greek philosophy and culture, with Roman law and social life; but as a moral force among the common people, its weakness was contemptible. It could sway the wavering multitude with superstitious fancies, and cast a subtler spell upon the noblest Christian teachers; but its own adherents it could hardly lift above their petty quest of pleasure. Julian called aloud, and called in vain. A mocking echo was the only answer from that valley of dry bones.

Christianity on the other hand had won the victory almost without a blow. When the great army of heathenism turned out to be a crowd of camp-followers, the alarm of battle died away in peals of defiant laughter. Julian's renegades were a sorry comedy[1], his hecatombs a broad farce of impious presumption. Instead of ever coming to grapple with its mighty rival, the great catholic church of heathenism hardly reached the stage of apish mimicry[2]. Yet the alarm was real, and its teachings were not forgotten. It broke up the revels of party strife, and partly roused the churches to the dangers of a purely heathen education. Above all, the near approach of danger shewed that the life of Christianity is not in the multitude of converts, or in the privileges accorded by the state. Renegades on one side, fanatics on the other, were ancient scandals of the Christian cause; and signs were not wanting that the touch of persecution would wake up the old heroic spirit which had fought the Empire from the catacombs and overcome it.

Julian was the last survivor of the house of Constantine[3], so that his lieutenants were free to choose the worthiest of their comrades. Victor and Arinthæus formed a Syrian, Dagalaifus and Nevitta a Gaulish faction. It was well that the four barbarian generals were agreed in deference for the prefect Sallust. But when Sallust declined the purple, the debate went on. Suddenly one or two voices hailed the *primus domesticorum*[4] Jovian as emperor. The cry was taken up; and in a few moments the young officer found himself the successor of Augustus.

The stately form of Jovian was animated by a spirit of cowardly selfishness. His only thought was to make sure of his undeserved election. Perhaps even that end might have been better served if he had fought his way to the mountains of Carduene. But Jovian preferred to save the relics of an army he might need for civil war by patching up a disgraceful peace with Persia[5]. The five provinces conquered by Galerius were

---

[1] So Asterius of Amasea, p. 208.
[2] Greg. Naz. *Or.* iv. p. 139.
[3] Only his distant relative Procopius was left, besides the infant daughter of Constantius. But Procopius may have been a connexion of Basilina, and therefore not a Flavian at all.
[4] Ammianus xxv. 5, 4. Later writers make him *comes domesticorum*: but that high office was occupied at the time by Dagalaifus and Arinthæus.

[5] We may say broadly that the heathen writers blame Jovian for consenting to a disgraceful peace, while the Christians clear him on the ground of hard necessity.
Opposite prejudices must be taken into account, for if one side is too ready to convict Jovian of cowardice, the other is equally determined to throw the blame on Julian's rashness. In this case we must decide for the

restored to Sapor, and the impregnable fortress of Nisibis given up to his commissioner by Jovian's own imperial command.

Jovian was a decided Christian, though his morals illustrated neither the purity of the gospel nor the dignity of his imperial position[1]. The immunities abolished by Julian were restored to the churches, but fiscal necessity allowed only a partial restitution of the endowments. No attempt however was made to disturb the general toleration. If Athanasius was graciously received at Antioch, even the Arians were told with scant ceremony that they could hold their meetings as they pleased at Alexandria[2].

About this time the Anomœans organized their schism. Nearly four years had been spent in uncertain negotiations since the condemnation of Aetius at Constantinople. Eudoxius does not seem to have been very much in earnest about the matter, but it was not till Jovian's time that the Anomœans made up their minds to set him at defiance by consecrating Pœmenius to the bishopric of Constantinople. Other appointments were made at the same time[3], and Theophilus the Indian was sent to Antioch in the hope of winning over Euzoius. Henceforth the Anomœans were an organized sect.

But the most important document of Jovian's reign is the acceptance of the Nicene Creed by Acacius of Cæsarea and more than twenty of his friends, amongst whom we find

[1] Ammianus xxv. 10, 15 is perfectly clear on this point, and it is mere special pleading to set aside his evidence as hearsay.

Bishop Wordsworth *Ch. Hist.* ii. 186—196 writes of Jovian with almost unqualified admiration. But Jovian's immorality was open and scandalous, and it must not be condoned for the sake of his formal orthodoxy. We hardly find so clear a case among his successors before that of Michael the Drunkard.

[2] The story is given in some fragments printed in the works of Athanasius; and their authenticity is fairly vouched for by the undignified conduct ascribed to Jovian.

[3] Philost. viii. 2. The distribution of the Anomœan bishoprics is instructive. They were constituted for (1) Constantinople, (2) Lydia and Ionia, (3) Lesbos, (4) Pontus and Galatia, (5) Cilicia, (6) Syria, (7) Palestine, (8) Libya and Egypt. The sect must have been strongest in the Asiatic and Syrian dioceses, weak in the Pontic and Egyptian.

heathens. The difficulty indeed was so great that we cannot blame Jovian merely for not having been able to overcome it: but it is clear from the circumstantial narrative of Ammianus that he made supine delays, and that he scarcely attempted to keep up the discipline of the army; and this is enough to condemn him.

Philostorgius viii. 1 tells us that the army was reduced to a tenth of its numbers before the peace was made; but this is not likely.

Meletius of Antioch and Athanasius of Ancyra[1]. Acacius was only returning to his master's steps when he explained ὁμοούσιον in the sense of ὁμοιούσιον, and laid stress on the care with which "the Fathers" had guarded the meaning of the word[2]: but the transaction helped to widen the breach between Meletius and the older Nicenes.

All these movements came to an end at the sudden death of Jovian (Feb. 16, 364). Once more the prefect Sallust reconciled contending factions[3]; and this time it was with full consent and after full debate that the army chose the Pannonian Valentinian for emperor. A month later he assigned the Eastern prefecture to his brother Valens, and the two *Augusti* went on together as far as Sirmium before they parted, reaching Milan and Constantinople before the end of that strange consulship of Divus Jovianus and Varronianus.

Valentinian decidedly belongs to the better class of emperors. We cannot but approve the preference of Ammianus[4] for his old commander; yet history is bound to confess that Julian's philosophy was not ill replaced by a soldier's sense of duty. If Valentinian had little of Julian's brilliancy and none of his kindliness, he was a stranger also to Julian's Quixotic enthusiasm and fussy restlessness. Instead of plunging into the desert in quest of Sapor, he was content to keep a sober watch on the Rhine and the Danube. His reign was a laborious and honourable struggle with the enemies of the republic; and when the Alemanni claimed his presence on the Rhine, he left his brother to make head alone[5] against Procopius. An uncultivated man himself, he still could honour learning and carry

---

[1] Of the others we may notice Pelagius of Laodicea, Titus of Bostra, Isaac of Armenia, and Eusebius of Samosata. We shall see presently the light this list throws on the rise of the new Nicenes in Cappadocia. It is given by Socr. iii. 25 from the collection of Sabinus.

[2] Socr. iii. 25 ἀσφαλοῦς τετύχηκε παρὰ τοῖς πατράσιν ἑρμηνείας is a strange contradiction of the Sirmian διὰ τὸ ἁπλούστερον ὑπὸ τῶν πατέρων τεθεῖσθαι.

[3] Philostorgius viii. 9 has a touch of truth when he names Dagalaifus aud Arinthæus as the chief agents after Sallust and Datianus. We have only to note that Victor was by this time sent to Egypt, and Nevitta removed from office. Valentinian's elevation on a shield is one more hint that the empire was already in the gift of the barbarians. The ceremony seems first recorded in Julian's case, and is afterwards found even in the East, as in that of Justin II.

[4] Ammianus xxvi. 10, 9 *nec similes ejus nec suppares*, of Valentinian and Valens.

[5] Except that Aequitius in Illyricum must have acted on orders from Paris.

further the legislative reforms of Constantine. In religious matters his policy was a comprehensive and honourable toleration[1]. If he refused to displace the few Arian Bishops like Auxentius of Milan in possession of Western sees, he left the churches free to choose Nicene successors. Under his wise rule the West soon recovered from the strife Constantius had introduced.

Valens was altogether a weaker character—timid, suspicious and inert, yet not without a certain gentleness in private life. He was as uncultivated as his brother, but not inferior to him in scrupulous care for the interests of his subjects. Only Valens was no soldier, so that he preferred remitting taxation to taking a personal share in the defence of his frontiers. In both ways he is entitled to head the series of financial rather than unwarlike sovereigns whose cautious policy brought the Empire safely through the great barbarian invasions of the fifth century.

The contest entered on a new stage in the reign of Valens. The friendly league of church and state established at Nicæa had given place to a struggle for supremacy. On the one hand Constantius endeavoured with high-handed violence to dictate the faith of Christendom according to the pleasure of his eunuchs; on the other, the fathers of Ariminum stood out for clerical privileges, and Athanasius reigned in Egypt like a rival for the Empire. The tyranny of Paul *Catena* and the outrages of George contributed to make Nicenes and Luciferians nearly as rebellious as the Donatists: and if Julian's reign sobered party spirit, it brought home to all the possibility that an emperor could again sit in Satan's seat. Valens had an obedient Homœan clergy, but the moral strength of Christendom lay elsewhere. No trappings of official splendour could enable Eudoxius or Demophilus to rival the imposing personality of Athanasius or Ambrose. Thus the Empire lost the moral help it looked for, and the church became embittered with its wrongs.

---

[1] Of course de Broglie v. 111 views it unfavourably, though Hertzberg *Gesch. Griechenlands* 33 forgets Theodoric when he speaks of Valentinian as *für lange Jahrhunderte der letzte fürstliche Vertreter allgemeiner Religionsfreiheit.*

The breach involved a deeper evil. The Roman world had been decaying through four hundred years of hopeless servitude. Vice and war and latterly taxation had steadily dried up the sources of prosperity, and even of population, till Rome was perishing for lack of men. Cities had dwindled into villages, and of villages the very names had often disappeared. The stout Italian yeomen had been replaced by gangs of slaves, and these again by thinly scattered serfs. In vain the Empire hired Teutonic swords to fight its battles, and even Saracens and Moors and Persians helped to swell its motley armies. In vain whole nations were brought over from the wastes of Germany to fill the solitudes of Gaul. But if Rome grew weaker every day, her power for oppression seemed only to increase. Ruthless and crushing like the laws of Nature, her legislation coiled tighter and tighter round the unfortunate *curiales*, till they fled in all directions from her tyranny. Numbers of them took to the road; and the Alps, the Taurus and the Balkans swarmed with robbers[1]. The outlaws of Gaul flourished beyond the Rhine till it was hard to tell the Roman from the German bank, while the provincials of Spain were ready to welcome even the Vandals as deliverers[2]. It was time for the Empire to give place to something better. But in the East men were more inclined to look for refuge to the desert, where as many a legend told, there was neither oppressor nor oppressed, nor rumour of the dreadful tax-gatherer, but a people of brethren dwelling together in unity and serving God in peace[3].

We have no occasion here for any full discussion of the early history of monachism. Let it suffice to say that the ascetic

---

[1] Brigands were a chronic nuisance even in the better times of the Empire. Thus Juvenal iii. 307 of the Pomptine marshes, and Jul. Capitolinus *M. Ant. Phil.* 21, where Marcus arms the *latrones* of Dalmatia and Dardania, and sends Avidius Cassius against the *bucolici* of the Delta. The Gaulish *Bagaudæ* are well known.

The evil had not diminished in the fourth century. Besides the usual sources of brigandage in runaway slaves and such like desperadoes, there were the marauding *veterani* (*C. Th.* vii. 20, 7), and the misuse of the *cursus publicus* by *abactores*. Brigands are expressly mentioned in Lucania (*C. Th.* ix. 30, 1), the Alps (*C. Th.* vii. 18, 1), the Taurus (Isaurians till Zeno's time), and the Balkans (Ammianus xxxi. 6, 5, and even Basil *Ep.* 268); and the laws against *latrones* and their abettors are too numerous to quote.

Here again we are reminded of France before the Revolution.

[2] Orosius vii. 41—before the expedition of Castinus: Salvian *de Gub. Dei* v. 5.

[3] *Vita Antonii* 44.

spirit which "hovered on the outskirts of Christianity" long before the Nicene age[1] was only then beginning to assume the familiar shape of monasticism. Earlier ascetics knew how to devote themselves to fasting and prayer without renouncing the natural duties of social life. Before the end of the third century we come upon an occasional hermit like Narcissus of Jerusalem, and in Egypt there were perhaps the beginnings of ascetic communities; but monks are not a power the historian has to reckon with till the reign of Julian at earliest[2]. Even then the wildest austerities belong to the novels rather than to real life. The Clementines and the romance of Paul and Thecla were succeeded by the foolish tales of Jerome and Palladius[3]. Clement of Alexandria's wise rebuke was soon forgotten; and by Julian's time[4] the successors of Marcion and Montanus had already

[1] Hatch *Organization* 152.

[2] *C. Th.* xii. 1, 63 is our first trace of monks in the law books, and must be dated in 373.

As it stands in the *Codex*, it is addressed through the Prefect Modestus to the *comes Orientis*, and dated from Berytus Jan. 1, in the consulship of Valentinian and Valens. This will be 365—a date further supported (*a*) by the order of the *Codex*, (*b*) by our knowledge from Epiphanius *Hær.* 80, 2 of the vexation of the Massalians about 365 by Λουππικιανὸς ὁ στρατηλάτης. Now if the rescript had really been issued in 365, the *magister militum* Lupicinus was the very person who would have had to carry it out.

On the other hand, Modestus was not Prefect before 370, and Valens was not at Berytus at the beginning of 365, but at Constantinople (Ammianus xxvi. 5, 6). Replacing then a numeral (which must have fallen out before 438), in order to refer the law to one of his later consulships, we find him on the Danube in the winter of 367—8, and at Constantinople at the end of 369 (*C. Th.* v. 1, 2—Dec. 29). Hence we must fall back with Godefroy on the consulship of 373, when we know that he was in Syria.

Sievers *Einl.* p. 119 puts it in 370, of course altering *data* to *reddita*, and reading *Auxonium* for *Modestum*. For this bold course his only reason is that a law against Egyptian monks would not be addressed to the *comes Orientis* while there was a prefect in Egypt. This by the way rests on an evident misunderstanding of Larsow's *Festbriefe*.

Rufinus ii. 1 first fixes the "persecution" for the years 367—370 by naming the prefect Tatianus, then adds *sed hæc omnia post Athanasii obitum* in May 373, "for Valens attempted nothing of the sort while Athanasius lived."

[3] Novel-writing formed a part of the ascetic movement. It came from the same quarters, bore the same heathen characters, and was adopted by the churches about the same time. The last fragments of the *Monumenta Vetera* are Arian novels, though they may fall outside our period.

The writing of these ἄτοπα πάντη καὶ δυσσεβῆ was not always considered innocent. The Asiatic presbyter who forged the *Acts of Paul and Thecla* was deposed for his pains; and the writer of the *Acts of Andrew* is known in history by the title of *discipulus diaboli*. Jerome and Palladius have been fortunate enough to escape the censures of the church.

[4] Julian *Fragm.* p. 288 εἰσὶ δὲ οἳ καὶ τὰς ἐρημίας ἀντὶ τῶν πόλεων διώκουσιν, ὄντος τἀνθρώπου φύσει πολιτικοῦ ζῴου καὶ ἡμέρου, δαίμοσιν ἐκδεδομένοι πονηροῖς, ὑφ᾽ ὧν εἰς ταύτην ἄγονται τὴν μισανθρωπίαν. ἤδη δὲ καὶ δεσμὰ καὶ κλοιοὺς ἐξηῦρον οἱ πολλοὶ τούτων. Also *Or.* vii. p. 224.

made good their footing in the churches. Inside Mount Taurus the movement came chiefly from the Semiarian side. Eustathius of Sebastia has the credit of starting it in Pontus[1], while Eleusius and Marathonius were as busy on the Hellespónt. Acacians and Anomœans held more aloof, though they could not escape an influence which even Julian felt. Their Nicene opponents tax them with indifference to the good cause; but the charge is hardly borne out by what we know of their hagiology[2].

Absolutely as the loving sympathy of Christian self-denial is opposed to the selfish cowardice of the monastic life, the two are often strangely intermingled. In an age of indecision and frivolity like the Nicene, the most earnest striving after Christian purity will often degenerate into its ascetic caricature. Thus there was an element of true Christian zeal in the enthusiasm which swept over the Eastern churches at the end of the fourth century; and thus it was that the rising spirit of asceticism naturally attached itself to the Nicene faith as the strongest moral power in Christendom. It was a protest against the whole framework of society in that age; and therefore the alliance was cemented by a common enmity to the Arian Empire. It largely helped to conquer Arianism, but it left a lasting evil in its lowering of the Christian standard; for the ascetic's conception of common life is quite as low as that of any sinner. Henceforth the victory of faith was not to overcome the world but to flee from it. Far be it from us to apologize in the least for heathen immorality: yet it was hardly more ruinous to both church and state than the unclean ascetic spirit which defames God's holy ordinance, and sees in it

---

[1] Hatch *Organization* 155 says that "there are some, though not considerable, traces of monasticism in Armenia at the beginning of the fourth century." If so, it must have existed still earlier in Pontus. But can we fully trust the history of Agathangelus in its present form? The life of Gregory the Illuminator is embellished with almost as many legends as that of Gregory the Wonderworker.

[2] We have touched on Arian hagiology at p. 134. The special charge of despising saints and relics is found in Jerome *c. Vigilantium* 8 and Asterius of Amasea, p. 324.

There seems little ground for it, except that the exaggerated estimate of knowledge by the Anomœans would tend to a Gnostic contempt of practice. So Epiph. *Hær.* 76, 4, Aug. *de Hær.* 54. Yet Philostorgius the Anomœan is much more credulous than the orthodox Socrates.

nothing essentially better than a form of sinning which a too indulgent Lord will overlook[1].

It was some time before Valens had a policy to declare. He was only a catechumen, and perhaps cared little for the controversies before his elevation. Even then he needed caution, depending as he did upon his brother instead of inheriting an assured position like Constantius[2]. So for the present there was peace in the churches.

Events continued to develop naturally. The Homœan bishops retained their sees, but their influence was fast declining. The Anomœans were forming an extensive schism on one side, the Nicenes recovering power on the other. Episcopal belief resumed its natural course when Julian took off the pressure of the court. Unwilling signatures to the Homœan creed were disavowed in all directions: while some even of its authors declared for Arianism with Euzoius, and others drew nearer to the Nicene faith like Acacius. On all sides the simpler doctrines were driving out the compromises. It was time for even the Semiarians to bestir themselves. A few years before they were an undoubted majority in the East; but this was not so certain now. The Nicenes had made an immense advance since the council of Ancyra, and assumed a less conciliatory tone. Lucifer had compromised them by excess of zeal in one direction, Apollinarius in another, and even Marcellus had never been explicitly disavowed: yet the Nicene cause advanced. But the controversy was beginning to turn on the doctrine of the Holy Spirit. While the Semiarians were coming to accept the Athanasian proof of the Lord's divinity, the Nicenes were beginning to see that similar reasoning proved the same for the Holy Spirit.

This question however was only now beginning to emerge from obscurity. The first note of alarm was sounded by Athanasius during his third exile (356—362), in his letters to Serapion[3]. In 362 the council of Alexandria is sometimes

---

[1] Thus Tert. *Exh. Cast.* 9 *nuptiæ ex eo constant, quod est stuprum*, Baur's strictures E. Tr. ii. 257—269 are not too severe. Like a good advocate, Tertullian has much-quoted phrases on the other side: but it is easy to see which of his two inconsistent principles he held more firmly.

[2] Broglie v. 79.

[3] The Letters to Serapion are dis-

understood to have demanded from the returning Arianizers not only a subscription to the Nicene creed, but also a condemnation "of those who say that the Holy Spirit is a creature and distinct from the essence of the Son[1]." But the last was not made a formal condition of their reception. Though it must have been well known to Liberius, we find no mention of it in his correspondence with the Semiarians, and Athanasius himself seems to have waived it in his directions to the bishops of Pontus[2]. We may therefore conclude that the question was not yet considered one of primary importance.

For the present then their chief efforts were directed against the Homœans. Under the guidance of Eleusius of Cyzicus and Hypatianus of Heraclea, they endeavoured to establish the decisions of Seleucia. Permission to hold a council was easily obtained from Valentinian as he left Constantinople in April 364. It sat two months at Lampsacus, and reversed the acts of the Homœans at Constantinople four years before. Eudoxius was deposed, and the Semiarian exiles declared entitled to resume their sees. With regard to doctrine they adopted the formula ὅμοιον κατ᾽ οὐσίαν, on the ground that while likeness was needed to exclude a Sabellian (Nicene) identity, its express extension to essence was required as against the Arians. Nor did they forget to reissue the Lucianic creed for the acceptance of the churches. They also discussed the deity of the Holy Spirit, but it seems without coming to any formal conclusion. Eustathius of Sebastia for one was not prepared to commit himself to any decision on the matter[3]. As soon as the council

cussed by Nitzsch *Grundriss* 294. They are partly directed against Patrophilus and Acacius. The latter was following his master (Eus. *Eccl. Theol.* p. 174) in declaring the Holy Spirit a creature.

So reckless is the assertion of Basil *c. Eunom.* ii. 33, that Eunomius invented the heresy.

[1] Ath. *ad Ant.* 3, p. 616.

[2] Basil *Ep.* 204 tells us in 375 that Athanasius directed him "to receive without hesitation all who confessed the Nicene creed." This implies that nothing further was to be required.

That Athanasius considered the deity of the Holy Spirit implicitly contained in the Nicene creed is clear from *ad Ant.* 3, p. 616, *Ep. ad Jovianum*, p. 623, and *Ep. ad Afros* 11, p. 718. But there is all the difference between logical implication and formal requirement. Even in his *ad Antiochenos* he repeatedly denounces any attempt to go beyond the Nicene creed, "as if it was in any respect deficient"; and it is also clear not only that Basil did not refuse communion to the *Pneumatomachi*, but that he was blamed by the stricter Nicenes for his οἰκονομία in avoiding any open attack on them.

[3] Socr. ii. 45.

broke up, its decisions were laid before Valens, who was by this time at Heraclea on his return from Sirmium[1].

But Valens was already falling into bad hands. Julian had scattered the vultures of the court; but Jovian restored the eunuchs[2], and under Valens the unclean tribe came back in multitudes. Amongst these intriguers Eudoxius had already obtained a decisive influence. The emperor ordered the deputies of Lampsacus to hold communion with the bishop of Constantinople, and exiled them on their refusal[3].

Looking back from the nineteenth century, we should say that Valens chose an unpromising policy in his support of the Homœans. They had been in power before; and if they had not then been able to establish peace in the churches, they were not likely to succeed any better after their heavy losses in Julian's time. It is therefore the more important to see how the emperor's decision is to be explained.

In the first place, personal influences must count for a good deal with a man like Valens, whose private attachments were so steady[4]. Eudoxius was after all a man of experience and learning, whose mild prudence[5] was just the help which Valens needed. The empress Dominica was also a zealous Arian, so that the courtiers were Arians too. It is not surprising to find their master sincerely attached to the doctrines of his friends.

But Valens was not strong enough to impose his own likings on the Empire. No merit raised him to the throne, but only his brother's favour; and his dependence was so open that the courtiers could even turn it into a compliment[6]. Neither education nor experience prepared him for the august dignity he only reached in middle life; so that he was more dependent on official help than most of his predecessors. With all his exertions he could never firmly control the administration. His

---

[1] Note M. *The Chronology of the Council of Lampsacus*.
[2] Athanasius, p. 626.
[3] Soz. vi. 7 τοὺς μὲν ὑπεροραν οἰκεῖν προσέταξε. It was a mild exile which allowed Eustathius to go to Rome next year on behalf of the Semiarians. So also in 372 Meletius is living undisturbed on his estate at Getasa in Armenia, notwithstanding his ὑπεροπία φυγή. It is therefore clear that exile under Valens was sometimes no more than an order to find some other residence.
[4] Ammianus xxxi. 14, 2.
[5] Philostorgius iv. 4—we may accept an enemy's evidence in his favour.
[6] Themistius *Or*. ix. p. 126 ὦ πάντα σὺ τὸν ἀδελφὸν ἐζηλωκώς.

very conscientiousness increased his irresolution, so that it was not an unmixed evil when Modestus persuaded him to give up hearing causes in person[1]. He had no Flavian prestige to fall back upon, and Valentinian's toleration prevented him from buying support with the spoils of the temples.

Under these circumstances it is hard to see what other policy was open to him. Heathenism had failed in Julian's hands, and an Anomœan course was still more hopeless. A Nicene policy might do well enough in the West, but it was not likely to find much support in the East outside Egypt. The only alternative was to favour the Semiarians; and even this was full of difficulties. After all, the Homœans were still the strongest party in 365. They were in possession of the churches and commanded most of the Asiatic influence, and had no enmity to contend with which was not quite as bitter against the other parties. They also had astute leaders, and their doctrine had not lost its attractions for the quiet men who were tired of controversy. Upon the whole, the Homœan policy was the easiest for the moment.

Some will find a close connexion between the despotism of the Empire and the Arian doctrine of the unity of God[2], which is very much a deification of despotic caprice. The Empire then was Arian in the same way as Mohammedan kings are despots. But in that case why did it ever cease to be Arian? Why at least did it never for a moment return to Arianism? Monotheletism and Iconoclasm had their revivals under Philippicus Bardanes and the Amorians, and Monophysitism at least neutralized the council of Chalcedon with the Henoticon of Zeno; but when Arianism fell, it fell for ever. Neither is there a true parallel in Mohammedan despotism, for the Arians were no fatalists. Without denying the existence of such a connexion, we may fairly say that we see very little of it in history. The Empire did not become less despotic even in spiritual matters after the fall of Arianism. If the Homœans obeyed Valens too implicitly, the conservatives were quite as

---

[1] Ammianus xxx. 4, 2. In many ways Valens reminds us of Claudius. But he was no pedant, and Dominica was not a Messalina.
[2] Chastel *Destr. du Paganisme* 58.

servile to Constantius, and the Nicenes hardly less so under Theodosius[1], whereas Aetius and Eunomius with the genuine Arians entirely repudiated the emperor's interference. It is a strange reading of history which turns Ambrose and Basil into champions of liberty.

In the spring of 365 an imperial rescript commanded the municipalities under a heavy penalty to drive out from the cities the bishops who had been exiled by Constantius and restored by Julian. The order may have been carried out under the emperor's eyes at Antioch, but the attempt was a failure at Alexandria. The populace declared that the law did not apply to Athanasius, who certainly had not been restored by Julian. A series of dangerous riots followed, which obliged the prefect Flavianus to refer the question back to Valens. Other bishops however were less fortunate. The persecution fell chiefly on Semiarians and Nicenes, but the Novatians were not forgotten, and even the Massalian enthusiasts of Melitene failed to escape the hand of Lupicinus the *magister militum*.

The Semiarians looked to Valentinian for help. He had received them favourably the year before: and if they could obtain his intercession now, it was not likely to be in vain. Eustathius of Sebastia was therefore sent to the court at Milan together with Silvanus of Tarsus and Theophilus of Castabala. Unfortunately Valentinian had started on his Gaulish campaign before their arrival[2], and they were not prepared to follow him

---

[1] Here we may be reminded of the penance of Theodosius. But if the Arians never had a bishop like Ambrose, neither did Constantius or Valens ever perpetrate a massacre like that of Thessalonica. Perhaps Demophilus would not have been found wanting if Valens had descended to so brutal a crime as this of Theodosius.

[2] The primary date for this part of the history is that of Valentinian's departure from Italy in 365. Unfortunately it is not an easy one to settle. Valentinian entered on his consulship at Milan, and was at Paris by the end of October (Ammianus xxv. 5, 6; 8). Nevertheless in the corrupt inscriptions of the *Codex Theodosianus* he dates from Milan throughout the year. We therefore have to disentangle his stay at Milan in the earlier part of 365 from another visit in one of his later consulships.

Now Symmachus was P.U. in 365 at least till Mar. 10. Laws are addressed to him from Aquileia Sept. 27, and from Milan Oct. 23, Nov. 18, Dec. 20; but these are inconsistent with the emperor's arrival in Paris. Knowing then (Ammianus xxvii. 3, 5) that Lampadius succeeded Symmachus, we may safely refer to the second visit of Valentinian the laws of Apr. 3, June 28, Aug. 10, addressed *ad Volusianum* P.U. And these must be placed in 373. In 368 the emperor was in

across the Alps. The envoys therefore presented to Liberius of Rome an acceptance of the Nicene creed[1], signed by fifty-nine Semiarians and purporting to come from the council of Lampsacus and other Asiatic synods. The deputation was well received at Rome, and in due time returned to Asia to complete their reconciliation with the West.

Meanwhile the journey of Valens eastward was interrupted in October (and his schemes of persecution with it) by the news that Julian's relative Procopius had declared himself emperor and seized Constantinople. There was a stir among the heathens, who still hoped to see another emperor like Julian[2]. Procopius won over to his side some of the best legions of the Empire, while his connexion with the house of Constantine secured him the formidable alliance of the Goths[3]. But the great generals kept their faith to Valens. Arbetio and Arinthæus led his army and Lupicinus hurried up the Syrian troops, while Aequitius in Illyricum checked the westward spread of the revolt. The usurper's power melted away before them. His Gothic[4] soldiers gave up their commander to the Gothic hero Arinthæus, and his Frankish generals Gumoarius and Agilo deserted to their old battle-mate Arbetio. The decisive battle was fought in May 366 at Nacolia in Phrygia, and the next consulship rewarded the victors of the year—Lupicinus in the East, and Jovinus in the West.

The war being ended, the executions began, for Valens

Gaul; and 370 is excluded by laws dated Mar. 10, Apr. 4, from Trier to Olybrius P.U.

If this be the case, the last of the Milan laws which can be assigned with certainty to 365 are those of May 25 and 31, to Jovinus the *magister equitum*, who was succeeded by Theodosius in 369 or 370. The rescripts of July 19 and 31 must be left uncertain.

Valentinian therefore did not leave Italy in 365 before June; perhaps not till August.

[1] They give it in full. The only variation of consequence is $μονογενῆ$ $θεὸν$ before $κύριον$ 'I. X., which of course alters the connexion of $τοῦτ'$ $ἐστὶν$ $ἐκ$ $τῆς$ $οὐσίας$ $τοῦ$ Π. It seems to have caused no difficulty. Hort *Two Diss.* 23.

[2] Procopius may or may not have been an avowed heathen; but he certainly surrounded himself with heathens, such as his prefects Araxius and Phronemius (both of them friends of Julian—*Ep. ad Themistium*, p. 259, Ammianus xxvi. 10, 8), and Heraclius the Cynic (Eunapius, p. 73), to whom Julian inscribes *Or.* vii. On this Sievers *Libanius* 141.

[3] Ammianus xxvi. 10, 3 *Gothorum tria millia ad auxilium erant missa Procopio, Constantianam prætendenti necessitudinem:* also xxvii. 5.

[4] The conjecture seems reasonable, and will fairly explain an incident we should be inclined to reject as legendary if it were not related by Ammianus xxvi. 8, 5.

had been too thoroughly frightened to think of mercy. The slaughter fell heavily on Julian's heathen favourites. Phronemius the prefect was exiled, the philosopher Maximus[1] and the renegade Elpidius imprisoned, and Aetius the Anomœan narrowly escaped the executioner. Still no attempt was made to alter the general system of toleration which Julian had established. Even magic was not interfered with till the end of 370[2], and heathen rites were performed under the eyes of Valens at Antioch till the end of his reign[3].

Events could hardly have fallen out better for Eudoxius and his friends. Valens had already taken their side; and now his zeal was quickened by the mortal terror he had undergone. In an age when perhaps the larger number of professing Christians were content to spend most of their lives as catechumens, it was a decided step for an emperor to come forward and apply for baptism[4]. This however was the step taken by Valens in 367, before the opening of the Gothic war[5]: and it finally committed him to the Homœan side. The policy of Constantius was to be definitely resumed, and the teachers of false doctrine to be driven out at the dictation of Eudoxius.

The blow fell most heavily on the Semiarians. Their district had been the seat of the revolt, and their disgrace had not been removed by the embassy to Rome. So divided also were they that while some of them assembled a synod at Tyana to welcome the return of the envoys, others met in Caria to ratify the Lucianic creed again. Everything therefore seemed to favour the complete establishment of the Homœan supremacy.

[1] The imprisonment of Maximus is fixed for 366 by Eunapius *Max.* p. 60 (proconsulship of Clearchus, and prefecture of Sallust); his execution was after 372 (proconsulship of Festus, and Valens at Antioch).

[2] The only law of Valens on the subject is *C. Th.* ix. 16, 8. This is usually dated in 365, but is fixed for 370 by its address from Constantinople to Modestus. Godefroy connects it with the persecution of the philosophers; but the affair of Theodorus was after Valens came to Antioch in April 372.

[3] This is the complaint of Theodoret iv. 24, and again v. 21.

[4] Constantine, Constantius and Theodosius were baptized in dangerous illnesses, from which only the last recovered. Constans also (Ath. *Apol. ad Ctium* 7, p. 237) was baptized, and there is nothing to connect his baptism with any illness. Of Valentinian and the younger Constantine there seems no record; and Jovian was probably never baptized at all.

[5] Whatever were the earlier relations of Valens to Eudoxius, we need not doubt the explicit statement of Jerome *Chronica* and Theodoret iv. 12, that he was baptized just before the Gothic war.

Unfortunately however for Eudoxius, Valens had already entangled himself in a war with the Goths, which left him no leisure to revisit Asia before 370. Meanwhile there was not much to be done. Athanasius had been formally restored to his church during the Procopian panic by Brasidas the notary (Feb. 1, 366), and was too strong to be molested again. Meletius also[1] and probably others had been allowed to return about the same time, and the emperor was not strong enough to disturb them. Thus there was a sort of truce for the next three years. Of Syria we hear scarcely anything, and even in Pontus the strife must have been abated by the famine of 368. The little we find to record seems to belong to the year 367. On one side Eunomius the Anomœan was sent into exile, but before long recalled on the intercession of the old Arian Valens of Mursa[2]. On the other the Semiarians were not allowed to hold the great synod at Tarsus which was intended to complete their reconciliation with the Western Nicenes.

For three years the emperor was busy on the Danube. The war proved a more serious task than he had expected. It was not very hard to drive the Goths into the Transylvanian mountains, but Athanaric was not reduced to ask for peace till the third campaign. The terms granted were not dishonourable to the Empire[3], but they were such as did it rather harm than good. The Gothic chiefs lost the pensions which controlled them in the Roman interest, and the Gothic people saw its

[1] Socrates iv. 2 and Sozomen vi. 7 expressly state that Meletius was exiled during this visit of Valens to Antioch, and the fact is also implied by his three exiles (in 360, 365 and 372) mentioned by Greg. Nyssa *de S. Meletio* ii. 857 Migne. The question is discussed by Tillemont *Mém.* viii. 764, but he is much hampered by the old chronology which placed the rescript of Valens in 367.

The recall of Meletius is nowhere formally recorded, but it is proved (*a*) by the *three* exiles mentioned *supra* by Gregory of Nyssa, (*b*) by Chrysostom's baptism about 370, after three years' teaching. No time can be named more likely than the winter of 365-6. In this case there would be a general amnesty for the exiles, as is further indicated by the return of Eustathius to Sebastia.

[2] From Philost. ix. 8 we find that Eunomius was exiled by Auxonius during winter, and while Eudoxius was at Marcianopolis. These three data fix the event for the end of 367. Valens of Mursa was still active in the defence of Arianism, as we know from his controversy with Germinius the year before. Eunomius was exiled a second time (Philost. ix. 11) by Modestus, and therefore not before 370; but in 380 we find him living near Constantinople.

[3] Aschbach *Gesch. d. Westgothen* 27 puts them too favourably for the Goths. Contrast Wietersheim-Dahn *Völkerwanderung* i. 546, and Gibbon.

civilizing commerce with the Empire limited to two cities on the Danube[1]. The parsimony of Valens was never more misplaced. Roman pride might cry out at the idea of "tribute to barbarians"; but the trifling sums stigmatized with this name could hardly have been better spent than in restoring the alliance which had already secured a hundred years of almost unbroken peace on the lower Danube[2].

Valens was glad of peace; but we can see by the light of Hadrianople that the friendship of the Goths was fast becoming a question of life and death for Rome. Nothing indeed more clearly shews the exhaustion of the Empire than the increasing importance of the free peoples on its borders. The advance of Sapor after Julian's death was checked more by the valour of the Armenians than by the discipline of the legions behind them. The Roman power along the Rhine depended on the Franks, and the Goths themselves had repeatedly tasked the utmost efforts of Constantine. Even the puny state of Cherson was strong enough to give him welcome and long remembered help[3]. The Empire still bore up manfully and still had vast reserves of strength, but its elaborate officialism was no match for the living spirit of freedom in the last of the Greek republics. Valens might thank the generalship of Arinthæus and Victor, and still more the financial skill of his prefect Auxonius, for the successful ending of the Gothic war.

Though Valens returned to Constantinople before the end of 369, he was still detained for another year in the Hellespontine district[4] before he could resume his schemes of persecution. Meanwhile he lost two of his best advisers. The prefect Auxonius was succeeded by the vulgar flatterer Modestus, and Eudoxius of Constantinople was ill replaced by the rash

---

[1] The conditions are given by Themistius *Or.* 10, p. 135. Zosimus iv. 11 merely says they were "not disgraceful," and Ammianus xxvii. 5, 9 does not tell us what they were.

[2] Gibbon is a thorough heathen in this matter. Finlay i. 166 takes the truer view, that the payment of a subsidy is not always a confession of weakness. If the American government allows a few blankets by the year to Sitting Bull to keep him quiet, some of our fire-eaters will tell us that Sitting Bull is the real master of America.

[3] The story is told by Constantine Porphyrogenitus *de Admin. Imp.* 53.

[4] Note N. *The Story of the Eighty Clerics.*

Demophilus. But before we trace the emperor's eastward journey, let us glance at the condition of the churches.

The Homœan party was the last hope of Arianism. The original doctrine of Arius had been decisively rejected at Nicæa, the Eusebian coalition was broken up by the Sirmian manifesto; and if the Homœan union also failed, the fall of Arianism could not be much longer delayed.

The real weakness of the Homœan power is shewn by the growth of a new Nicene party in the most Arian province of the Empire. Cappadocia is an exception to the general rule that Christianity flourished best where cities were most numerous. The polished vice of Antioch or Corinth presented fewer difficulties in its way than the rude ignorance of country villages. Now Cappadocia was essentially a country district. The walls of Cæsarea lay in ruins since its capture by Sapor in the reign of Gallienus, and the other towns were small and few, so that the province chiefly consisted of thinly-peopled *regiones*. Yet Julian found it incorrigibly Christian[1], and we hear very little of heathenism from Basil. The *chorepiscopi* who abounded in the Pontic diocese[2] were often ignorant or corrupt: but Christianity was nevertheless supreme. Yet we cannot suppose that the Cappadocian boors were civilized enough to be out of the reach of heathen influences. It rather seems that the *paganismus* of the West was partly represented by Arianism. In Cappadocia the heresy found its first great literary champion in the "many-headed" sophist Asterius. Dianius of Cæsarea was his patron, and from Cæsarea came also Euphronius of Antioch[3]. Gregory and George were brought to Alexandria from Cappadocia, and afterwards Auxentius to Milan, and Eudoxius[4] to Constantinople. Philagrius also, the prefect who drove out Athanasius in 339, was another of their countrymen. Above

---

[1] Julian *Ep.* 4. Compare Greg. Nyss. *de euntibus Hierosolymam.*

[2] Eleven signatures of *chorepiscopi* at Nicæa come from the Pontic diocese and the adjacent province of Isauria: the other three from Syria. The *chorepiscopi* are frequent in Basil's letters. The Benedictines say that those mentioned in *Ep.* 53 must be bishops, because only bishops can ordain presbyters. But this is begging the question.

[3] Eusebius *V. C.* iii. 62.

[4] Eudoxius was a native of Arabissus in Cappadocia, and held for many years the see of Germanicea, just across the mountains.

all, the heresiarch Eunomius came from Cappadocia, and found abundance of admirers in his native district.

In this old Arian stronghold the league was formed which decided the fate of Arianism. Serious men like Meletius had only been attracted to the side of the Homœans by their professions of reverence for the Person of the Lord. When therefore it appeared that Eudoxius and his friends were only Arians after all, these men began to look back to the decisions of "the great and holy council" of Nicæa. There at any rate they would find something independent of eunuchs and cooks. Of the old conservatives also, who were so strong in Pontus, there were many who felt that the Semiarian position was unsound, and yet could find no satisfaction in the indefinite doctrine professed at court. Here then was one split in the Homœan, another in the conservative party. If only the two sets of malcontents could form a union with each other and with the older Nicenes of Egypt and the West, they would ultimately be the arbiters of Christendom. And if they could secure Valentinian's intercession, they might even be able to obtain religious freedom at once.

Such seems to have been the plan laid down by the man who was now succeeding Athanasius in the leadership of the Nicene party[1]. Basil of Cæsarea was a disciple of the Athenian schools, and a master of heathen eloquence and learning. In later years he still cultivated the friendship of rhetoricians like Libanius and Sophronius, and even of the double renegade Modestus. Notwithstanding his want of interest in political matters, he was man of the world enough to secure the friendly interest of men of all sorts[2]. The connexions however of his earlier years were mostly with the conservatives. He owed his baptism to Dianius of Cæsarea, and much encouragement in asceticism to Eustathius of Sebastia. The young deacon was soon recognized as a power in Asia. He accompanied Basil of Ancyra from Seleucia to the conferences at Constantinople, and on his

---

[1] Fialon *Basile* 120 for Basil's plans.

[2] His relations were somewhat miscellaneous. We also find him on friendly terms with the generals Arinthæus, Terentius and Victor, the *præsides* Elias and Maximus, Harmatius the heathen citizen of Cæsarea, and for some time even with the respected Arian Euippius.

return came forward as a firm opponent of Arianism at Cæsarea[1]. He received the dying recantation of Dianius, and guided the choice of his successor in 362. Yet he still acted with the Semiarians, and helped them with his counsel at Lampsacus and Heraclea[2]. In his own city of Cæsarea the bishop Eusebius found Basil indispensable. When he attempted to do without him, he was forced by the popular clamour to recall him on the approach of Valens in the spring of 365. Thenceforth Basil practically governed the church of Cæsarea, till in the summer of 370 he succeeded to the bishopric himself.

The crisis was near. By the spring of 371 Valens had fairly started on his progress to the East. He travelled slowly through the famine-wasted provinces, only reaching Ancyra in July, and Cæsarea in time for the great winter festival of Epiphany 372. Nicene misbelief in Cappadocia was not the least of the abuses he had undertaken to reform. Many of the lesser bishops yielded, but their metropolitan remained unshaken. The rough threats of Modestus succeeded no better than the fatherly counsel of Euippius; and when Valens himself and Basil met face to face, the emperor was overawed. More than once the order was prepared for the obstinate prelate's exile, but for one reason or another[3] it was never issued. Valens went forward on

---

[1] Basil *Epp.* 8, 9 are doctrinal statements written in 360. They shew some connexion with the *de Synodis* of Athanasius. A few leading phrases may be set down.
Ep. 8. ἕνα Θεόν, οὐ τῷ ἀριθμῷ ἀλλὰ τῇ φύσει, ὁμολογοῦμεν...ὁ γὰρ ἀριθμός ἐστι τοῦ ποσοῦ......οὔτε ὅμοιον οὔτε ἀνόμοιον...ὅμοιον γὰρ καὶ ἀνόμοιον κατὰ τὰς ποιότητας λέγεται (*de Syn.* 53, p. 612)... ὁ γὰρ κατ' οὐσίαν Θεὸς τῷ κατ' οὐσίαν Θεῷ ὁμοούσιος.
Ep. 9. ἐγὼ δέ, εἰ χρὴ τοὐμὸν ἴδιον εἰπεῖν, τὸ ὅμοιον κατ' οὐσίαν, εἰ προσκείμενον ἔχει τὸ ἀπαραλλάκτως, δέχομαι τὴν φωνὴν ὡς εἰς ταὐτὸν τῷ ὁμοουσίῳ φέρουσαν, κατὰ τὴν ὑγιῆ τοῦ ὁμοουσίου διάνοιαν ...εἰ δέ τις τοῦ ὁμοίου τὸ ἀπαράλλακτον, ὑποπτεύω τὸ ῥῆμα...ἐπεὶ οὖν ἧττον οἶμαι κακουργεῖσθαι τὸ ὁμοούσιον, οὕτω καὶ αὐτὸς τίθεμαι. We may trace the influence of Basil of Ancyra in the acceptance of the Athanasian definition (*de Syn.* 41, p. 603) of ὅμοιον κατ' οὐσίαν together with ἐκ τῆς οὐσίας as amounting to ὁμοούσιον. The letter however is addressed to Maximus, whom the Benedictines identify with the Egyptian Cynic, and discusses Dionysius of Alexandria in a slightly different tone from that of Ath. *de Syn.* 45, p. 605. Altogether we see a Semiarian position modified by an Athanasian influence.

On the new meaning given to ὁμοούσιον by Basil and the later Nicenes, Zahn *Marcellus* 87.

[2] The Benedictines (*Life* p. 87) do not allow that Basil was present himself; but he seems to say so in *Ep.* 223.

[3] Gibbon complains with justice of the "thick coat of rhetoric and miracle" with which this famous story has been invested. Perhaps the influence of Terentius and Arinthæus is enough to explain the unexpected mildness of Valens.

his journey, leaving behind a princely gift for Basil's poorhouse. He reached Antioch in April[1] and fixed his quarters there for the rest of his reign, never again leaving the Oriental diocese till the disasters of the Gothic war called him back to Europe.

Armed with spiritual power which in some sort extended over Galatia and Armenia, Basil could now endeavour to carry out his plan. Homœan malcontents formed the nucleus of the league, but conservatives soon began to join it, and Athanasius gave his patriarchal blessing to the scheme[2]. But the difficulties were immense. It was not merely that the whole enterprise was a secret plot, so that every step had to be taken in personal interviews or committed to the care of trusty messengers[3]. The league was full of jealousies. Athanasius indeed might frankly recognize the orthodoxy of Meletius, though he was committed to the other side at Antioch. But others were less liberal, and Lucifer of Calaris was even forming a sort of Donatist schism upon the question of his recognition. Some again were lukewarm in the cause and others sunk in worldliness, while men like Eustathius of Sebastia or Anthimus of Tyana were easily diverted from their purpose. But the sorest trial of all was the selfish coldness of the West. Basil might find here and there a kindred spirit like Ambrose of Milan or Valerianus

---

[1] To this period belongs the third exile of Meletius. Basil *Ep.* 68 seems to shew that he was still at Antioch in 371, whereas in *Epp.* 99, 128 we find him at Getasa in 372. Eusebius of Samosata was not exiled till the summer of 374 at earliest.

[2] Basil *Ep.* 92 is a circular to the Westerns, signed by thirty-two bishops. The sees are not given, but Tillemont (*Mémoires* ix. 172) traces fifteen of them.

Accepting his identifications, adding the name of Paul of Emesa, and neglecting a few whom we know only by their possible signatures at Constantinople, we have—

(1) Six Homœan malcontents, recognized as such by their signatures at Seleucia or in the address to Jovian— Meletius of Antioch, Eusebius of Samosata, Paul of Emesa, Pelagius of Laodicea, Abraham of Urimi and Isaac of Armenia. To these we may perhaps add Gregory of Nazianzus, who had signed the creed like the rest.

(2) Six new Nicenes, recognized as such by their conduct before 378— Basil of Cæsarea, Zeno of Tyre, Anthimus of Tyana, Otreius of Melitene, Theodotus of Nicopolis, and Barses of Edessa. On the other hand, Gregory of Nyssa cannot have signed the document with Anthimus of Tyana, unless we alter the date.

The only possible Semiarian is Eustathius of Sebastia, who may have been willing to sign in 372, but not later.

[3] Basil *Ep.* 48 complains that he could hardly get a messenger to go to Samosata, "for our countrymen are too much afraid of the winter to set foot out of doors." Yet *Ep.* 156 he tells us that the Armenian passes in winter are too much for even a strong man. But on this occasion the excuse is for himself.

of Illyricum; but the confessors of 355 were mostly gathered to their rest, and the church of Rome paid no regard to sufferings which were not likely to reach herself.

Nor was Basil quite the man for such a task as this. His courage indeed was indomitable. He ruled Cappadocia from a sick bed, and bore down opposition by sheer strength of his inflexible determination. The very pride with which his enemies reproached him was often no more than a strong man's consciousness of power. And to this unwearied energy he joined an ascetic fervour which secured the devotion of his friends, and a knowledge of the world which often turned aside the fury of his enemies. Yet after all we miss the lofty self-respect which marks the later years of Athanasius. Pride and suspicion were constant sources of difficulty to Basil. We cannot imagine Athanasius turning two presbyters out of doors as "spies," or allowing himself to be entangled in an undignified affair like that of the convoy. But the ascetic is usually too full of his own purposes to feel sympathy with others, too much in earnest to feign it like a diplomatist. Basil had enough worldly prudence to dissemble his belief in the Holy Spirit[1], but not enough to protect his closest friends from the outbreaks of his imperious temper[2]. Small wonder if the great scheme met with many difficulties.

The dispute with Anthimus was little more than a personal quarrel, so that it was soon forgotten. The old Semiarian Eustathius of Sebastia was able to give more permanent annoyance. It was difficult indeed to deal with a man too active to be ignored, too unstable to be trusted, and yet too famous for ascetic piety to be lightly made an open enemy. His friendship was compromising, his enmity dangerous. We left him in 367, professing the Nicene faith before the council of Tyana. For the next three years we lose sight of him[3]. He reappears as a friend of Basil

---

[1] Greg. Naz. *Ep.* 20.
[2] Greg. Naz. *Ep.* 33.
[3] It appears from Basil *Ep.* 244 εἶδον γὰρ Κύζικον, καὶ μετ' ἄλλης πίστεως ἐπανῆλθον that Eustathius of Sebastia signed an Arian formula at Cyzicus some time or other before 376. The event has been placed either after his return from Rome in 366, or during the stay of Valens at Cyzicus in 370; but it is best connected with his overtures to the Arians in 375. For (1) Basil knows the formula imperfectly, and lays stress on τὰ νῦν περιφερόμενα; (2) he would scarcely have been on friendly terms with Eustathius in 370,

in 370, and the bishop of Cæsarea long clung to his old ascetic teacher, though the increasing distrust of staunch Nicenes like Theodotus of Nicopolis was beginning to attack himself. His efforts at pacification in 372–3 were worse than a failure. First he offended Theodotus, then he alienated Eustathius. The suspicious zeal of Theodotus was soothed; but Eustathius never forgave the imperious determination which forced on him a stringently Nicene confession[1].

The Arian controversy was exhausted for the present, and new questions were already beginning to take its place. While Basil and Eustathius were preparing the victory of asceticism in the next generation, Apollinarius had already essayed the christological problem of Ephesus and Chalcedon; and Apollinarius was no common thinker. If his efforts were premature, he at least struck out the most suggestive of the ancient heresies. Both in what he saw and in what he failed to see, his work is full of meaning for our own time. Apollinarius and his father were Christian literary men of Laodicea in Syria, and stood well to the front of controversy in Julian's days. When the rescript came out which forbade the Galileans to teach the classics, they promptly undertook to form a Christian literature by throwing Scripture into classical forms. The Old Testament was turned into Homeric verse, the New into Platonic dialogues. Here again Apollinarius was premature. There was indeed no reason why Christianity should not have as good a literature as heathenism, but it would have to be a growth of many ages. In doctrine Apollinarius was a staunch Nicene, and one of the chief allies of Athanasius in Syria. But he was a Nicene of an unusual type, for the side of Arianism which specially attracted his attention was its denial of the Lord's true manhood. It will be remembered that according to Arius the created Word assumed human flesh and nothing more. Eustathius of Antioch had long ago pointed out the error, and the Nicene council shut it out by adding *was made man* to the

if the latter had so lately signed a heretical creed; and (3) he would not have omitted so damaging a fact in the hostile account he gives in *Ep.* 263 of the past life of Eustathius. Nor is it needed to explain the latter's return to his diocese.

The Cyzicene formula seems alluded to again by Basil *Ep.* 251 ἡ νῦν περιφερομένη in 376.

[1] Note O. *Eustathius of Sebastia*.

was made flesh of the Cæsarean creed. It was thus agreed that the lower element in the incarnation was man, not mere flesh; in other words, the Lord was perfect man as well as perfect God. But in that case, how can God and man form one person? In particular, the freedom of his human will is inconsistent with the fixity of the divine. Without free-will he was not truly man; yet free-will always leads to sin. If all men are sinners, and the Lord was not a sinner, it seemed to follow that he was not true man like other men. Yet in that case the incarnation is a mere illusion. The difficulty was more than Athanasius himself could fully solve. All that he could do was to hold firmly the doctrine of the Lord's true manhood as declared by Scripture, and leave the question of his free-will for another age to answer.

The analysis of human nature which we find in Scripture is twofold. In many passages there is a moral division into the spirit and the flesh—all that draws us up towards heaven and all that draws us down to earth. It must be carefully noted (what ascetics of all ages have overlooked) that the flesh is not the body. Envy and hatred are just as much works of the flesh[1] as revelling and uncleanness. It is not the body which lusts against the soul, but the evil nature running through them both which refuses the leading of the Spirit of God. But these are practical statements: the proper psychology of Scripture is given in another series of passages. It comes out clearly in 1 Thess. v. 23—"your whole spirit, and soul, and body, be preserved blameless unto the coming of our Lord Jesus Christ." Here the division is threefold. The body we know pretty well, as far as concerns its material form. The soul, however, is not the "soul" of common language. It is only the seat of the animal life which we share with the beasts. Above the soul, beyond the ken of Aristotle, Scripture reveals the spirit as the seat of the immortal life which is to pass the gate of death unharmed. Now it is one chief merit of Apollinarius (and herein he has the advantage over Athanasius[2]) that he based his system on the true psychology of

[1] Gal. v. 19—21.
[2] On the psychology of Athanasius, Harnack *D. G.* ii. 146.

Scripture. He argued that sin reaches man through the will, whose seat is in the spirit. Choice for good or for evil is in the will. Hence Adam fell through the weakness of the spirit. Had that been stronger, he would have been able to resist temptation. So it is with the rest of us: we all sin through the weakness of the spirit. If then the Lord was a man in whom the mutable human spirit was replaced by the immutable Divine Word, there will be no difficulty in understanding how he could be free from sin. Apollinarius, however, rightly chose to state his theory the other way—that the Divine Word assumed a human body and a human soul, and himself took the place of a human spirit. So far we see no great advance on the Arian theory of the incarnation. If the Lord had no true human spirit, he is no more true man than if he had nothing human but the body. We get a better explanation of his sinlessness, but we still get it at the expense of his humanity. In one respect the Arians had the advantage. Their created Word is more easily joined with human flesh than the Divine Word with a human body and a human soul. At this point, however, Apollinarius introduced a thought of deep significance—that the spirit in Christ was human spirit, although divine. If man was made in the image of God, the Divine Word is not foreign to that human spirit which is in his likeness, but is rather the true perfection of its image. If, therefore, the Lord had the Divine Word instead of the human spirit of other men, he is not the less human, but the more so, for the difference. Furthermore, the Word which in Christ was human spirit was eternal. Apart then from the incarnation, the Word was archetypal man as well as God. Thus we reach the still more solemn thought that the incarnation is not a mere expedient to get rid of sin, but the historic revelation of what was latent in the Word from all eternity. Had man not sinned, the Word must still have come among us, albeit not through shame and death. It was his nature that he should come. If he was man from eternity, it was his nature to become in time like men on earth, and it is his nature to remain for ever man. And as the Word looked down on mankind, so mankind looked upward to the Word. The spirit in man is a frail and shadowy thing apart from Christ, and men are not true men till they have found in him their immutable and sovereign guide. Thus the Word and man do not confront each other as alien beings. They are joined together in their inmost nature, and (may we say it?) each receives completion from the other.

The system of Apollinarius is a mighty outline whose details we can hardly even now fill in; yet as a system it is certainly a failure. His own contemporaries may have done him something less than justice, but they could not follow his daring flights of thought when they saw plain errors in his teaching. After all, Apollinarius reaches no true incarnation. The Lord is something very like us, but he is not one of us. The spirit is surely an essential part of man, and without a true human spirit he could have no true human choice or growth or life; and indeed Apollinarius could not allow him any. His work is curtailed also like his manhood, for (so Gregory of Nyssa put it) the spirit which the Lord did not assume is not redeemed. Apollinarius understood even better than Athanasius the kinship of true human nature to its Lord, and applied it with admirable skill to explain the incarnation as the expression of the eternal divine nature. But he did not see so well as Athanasius that sin is a mere intruder among men. It was not a hopeful age in which he lived. The world had gone a long way downhill since young Athanasius had sung his song of triumph over fallen heathenism. Roman vice and Syrian frivolity, Eastern asceticism and Western legalism, combined to preach, in spite of Christianity, that the sinfulness of mankind is essential. So instead of following out the pregnant hint of Athanasius that sin is no true part of human nature (else were God the author of evil), Apollinarius cut the knot by refusing the Son of Man a human spirit as a thing of necessity sinful. Too thoughtful to slur over the difficulty like Pelagius, he was yet too timid to realize the possibility of a conquest of sin by man, even though that man were Christ himself[1].

---

[1] On Apollinarius, Dorner *Person of Christ* ii 352—399; Harnack *D. G.* ii. 312 sq.

Apollinarius and his school contributed not a little to the doctrinal confusion of the East. His ideas were current for some time in various forms, and are attacked in some of the later works of Athanasius; but it was not till about 375 that they led to a definite schism, marked by the consecration of the presbyter Vitalis to the bishopric of Antioch. From this time Apollinarian bishops disputed many of the Syrian sees with Nicenes and Anomœans. Their adherents were also scattered over Asia, and supplied one more element of discord to the noisy populace of Constantinople.

The declining years of Athanasius were spent in peace. Valens had restored him in good faith, and never afterwards molested him. If the heathens burnt the Cæsareum, they were severely punished for the outrage. If Lucius returned to try his fortune, he met with no connivance from the officials—nothing more than sorely needed shelter from the fury of the mob. Heathenism was still a living force at Alexandria, but the Arians were nearly extinct.

One of the last public acts of Athanasius was his reception of an embassy from Marcellus, who was still living in extreme old age at Ancyra. About the year 371[1] the deacon Eugenius presented a confession at Alexandria on behalf of the "innumerable multitude" who still owned Marcellus for their father. "We are not heretics as we are slandered. We specially anathematize Arianism, confessing like our fathers at Nicæa that the Son is no creature, but of the essence of the Father and coessential with the Father. And by the Son we mean no other than the Logos. Next we anathematize Sabellius, confessing as we do the eternity and reality ($ὑφεστὸς$) of the Son and of the Holy Spirit; for we do not maintain an unreal ($ἀνυπόστατον$) Trinity. Also we anathematize the Anomœans, who profess not to be Arians. We are confident that there is nothing superinduced and nothing created in the Trinity; and therefore we anathematize both the Sabellian doctrine of a solitary Monas, and the Arian of a solitary Father. With

---

[1] The Benedictines (*Life of Basil* p. 225) date the Marcellian embassy in 363, and it must be confessed that there is no very strong case on either side.

regard to the Incarnation, we believe that the Logos did not come down as on the prophets, but really became flesh and took a servant's form, and as regards flesh was born as a man. We believe that the Trinity is perfect and eternal, and therefore indivisible. We anathematize also the doctrines of Photinus and Paul of Samosata, and also the Arianizers who separate the Logos from the Son, giving the latter a beginning at the Incarnation because they do not confess him to be very God[1]."

To Basil's great sorrow, Athanasius accepted the confession, and could not be induced to sacrifice the old companion of his exile. Even the great Alexandrian's comprehensive charity is hardly nobler than his faithfulness to erring friends. Meaner men might cherish the petty jealousies of controversy, but the veterans of the great council once more recognized their fellowship in Christ. They were joined in life; and in death they were not divided.

The school of Marcellus expired with him. Four years later (in 375) his surviving followers drew up a memorial[2] in a different spirit, studiously confessing the eternal Sonship so long evaded by their master. Being an overture for closer union with the Nicenes, it was naturally addressed to the surviving friends of Athanasius in exile at Sepphoris. Basil took no small offence at their reception of the memorial. "They were not the only zealous defenders of the Nicene faith in the East, and should not have acted without the consent of the Westerns and of their own bishop Peter. In their haste to heal one schism they might cause another, unless they made it clear that the heretics had come over to them, and not they to the heretics[3]." Nevertheless the Marcellians had taken the decisive step, so that their formal reconciliation cannot have been a matter of difficulty. The West held out for Marcellus after his own disciples had given up his teaching, so that he was not condemned at Rome till 380, nor by name till 381.

---

[1] Zahn *Marcellus* 88—94.
The confession of Eugenius has some significant coincidences with the creed ascribed to Gregory of Neocæsarea. Thus πατέρα ἀΐδιον υἱοῦ ἀϊδίου ὄντος καὶ ὑφεστῶτος...οὐδὲν ἐπείσακτον οὐδὲ κτίσμα ἐστὶν ἐν τῇ Τριάδι. πνεῦμα γὰρ ἁγιωσύνης ἐστίν...τελεία καὶ ἀΐδιός ἐστιν ἡ Τριάς. Other traces of it may be found in *Ep*. 105.

[2] Epiphanius *Hær.* 72, 10—12: discussed by Zahn *Marcellus* 95.

[3] Basil *Epp.* 265, 266.

Meanwhile the churches of Asia seemed in a state of universal dissolution. Disorder under Constantius had become confusion worse confounded under Valens[1]. The exiled bishops were so many centres of disaffection, and personal quarrels had full scope everywhere. When for example Basil's brother Gregory was expelled from Nyssa by a riot got up by Anthimus of Tyana, he took refuge under the eyes of Anthimus at Doara, where another riot had driven out the Arian bishop[2]. Pastoral work was carried on under the greatest difficulties. What indeed could be expected from exiles like Cyril and Meletius, or from such selfish schemers as Fronto and Atarbius?

Creeds were in the same confusion. The Homœans as a body had no consistent principle at all beyond their rejection of technical terms, so that their doctrinal statements are of the most multifarious character. They began with the indefinite Sirmian creed, but the confession they imposed on Eustathius of Sebastia was purely Macedonian. Some of their bishops were genuine Nicenes, others genuine Anomœans. There was room for all in the happy family presided over by Demophilus. In this anarchy of doctrine the growth of irreligious carelessness kept pace with that of party bitterness. Ecclesiastical history records no clearer period of decline than this. There is a plain descent from Athanasius to Basil, a rapid one from Basil to Theophilus and Cyril. The victors of Constantinople were only the Epigoni of a mighty contest, though they still rank far above the combatants of Ephesus.

Hopeful signs indeed were not entirely wanting. If the Nicene cause did not seem to gain much ground in Pontus, it was at least not losing. While Basil held the court in check, the rising power of asceticism was declaring itself every day more plainly on his side. One schism was healed by the reception of the Marcellians; and if Apollinarius was forming another, he was at least a determined enemy of Arianism. The submission of the Lycian bishops in 375[3] helped to isolate the

---

[1] Basil's works are full of the subject. It will be enough to mention *Ep.* 92 (in 372) and *de Sp. Sancto* 77 (in 375).

[2] Montaut *Questions historiques* 91.
[3] Basil *Ep.* 218. He is thankful to hear that orthodox bishops are to be found at all in Asia.

Macedonians in Asia, and the Illyrian council held in the same year by Ambrose[1] was the first effective help from the West. It secured a rescript from Valentinian in favour of the Nicene doctrine; and if he did not long survive, his action was enough to shew that Valens might not always be left to carry out his plans undisturbed.

The fiftieth year from the great council came and went, and brought no relief to the calamities of the churches. Meletius and Cyril were still in exile, East and West were still divided over the consecration of Paulinus, and now even Alexandria had become the prey of Lucius. The leaden rule of Valens still weighed down the East. Upright and moderate as he was, his economy could scarcely lighten the heavy fiscal burdens of the Empire, while his fears allowed a reign of terror to grow up round him. And Valens was scarcely yet beyond middle life, and might reign for many years longer. The deliverance came suddenly, and the Nicene faith won its victory in the confusion of the greatest calamity which had ever yet befallen Rome.

In the year 376 the Empire still seemed to stand unshaken within the limits of Augustus. If the legions had surrendered the outlying provinces of Dacia and Carduene, they more than held their ground on the great river frontiers of the Euphrates, the Danube and the Rhine. Julian's death had seemed to let loose on Rome all her enemies at once: but they had all been repulsed. While the Persian advance was checked by the obstinate patriotism of Armenia, Valens reduced the Goths to submission, and his Western colleague drove the Germans out of Gaul and recovered Britain from the Picts. The Empire had maintained itself through twelve years of incessant warfare. And if there were serious indications of exhaustion in the dwindling of the legions and the increasing numbers of the barbarian auxiliaries, in the troops of brigands who infested every mountain district, in the alarming decrease of population, and above all in the ruin of the provinces by excessive taxation, it still seemed inconceivable that real danger could ever menace Rome's eternal throne.

[1] Theodoret iv. 8, 9. It seems rightly dated by Theophanes in 375. So Swete *Doctrine of the Holy Spirit* 58.

But while the imperial statesmen were watching the Euphrates[1], the storm was gathering on the Danube. The blow which shook the Empire was to come from a nobler enemy than Persia. The Goths in Dacia had been learning husbandry and Christianity ever since Aurelian's time, and bade fair soon to become a civilized people. Heathenism was already half abandoned and their nomad habits half laid aside. But when the Huns came up suddenly from the steppes of Asia, the stately Gothic warriors fled almost without a blow from the hordes of wild dwarfish horsemen. Such miscreated forms could only spring, as legends told, from some infernal birth. The Ostrogoths became the servants of their conquerors, and the heathens of Athanaric betook themselves to the recesses of the Transylvanian forests. But Fritigern was a Christian, and looked southward. A whole nation of panic-stricken warriors crowded to the banks of the Danube. There was but one inviolable refuge in the world, and that was beneath the shelter of the Roman eagles. Only let them have some of the waste lands in Thrace, and they would be glad to do the Empire true and faithful service.

With such an opportunity as this before him, a statesman in the place of Valens might have outdone the work of Constantine. The Vandals in Pannonia were among the quietest subjects of the Empire; and there was nothing to prevent the success of a new Teutonic colony in Thrace. The Goths were not mere barbarians, but might have been trusted to settle down peaceably for the present. Fritigern had the more civilized part of the nation with him, and they would certainly have assimilated to the Empire more quickly in Thrace than under jealous restrictions of commerce beyond the Danube.

In one sense the opportunity was not unrecognized. The flatterers of Valens told him that his army would be more invincible than ever when he had secured (and that for nothing) the services of two hundred thousand Goths; while officials of the school of Sallust or Auxonius hoped to lighten the crushing

---

[1] Hodgkin *Italy* 92 notices that Valens gave his chief attention to the eastern frontier. Such a policy was natural after Julian's failure; and Valens moreover personally disliked Constantinople.

taxation of the Empire by an extensive substitution of barbarian colonists for conscript serfs in the Roman army[1].

The scheme was wrecked partly by the excessive caution of the court, partly by official corruption and rapacity. First imperial timidity imposed hard and degrading conditions on the panic-stricken host waiting by the Danube. Every free Gothic warrior was required to give up his arms before crossing. Then the details of the arrangements were left to miscreants like Maximus and Lupicinus, whose only thought was to make the famished barbarians a prey to their own rapacity and lust. Before long the Goths were congregated south of the Danube, an armed multitude full of indignation at the sacrifices to which they had been reduced in order to retain their weapons. The commissariat was utterly neglected, famine arose, and still organized plunder went on through that miserable winter. Well did the Goths keep their allegiance to the emperor whose bread they were not allowed to eat. But it was not in human nature to endure this for ever. When discontent arose, Maximus and Lupicinus could devise no better expedient than the assassination of the Gothic chiefs at a banquet. But Fritigern had not drunk deep like Para, and cut his way out sword in hand.

The die was cast, and there was war with the Goths. Once more Lupicinus tried to stop the conflagration. He was hopelessly defeated, and the Goths marched on Hadrianople. But they could do nothing against the stone walls of a city fortified by Roman engineers.

Repulsed from Hadrianople, the Gothic host spread over Thrace and Dacia, destroying whatever cultivation had survived the desolating misgovernment of the Empire. Crowds of outlaws and deserters volunteered to guide them, and only the most inaccessible recesses escaped their devastations. Valens patched up a truce in all haste with Persia, and sent the Asiatic troops under Trajan and Profuturus into Thrace. They were supported for awhile by a small force of Western cavalry under the *comes domesticorum* Richomer[2]—as large as Merobaudes could

---

[1] The abuses of the conscription (*prototypiæ*, &c.) may be seen in *C. Th.* xi. 23, 2.

[2] Richomer's military services are traced by Godefroy on *C. Th.* vii. 1, 13.

spare[1] from the defence of the Rhine. But the legions of Armenia were overborne in a stubborn fight beneath the Balkans[2]; and though a reinforcement of cavalry under the veteran Saturninus enabled the imperial generals to keep the field, fresh hordes of barbarians came in across the Danube, found their way through the unguarded pass of Succi, and swept over Thrace.

The victories of Claudius and Aurelian had stayed for a century the tide of northern war; but now the Empire was reduced again to fight on its own territory, no more for glory but for bare existence[3]. For awhile her rulers seemed to understand the crisis. Rome could still fight with iron and not with gold. The East was drained of all available troops; and Sebastian the Manichee, the idol of the Western army[4], was summoned from Italy to take the command in Trajan's place. Gratian hurried Thraceward with the Gaulish legions, and even Valens thought it time to leave his pleasant home at Antioch for the field of war. Clamours of impatience and alarm greeted his return to Constantinople. "Only give us arms," the whole circus shouted, "and we will fight the Goths ourselves."

Hunted from his capital by the jeers of the rabble, Valens devoted a few weeks at Melanthias to the cultivation of popularity with the army, and before long found himself encamped at Hadrianople, with the Goths hovering round him. Evil omens beset his march, but no omen could be worse than his own impulsive rashness. Valens at Hadrianople was reduced to no such distress as Claudius before Naissus. He had with him an ample force, and generals of no mean ability, who had kept the Goths in check with fair success. Sebastian had made a good beginning, and every day's delay was so much gain.

---

[1] This is my interpretation of the rumour (Ammianus xxxi. 7, 4) that it was Merobaudes who induced most of them to desert.

[2] Ammianus xxxi. 7, 5 *prope oppidum Salices*. This would indicate a site in the Dobrudscha; but Wietersheim (*Völkerwanderung* iv. 80 Anm. 14) shews that the battle must have been fought *ad Radices*, between Philippopolis and the Danube.

[3] Jerome *Ep.* 123 *ad Ageruchiam*. *Quis hoc credet?...Romam in gremio suo, non pro gloria, sed pro salute pugnare? imo ne pugnare quidem, sed auro et cuncta supellectile vitam redimere?* Hodgkin *Italy* i. 379 seems to date this after the capture of Rome in 410, but the allusion is only to the capitulation of 408. The letter however more or less refers to the whole period since 376. *Epp.* 127, 128 were written later.

[4] Ammianus xxx. 10, 3 *militari favore sublatum* in 375, and therefore removed from his command as a possible rival to Gratian.

The Gaulish legions were marching to his aid, their vanguard under Richomer had already joined him, and Gratian earnestly besought him to await their coming. But Valens was only anxious to snatch an easy victory before his Western colleague could arrive to share it. In vain the Sarmatian Victor gave his voice for the delay which common sense required. Sebastian and the courtiers overruled him, and on the ninth of August Valens left the shelter of Hadrianople to attack the Gothic camp. It was a rugged march, and the legions fell into disorder. Fritigern negotiated, wasting the day in useless embassies, while his famished enemies, burdened with heavy armour, were fainting in the noonday heat. Tracts of burning grass delayed their progress; and it was past two in the afternoon when they neared the line of waggons. It was later still before the Gothic trumpet sounded; but the Roman army was in hopeless rout at sundown, outgeneralled, surrounded and overpowered. The Goths came down "like lightning on the mountain-tops," and in a moment all was lost. The cavalry had fled; and far into the night sword and fire completed the destruction of the jammed and helpless infantry. It was a butchery like Cannæ, with the added horrors of the conflagration. The emperor had fallen—a soldier's death like that of Decius[1], and his corpse was never found. Full two-thirds of the Roman army perished in the slaughter. There fell Sebastian the Manichee, the old enemy of Athanasius, and the orthodox Trajan with him; Potentius the son of Ursicinus, illustrious for his father's merits and his own; and as many as five and thirty officers of rank[2]. Richomer and Victor drew off a remnant of the broken army; and with them, under cover of the moonless night, escaped Saturninus and the Iberian Bacurius[3].

Beneath that crushing blow the everlasting Empire shook from end to end. The whole power of the East had been

---

[1] History may perhaps be allowed to draw an impartial vail over the *diris pavoribus circumsæptus* of Ammianus xxxi. 13, 8 and the panegyric of Libanius. The main point is that Valens fell in battle: his conduct is a very minor matter. It was four hundred years before another emperor shared his fate.

[2] *Tribuni vacantes* Ammianus xxxi. 13, 18.

[3] The new moon fell on the afternoon of the battle. Bacurius is not named by Ammianus, but his escape is proved by later notices of him, such as Zosimus iv. 57, 58.

mustered with a painful effort to the struggle; and the whole power of the East had been shattered in a summer's day. Down the Morava valley fled Victor's broken cavalry; and when the tidings of disaster reached him, Gratian fell back on Sirmium. For the first time since the days of Gallienus, the Empire could place no army in the field. The mere loss of men was more than could be replaced by an administration which more and more preferred to lean on barbarian mercenaries, and anxiously forbade its taxpayers the use of arms. The Empire was still populous enough to crush its enemies, if only the provincials had been allowed to take some interest in their own defence[1]. Instead of this, the codes are full of laws which bind the *curialis* to his town, the workman to his guild, and the labourer to his master's farm[2]. And therefore other laws had to denounce the severest penalties against deserters—as many as six[3] were issued during the Gothic war. This rather than the mere loss of men was the worst effect of the defeat of Hadrianople. The great cities were in no immediate danger. Fritigern had long ago made his peace with stone walls[4], and the empress Dominica found a few Saracen cohorts enough to secure the capital, while a treacherous massacre freed Asia from the fear of a Gothic rising. Hadrianople itself repulsed the conquerors the morning

---

[1] It is possible to lay too much stress on the depopulation of the Empire as a cause of its fall. No doubt there were immense wastes in every province, and some provinces were little else than waste. But were they all in as bad a state as Lucania or Etruria? Were the great cities empty too? How many thousand men of fighting age could Rome or Antioch have turned out? Such lazzaroni might not be the best of raw material, but even the rabble of Constantinople did good service when they were allowed to fight the Goths. The difficulty of keeping up the army was due not so much to absolute want of men as to the necessity of leaving taxpayers enough to maintain them. This was what made it so much cheaper to hire barbarian mercenaries than to arm the taxpaying provincials. And the difficulty was increased far beyond its legitimate dimensions by the wasteful caste system which had become the corner-stone of the imperial finance.

[2] Broglie ii. 256 on this policy of the Empire. Even the sons of the *veterani* were required to be soldiers.

[3] It was not for nothing that recruits were branded to prevent escape from their hereditary servitude. Themistius (quoted by Reitemeier on Zosimus ii. 34) has a dreadful picture of the *Russian* peculation which consumed the Roman armies. No doubt it was at its worst under such scoundrels as Maximus and Lupicinus. A few years later, the title *de desertoribus* of the *Codex Theodosianus* swells out suddenly during the Gothic war. *C. Just.* vii. 134 (380) sets slave-informers free.
Cod. Theod. VII. xviii. 2—7, all dated 379—383.

[4] Ammianus xxxi. 6, 4 *pacem sibi esse cum parietibus memorans*, after his first repulse from Hadrianople.

after the battle. But the Goths ranged over the open country from Sirmium to Thessalonica; and as they could not be dislodged, there was nothing for it but to let them settle there. As Aurelian surrendered Trajan's Dacia, so Theodosius gave up Aurelian's Dacia to the Goths—a position which equally commanded Rome and Constantinople, and almost cut the Empire in two. Theodosius was a brilliant soldier, and almost stepped into Athanaric's place as a chief of the Goths. Constantine himself would have disdained to fill the legions with barbarians, and it was even now a dangerous policy; but after the calamity of Hadrianople the Empire was forced to lean upon its conquerors. Once more the Goths became the servants and allies of Rome, the clients of Theodosius as they had been of Constantine. And a mere tincture of Roman discipline was enough to make them irresistible. They drove the mutineers of Britain over the Julian Alps, and triumphantly scaled the impregnable walls of Aquileia to seize the tyrant Maximus. A worthier enemy met them on the Frigidus and more than held his ground through the whole day of stubborn fighting, but in the end even the Franks of Arbogast went down before the Gothic onset. The legions never fought with more splendid valour than when their ranks were filled with Goths. Twice they conquered Italy for Theodosius; but the third time it was for themselves and for Alaric their king.

Had Theodosius possessed a statesman's genius in addition to his Spanish courage[1], he would have called his people to his aid and formed a new army of provincials. Money for it might have been found by a clearance of the palace like Julian's and a remorseless abolition of the corn largesses. It would have been a harder task to interest the people in their own fate; but even this might have been done by freeing the *curiales* from their servitude and reducing the heavy taxes which impeded commerce. Nor was the Empire too effete for such reforms. It was yet a thousand years above the wretched civil wars of Palæologus and Cantacuzene. The reforms were all more or less carried out by Zeno and Anastasius; and their issue was the splendid power wasted by Justinian. Had they been accom-

[1] Hodgkin *Italy* i. 197 for the *Spanish* character of Theodosius.

plished by Theodosius a century earlier, the Empire might have become Greek and homogeneous, not merely from Mount Taurus to the wall of Anastasius, but over the whole extent of the Macedonian conquests, from Antioch to Belgrade, and from the waters of the Hadriatic to the cliffs of Anium. Belisarius would at least have been able to fight Zabergan on the Danube instead of in the suburbs of Constantinople.

Even as it was, the Illyrian emperors had not fought in vain; nor were the hundred years of respite lost. If the dominion of Western Europe was transferred for ever to the northern nations, the walls of Constantinople had risen to bar their eastward march, and Christianity had shewn its power to awe their boldest spirits. The Empire rose again with almost undiminished majesty from the catastrophe of Hadrianople. Centuries of splendour were still before it; and the Hannibalic war itself can scarcely shew a more heroic record than that last great strife of Rome and Persia, when the Christian legions drove the King of Kings in headlong rout before them from Chalcedon to the gates of Ctesiphon, and dictated peace from the fort which crowns the sevenfold wall of old Ecbatana[1].

Fast rose the storm which overthrew the ancient world. The old barriers of civilization on the Danube and the Rhine were broken through at Hadrianople, and thenceforth for six hundred years the barbarians poured in like a flood of mighty waters overflowing. Wave after wave engulfed some relic of antiquity; and when the waters of the deluge abated hardly a wreck was left which recalled the old heathen world of Julian and Ammianus. The Roman Empire and the Christian Church alone stood unshaken, though strangely metamorphosed by Teutonic influences; but the Christian Church was founded on the everliving Rock, the Roman Empire rooted deep in history. Arianism was a thing of yesterday and had no principle of life, and therefore it vanished in the crash of Hadrianople. The Homœan supremacy had come to rest almost entirely on imperial misbelief. The mob of the capital might be in its favour, and the virtues of

---

[1] It is fair to add that Rawlinson's identification of Ganzaca with the Ecbatana of Herodotus i. 90 has been disputed: e.g. by Bunbury, *Hist. Anc.* *Geography* i. 258. Its currency in the fourth century is proved by Moses of Chorene ii. 87.

isolated bishops might win it some support elsewhere; but serious men were mostly either Nicenes or Anomœans. Demophilus of Constantinople headed the party, and his blunders did it almost as much harm as the profanity of Eudoxius. At Antioch the last of the early Arians had been replaced by Dorotheus. Milan under Ambrose was aggressively Nicene, and before long the Homœans at Alexandria hardly ventured to dispute the rule of Peter. On the other hand, the mightiest champions of the Nicene cause too had passed away, and few were left besides Auxano who could remember the great council's meeting. Athanasius and Hilary were dead, and even Basil hardly lived to greet an orthodox emperor. Meletius of Antioch was in exile, and Cyril of Jerusalem, and the venerated Eusebius of Samosata. If none of the living champions of the Nicene cause could pretend to rival Athanasius, they at least outmatched the Arians.

The first results of the battle of Hadrianople were in favour of toleration. Whether Gratian ascribed the catastrophe to the divine wrath (as Ambrose put it) against his uncle's persecutions, we cannot say; but he had sense enough to see that it was no time to cultivate religious quarrels when the Empire was fighting for existence. The heathens had not very much to complain of. If Gratian had disestablished them in the West, and Valens had made bloody inquisition for magic in Syria, both emperors had upon the whole adhered to Valentinian's policy of toleration. Sacrifices were still offered publicly, even at Rome and Alexandria, and victors at Olympia were still recorded, the Eleusinian mysteries still celebrated. Though the schools of Athens were declining, education still remained very much in heathen hands, for monastic jealousy was not yet fully roused against the ancient classics. Heathenism was rather perishing of neglect than sinking under persecution. It was beginning its final retreat to the rude villages and country districts, where it held its ground for a surprising length of time[1], till in the

[1] Notice for example the prohibition of sacrifices by Anthemius in 472, the suppression of the temples at Augila and Philæ in Justinian's time, the continuance of open heathenism in Italy during Gregory's pontificate, and in Spain in the seventh century, and in particular the conversion of the Mainotes in Laconia near the end of the ninth.

end it was quite as much adopted or absorbed as overcome by Christianity.

There was no legal persecution even in the East. Toleration was still the general theory of imperial policy, though Valens had infringed it by frequent exiles of individual bishops[1]. None therefore but the Nicenes gained anything when Gratian proclaimed liberty for all but Anomœans and Photinians. The exiles found little difficulty in resuming the government of their flocks, and even in attacking Arian strongholds with missions like that undertaken by Gregory of Nazianzus at Constantinople. The Macedonians were divided. Large numbers of them joined the Nicenes, and the remainder took up an independent position. Thus the Homœan power in the provinces collapsed of itself before it was touched by persecution. Nor did it even struggle very hard against its fate. Though party spirit ran as high as ever at Jerusalem, and local outrages were perpetrated like the murder of Eusebius of Samosata or the desecration of Gregory's chapel at Constantinople, we find few traces of serious resistance on the part of Arianism.

The young emperor's next step was to share his burden with a colleague. If the care of the whole Empire had been too heavy for Valentinian or Diocletian, Gratian's were not the Atlantean shoulders which could bear its undivided weight. Couriers were sent to Spain in quest of Theodosius, the son of the *magister militum* who had been so unworthily rewarded for his recovery of Britain and Africa[2]. Early in 379 Gratian entrusted to him the conduct of the Gothic war. With it went the Empire of the East, this time including the Illyrian dioceses of Macedonia and Dacia.

---

[1] *C. Th.* xvi. 5, 3 is the only persecuting law dated between 326 and 375. It is an edict of Valentinian against the Manichees: yet Sebastian the Manichee was not displaced from his command in Illyricum. Persecution, however, as we have seen in the reign of Constantius, is not always traceable in the law books.

[2] The execution of the elder Theodosius is by some ascribed to the influence of Valens. Richter *Weström. Reich* 410 points out that the jealousy of Merobaudes may have had something to do with it. We know that the Frankish general favoured Romanus; and he may well have thought strong measures needed against a more active rival than Sebastian. We find no resentment against Merobaudes on the part of Theodosius; but he never was in a position to shew any.

Though Theodosius had seen service before in Mœsia, we may upon the whole regard him as a Western stranger, endued with a full measure of Spanish courage and intolerance. As a general he was the most brilliant Rome had seen since Julian's death. Men compared him to Trajan, and in a happier age he might have rivalled Trajan's fame. But the Empire could not now aspire to wars of conquest. The beaten army was hopelessly demoralized, and could not do more than watch the Goths from Thessalonica and cut off stragglers as occasion served. It was not till Theodosius had formed a new army of barbarian legionaries that the old tradition of Roman superiority resumed its wonted sway. It soon appeared that if the Goths could do nothing with their victory, they would sooner or later have to make their peace with Rome. Theodosius drove them inland in the first campaign; and while he lay sick at Thessalonica in the second, Gratian or his generals received the submission of the Ostrogoths. Fritigern died the same year, and his old rival Athanaric was a fugitive before it ended. When the returning Ostrogoths drove him out from his Transylvanian forests, he was welcomed with honourable courtesy by Theodosius in person at Constantinople. But the old enemy of Rome and Christianity had only come to lay his bones on Roman soil. In another fortnight the barbarian chief was carried out with kingly splendour to his Roman funeral. Theodosius had nobly won Athanaric's inheritance. His wondering Goths at once took service with their conqueror: chief after chief submitted, and the work of peace was completed by Saturninus on the Danube in the autumn of 382[1].

---

[1] The Gothic war of Theodosius is one of the most intricate parts of our history, and I have done no more than trace its course. The accounts of Gibbon, of Pallmann *Völkerwanderung* i. 139—144 and of Wietersheim-Dahn *Völkerwanderung* ii. 64—67 are all corrected by Kaufmann in *Forschungen z. Deutschen Gesch.* xii. 414—438.

One disputed point is whether Athanaric had succeeded Fritigern as chief of the Goths. Here Pallmann and Dahn seem to have the best of it. Kaufmann shews clearly enough that he reached Constantinople as a fugitive; but this does not prove that the Goths generally did not profess to acknowledge him. On the other hand Dahn points out that his treatment by Theodosius implies that he was the real chief. And this consideration seems decisive.

We can now return to ecclesiastical affairs. The dangerous illness of Theodosius in 380 led to important consequences, for his baptism by Ascholius of Thessalonica was the natural signal for a more decided policy. Its first result[1] was a law dated Feb. 27, commanding all men to follow the Nicene doctrine, "committed by the apostle Peter to the Romans and now professed by Damasus of Rome and Peter of Alexandria," and threatening to impose temporal punishments on the heretics. In this it will be noticed that Theodosius abandons Constantine's test of orthodoxy by subscription to a creed, returning to Aurelian's requirement[2] of communion with the chief bishops of Christendom. The choice of Rome is natural, the addition of Alexandria shews that the emperor was still a stranger to the mysteries of Eastern partizanship.

There was no further reason for delay when the worst dangers of the Gothic war had been overcome. Theodosius made his formal entry into Constantinople Nov. 24, 380, and at once required the bishop either to accept the Nicene faith or to leave the city. Demophilus honourably refused to give up his heresy, and adjourned his services to the suburbs. But the mob of Constantinople was still Arian, and their stormy demonstrations when the cathedral of the Twelve Apostles[3] was given up to Gregory of Nazianzus were enough to make Theodosius waver. A milder rescript was issued, and the emperor even consented to an interview with the heresiarch Eunomius, who was then living near Constantinople[4]. This however was prevented by the empress Flacilla, and before long Theodosius took another step. A second edict in Jan. 381 forbade all heretical assemblies inside cities, and ordered the churches everywhere to be given up to the Nicenes[5].

[1] *C. Th.* xvi. 1, 2. Socrates v. 6 puts the baptism of Theodosius "a few days" before Nov. 24: but Soz. vii. 4 dates it before Feb. 27. This seems a more natural arrangement, and is followed by Gibbon and by Wietersheim-Dahn ii. 65.

[2] Eus. *H. E.* vii. 30 οἷς ἂν οἱ κατὰ τὴν Ἰταλίαν καὶ τὴν Ῥωμαίων πόλιν ἐπίσκοποι τοῦ δόγματος ἐπιστέλλοιεν.

[3] Ullmann *Gregorius* 153 for the proof that this was then the cathedral of Constantinople.

[4] Soz. vii. 9. Valesius sets this down for a piece of Anomœan scandal, forgetting that Theodosius hesitated more than four years before finally committing himself to a policy of persecution, and married an Arian wife as late as 387. Kaufmann *Deutsche Gesch.* i. 294 appreciates the position much better.

[5] *C. Th.* xvi. 5, 6. Heretics of

THEODOSIUS AND THE ARIANS.

Thus was Arianism put down as it had been set up, by the civil power. Nothing was left now but to clear away the disorders which the strife had left behind. Once more an imperial summons went forth for a council of the Eastern bishops, to meet in May 381. It was a sombre gathering. The bright hope which lighted the Empire at Nicæa had long ago died out, and the conquerors themselves had no more joyous feeling than that of thankfulness that the weary strife was coming to an end[1]. Only 150 bishops were present, and none of these were Westerns[2]. The Macedonians however mustered 36, under Eleusius of Cyzicus.

The bishops were greeted with much splendour, and received a truly imperial welcome in the form of a new edict against the Manichees[3]. Meletius of Antioch presided in the council, and Paulinus was ignored. Theodosius was no longer neutral. The Egyptians were not invited to the earlier sittings, or at any rate were not present. The first act of the assembly was to ratify the choice of Gregory of Nazianzus as bishop of Constantinople[4]. The next move was to find out whether the Semiarians were willing to share in the Nicene victory. They were still a strong party in the Hellespontine district, so that their friendship was important. Theodosius also was less of a zealot than some of his admirers imagine. The sincerity of his desire to conciliate Eleusius is fairly guaranteed by his effort two years later to find a scheme of comprehension even for the Anomœans.

But the old soldier was not to be tempted by hopes of imperial favour. However he might oppose the Anomœans, he could not forgive the Nicenes their inclusion of the Holy Spirit

---

all sorts are denounced, but only "Photinians, Arians and Eunomians" are specially named. The "Arians" are the Homœans, as in *Can.* 1 Ctp. τὴν τῶν 'Αρειανῶν, εἴτουν Εὐδοξιανῶν.

Godefroy discusses a possible transfer of the edict to June or July. But this breaks the order, and has nothing in its favour.

[1] This is very conspicuous in their letter to Damasus, Theod. v. 9.
[2] Rejecting the signature of *Agrius*

Immontinensis, Thessalonica is the most western see represented. There is really nothing to distinguish the council from many others; and how it was discovered to be œcumenical is not easily explained. It is however so called even in the letter to Damasus.
[3] *C. Th.* xvi. 5, 7.
[4] The intrigue of Maximus the Cynic is discussed by Montaut *Quest. hist.* 97—131. It need not detain us now.

in the sphere of co-essential deity. Those of the Semiarians who were willing to join the Nicenes had already done so, and the rest were obstinate. They withdrew from the council and gave up their churches like the Arians[1].

Whatever jealousies might divide the conquerors, the Arian contest was now at an end. Pontus and Syria were still divided from Rome and Egypt on the question of Paulinus, and there were the germs of many future troubles in the disposition of Alexandria to look for help to Rome against the upstart see of Constantinople. If Peter had been disappointed by his Western allies in the intrigue of Maximus the Cynic, his successors might hope to be more fortunate another time. But against Arianism the council was united. Its first canon was a solemn ratification of the Nicene creed in its original shape[2], and a formal condemnation of all the Arianizing parties. The remainder of the canons deal with various irregularities which had been overlooked during the recent troubles[3].

The council having ratified the emperor's work, it only remained for the emperor to complete that of the council. Another edict in the middle of July[4] forbade Arians of all sorts to build churches even outside cities; and at the end of the

---

[1] Sozomen iv. 27 says that they had neither church nor bishop at Constantinople till the reign of Arcadius. A modern writer repeats his strange statement that this was "owing to the intolerance of the stricter Arians"—under Theodosius, doubtless.

[2] We surely need not condescend to discuss the story that the council of Constantinople solemnly revised the Nicene creed. Dr Hort *Two Dissertations* has conclusively shewn that the document in question is not a revision of the Nicene creed at all, but of Cyril's Jerusalem formula, and that it cannot have had any sanction from the council beyond an incidental approval when Cyril's case came before them.

Bishop Wordsworth (of Lincoln) *Ch. Hist.* ii. 332—5 tells the old story all the better for his ignorance that it had ever been disputed. He only alludes to recent doubts in a postscript. Recently it has found a more serious defender in Bright *Canons of the First Four General Councils*, 80—82. But he lays unaccountable stress on the assertion of Aetius at Chalcedon, makes no new point whatever, and seems not to have met with Dr Hort's decisive work. At any rate, he absolutely fails to touch its arguments. Nor is his own account of the matter free from serious objection. When he tells us that "this creed was in effect the Nicene confession expanded," he forgets that there is something more than expansion in it. Surely Athanasius would have had an anathema for the men who left out the all-important ἐκ τῆς οὐσίας.

[3] Canon 2 deserves notice, for the intrusion of bishops in other men's dioceses was a chronic difficulty in times of persecution. The Meletian schism in Egypt had arisen from just this cause, and the council was fortunate in escaping a repetition of it.

[4] *C. Th.* xvi. 5, 7.

month Theodosius issued an amended definition of orthodoxy[1]. The true faith was henceforth to be guarded by the demand of communion, no longer with Rome and Alexandria, but with Constantinople, Alexandria, and the principal bishops of the East.

As far as mere numbers went, the cause of Arianism was not hopeless even yet. It was still fairly strong in Asia, and counted adherents as far west as the banks of the Danube[2]. At Constantinople it could raise dangerous riots, and at the court of Milan it had a strong supporter in the empress Justina. But its fate was none the less a mere question of time. Its cold logic generated no such fiery enthusiasm as sustained the African Donatists, and its recent origin allowed no venerable traditions to grow up like those of heathenism, while its imperial claims and past successes cut it off from the appeal of Nestorians and Monophysites in the next century to provincial separatism. When therefore the last overtures of Theodosius fell through in 383, the heresy was quite unable to bear the strain of persecution.

But if Arianism ceased in a few years to be a power inside the Empire, it still remained the faith of the barbarian invaders. The work of Ulfilas was not in vain. Roman law concerned the Romans only, for even Justinian never ventured to meddle with the belief of his Gothic soldiers. They remained privileged heretics in the midst of the orthodox Empire, for the most intolerant of Byzantine sovereigns never disdained the services of stout misbelievers like Aligern or Harold Hardrada[3].

---

[1] *C. Th.* xvi. 1, 3. The choice of bishops appears to be determined partly by their own importance, partly by that of their sees. Gregory of Nyssa may represent one class, Helladius of Cæsarea the other.

Some of the omissions are remarkable. Antioch and Jerusalem may have been left out on account of the special relation of the council to Flavian and Cyril, though this would have been as good a reason for omitting Constantinople itself. Ephesus again may have had a Semiarian bishop, but Euphrasius of Nicomedia signs the canons. We shall hardly go far wrong if we suppose that he was omitted in order to leave a clear field for the supremacy of Constantinople. In the same way Marcianopolis and Tomi are represented, but no bishopric south of the Balkans.

[2] Palladius and Secundianus were mere outliers, as is stated by the Aquileian bishops in Ambrose *Ep.* 12 *per Occidentales partes duobus in angulis tantum, hoc est in latere Daciæ Ripensis ac Mœsiæ, fidei obstrepi videbatur*, and more than once elsewhere.

[3] Kaufmann *Deutsche Gesch.* ii. 95.

In the fifth century the Teutonic conquest of the West gave Arianism another lease of power. Once more the heresy was supreme at Ravenna, Toulouse and Carthage. To the barbarian as well as to the heathen it was a half-way halting place on the road to Christianity. Yet to the barbarian also it proved only a source of weakness. It lived on and in its turn perpetuated the feud between the Roman and the Teuton which involved the destruction of the earlier Teutonic kingdoms in Western Europe. The provincials or their children might forget the wrongs of conquest, but heresy was a standing insult to the Roman world. Religious disaffection was a growing trouble even to Theodoric, and his successors were much less able than himself to overcome it. Totila was a model of barbarian justice; yet even Totila could never venture to arm the provincials against the orthodox oppressor. And if the isolation of Arianism fostered the beginnings of a native literature[1], it also blighted every hope of future growth. The Goths were not inferior in capacity to the English, yet their history can boast no native names to compare with those of Bede or Cædmon. Jordanis is not much to set against them, and even Jordanis was not an Arian.

The sword of Belisarius did but lay open the internal disunion of Italy and Africa. The Vandal kingdom disappeared at a blow, and all the valour of the Ostrogoths availed only to win for theirs a downfall of heroic grandeur. As the last desperate struggle for a nation's life, the battle of the Lactarian mountain may take its place in history beside the fall of Carthage or Jerusalem. Ildibad and Totila, Teja and Aligern fought in vain. Sooner or later every Arian nation had to purge itself of heresy or vanish from the earth. Even the distant Visigoths were forced to see that Arians could not hold Spain. Franks and Romans together almost overcame the strong Leovigild, and his successor prudently gave up the hopeless cause. The Lombards in Italy were its last defenders: and they too yielded a few years later to the efforts of

---

[1] The scholar will hardly need to be reminded that the noble Codex Argenteus appears to date from the reign of Theodoric in Italy. A Roman education was not unfrequent: King Theodahad was respectable for his learning, if for nothing else.

Gregory and queen Theodelinda. Of continental Teutons the Franks alone escaped the plague of Arianism. It was in the strength of orthodoxy that they drove the conquerors of Rome before them on the field of Vouglé, and brought the green standard of the Prophet to a halt upon the Loire. The Franks were neither better nor more civilized than the Ostrogoths and Lombards; so that it was nothing but their orthodoxy which won for them the prize Theodoric and Aistulf had missed, and brought them through a long career of victory to that proud day of culminating triumph when the strife of ages was forgotten, and Arianism with it, when after three hundred years of desolating anarchy the Latin and the Teuton joined to vindicate for Old Rome her just inheritance, and to set the holy diadem of empire on the head of Karl the Frank.

Now that we have traced the history of Arianism to its final overthrow, let us once more glance at the causes of its failure. Arianism was an illogical compromise. It went too far for heathenism, not far enough for Christianity. It conceded Christian worship to the Lord, though it made Him no better than a heathen demigod. As a scheme of Christianity it was overmatched at every point by the Nicene doctrine, as a concession to heathenism it was outbid by the growing worship of saints and relics. Debasing as was the error of turning saints into demigods, it seems to have shocked Christian feeling less than the Arian audacity which degraded the Lord of Saints to the level of His creatures.

The crowning weakness of Arianism was the incurable badness of its method. Even apart from Christianity, we may well believe that some mysterious plan runs through the vast complex of life around us, and that some high power watches over its majestic evolution. Nature indeed may not know that power's name; but if we are verily the sons of God in Christ, we know that truth in all its forms in more than worldwide range expresses but a single purpose of eternal Love. Thus the theologian's problem is not so far removed from that of the historian or the zoologist, or any other man of science. His data are partly the same, his method is wholly analogous. He has treasures which peradventure they have not; but he is unworthy of his prerogative among them if he ventures to imagine that their work does not concern him. Even the theologian must be a learner like the rest, and if need be learn from them the scientific spirit of patient reverence and wary independence. The Lord's freedman cannot lord it over others without himself becoming the slave of men. "Unanimous consent of Fathers" can no more "prove" the Chalcedonian system than the Ptolemaic; and it is mere irreverence to look upon the fluctuating majorities of arbitrarily selected councils as the proper mouthpiece of God's Holy Spirit. The Gnostic had some excuse for making nature and "history give place to dogma"; but for Christians to do the same is to glory in the falsehood of our dogma, to renounce our Master's teaching, and to make our God a liar. Not even a revelation from above can dispense us from the elementary duty of receiving truth from whatever quarter it may come to us.

Now whatever were the errors of Athanasius—and on details they were not a few—his work was undoubtedly a faithful search for truth by every means attainable to him. Little as he knew of nature, that little has its place in his theology. In breadth of view as well as grasp of doctrine he is beyond comparison with the rabble of controversialists who cursed or still invoke his name. It was far otherwise with the Arians. On one side their doctrine was a mass of presumptuous theorizing, supported by alternate scraps of obsolete traditionalism and uncritical text-mongering, on the other it was a lifeless system of unspiritual pride and hard unlovingness. And therefore Arianism perished.

So too every system of science or theology must likewise perish which presumes like Arianism to discover in the feeble brain of man a law to circumscribe the revelation of our Father's love in Christ.

NOTE M.

THE CHRONOLOGY OF THE COUNCIL OF LAMPSACUS.

THE above account of the council of Lampsacus is mostly derived from Sozomen vi. 7. He seems usually well informed on the Semiarian movements, and in this case is incidentally supported by Philostorgius ix. 3, who complains that Valens "honoured Eudoxius" on his return from Illyricum before the rising of Procopius, and therefore towards the end of 364.

Socrates iv. 2—4 gives a different account. He tells us that the Macedonians came and asked Valens for a new council shortly after his return from Illyricum. The emperor gave permission in ignorance of their quarrel with Eudoxius, and hurried ($\tilde{\eta}$ τάχος) to Antioch, where he carried on a vigorous persecution of the Nicenes. The council was held in 365 (consuls named), during the Procopian troubles, in the seventh year from the council of Seleucia, and Valens quashed its decisions after the civil war.

Before discussing this further, let us note the agreement of Socrates with Sozomen in telling us that Valens reached Antioch in 365 and carried on a persecution there. They may give an exaggerated account of it, but there seems no reason to doubt the fact. In Ammianus xxvi. 6, 11 : 7, 2 Valens is *consumpta hieme festinans in Syriam*, and yet in October we find him at Cæsarea Mazaca, waiting for cooler weather to cross the Cilician marshes. Ammianus therefore leaves ample time for the spring visit to Antioch recorded by Socrates and Sozomen.

Other traces of such a visit may be pointed out. (1) *C. Th.* xii. 6, 5 is dated from Cæsarea, July 4. If Valens left the capital when the winter was over, he must have reached Cæsarea before July; and if he was in a hurry, he would hardly wait there three months longer. The law is therefore best assigned to his return from Syria. (2) *C. Th.* xii. 6, 8 (= *C. Just.* x. 70, 2) is dated from Constantinople, July 30. The date is faulty, for the law before it is dated Aug. 4; but Godefroy *Chronol.* lxxiv. does not mend the matter by reading *reddita* for *data*. However this may be, the order of the *Codex* positively fixes it somewhere between July 18 and Aug. 31. During this interval then Valens must have visited Constantinople. We have also (3) the account of the *Hist. Aceph.* on which (Sievers *Einl.* § 18) Sozomen is possibly dependent. According to this, a rescript of Valens reached Alexandria May 5, which ordered the expulsion of all bishops "who had been ejected by Constantius and restored by Julian." The populace maintained that this did not apply to Athanasius, and the question was referred back to Valens, whose answer was received June 8. From this we may infer (*a*) that the rescript was issued either before Mar. 19 (when Valens was still at Constantinople) or not long after, (*b*) that it was aimed at Semiarians as well as Nicenes, (*c*) that Valens was most likely in Asia towards the end of May, for time must be allowed for the riots at Alexandria before Flavianus ventured to send off the appeal.

These conclusions harmonize perfectly with all our data except the time fixed by Socrates for the operations of the Semiarians. If Valens was under the influence of Eudoxius at Antioch, that influence must have been established before he left Constantinople, as it might well have been during a stay of more than three months.

It may further be noted (*a*) that Socrates is frequently inaccurate when he ventures to fix a consulship, (*b*) that Basil *Ep.* 223 seems to imply that some conference at Heraclea succeeded the council of Lampsacus.

It may also be well to add that Hefele *Councils* § 88 has made no serious attempt to observe any chronological order.

There is not much to be said on the other side. Godefroy (on Philost. ix. 5) has a theory that Procopius seized the capital as early as July or August, but the Idatian *Fasti* give Sept. 28 for the date; and this is confirmed by the statement of Ammianus xxvi. 5, 8 that the news reached Valentinian near Paris at the end of October.

NOTE N. THE STORY OF THE EIGHTY CLERICS.

To this period belongs the story of the eighty clerics burnt at sea by Modestus. It is the worst story connected with the reign of Valens. Fortunately it seems unhistorical.

Socrates iv. 16 and Sozomen vi. 14 relate it between the death of Eudoxius in 370 and the meeting of Basil and Valens in 372; and it is further determined for 370—1 by the emperor's presence at

Nicomedia, and by the attendance at Modestus, who only became prefect at the end of 369. Theodoret iv. 24 lays the scene at Constantinople, and puts it later. An allusion may be found (so Zonaras xiii. 16) in Greg. Naz. *Or.* xliii. 46, πρεσβυτέρων ἐμπρησμοὶ θαλάττιοι, perhaps also in Greg. Nyss. *in Eunomium* i. p. 289, μετὰ τὰς τραγῳδίας ἐκείνας, ἃς κατὰ Βιθυνίαν ἐξειργάσατο. Some will discover yet another in Epiph. *Hær.* 69, 13 ὅσα γέγονε...ἐν Νικομηδείᾳ. We may add that the famine in Phrygia which followed may be that of 373; and that Modestus was *aptus ad hæc et similia*, as Ammianus xix. 12, 6 says of his doings on the Scythopolis commission in 359.

Richter *Weström. Reich* (note 132) rejects the whole story without discussion: but so far all seems clear and circumstantial. There are only two objections; and these seem fatal.

In the first place the story is one of the very worst on record. Such a wholesale butchery of ecclesiastics might have staggered Galerius himself, and could scarcely have failed to bring a curse on Valens from every writer of the time. Ammianus and Libanius were not wanting in humanity, Rufinus and Chrysostom in hatred of the persecutors; yet one and all they pass it over. Still more unaccountable is the silence of Basil if so monstrous a crime was really carried out; and his friendly correspondence with Modestus is surely something worse than unaccountable.

Another difficulty is pointed out by Sievers *Libanius* 231. When Gregory of Nazianzus *Or.* xxv. 10 is saying the worst he can of Valens, he distinctly tells us that a single presbyter (τῶν πρεσβυτέρων ἕνα) was burnt at sea. The plural in *Or.* xliii. will therefore be a rhetorical flourish. Ultimately then the whole story comes to rest on the single authority (not Rufinus this time) followed by Socrates and Sozomen.

Upon the whole it seems to be a true story grossly exaggerated— one victim grown into eighty. Bad as it is at best, it is no more than the ordinary barbarity of the criminal law; and in the absence of better information, we cannot even be sure that religion had anything to do with the matter more than in the case of Artemius.

NOTE O. EUSTATHIUS OF SEBASTIA.

THE common account of Eustathius is an enigma. Such a record of meaningless instability in a man of his high character reads more like satire than history. Perhaps however he was not so fickle after all. His changes become fairly intelligible if we suppose that his adoption of Macedonian views was gradual. He started from a neutral position (Socr. ii. 45) about 364, and by 377 had become (Basil *Ep.* 263) "a ringleader of the Macedonians." Towards Basil he was drawn by old friendship and a common love of asceticism, but equally repelled by the imperious orthodoxy of a stronger will than his own. Two ascetics are sure to have misunderstandings; and in this case there was a growing difference of doctrine to widen the breach.

Some such view of him is suggested by the following considerations—

(1) Eustathius was not at all " one of those who are usually to be found on the side of authority." We cannot set down as a mere timeserver the man who defended Semiarianism at Seleucia and Tyana, who supported Basil (*Ep.* 79) in the crisis of his strife with Valens, and who was content to remain for nearly ten years in consistent opposition to the court. If he ultimately yielded at Constantinople in 360, we have already seen that he did not sign another Homœan creed before his quarrel with Basil.

(2) We really cannot ascribe to Eustathius the unmeaning folly of coming to Nicopolis in 373 with the deliberate purpose of first signing and then disavowing the stringent confession we find in Basil *Ep.* 125. His relations with his old friend were already seriously strained by the affair of Sophronius (Basil *Ep.* 119) and by the misunderstanding of the year before; and if he was now persuaded by importunity to sign for the second time in his life what he ought not to have signed, we know that there were plenty of mischiefmakers at Sebastia ready to inflame his resentment into an open quarrel.

(3) And such a quarrel might easily carry him over to the Homœan side. However rudely Basilides and Ecdicius might treat him, they did not ask him like Basil to strain his conscience. The formula laid before him at Cyzicus contained nothing offensive to him. Its $\H{o}\mu o\iota o\nu$ $\kappa\alpha\tau$' $o\vec{\upsilon}\sigma\iota\alpha\nu$ was exactly the Nicene $\H{o}\mu oo\vec{\upsilon}\sigma\iota o\nu$ in the sense adopted by the Semiarians, and its denial of the Holy Spirit was quite consistent with his confession to Liberius. Rather the Nicene doctrine on the subject was a growing offence to the $\mu\epsilon\sigma\acute{o}\tau\eta s$ on which Eustathius (Basil *Ep.* 128) prided himself as much as Sophronius of Pompeiopolis and the rest of the Macedonians. Full discussion in Loofs *Eustathius v. Sebaste.*

APPENDIX I.

THE GREAT OFFICIALS OF THE EMPIRE DURING THE REIGNS OF
CONSTANTIUS AND VALENS. A.D. 337—378.

In the absence of any indication to the contrary, it will be understood that the data of the following table are derived from the inscriptions of the laws in the *Codex Theodosianus*. These however have come down to us in a very corrupt state, and the errors not unfrequently seem beyond the reach of critical emendation. Account however has been taken of the labours of Godefroy, Tillemont, Clinton and Haenel, of the Benedictine life of Basil, and of the admirable *Leben des Libanius* of Sievers.

Of contemporary writers Ammianus and Libanius are by far the most important, though much help has been derived from the inscriptions collected by Boeckh and Orelli. A secondary rank may be assigned to Athanasius and the ecclesiastical historians, to Julian and Eunapius, while stray facts may be gleaned from almost every writer of our period, from the late Byzantines, and even from Moses of Chorene and the Jerusalem Talmud.

There are few special helps for the individual sections of the table. In the case however of the urban prefects we have a list as far as 354 in the Ravenna Chronographer of that year, with Mommsen's discussion of it; also monographs by Corsini and Léotard; and in that of the *magistri militum* the tangle is partially unravelled by Bethmann-Hollweg *Römischer Civilprozess*, iii. 81—83; but there is still much wanting.

The sign † denotes a Christian, ‡ a heathen; the remainder are unknown, except that Sebastian was a Manichee. Renegades are noted according to their profession for the time being, and barbarian *magistri militum* are given in italics.

§ 1.

PRÆFECTUS URBIS ROMÆ.

L. Aradius Valerius Proculus Populonius, Mar. 337—Jan. 338[1].
Mecilius Hilarianus, Jan. 338—July 339[2].
L. Turcius Apronianus, July—Oct. 339[3].
‡ Tib. Fabius Titianus, Oct. 339—Feb. 341[9].
Aurelius Celsinus, Feb. 341—Apr. 342.
Fl. Lollianus Mavortius, Apr.—July 342[4].
? ‡ Aconius Catullinus, July 342—Apr. 344[5].
Quintus Junius Rusticus, Apr. 344—July 345.
Petronius Probinus, July 345—Dec. 346[6].
‡ M. Mæcius Memmius Furius Balbinus Cæcilianus Placidus, Dec. 346—June 347[7].
Ulpius Limenius, June 347—Apr. 349[8].
(Interval of 41 days.)
Hermogenes, May 349—Feb. 27, 350.
‡ Tib. Fabius Titianus II., Feb. 27, 350—Mar. 1, 351[9].
Aurelius Celsinus II., Mar. 1—May 351.
Cœlius Probatus, May—June 351[9a].
Clodius Adelfius, June—Dec. 351[10].
Valerius Proculus II., Dec. 351—Sept. 9, 352.

---

[1] Consul 341. He seems from Orelli 3672 (where the date is wrong) to have held also a prætorian prefecture at some time or other.

[2] Consul 342.

[3] The prefecture of Apronianus is mentioned in Orelli 603, 1099, 1100, 6475. *C. Th.* xi. 30, 18 *Anicio Juliano P.U.* June 339 belongs to 326.

[4] On Lollianus, § 3[5].

[5] Consul 349. Mentioned Orelli 2361: Prætextatus married his daughter. Some error in the title of *C. Th.* xv. 8, 1 *ad Severum P.U.*, which being dated from Hierapolis in July 343, cannot refer to Rome at all.

[6] Consul 341. Orelli 4035.

[7] Consul 343. Augur in Orelli 3191, where his name is given at length. *C. Th.* xvi. 10, 3 *ad Catullinum P.U.* in Nov. 346 must be removed to 342. Henzen distinguishes the Placidus of Orelli 5699.

[8] Corsini *de Præf. Urb.* notices the remarkable union of the urban and Italian prefectures by Limenius and his successor Hermogenes. We have a Limenius proconsul of Constantinople, who expelled Libanius early in 343, and a Limenius consul in 349. Sievers *Libanius* 53 identifies the two: but since the other consul Catullinus was a western official, it is safer (so Corsini) to keep them distinct.

[9] Titianus in Orelli 17 repairs a temple as P. U. in 341 or 350. Henzen refers to him the lacuna in Orelli 5587 *Præf. urbi iterum*, apparently under Magnentius: but it would equally suit Proculus or Celsinus.

[9a] Aurelius Victor *Cæs.* 42 *cæso Urbi præfecto* in the riot of Nepotianus. The time of year would suit Cœlius Probatus, and so Valesius understands it. But the riot is firmly settled for 350 (Zos. ii. 48—Magnentius not left Gaul; Jerome *Chron.*, Idat. *Chron. Pasch.*), and Ammianus xxviii. 1, 1 *sexto decimo anno et eo diutius* (referring to 368) is too vague to warrant us in putting it later.

[10] Ammianus xvi. 6, 2.

APPENDIX I.

Septimius Mnasea, Sept. 9—26, 352.
Neratius Cerealis, Sept. 26, 352—Dec. 353[11].
‡ Memmius Vitrasius Orfitus, Dec. 353—Mar. July 355[12].
Leontius, 355, Nov. 356[13].
? Decimus Simonius Julianus, Feb. 357[14].
‡ Memmius Vitrasius Orfitus II., June, July, Oct. 357, June 358, Mar. 359[12].
† Junius Bassus, died Aug. 25, 359[15].
‡ Tertullus, Oct. 359, Dec. 361[16].
‡ Clytholias Maximus, Dec. 361, Feb. 363[17].
‡ Apronianus, Feb. 363, 364[18].

[11] Consul 358. Uncle of Gallus (Ammianus xiv. 11, 27) *C. Th.* vii. 20, 7 *Evagrio P. U.* in Aug. 353 must be altered to *Pf. P.* (of Italy). We have Orelli 1101 to Constantius by Cerealis.
Jerome *Ep.* 127 *ad Principiam* names him as a suitor of Marcella.

[12] The first prefecture of Orfitus seems fairly marked. Removing to 354 a few laws addressed to him in 353, we find the other limit of his tenure in *C. Th.* xiv. 3, 2, in June 355. *C. Th.* ix. 17, 3 must be removed to 357.
Then *C. Th.* xi. 34, 2 (Jan. 355) and *C. Just.* vi. 22, 6 (Feb. 355) in which Volusianus is addressed as P. O. and P. U. are to be explained by iii. 12, 2 (April 355), where he is only *Vicarius urbis*. Probably also *C. Th.* xi. 36, 11, and two other laws dated in July: but Volusianus may have held the prefecture for a short time before Leontius. There is more difficulty in Orelli 5587 *Fabius Felix Pasiphilus Paulinus P.U.*, dated May 31, 355, which seems to require a change in *C. Th.* xiv. 3, 2.
The second prefecture of Orfitus is clear enough at the visit of Constantius to Rome, and may have extended to Mar. 359. In *C. Th.* xiii. 5, 9 *Olybrio P. U.* Godefroy reads *Orfito*. To the second term of Orfitus belong Orelli 3184 (Orf. priest of Vesta), 3185, 5585. Q. Aur. Symmachus P.U. 384, 418 (*Epp.*ix.131, x. 54) married Rusticiana, the daughter of Orfitus. Orelli 3181 is a few years earlier.

[13] Leontius first appears *C. Th.* viii. 18, 5 in Apr. 349 as *comes Orientis*. In 353 he was sent out to replace Montius as quæstor in Syria (Ammianus xiv. 11, 14), and no doubt returned with Gallus to Europe in the autumn of 354. We find him (Ammianus xv. 7, 1 ; 6) P. U. after the revolt of Silvanus in the spring of 355, and again at the exile of Liberius.
C. Th. xvi. 2, 13 *ad Leontium P. U.* must be removed to 356, for Leontius was no longer P. U. in Nov. 357.

[14] Corsini *de Præf. Urbana* 215— 220, on the authority of (*a*) Inscription at Thermæ which calls him *præses Daciarum.* (*b*) Inscription in Etruria which calls him *P. U.* (*c*) *C. Th.* xiv. 1, 1 *sublimitas tua* suits the dignity of P. U. If so, Julianus will divide the second prefecture of Orfitus in two.

[15] Ammianus xvii. 11, 5. Orelli, 2527 *Junius Bassus in ipsa præfectura urbis neofitus iit ad Deum*, dated Aug. 25, 359. Hence not the Terracius Bassus P. U. of Orelli 6430, Ammianus xxviii. 1, 27, Symm. *Ep.* x. 43.

[16] Ammianus xix. 10, 1 ; xxi. 10, 7. His heathenism is shewn by Ammianus xix. 1, 4.

[17] Symmachus *Ep.* x. 54. He was a nephew of Vulcatius Rufinus (Ammianus xxi. 12, 24), and therefore a first cousin of Gallus. Probably heathen, being Julian's nominee.

[18] The appointment of Apronianus is recorded by Ammianus xxiii. 1, 4 after the death of Julian the *comes Orientis :* but *C. Th.* v. 12, 1 *ad Maximum P. U.*, dated Feb. 26, 363, shews that it must have been one of the emperor Julian's last acts before quitting Antioch. Ammianus xxvi. 3, 1 names him again in 364. Orelli 3166 is referred to this Apronianus rather than to his father (P. U. in 339). His second prefecture in 372 depends on *C. Just.* i. 40, 5, *ad Apronianum P. U.* where however Godefroy *Prosopogr.* conjectures *Ampelium.*

‡ L. Aur. Avianius Symmachus, Apr. 364—May 365 (or later)[19].
Lampadius 366[20].
Viventius, Dec. 366, Apr., May 367[21].
‡ Vettius Agorius Prætextatus, Aug., Oct., Dec. 367, Jan., Sept. 368[22].
‡ Clodius Hermogenianus Cæsarius Olybrius, Jan. 369—Aug. 370[23].
Ampelius, Jan. 371—July 372[24].
Bappo, Aug. 372.
? Apronianus II., 372[18].
‡ Ceionius Rufius Albinus Volusianus, Feb.—Sept. 373[25].

[19] The offices held by Symmachus are recounted by Orelli 1186, but his consulship is not easily dated. As he succeeded Apronianus (Ammianus xxvii. 3, 3), we may presume that Volusianus was only *Vicarius Præfecturæ Urbis* in April 364, when *C. Th.* xi. 14, 1 was addressed to him. We may also safely follow Godefroy in reading *Symmachum* in the title of *C. Th.* xiv. 3, 7 *ad Viventium P. U.*, dated Oct. 364.

Next comes the usual medley of laws which ought *not* to be dated in 365. We may refer *C. Th.* viii. 5, 25 *ad Symmachum correctorem Lucaniæ* to his son Q. Aur. Symmachus. Sundry laws addressed between Feb. and Sept. to Volusianus may be removed to 373. Next *C. Th.* i. 6, 6 *ad Prætextatum P. U.* in Sept. must be transferred to 368, while *C. Th.* xi. 31, 3 and others *ad Olybrium P. U.* between March and Aug. will belong to 370.

[20] Ammianus xxvii. 3, 5 *Lampadius ex-Pf. P.* (Italy in 354).

[21] Succeeded Lampadius before Dec. 366 (Ammianus xxvii. 3, 11: mentioned by Symmachus *Ep.* x. 50). Then *C. Th.* ix. 40, 10 *ad Prætextatum P. U.* must belong to Oct. 367.

There is more difficulty in *C. Th.* ix. 1, 9 *ad Valerianum P. U.* in Dec. 366. It is not likely that Ammianus has overlooked him. Corsini de *Præf. Urb.* 239 calls him Severianus and doubts him : indeed there is no proof from Symm. *Ep.* iii. 87 that a Severianus was P. U. about this time. Nor can we read *Volusianum* and shift to 371. Upon the whole Godefroy's view is the best, that Valerianus (*C. Th.* i. 16, 10 *ad Valerianum Vicarium Hispaniarum* in 365) was *Vicarius Præfecturæ urbi* in the interval between Lampadius and Prætextatus. See Haenel's notes.

[22] Prætextatus is mentioned Boeckh 2594, Orelli 2362 (priest of Bacchus) 2354 (augur, tauroboliated, &c. and twice Pf. P. of Italy and Illyricum before 387). Then *C. Th.* xiii. 3, 8 *ad Prætextatum P. U.* must be thrown back to Jan. 368.

[23] We must remove to 370 all the laws addressed to Olybrius in 365; also *C. Th.* xi. 31, 5, dated in Aug. 373. *C. Th.* xii. 1, 72 *ad Olybrium consularem Tusciæ* also needs correction : but it may best be placed in 373, in order to keep the order.

Olybrius was in weak health during his prefecture, so that his power was mostly exercised by the savage Maximin. Ammianus xxviii. 1, 4 ; 12, xxix. 2, 3 distinctly marks the vicarious character of Maximin's authority, and the *Chron. Pasch.* puts the severities of Valentinian in 369. Similarly we may explain *C. Th.* xiii. 3, 10 *ad Principium P. U.* in Apr. 370 (removing a difficulty of Clinton *F. R.* ii. 118).

Orelli 4321 gives his name as Pf. P. and P. U. on a dog's collar (*noli me tenere : non exped(i)et*). The former dignity is not easy to verify. Olybrius was consul with Ausonius in 379. The name Cæsarius comes from Orelli 1900. It scarcely refers to Olybrius the son of Probus, consul 395.

[24] *C. Just.* i. 40, 5 *ad Apronianum P. U.* in May 372. Godefroy reads *Ampelium*.

[25] The years 365, 368, and 370 being occupied by Symmachus, Prætextatus and Olybrius, the laws addressed between Feb. and Sept. 365 to Volusianus must be referred to 373.

A genealogy of Volusianus is given

APPENDIX I. 283

Eupraxius, Feb. 374[26].
Claudius, May 374[27].
? Maximinus, Nov. 374, Apr. 376[28].
Rufinus, July 376[29].
† Publicola Gracchus, Dec. 376, Jan. 377[28].
Probianus, Sept. 377[30].
Marinus, Mar. 378.

§ 2.

PRÆFECTUS PRÆTORIO GALLIARUM.

Aurelius Celsinus, June 338, Jan. 339[1].
? Antonius Marcellinus, Apr., June 340[2].

by Itasius Lemniacus on Rutilius Namatianus *de reditu suo* i. 168. We find him in Orelli 2305 priest of Sun, in 2355 *P. U.* and *Pf. P.* and tauroboliated in 370. The Rufia Volusiana tauroboliated in the same year with her husband (Orelli 6040) may have been his daughter. There is no other trace of him as Pf. P. except *C. Just.* i. 19, 5, *ad Volusianum P. O.* dated from Rome, Sept. 18, 365. As Valentinian never visited Rome, and 365, 368, 370 and 373 are all for various reasons inadmissible, there seems no choice but to alter the inscription.

[26] Also Orelli 1116, as Henzen supplies the lacuna.

[27] Allusions in Ammianus xxvii. 3, 2, xxix. 6, 17; perhaps also Symmachus *Ep.* i. 28. There seems to be some error in *C. Just.* i. 4, 2 (copied vii. 65, 4ᵇ) *ad Claudium P. P.* in July 369. Similarly *C. Th.* xi. 36, 20 *ad Claudianum P. U.* of the same date and on the same subject. Can they be for *Clodius* Herm. Olybrius?

[28] If Maximin (or Maximus) was ever P. U. he may come in here. His career is traced by Ammianus xxviii. 1.

In the *C. Th.* we find him ix. 1, 8, *corrector Tusciæ* in Nov. 366, and *præf. annonæ* at Rome 368—370. He seems also to have been *vicarius urbis* during the illness of Olybrius, and *Cod. Vatic.* in Haenel *Index Legum* 224 as late as 371, when Ampelius was P. U. In 372 he was Pf. P. (Ammianus xxix. 3, 1; 4: 6, 3. Jerome *Chron.* 372) in Gaul (Jurisdiction at Mogontiacum), while at Rome he was replaced by Ursicinus as *præf. annonæ*

(*C. Th.* xiv. 3, 14, in Feb. 372) and by Simplicius as *vicarius urbis* (Ammianus xxviii. 1, 45, *C. Th.* ix. 29, 1, in Mar. 374).

The question is closely connected with that of the prefecture of Gracchus, on which see Godefroy on *C. Th.* ii. 2, 1; and for the other side Vallarsi on Jerome *Ep.* 107 *ad Lætam*, where Gracchus is dated after 378. In any case the present is the latest possible date of Maximin as P. U., for (Ammianus xxviii. 1, 53) he was executed by Gratian. Corsini *de Præf. Urb.* 239 puts him in 366, which cannot be admitted. The error comes from Rufinus ii. 10, copied by Socr. and Soz.

[29] Here Corsini inserts Rufinus the ex-P. U. mentioned by Symmachus, *Ep.* vii. 126. So also *C. Th.* i. 6, 7.

Vindaonius Magnus (another of Corsini's prefects) belongs to Constantinople.

[30] On Petronius Probianus some indifferent verses of the elder Symmachus *Ep.* i. 2.

---

[1] Godefroy leaves it undecided which prefecture Celsinus held. But from *C. Th.* xii. 1, 7, *Have Celsine*, which concerns the *curiales* of Carthage, and is dated by Constantine II. from Trier in Jan. 339, it seems safest to assign him the Gaulish prefecture, for the moment including Africa.

[2] With some hesitation I place here the name of Marcellinus, to whom *C. Th.* xi. 12, 1, and vi. 22, 3, are addressed. The former law seems from its allusion to *publicus et noster inimicus*

‡ Ti. Fabius Titianus, June 343, 344, May, Nov. 349[3].
Vulcatius Rufinus, Dec. 349, summer 350, summer 354, 356[4].
Honoratus[5].
Florentius, summer 357, 359, Jan. 360[5].

(which Godefroy refers to Constantine II.) to suit the Gaulish prefecture. Antonius Marcellinus (Orelli 4035, for the *prænomen*) was consul in 341.

This Marcellinus will be distinct from the contriver of the Magnentian plot, who was *comes S. L.* in Jan. 350, (Zos. ii. 41), *magister officiorum* a few months later (Zos. ii. 43: defeat of Nepotianus), and disappeared at Mursa. The office indeed of *comes S. L.* was sometimes held by ex-prefects (Germanianus and perhaps Florentius under Valentinian): but in this case the interval of time seems too great.

A third Marcellinus was *præses Phœniciæ* in 342, and *comes Orientis* in 349.

Paulinus *Vita Ambrosii* 3, gives the Gaulish prefecture to the saint's father Ambrosius at the time of his birth. This may fall in 333, or more likely 340. But Paulinus is very inaccurate, and may have placed Ambrosius in a higher rank than he really held. In the same way Jerome, *Chron.* 335 assigns it to Tiberianus, who appears in *C. Th.* iii. 5, 6, as *Vicarius Hispaniarum* in 335–6.

[3] Consul 337. *C. Th.* xii. 1, 36, *ad Titianum* (rank omitted) in June, 343, supported by Jerome *Chron.* 344.

The other dates (May, Nov. 349) depend on *C. Th.* vii. 1, 2, and ix. 24, 2, emended. We have *C. Th.* ii. 1, 1, *ad Eustathium P. O.*, dated March 349, and published at Rome. Here however (Tillemont *Empereurs*, iv. 672) we must read *C. R. P.* for (*a*) the prefectures of Rome and Italy are accounted for in 349, (*b*) we find Eustathius *comes R. P.* about 345 in Philost. iii. 12, and *C. Th.* x. 10, 7.

[4] Uncle of Gallus (Ammianus xiv. 11, 27). Orelli 5583 seems to imply that he was Pf. P. (of Italy, to judge from the allusion of *C. Th.* xi. 1, 6, where see Godefroy's note) before his consulship in 347. The dates given depend—Dec. 349, on *C. Just.* vi. 62, 3 (when Hermogenes held Italy); 350 on Peter Patricius, p. 129, Bonn Edition; 354 and 356 on Ammianus, xiv. 10, 4 and xvi. 8, 13. Rufinus seems to have been an unpolitical character, acceptable both to Magnentius and to Constantius, and afterwards to Valentinian; hence it is not unlikely that he remained in office from 349 to 356 without a break.

Godefroy transfers to 352 the laws *C. Th.* vi. 35, 3 and iii. 5, 2 *ad Rufinum P. P.*, dated in April and May, 319. But thus he breaks the order. He forgets moreover that Constantius could have had no power over the Gaulish prefect in 352.

The following genealogy may be given:

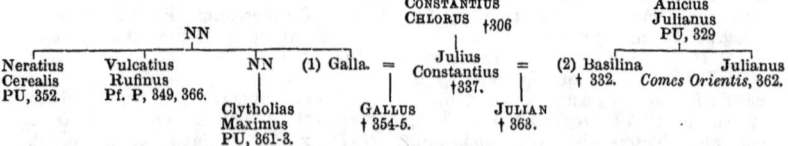

Rufinus and Cerealis were certainly brothers of Galla; but perhaps only by marriage.

[5] Libanius *Ep.* 389, and Jerome *Chron.* 360, imply that Honoratus held the Gaulish prefecture. If so, it must have been between his proconsulship at Constantinople in 354 and his appointment to the East in 359. Then he must come before Florentius, who was prefect (Ammianus xvi. 12, 14), before the battle of Argentoratum in 357, and remained in office till his flight in Jan. 360 (Ammianus xx. 8, 20).

APPENDIX I.

Nebridius, 360, summer 361[6].
‡ Fl. Sallustius, 361, Jan.—Sept. 362[7].
‡ Germanianus, Dec. 362—Apr. 366[8].
‡ ? Probus, May 366[9].
Florentius, June 367[10].
Viventius, Apr. ? Sept. 368—May 371[8].
Maximinus, 371—373[11].
Antonius, Sept. 376—Dec. 378.
† D. Magnus Ausonius, 378[12].

§ 3.

PRÆFECTUS PRÆTORIO ITALIÆ.

‡ Aconius Catullinus, June 341[1].

It is not likely that Sallust held the office when he was sent with Julian to Gaul. Zosimus iii. 1; 5 only calls him ἕνα τῶν συμβούλων αὐτοῦ, and wrongly puts his recall before the battle of Argentoratum about August, 357. Julian *ad S. P. Q. Athen.* p. 282, leaves an interval; and elsewhere (*Or.* viii. p. 251—2) mentions his journey to the emperor in Illyricum, where we find Constantius in December certainly, perhaps also about August.

[6] Ammianus xx. 9, 5, xxi. 5, 11. Nebridius was appointed by Constantius after the mutiny at Paris, and allowed by Julian to remain till he opposed the eastward march in 361.

[7] Fl. Sallustius (so Orelli 6471) was Julian's friend in Gaul, and by him appointed to succeed Nebridius in 361. He can be traced in *C. Th.* xii. 1, 53 as late as Sept. 362. Next year he was consul (Ammianus xxiii. 1, 1). Despatches from him reached Julian at Circesium (Ammianus xxiii. 5, 4). We may safely set him down as a heathen, and Germanianus with him.

If there be any truth in the story of Rhodanius, it must be connected with the Gaulish Sallust, though *Chron. Pasch.* 369, Moses of Chorene iii. 26, and Malalas, 340, Bonn Edition, tell it of the Eastern prefect, and Zonaras xiii. 15 does not mention Sallust at all. The story is quite in character with Valentinian (compare the case of Diocles in Ammianus xxvii. 7, 5), and there may be a trace of reality in the designation of Sallust as *patrician*, though some of the late Byzantines give that title to the Eastern Sallust. Moses and Malalas (the two often run very much together) seem to have taken it from the same authority as the *Chron. Pasch.* If this be the old Homœan writer, it will be contemporary. On the other side we may set the silence of Ammianus, Zosimus and the ecclesiastical writers. Nor does the story seem to come from Eunapius.

[8] The prefecture of Germanianus can be traced in the *Cod. Theod.* from Dec. 362, (xi. 30, 30—reading *Jan.* for *Jul.*) to Apr. 366, (viii. 7, 9). Next month (v. 13, 20) we find him *comes S. L.*

Then *C. Th.* vii. 13, 5 and xiii. 10, 4, *ad Viventium P. O. Galliarum* in Apr. and Nov. 365 must be removed to 368 or 370. And as Ammianus xxvi. 5, 5 expressly tells us that Germanianus was ruling Gaul at the election of Valentinian, we must not add *Pf. P.* (as Godefroy does) to *C. Th.* viii. 5, 17 *ad Menandrum* in March (rather May), 364.

Then Viventius first appears as Pf. P. in April, 368. From this point we can trace him as far as *C. Th.* xii. 1, 75 in May, 371.

[9] On Probus, § 3[8].
[10] Ammianus xxvii. 7, 7. Better not identified with Julian's enemy, the consul of 361.
[11] On Maximinus, § 1[28].
[12] On Ausonius, § 3[9].

---

[1] *C. Th.* viii. 2, 1; xii. 1, 31, both dated from Lauriacum. On Catullinus see (I) (5).

‡ Placidus, May 344².
? Vulcatius Rufinus, 346⁷.
Ulpius Limenius, June 347—Apr. 349³.
Hermogenes, May 349—Feb. 350³.
Anicetus, spring 350⁴.
Evagrius, Aug. 353, Sept. 354⁵.
‡ Q. Flavius Mæcius Cornelius Egnatius Severus Lollianus Mavortius, July 355⁵.
Taurus, Sept. 355, July, Dec. 356, Apr. 356—July 358, Feb., June 359, June, July 360, Aug. 361 : flees before Julian's advance⁵.
‡ Claudius Mamertinus, Dec. 361—Aug. 365⁶.

---

² Consul 343. *C. Th.* xii. 1, 37 *ad Placidum Pf. P.* Placidus did not hold the urban prefecture till Dec., 346. We find Anatolius in Illyricum in May, 346, and Placidus may have preceded him there. But Italy is more likely from Orelli 3191, *Placidus Pf. P.* at Naples after 343. He is *Pf. P.* again in Orelli 6472.

³ On Limenius see § 1⁸, and on Hermogenes § 5⁶.

⁴ Zos. ii. 43. Appointed by Magnentius before the rising of Nepotianus.

⁵ Lollianus was P. U. in 342, consul in 355. In Orelli 2284, 6481 he appears as an augur. His full name in Orelli 3162, 3163. The heathen Julius Firmicus Maternus dedicated his Astrology to Lollianus about 355.

His prætorian prefecture is beset with difficulties, and I cannot flatter myself that I have fully disentangled them. It is alluded to in 355 by Ammianus xvi. 8, 16, and seems fixed for Italy by *C. Th.* xi. 30, 25 *P. P. Capuæ*, and dated in July, 355. Now let us note first (*a*) that Volusianus, to whom laws are addressed in Feb., Apr., July, Dec. 355, was only *Vicarius urbis;* and (*b*) that the prefectures of Gaul, the East and Rome are accounted for. We have then laws addressed (*a*) to Evagrius, Aug. 353, (*C. Th.* vii. 20, 7; xvi. 8, 6 and 9, 2 are also best shifted here) and Sept. 354, (*b*) to Taurus, July 353, Dec. 346 (*C. Th.* xvi. 10, 4—should be 353), Apr., July, Sept. 355, and from June, 356 onward; also (*c*) allusions to Lampadius as Pf. P. at the beginning

(Zos. ii. 55) and end (Ammianus xv. 5, 3) of 354.

Given these data, there is but one solution. Taurus must have been three times prefect—twice of Illyricum in 353 and 355, with Lampadius interposed in 354 and Anatolius succeeding in 356—the third time in Italy, with Evagrius and Lollianus for his predecessors. The beginning of this term of office will be marked by *C. Th.* xi. 7, 8, which was received at Carthage in Nov. 355.

The prefecture of Evagrius depends on (*a*) *C. Th.* vii. 20, 7, where Godefroy reads *Pf. P.* for *P. U.*, and fixes on Gaul as the part of the Empire most likely to be troubled with marauding *veterani* in 353—a chronic evil by the way, as is plainly hinted even in Constantine's quieter time by *C. Th.* vii. 20, 3: also (*b*) *C. Just.* ii. 20, 11, where there is nothing to fix the prefecture.

We find Taurus at Ariminum in 359, and consul 361, but whether he was the *Taurus quæstor* sent into Armenia in 354 (Ammianus xiv. 11, 24) is best left open.

⁶ The Illyrian prefecture was given by Julian to Mamertinus before the end of 361 (Ammianus xxii. 12, 25; Mamertinus *Gr. Actio* 22—in *c*. 17 he gives his *prænomen*). As Taurus fled together with Florentius, the Italian prefecture was vacant also. Its tenure by Mamertinus is proved by Ammianus xxii. 12, 20 (jurisdiction at Aquileia). He held both prefectures at Jovian's death in 364 (Ammianus xxvi. 5, 5), and retained his office (*C. Th.* xii. 6, 7) as late as Aug. 365. In *C. Th.* viii.

APPENDIX I.

Vulcatius Rufinus, Nov. 366, May 367, Jan., June, Sept. 368[7].
‡ Sextus Anicius Petronius Probus, Nov. 368, 370—373, Feb.—Dec. 374[8].
† D. Magnus Ausonius, 376[9].
Hesperius, Jan. 377—380[10].

§ 4.
PRÆFECTUS PRÆTORIO PER ILLYRICUM.

‡ Anatolius, May 346, Apr. 349[1].

11, 3, dated Feb. 369, we must read *ad Probum P. O.*
Mamertinus was consul in 362.
At this point we have serious difficulties arising from the perpetual confusion of the successive consulships of Valentinian and Valens in 365, 368, 370 and 373. The best solution may be to remove *C. Th.* xii. 6, 10 *ad Mamertinum P. O.*, dated Oct. 31, 365, to an earlier month, while *C. Th.* viii. 6, 1 *Rufino P. O.*, dated Jan. 365 is shifted to 368. Sundry laws *ad Probum P. O.* in 365 must be placed later.

[7] Vulcatius Rufinus succeeded Mamertinus (Ammianus xxvii. 7, 2), apparently in both prefectures, and died in 368. On his earlier prefecture, see § 2[4].
We lose sight of him for nearly ten years before 366, unless *C. Th.* xv. 1, 10 (so Godefroy) gives us a trace of him at Aquileia in 362.

[8] Probus first appears in *C. Th.* xi. 36, 13, as proconsul of Africa in 358. He was summoned from Rome on the death of Rufinus in 368 (Ammianus xxvii. 11, 1; also *C. Th.* i. 29, 3, if we shift it to Nov. 368), and held the double prefecture of Italy and Illyricum. Ambrose was a member of the prefect's council before his promotion to be *consularis* of Liguria (Paulinus *Vit. Ambr.* 5), and (*id.* 25) remained on friendly terms with him afterwards. Probus was also prefect for Valentinian II., and fled eastward in 384, when Maximus entered Italy (Socr. v. 11).
His Gaulish prefecture in 366 is established by (*a*) *C. Th.* xi. 1, 15, dated May 366. (*b*) *C. Just.* iv. 60, 1: vii. 38, 1 addressed to him by Valentinian and Valens, and therefore (if correct) before Aug. 24, 367. Orelli 1130 shews that he had been four times prefect before the consulship of his sons in 395, and had held Italy, Illyricum, Africa and Gaul. The last however is not clear in Claudian *in cons. Prob. et Olybr.* 168, and is not mentioned in Orelli 3063, dated 378. It might be placed in 380—383, when Italy was held by others; but best suits 366.
Boeckh 2593 names a Probus three times Pf. P.; but he seems a generation later.

[9] Ausonius *Gratiarum Actio,* and frequently. Gratian made his old tutor first Quæstor, then Pf. P. of Illyricum of Italy (we may presume he held them together), then Pf. P. of Gaul and finally consul in 379. His Italian prefecture therefore follows that of Probus.
It may be noted that his appointment to Illyricum proves that Greece was not annexed by Valens in 375. The case is not altered if his office was merely titular, as Tillemont *Empereurs* v. 149 supposes.

[10] *C. Th.* i. 32, 2 Hesperius was proconsul of Africa in July 376. Hence shift *C. Th.* xvi. 5, 4 *ad Hesperium P. O.* in April 376 to 378, and omit *proc. Africæ* in *C. Just.* xi. 65, 3, dated after Aug. 378.

[1] *C. Th.* xii. 1, 38; 39. Anatolius is discussed by Sievers *Libanius* 235—238. The story in Eunapius of the rhetorical contest before him at Athens in the time of Constans shews that he held the Illyrian prefecture. There must therefore be some mistake in *C. Th.* xii. 1, 39, which is dated from Antioch in 349, when Philippus undoubtedly held the Eastern prefecture.
We hear nothing for certain of

? Taurus I., 353².
? Lampadius, 354².
Taurus II., Apr., July, Aug. 355².
‡ Anatolius II., 356, to his death in 360¹ (p. 279).
Florentius, 361.
‡ Claudius Mamertinus, 361—Oct. 365.
Vulcatius Rufinus, Nov. 366—Sept. 368.
‡ Sextus Anicius Petronius Probus, Nov. 368, 370—373, Feb.—Dec. 374.
† D. Magnus Ausonius, 376.
? Hesperius, 377—380.

§ 5.
PRÆFECTUS PRÆTORIO PER ORIENTEM.
† Ablavius, May 337¹.
Dometius Leontius, Oct. 338².
Acindynus, Dec. 338, Apr. 340³.
Dometius Leontius II., May 342—June 343, July 344².
Philippus, July 346, Sept. 349, 350⁴.

Anatolius during the Magnentian troubles; and the city prefecture assigned to him by Sievers in the spring of 355 must be rejected, for the dignity was then held by Orfitus. He returned to office early in 356 (Sievers), or at least in the course of the year, as prefect of Illyricum. As such we find him (Ammianus xix. 11, 2) in 359, and in that office he died (Ammianus xxi. 6, 5) in 361.
² On Lampadius and Taurus, § 1²⁰ and § 3⁵.

¹ Zos. ii. 40.
² The first prefecture of Leontius depends on *C. Th.* ix. 1, 7; the second is marked by i. 5, 4 (July 342), xii. 1, 35 (June 343) and xiii. 4, 3 (June 344). There must be some error in the title of xv. 8, 1 *ad Severum P. U.* from Hierapolis in June 343.
³ Consul 340. The prefecture of Acindynus has a famous story connected with it, and is therefore frequently referred to. Its termination may be marked by *C. Th.* xvi. 8, 2 *ad Madalianum agentem vicem Pf. P.*, in 341.
⁴ Consul 348. We have two difficulties here. The first is *C. Th.* xi. 30, 20 *Philippo Pf. P....P.P. V Id. Jun.* (surely *Jan.*) *post cons. Constantii iterum et Constantis A. A.* (340). Godefroy transfers it to 347, breaking the order. Rather the inscription *Pf. P.* is corrupt. The other is *C. Th.* xvi. 10, 4 *ad Taurum Pf. P.*, Dec. 346. But this may perhaps be shifted to 353, reading... *Kal. Dec.* and *Constante Cæs.* i.e. Gallus.
The date 351 is given by the final expulsion of Paul from Constantinople. Socrates ii. 16 seems to distinguish it from the exile ii. 13 of 342, and expressly says that Philippus was prefect at the time. Sozomen iv. 2 relates it after the rising of Magnentius; and so (with much confusion) the worthless *Vita Pauli* in Photius *Cod.* 257. We also find Philippus in high favour (Zos. ii. 46) just before the battle of Mursa in Sept. 351: whereas Athanasius *Hist. Ar.* 7 p. 275 tells us that he was disgraced within a year of Paul's death. He was certainly prefect in 350 (Ath. *Hist. Ar.* 51 p. 296). Sievers *Libanius* 55 n. A statue of Philippus was standing at Chalcedon in the time of Joannes Lydus *de magistr.* iii. 9, p. 175.
C. Th. viii. 7, 2 *ad Philippum Pf. P.* is dated by Constantine from Arles, Nov. 3, 326. As Philippus was not then Pf. P., Godefroy removes it to 353,

APPENDIX I.

Thalassius, 351—353⁵.
Domitianus, 353⁵.
† Musonianus (Strategius), winter 353—June 358⁶.
Hermogenes, Aug. 358, May 359⁶.
† Elpidius, Feb., Nov. 360, Nov. 361⁶.
‡ Sallustius Saturninius Secundus, Dec. 361—July 365⁷.
Nebridius, Sept. 365⁷.
[Araxius, Sept. 365⁸.]
‡ Sallustius Saturninius Secundus II., Dec. 365, Apr. 366, May 367⁷.
‡ Auxonius, May 367, Sept. 368—Dec. 369⁹.
† Domitius Modestus, June 370—Nov. 377⁹.

and reads Philagrius for Philippus in Athan. *supra*. But thus he breaks the order and leaves no time for the prefecture of Thalassius before 353. Nor is anything gained by removing to Arelape in Noricum, or dating in 346. The law is therefore best referred to another Philippus, who appears in *C. Th.* x. 4, 1 as *Vicarius urbis* in 313, or rather (being dated from Heraclea) in 315.

⁵ Ammianus xiv. 1, 10; 7, 9 (where Gardthausen reads *eum odisse* for *obisse*). Thalassius was apparently sent into the East with Gallus, and replaced in 353. He was still alive in 362 (Ammianus xxii. 9, 16). But Libanius *Ep.* 1209 seems to speak of his death before that of Anatolius in 360. Sievers *Libanius*, p. 227. In any case there is an error in *C. Th.* xvi. 8, 7, addressed to Thalassius as Pf. P. in May 357.

⁶ The prefectures of Musonianus, Hermogenes and Elpidius are fully discussed by Sievers *Libanius* 222—227. To his refs. add the allusion to Hermogenes in Soz. iv. 24, which may be as early as June 358.

⁷ The career of Sallustius Saturninius Secundus is traced in Orelli 3192. He was appointed by Julian in Dec. 361 (Ammianus xx. 3, 1), negotiated together with Arinthæus the peace of 363, and remained in office at least till July 4, 365. The *Chron. Pasch.* 364 has a story (also in later writers) of his momentary displacement by Valentinian; but it looks rather legendary. Nebridius (perhaps the faithful Gaulish prefect of 361) succeeded him shortly before the rising of Procopius, Sept. 28, 365 (Ammianus xxvi. 7, 4, Zos. iv. 4): but Sallust was restored before Dec. 1, 365 (*C. Th.* vii. 4, 14). His final retirement is fixed for May 367 by the presence of Valens at Martianopolis and the preparations (Zos. iv. 10) for the Gothic war. His death before 374 is intimated (Sievers *Libanius* 185) by Ammianus xxx. 2, 3.

⁸ Appointed by Procopius (Ammianus xxvi. 7, 6; 10, 7). He was a favourite of Julian (*Ep. ad Themistium* p. 259), but escaped with a short exile in the proscription of 366. This good fortune he owed to the good offices of his son-in-law, the traitor Agilo.

⁹ The prefectures of Auxonius and Modestus are seriously confused by the difficulty of distinguishing the joint consulships of Valentinian and Valens in 365, 368, 370 and 373. However, we have some firm ground to go upon. Auxonius was still Pf. P. (*C. Th.* v. 1, 2) in Dec. 369, whereas Valens found him dead (Zos. iv. 11) on his return from the Gothic war, which is fixed by the death of Eudoxius to the beginning of 370. Hence we must remove to 368 certain laws addressed to Auxonius— *C. Th.* x. 16, 1; vii. 6, 2; x. 20, 4 (dated Sept. Nov. Dec. 365); also xi. 24, 2 (dated Nov. 370).

Similarly we must remove from the year 365 three laws addressed to Modestus, placing *C. Th.* xi. 36, 17 (Cyzicus) in June 370, ix. 16, 8 (Constantinople) in Dec. 370, and xii. 1, 63 (Berytus—against the monks) in Jan. 373.

There is more difficulty in *C. Th.* xi. 30, 35 (Martianopolis, Aug. 365), for Valens was not at Martianopolis in 370 or 373, or (Ammianus xxvii. 5, 5) in the summer of 368. Haenel therefore reads *Hierapoli*, and places

§ 6.

PRÆFECTUS URBIS CONSTANTINOPOLITANÆ.

[Proconsuls only :—[1]
   Alexander, 342.
   Aurelius Limenius, 343, 346.
   ? *Montius*,   } 349—353.
   ‡ ? *Anatolius*,
   Honoratus, 354.
   Justinus, Sept. 355.
   ‡ *Araxius*, 356.
   ‡ *Themistius*, 358, 359.]
Honoratus, Dec. 11, 359[2].
‡ Themistius, 362[3].
‡ Domitius Modestus, 363[3].
? ‡ Jovius, Mar., Apr. 364.
Cæsarius, Sept. 365[4].

it in 370. It might however be shifted with a group of others to the Syrian Hierapolis in 373.

There remains *C. Th.* xi. 1, 14, *ad Modestum Pf. P.*, and dated May 1, 366, from Constantinople, then held by Procopius. Godefroy shifts it to 371; but in that case the next three laws must also be transferred. The date seems correct; but Valens was not then at Constantinople, and Modestus was neither Pf. P. nor P. U.

Thus we first find Modestus Pf. P. in June 370, and can trace him in *C. Th.* xi. 61, 5 at least as late as Nov. 377. He was consul 372.

On Modestus, Sievers *Libanius* 227—234. Auxonius being *corrector Tusciæ* under Julian, and also a favourite of Eunapius (Zos. iv. 10), we may set him down as a heathen.

---

[1] The list of proconsuls is given for the sake of completeness. It is copied from Sievers *Libanius*, 213—215. I have however considered *C. Th.* xi. 39, 4 sufficient proof that Limenius was proconsul in 346 also.

[2] Godefroy on *C. Th.* vi. 4, 16, and Bethmann-Hollweg *Römischer Civilprozess*, iii. 66, suppose the proconsuls to have been the ordinary *duumviri* of a Roman colony. Kuhn *Verfassung*, i. 181, (and apparently Hertzberg, *Griech. unter d. Römern*, iii. 265) makes them the proconsuls of Europa; but Sievers *supra* gives reasons for the theory that the city had a proconsul of its own from the first. We may however accept (Sievers notwithstanding) the mention by Constantine Porph. *de Them.* p. 45 Bonn of a Taurus proconsul of Thrace in Constantine's time.

Honoratus appears as *comes Orientis* under Gallus in 353, proconsul at Constantinople in 354, Pf. P. of Gaul 356 § 2[5], and P. U. Dec. 11, 359. So Socr. ii. 41 (τῶν ἀνθυπάτων καταπαύσας ἀρχήν), Soz. iv. 23, and with much confusion the *Chron. Pasch.* 359, where read δεκεμβρίων for σεπτεμβρίων.

[3] Themistius was appointed by Julian (Suidas, Θεμ.), and therefore held the office in 362; for Libanius *Epp.* 701, 1429[a] shews that Modestus came after him. Jovius may be Julian's *quæstor* in 361-2.

[4] Cæsarius was imprisoned with Nebridius by Procopius in Sept. 365 (Ammianus xxvi. 7, 4). Not to be identified with the brother of Gregory of Nazianzus, who in 368 was only quæstor of Bithynia. So Sievers *Libanius*, 107, n. 24.

APPENDIX I. 291

[‡ Phronemius, Sept. 365⁵.]
† Domitius Modestus II., 369⁶.
Sophronius, 370 or 371⁶.
‡ Clearchus, Apr., May 372, Aug. 373⁶.
Vindaonius Magnus, 375, May 376⁷.

§ 7.

COMES REI PRIVATÆ.

West.

Eusebius, Apr. 342¹.
Eustathius, May 345, Mar. 349.

Cæsarius, Feb.? 364⁴.
Florianus, Sept. 364, May 365,
  Oct. 367, Mar. 368,
  Mar. 368, Nov. 373⁵.

East.

Orion, Mar. 353.
† ? Arcadius 360².
Evagrius, Nov. 361².
‡ Elpidius, Oct. 362³.

Alexandrinus, May 367, Sept.—
  Dec. 369.
Fortunatianus, Apr. 369, 372 ?
  July 377⁶.

⁵ Appointed by Procopius, and afterwards exiled by Valentinian. Ammianus xxvi. 7, 4; 10, 8. Heathen, as being *divo Juliano acceptus.*
⁶ These three names must be taken together. *C. Th.* xiv. 13, *ad Clearchum P. U.* in Aug. 365 must be transferred to 373, when Valens was at Hierapolis. Clearchus also appears in the *Cod. Theod.* as P. U. in April and May 372, and Jerome *Chron.* names him in 373.
The second prefecture of Modestus is assigned to 369 by the Idatian Fasti, and cannot be placed later. On the other hand, the earthquake at Nicæa was in the autumn of 368, Cæsarius the quæstor died soon after, and in the course of the ensuing litigation, Gregory, *Epp.* 21, 29, wrote to the prefect Sophronius (Ammianus xxvi. 7, 2), whom we may therefore place in 370 or 371.
⁷ Corsini inserts Vindaonius Magnus among the Roman prefects; and *C. Th.* vii. 13, 3, Magnus is *Vicarius Urbis*

Romæ in 367. But *Chron. Pasch.* 375 relates the opening of the Carosian Baths at Constantinople, and *C. Th.* i. 28, 3 (unknown to Godefroy) is dated from Antioch.
Magnus may be the *comes largitionum* in Egypt in 373, who burnt the church at Berytus in Julian's time. Corsini takes Ambrose *Off.* iii. 7, *ille magnus vere probatus* as a proper name.

¹ Also Ammianus xv. 5, 4.
² Arcadius *C. R. P.* in Basil *Ep.* 15.
Evagrius *C. R. P.* in Ammianus xxii. 3, 7—exiled by Julian.
³ Philost. viii. 10—at closing of the church at Antioch.
⁴ *C. Th.* x. 1, 8: but *Feb.* is wrong.
⁵ *C. Th.* ix. 1, 10: but Valentinian was not at Martianopolis.
⁶ Also Zos. iv. 14, at the affair of ΘΕΟΔ.

§ 8.

COMES SACRARUM LARGITIONUM.

West.	East.
Marcellinus, 350¹.	
	Domitianus, before 353².
? ‡ Fl. Sallustius 355—357³.	Ursulus, 356, 360, Nov. 361⁴.
	‡ Claudius Mamertinus, summer 361⁵.
	‡ Felix, Mar., Oct. 362, died early in 363⁶.
	‡ Julianus, Feb. 363⁶.
Florentius, Sept. 364, Feb. 365, Sept. 366.	
‡ Germanianus, May 366, Jan., Apr. 367, Jan., Sept. 368⁷.	Felix, Mar. 368⁸.
	Archelaus, May, July 369⁹.
Philematius, May 371, Aug. 372?	
	Tatianus, Feb., Mar., May 374, Jan. 377.

§ 9.

QUÆSTOR.

Montius, 353¹,
Leontius, 353—4², } with Gallus in Syria.
Taurus, 353—4².
Nebridius,   to 360³ with Julian.
Leonas, 360⁴.

---

¹ Zos. ii. 42. Godefroy should not add *com. S. L.* in C. Th. xi. 12, 1, dated 342.
² Ammianus xiv. 7, 9.
³ Orelli 6471, *comes consistorii*, more likely before than after 363; and in Julian's case more likely *comes S. L.* than *comes R. P.*, though not certainly either. See § 2⁷.
⁴ Ammianus xx. 11, 5 (where see note of Valesius): xxii. 3, 7 (execution by Julian).
⁵ Ammianus xxi. 8, 1—Julian at Rauracum.
⁶ Ammianus xxiii. 1, 5. Scarcely the Felix refused by Julian in 360 (Ammianus xx. 9, 5), as *mag. off.*, and noted as an informer *ad S. P. Q. Ath.* 273. If so, his apostasy (θεοῖς δὲ νεωστὶ φίλος) was prompt. Philost. vii. 10 (where see Godefroy's note)—at closing of the church at Antioch.
⁷ This implies two *comites S. L.* in the summer of 366. It is not likely, but I do not see how to escape it.
⁸ C. Th. x. 17, 2, from Martianopolis in 365 is best removed to 368.
⁹ C. Th. iv. 12, 6, *comes Orientis:* and Haenel on *C. Th.* x. 16, 2, prefers *comes Orientis* there also.

---

¹ Ammianus xiv. 7, 12. Sievers *Libanius*, 216.
² Ammianus xiv. 11, 14.
³ Ammianus xx. 9, 5—named Pf. P. by Constantius. Orelli 3192 names Sallustius Saturninius Secundus as having been quæstor before 367.
⁴ Ammianus xx. 9, 3,—at Seleucia in 359, Leonas is called *comes*, but it does not follow that he was not already quæstor.

APPENDIX I.

‡ Jovius, summer 361, Mar. 362[5].
Viventius, summer 364—366[6].
Fl. Eupraxius, 367—after Sept. 368[7].
† D. Magnus Ausonius, 375[8].

§ 10.
MAGISTER OFFICIORUM.

West.	East.
Eugenius, 342[1] or 345.	
Marcellinus, 350[2].	
	Palladius, 353[3].
Musonius, 357[4].	
	Florentius, 355? 360[5].
	Evagrius, Nov. 361[5].
Pentadius, 360[6].	
? ‡ Anatolius, 360—363[7].	
Ursatius, summer 364[8].	
	(Euphrasius), 365[9].
Remigius, 368? 370, replaced by Leo before 373[10].	? Sophronius, 371—374[11].

[5] *C. Th.* xi. 39, 5. Ammianus xxi. 8, 1,—appointed by Julian (therefore heathen) at Rauracum: § 49 *postea quæstorem* in Dec. 361 must be an oversight.
[6] Ammianus xxvi. 4, 4; xxvii. 3, 11.
[7] Orelli 1116? Ammianus xxviii. 1, 25,—*Prætextatus ex P. U.*
[8] Ausonius, *Gratiarum Actio*—appointed by Gratian.

[1] Eugenius μάγιστρος in 342, at the interview of Athanasius with Constans, and still living in 357 (Ath. *Apol. ad Ctium*, 3, p. 235). Compare also Sievers *Libanius*, 94.
[2] Marcellinus was the contriver of the Magnentian plot (Zos. ii. 43), and disappeared at Mursa (Julian, *Or.* ii. p. 58 sq.).
[3] Palladius was only *notarius* in 350 (Ath. *Hist. Ar.* 52, p. 296), though soon afterwards *mag. off.* for Gallus (Ath. *Apol. ad Ctium*, 10, p. 239. Ammianus xxii. 3, 3).
[4] *C. Th.* viii. 5, 8.

[5] Florentius perhaps only *pro mag. off.* in 355 (Ammianus xv. 5, 12: no proof to the contrary in Libanius *Ep.* 424, dated by Sievers in 355). For 360, Ammianus xx. 2, 2, and correspondence in Lucifer, p. 935 Migne. For Evagrius, Ammianus xxii. 3, 7.
[6] Ammianus xx. 8, 19.
[7] Anatolius served Julian from 360 onwards, and was killed in Persia the same day. Ammianus xx. 9, 8 (Felix refused) xxv. 3, 14. Zos. iii. 29. Malalas p. 329—who depends on Magnus of Carrhæ, an eyewitness. Not the Illyrian prefect, who died in 360. Sievers *Libanius*, 235.
[8] Ammianus xxvi. 4, 4: 5, 7.
[9] To Procopius, Ammianus xxvi. 7, 4: 10, 8.
[10] Remigius is named *C. Th.* vii. 8, 2, which may belong to 368 or 370. He was in office in 370, and Leo did not succeed him before Maximin's prefecture (Ammianus xxvii. 9, 2, xxviii. 1, 41: 6, 8).
[11] Basil, *Epp.* 76, &c.

§ 11.
MAGISTER MILITUM.

The series of *magistri militum* is so difficult to trace that it seems the safest plan to set down a mere list of names and references. The signs prefixed are as follows :—

eq., ped., utr. = *M. equitum, peditum, utriusque militiæ.*
præs. = *M. M. præsentalis.* (Eastern or Western).
Gall. or *Ill.* = *M. M. per Gallias* or *per Illyricum.*
Or. or *Thr.* = *M. M. per Orientem* or *per Thracias.*

	eq.	Hermogenes, Nov. 342[1].
Or.		(?) Secundus, 345[2].
Or.	*eq.*	Bonosus, May 347[3].
præs.	*ped.*	Silvanus, May 349—355[4].
Ill.	*ped.*	† Vetranio, March 350[5].
Or.		(?) Lucillianus, 350[6].
		(?) Marcellinus, 351[7].
Or. } *Gall.* }	*ped.*	Ursicinus 352—355[8].
præs.	*eq.*	Arbetio, 354—361[9].

[1] Killed in the riot at Constantinople after the death of Eusebius—Ammianus xiv. 10, 2, Socr. ii. 13, and others.

[2] Chrysostom's father—Palladius, *Vita* c. 40: not a careful writer. For the date, Stephens *Life of Chrys.* 9.

[3] *C. Th.* v. 4, 1.

[4] Appointed by Constans *C. Th.* viii. 7, 3. *M. peditum* Aur. Victor *Cæs.* 42. A Frank: won over from Magnentius before the battle of Mursa, and rewarded with this rank. See Ammianus xv. 5, for his history. Tillemont *Empereurs,* iv. 674 has some minor difficulties on it.

[5] So called by Aur. Victor, *Cæs.* 41, and *Epit.* 41. For his religion, *Chron. Pasch.:* it is also fairly settled by the action of so zealous a Christian as Constantina appears in Orelli 1097.

[6] Left in command against the Persians in 350—Zos. ii. 45, probably as *M. M. per Orientem,* and defended Nisibis—Zos. iii. 8.

[7] For Magnentius, Peter Patricius p. 129 Bonn, uses the decisive word στρατηλάτης.

[8] Ursicinus may have been sent to the East in 349 (Ammianus xviii. 6, 2 *per decennium* in 359); but we first clearly trace him in the Jerusalem Talmud *Jebam* Col. 15, as commander in the Jewish war of 352; next as *mag. militum* in the East (Ammianus xiv. 9, 1), whence he was recalled by the eunuchs in 354. After his mission next year to assassinate Silvanus in Gaul, he was placed under the orders of Marcellus (Ammianus xvi. 2, 8), and summoned to court on his recall, though not till he had taken a share in the campaign of 357 (Ammianus xvi. 10, 21: 12, 1). From Sirmium he was sent back to Syria *quasi penuria meliorum,* and in the winter of 358—9, became *mag. peditum præsentalis* in the room of Barbatio (Ammianus xviii. 4, 2: 5, 5). He was finally removed from office after the fall of Amida (Ammianus xx. 2, 1).

He is probably the *Ursicinus comes* on whose representation Valentinian at Bonamansio in May 364 (*C. Th.* vii. 4, 12) forbade the exaction of *cenatica.* Godefroy gives an alternative of Ursicinus the Alemannic king, but it is not likely.

[9] Arbetio was a veteran of Constantine's wars, and rose from the ranks to his consulship in 355. We find him *mag. equitum* in 354 (Ammianus xv. 4, 1), and from this time onward to the death of Constantius in 361 (Am-

APPENDIX I.

præs.	ped.	Barbatio, 355—359[10].
Gall.	utr.	Marcellus, 355—356[11].
Gall.		Severus, 357—358[12].
præs.	ped.	Ursicinus, 359[8].
Or.	ped.	Sabinianus, 359[13].
Gall.	ped.	† Lupicinus, 359[14]—360.
præs.	ped.	Agilo, 360—361[15].

mianus xxi. 13, 3). After sitting on the Chalcedon commission (Ammianus xxii. 3, 1) he retired from the service. Roused from his retreat by Procopius, who plundered his house, he repaired to the camp of Valens (Ammianus xxvi. 8, 13: 9, 4), and took a leading part (Zos. iv. 7, from Eunapius, p. 73, Bonn) in the usurper's overthrow.

[10] Barbatio was *comes domesticorum* to Gallus, and took an active part in his murder. He succeeded Silvanus as *mag. peditum* in the spring of 355, and gave Julian much trouble by his misconduct in the campaign of 357. He was executed on suspicion of treason in the winter of 358—9. (Ammianus xiv. 11, 19; 24; xvi. 11, 2—8; xviii. 3, 1—6: Philost. iv. 1).

Libanius *Epp.* 470, 492, 1032, 1215, were written to Barbatio in Syria: but Sievers *Libanius* 218, can hardly be right in his identification of him with Bardio, a *comes* in attendance on Constantius (Ath. *Hist. Ar.* 22, p. 282) in 346. In Ath. p. 626 we find a eunuch Bardio.

[11] Marcellus was sent into Gaul with Julian (Zos. iii. 2) to supersede Ursicinus. He contributed much to the disasters of 356, and was recalled at the end of his campaign for his neglect to relieve Julian at Sens. Ammianus xvi. 2—7.

[12] Severus succeeded Marcellus in the summer of 357, commanded the left wing at Argentoratum, and helped to defeat the Franks in 358, but held back from the advance into Germany (Ammianus xvi. 10, 21: 12, 27; xvii. 10, 1).

Severus seems to have returned to active service under Valentinian. He was sent into Britain as *comes domesticorum*; apparently in 366, for we find him *mag. peditum* in the next summer (Ammianus xxvii. 8, 2: 6, 3). In his new rank he shared in the campaign of 368, was sent again into Britain in 370, and fought on the Rhine in 371 (Ammianus xxvii. 10, 6; xxviii. 5, 2; xxix. 4, 3). Our last trace of him is *C. Th.* vii. 1, 11, in April, 372. *C. Th.* viii. 7, 11 is a general law, and may have been sent by Valentinian to Syria.

Libanius *Epp.* 50, 66, 67 (Sievers dates them in 361) speaks of a "cursed Severus" at Constantinople. But this is more likely the *vicarius urbis* of *C. Th.* i. 6, 3, in 364; to whom perhaps also *C. Th.* xvi. 2, 12, *Severo suo* is addressed.

[13] Sabinianus was *mag. peditum* in Syria during 359, and by his misconduct caused the loss of Amida (Ammianus xviii. 5, 5; xix. 3, 1; xx. 2, 3).

[14] Lupicinus succeeded Severus as *magister peditum* in Gaul, and was sent into Britain against the Picts in the winter of 359. The mutiny at Paris occurred during his absence, but Lupicinus was superseded before the news reached Constantius (Ammianus xviii. 2, 7; xx. 1, 2: 4, 3: 9, 5). He was one of Julian's enemies, as we see from the hints in Julian *ad S. P. Q. Ath.* 281—283, and from the special precautions (Ammianus xx. 9, 9), taken against his return from Britain.

As Valens frequently employed Julian's enemies, we may presume that this is the Lupicinus whom Jovian made *magister equitum* in Syria, and who brought up the Eastern troops against Procopius in 366 (Ammianus xxvi. 5, 2: 8, 4: 9, 1). We find him in Epiph. *Hær.* 80, 2, persecuting the Massalians of Melitene, and Libanius (I. 108 Reiske) was relieved by him sometime later from a vexatious accusation. Consul 367; but hardly to be identified with the infamous *comes Thraciæ* in 376.

Lupicinus is discussed by Sievers *Libanius*, 145 n.

[15] Agilo the Frank succeeded Ursicinus as *mag. peditum præsentalis* after the campaign of 359. He was

296   ECCLESIASTICAL HISTORY.

Gall.	(*Gumoarius*), 360[16].
Ill.	Lucillianus, 361[17].
Ill. } *Gall.* }	eq. ? † Valens Jovinus, 362—369[18].
	eq. *Nevitta*, 360—363[19].
	utr. Lucillianus, 363—4[17].
	(*Malarich*), 363—4[18].
Ill.	Januarius, 363—4[20].
	eq. *Dagalaifus*, 363—366[21].

sent by Julian to assure the garrison of Aquileia of the death of Constantius, and served on the Chalcedon commission (Ammianus xx. 2, 5; xxi. 12, 16: 8, 49). After this he retired from the army in 362. He was recalled to active service in 365 by Procopius, with whom he had great influence, but whom he betrayed at Nacolia (Ammianus xxvi. 7, 4: 9, 7 also 7, 6: 10, 7; Zos. iv. 8).

[16] Gumoarius the Frank was appointed to succeed Lupicinus in Gaul in 360, but Julian refused him on account of his old treachery to Vetranio. He was therefore sent with Arbetio to defend the pass of Succi (Ammianus xx. 9, 5; xxi. 8, 1: 13, 16). After this he retired from the army in 362. He was recalled to active service in 365 by Procopius, whom he betrayed before the battle of Nacolia. (Ammianus xxvi. 7, 4: 9, 6; Zos. iv. 8).

[17] Lucillianus was *comes domesticorum* to Gallus in 354, and ambassador to Sapor in 358. He was *mag. militum* (Wietersheim-Dahn i. 459, strangely makes him *pro Pf. P.*) in Illyricum at the time of Julian's advance in 361, and we find him in command of Julian's fleet in 363 (Ammianus xiv. 11, 14; xvii. 14, 3; xxi. 9, 5; xxiii. 3, 9).

Lucillianus, the father-in-law of Jovian, was in retirement at Sirmium in 363. He was sent to Milan as *mag. equitum et peditum*, and perished in a tumult of the soldiery (Ammianus xxv. 8, 9: 10, 6).

[18] Valens Jovinus was appointed *mag. equitum* in Illyricum by Julian in 361, and sat on the Chalcedon commission; but was very soon removed to Gaul (Ammianus xxi. 8, 3: 12, 2; 3; xxii. 3, 1). Jovian was jealous of his merit, and named Malarich the Frank to supersede him, who however declined the office. Jovinus greatly distinguished himself in 366 and received the consulship next year. He was sent into Britain, apparently in 367. We meet him again in 368, and find him finally replaced in 369 or 370 by Theodosius (Ammianus xxv. 8, 11; xxvii. 2, 1: 6, 3: 10, 6; xxviii. 3, 9). Hardly the Jovinus mentioned by Libanius in 355 (Sievers *Libanius*, 221); nor is there any evidence to identify him with the Jovinus *comes* addressed by Basil *Ep.* 163.

[19] Nevitta was a rough barbarian, but a good cavalry officer. We first hear of him in 358. He succeeded Lupicinus as *mag. equitum* in 360, and next year seized the pass of Succi for Julian, whom he also accompanied on his Persian expedition. He sat on the Chalcedon commission, and to the disgust of Ammianus, received the consulship in 362 (Ammianus xvii. 6, 3; xxi. 8, 1; 3: 10, 2; 8; xxii. 3, 1; xxiv. 1, 2; xxv. 5. 2). As the name of Flavius Gaiso (colleague of Magnentius in 351) was erased from the *Fasti*, Nevitta is the first barbarian we find in them.

[20] Januarius being a relation of Jovian, was no doubt Jovian's appointment as *mag. militum* in Illyricum. He was one of the candidates discussed on Jovian's death (Ammianus xxvi. 1, 4).

[21] Dagalaifus appears to have been another barbarian. He was *comes domesticorum* under Julian, whom he followed from Gaul to Persia; and received his promotion from Jovian. He returned to Gaul with Valentinian, and was made consul in 366. His campaign however in that year was not very successful (Ammianus xxi. 8, 1; xxv. 5, 2; xxvi. 4, 1: 5, 2; xxvii. 2, 1).

APPENDIX I.

Or.	*eq.*	† Lupicinus, 363—4, 366, and later[14].
ped. } *eq.* }		† Arinthæus, 364, 367—369, 373[22]?
præs.	*eq.*	† Victor, 364 (?) 367, 378[23].
Ill.		Aequitius, 365, 375[24].
præs. W.	*ped.*	Severus, 367—372[12].
præs. W.	*eq.*	† Theodosius, 369—375[25].

[22] Arinthæus the Gothic Hercules served in Gaul as *tribunus militum* in 355, and afterwards in the East (Ammianus xv. 4, 10; xxv. 5, 2). He accompanied Julian as *comes domesticorum* in the Persian war, and was a chief negotiator of the peace (Ammianus xxiv. 1, 2; xxv. 7, 7; Philost. viii. 8; Zos. iii. 31; Chron. Pasch. and Malalas p. 335 Bonn, who both call him patrician). He was sent on a special mission to Gaul by Jovian, and appointed *mag. peditum* by Valens at Mediana (Ammianus xxv. 10, 9; xxvi. 5, 2). He distinguished himself in the civil war of Procopius (Ammianus xxvi. 8, 4), served against the Goths as *mag. equitum* in 367—9, and was afterwards sent into Armenia (Ammianus xxvii. 5, 4: 12, 13). Consul 372. Basil, *Ep.* 179 is addressed to Arinthæus, *Ep.* 269 to his widow. As this last must have been written before 379, we may set aside (or transfer to the war of 367—369) the story of Theodoret *H. E.* iv. 33, of Trajan's remonstrance in 378, seconded by Arinthæus and Victor. Arinthæus at one time owned Eutropius (Claudian *in Eutr.* i. 63).

[23] Victor the Sarmatian commanded the rearguard in Julian's Persian expedition, and was made *mag. militum* by Jovian (Ammianus xxiv. 1, 2; xxvi. 5, 2). He was stationed in Egypt in 364 (*C. Th.* vii. 4, 12, from Bonamansio, therefore in May: *C. Th.* xii. 12, 5, in Dec.), and was still at Alexandria from Oct. 365 to Jan. 366 (*Hist. Aceph.*). He served in the Gothic war of 367—369, and afterwards in Armenia, apparently remaining in the East till 378 (Ammianus xxvii. 5, 1; xxx. 2, 4; xxxi. 7, 1). This last detail is another argument against the story *supra* of Theodoret iv. 33. About 374 we must place his marriage with Mavia's daughter (Socr. iv. 36, who however seems to date it after 378).

Victor was consul in 369, and is complimented on it by Themistius *Or.* ix. p. 120, who also p. 128 claims him as a citizen of Constantinople. He voted for delay at Hadrianople, and escaped the slaughter after a brave effort to rescue Valens (Ammianus xxxi. 12, 6: 13, 9, where it is idle to distinguish Victor *comes* from the *magister militum*). Greg. Naz. *Epp.* 133, 134, are addressed to him in 382.

[24] Aequitius was mentioned as a candidate on Jovian's death, but considered too rough (Ammianus xxvi. 1, 4). Valentinian stationed him in Illyricum as *comes* in 364, and promoted him to be *magister militum* during the revolt of Procopius (Ammianus xxvi. 5, 3; 11: 7, 11: 10, 4: so also *C. Th.* vii. 1, 8, if we may shift the date from Sept. 365 to Nov. or Dec.,—but we must in any case read *reddita* and understand the Macedonian Heraclea). Aequitius was honoured with the enmity of Maximin, but received the consulship notwithstanding in 374, and remained in office till Valentinian's death (Ammianus xxix. 6, 3; xxx. 3, 1: 6, 2). He joined with Merobaudes in the elevation of the younger Valentinian in 375 (Jerome *Chronica*, Zos. iv. 19).

Compare Godefroy on *C. Th.* vii. 1, 8.

[25] Theodosius was sent as *dux* into Britain in 367—8, and only replaced Jovinus as *mag. equitum* in 369 or 370 (Ammianus xxvii. 8, 3; xxviii. 3, 9). He fought against the Alemanni in 370, on the Rhine in 372 (Ammianus xxviii. 5, 15; xxix. 4, 5), and seems to have ended his exploits with the conquest of Africa (Ammianus xxviii. 6, 26; xxix. 5, 1). About this time date Symmachus, *Ep.* x. 1. He was still at Carthage when he was executed in 375—6.

C. Th. iii. 14, 1, *ad Theodosium mag. equitum* is dated in May 365, but may very well be removed to 370 or 373.

W.   ped.   Merobaudes, 375—[26].
     ped.   † Trajan, 377, 378[27].
            (?) Profuturus, 377[28].
     ped.   Sebastian, 368? 375? 378[29].
Or.   Julius, 378[30].

[26] Merobaudes the Frank (Richter *Weström. Reich*, 283) is first found (Philost. viii. 1) in charge of Julian's corpse at Tarsus; apparently under the orders of Procopius. He was commander in chief in 375 (Zos. iv. 17), and consul 377 and 383. He was doubtless *magister militum*, though the fact is nowhere expressly stated by Ammianus.

[27] Trajan was *dux Ægypti* in Sept. 367 and May 368 (*Hist. aceph.* and index to *Festal Letters*), and seems to have gained the rank of *mag. militum* by later service in Armenia (Ammianus xxix. 1, 2; xxx. 1, 18). To this period (say 373) belong Basil *Epp.* 148, 149, and the murder of Para. He was sent into Europe against the Goths in 377 and commanded at Salices. He fell fighting at Hadrianople (Ammianus xxxi. 7, 1: 13, 8).

[28] Profuturus may have been *mag. militum* in 377 (Ammianus xxxi. 7, 1, *ambo rectores*).

[29] Sebastian the Manichee (Richter *Weström. Reich*, 282) was *dux Ægypti* in Lent, 357. (Ath. *de Fuga* 6, p. 256, *Hist. Ar.* 59, p. 300, Μανιχαῖον ὄντα καὶ ἀσελγῆ νεώτερον.) He was replaced by Artemius before 360 (Index to *Festal Letters*), and was sent with Procopius to operate from Nisibis in 363. He commanded the Illyrian and Italian troops in the campaign of 368, and took his share with Merobaudes in that of 375 (Ammianus xxvii. 10, 6; xxx. 5, 13). On Valentinian's death he left the service. Richter *supra* thinks he was very nearly chosen emperor; and Ammianus xxx. 10, 3, *militari favore sublatum* seems to favour the theory.

Sebastian was commander in chief in the Gothic war of 378, and voted to give battle at Hadrianople, where he perished (Ammianus xxxi. 11, 1: 12, 6: 13, 18).

Ammianus and Eunapius, p. 110, (copied by Zosimus iv. 23, and Suidas) speak well of Sebastian; and one of the worst charges of Athanasius against him is curiously cleared up (Bright, *Hist. Treatises*, lxxi.) from Augustine *de Mor. Manich.* 36, 53.

[30] Julius was *mag. militum trans Taurum* in 378, and planned the butchery of the Gothic hostages (Ammianus xxxi. 16, 8).

We may perhaps add the name of Majorianus, grandfather of the emperor Majorian, as *mag. utr. mil.* at Sirmium in Jan. 379, on the authority of Sid. Apoll. *Carm.* v. But his appointment was probably after the battle of Hadrianople.

APPENDIX II.

Movements of the Eastern Emperors.

The following table shews the movements of the eastern emperors, so far as I have been able to determine them for the period 337—381. They are chiefly taken from the *Codices* as given in Haenel's *Index Legum;* but the dates have needed a good deal of revision. When therefore laws are "rejected," it is only intended to set them aside as through some inaccuracy or other useless for the immediate purpose of fixing a date.

Fuller discussions are given by preference elsewhere. If then some changes seem arbitrary, the student may be warned that a very little examination will often shew the need for them.

Constantius.

337. May 22 in the East (*Chron. Pasch.*); perhaps at Antioch (Zonaras xiii. 4). Thence to CP, probably till after Sept. 8, and back to the East.

338. Meeting in Pannonia during the summer, but the laws all belong to Constantine II. Sept. 27 Antioch. Oct. 28 Emesa. Dec. 27 Antioch, wintering there.

339. Gregory sent from Antioch ἀπὸ τοῦ κομιτάτου (Ath. *Encycl.* 2, p. 89) in Jan. Feb. 1 Laodicea. Mar. 14 Heliopolis. Mar. 31 Antioch.

340. Sept. 9, 13 Antioch.

341. Feb. 12 Antioch: also at the Council of the Dedication some time between May 22 and Sept. 1.

342. Mar. 31, Apr. 5, 8, May 11 Antioch. Also in Nov. or Dec. at the time of the riot at CP. Thence (Socr. ii. 13) a hurried journey to CP and back to Antioch.

343. Feb. 18 Antioch. June 27, July 4 Hierapolis.
344. Antioch or thereabout after Easter, when Stephen was deposed.
345. May 12 Nisibis. At Edessa (Ath. *Apol. c. Ar.* 51, p. 134) about this time.
346. April? Antioch (third meeting with Athanasius[1]). May 7, Aug. 23 CP.
347. Mar. 8 Ancyra. May 11 Hierapolis.
348. At the battle of Singara.
349. Apr. 1 Antioch. Reject law dated Oct. 3 CP.
350. Jan., Feb. Edessa (Philost. iii. 22). Thence to Europe (by way of Alexandria, as some infer from Ath. *Hist. Ar.* 30, p. 285). Receives envoys of Magnentius and Vetranio at Heraclea (Zonaras xiii. 7), and Dec. 25 deposes Vetranio, probably (Zonaras) near Sardica.
351. Sept. 28 near Mursa.
352. Feb. 25, Mar. 5, June 24 Sirmium. Nov. 3 Milan.
353. July 21 Ravenna. Sept. 6 Lugdunum. Oct. 10 Arles, wintering there. Reject laws dated Dec. 3 Sirmium, and Dec. 6 Thessalonica.
354. Spring at Valentia (Ammianus xiv. 10, 2). Thence to Rauracum on the Rhine (snow still). Sept. 22 Aquileia. Winter at Milan. Reject laws dated Jan. 18 CP, May 22 Milan, Aug. 3 Antioch.
355. Jan. 1, Feb. 18 Milan. Mar. 3 Sirmium. Short campaign in Rhætia, halting at the Campi Canini. July 6, 17, 21, 22, 25 Milan. July 25 Messadensis close to Milan (Tillemont *Empereurs* iv. 683). Aug. 6 Milan. Sept. 2 (more likely June 2 or May 4) Dinumma in Rhætia. Oct. 31, Nov. 6, 30 Milan. Dec. 1 accompanies Julian (Ammianus xv. 8, 18) as far as Pavia.
356. Jan. 15, 19, Feb. 9, Mar. 8, Apr. 11, July 5 Milan; also late in the year, while Julian was besieged in his winter-quarters at Sens.
357. Jan. 25, Apr. 1, 2, 17 Milan. Apr. 28 till May 29 Rome (Ammianus xvi. 10, 20). June 13, 24, July 3[2] Milan, and thence by Trent into Illyricum. Nov. 10, Dec. 4, 6 Milan again. Dec. 18

---

[1] I can find no ground for the statement of Sievers *Studien* 228 (followed by Rendall *Julian* 286), that Constantius was never at Cæsarea between the limits 344—350, except in March 347. This was on his return from Constantinople: by what route did he go there the year before?

[2] This is better than reading the impossible *V. Non. Jun.*

Sirmium. Reject laws dated Feb. 24 CP, June 27 Valla in Africa, Apr. 29 Milan, June 1 Rome. In the last two there may be no more than a slip in the numeral.

358. Jan. 4, Mar. 3 Sirmium; there receiving Sapor's ambassador, who reached CP Feb. 23. After vernal equinox crosses the Danube (Ammianus xvii. 12, 4), and returns to Sirmium, where the envoys from Ancyra found him. May 22 Sirmium. June 7 Haerbillus. June 22, 23 Sirmium. June 27 Mursa, and about the same time (Philost. iv. 10) at Singidunum. Oct. 27, Dec. 19 Sirmium. Reject laws dated May 22, Jan. 11 Milan, July 5 Ariminum, and that of Dec. 29, whether issued from Doris or Dorylæum.

359. In early spring meets the Limigantes at Acimincum. May 22, 23 Sirmium. June 18 Singidunum, and thence (*supra*, p. 175) to Constantinople. Dec. 31, CP, wintering there. Reject laws dated Mar. 14 CP and Nov. 1 Rome.

360. Feb. 4, 15, 24 CP. Late in spring moves eastward. May 17 Hierapolis[1]. May 30 Synnada[2]. By Melitene, Lacotena and Samosata to Edessa, and thence after the equinox towards Amida (Ammianus xxii. 4). Repulsed from Bezabde. Winters at Antioch. Reject laws dated May 31 Milan.

361. Feb. 14 Antioch; and thence to Edessa. May 3 Gyfyra. Summer at Hierapolis, returning in late autumn to Antioch, and so by Tarsus to Nov. 3[3] Mopsucrenæ.

JULIAN.

361. Dec. 11, enters CP.

362. Jan. 1, 17, Feb. 1, Mar. 13, 23, Apr. 30, May 12 CP. Thence through Nicæa and Pessinus, leaving Ancyra June 29, passing through Tyana (*Ep.* 4), arriving at Antioch in July. Aug. 1 (*Ep.* 52), 18, 28, Sept. 3, 9, 18, 22, 25, Oct. 22, 26, Dec. 2, 6, 7 Antioch. Dec. 18 Emesa. Reject *C. Th.* vii. 4, 8, dated......*Kal. Aug.* from Nicomedia, and perhaps *C. Th.* i. 16, 8, dated from Antioch, July 28.

---

[1] This Hierapolis (Clinton) must be in Phrygia. Can the détour be connected with Eusebia's death about this time? Tillemont *Empereurs* iv. 688 removes it to the Syrian Hierapolis, and dates it Dec. 17.

[2] So Clinton. Godefroy alters *Sirmio* to *Syrimio* somewhere near Antioch. Clinton questions the date, observing that Julian was not Cæsar in December. But Constantius would not recognize him as more than Cæsar.

[3] Ammianus xxi. 15, 3 says Oct. 5. To other proofs that this is a mere slip, add the entry *Kustanteinaus thiudanis* under Nov. 3, in the Gothic calendar.

363. Feb. 12, 16, 21, Mar. 1 Antioch, leaving Mar. 6 (Ammianus xxiii. 1, 2) by Hierapolis to Callinicum Mar. 27, and Circesium Apr. 1. Killed in Persia June 26. Reject laws dated Feb. 26 CP, Mar. 9 Antioch (or shift to Jan. 7), Apr. 23 Salona.

JOVIAN.

363. June 27 elected in Persia. Sept. 27 Edessa, Oct. 23 Antioch. Nov. 12 Mopsuestia. Nov. 25, Dec. 9, 21 Antioch: thence by Tyana.

364. Jan. 1 Ancyra. Feb. 17 Dadastana.

VALENS.

364. Mar. 28 CP (Ammianus xxvi. 4, 3). Apr. 11, 17 CP. Apr. 29, May 13 Hadrianople. May 24, 25 Philippopolis (reading *Philippopoli* for *Philippis* in *C. Th.* xv. 1, 11, and ix *Kal. Jun.* for *Jul.* in *C. Th.* viii. 5, 19). May 27 Bonamansio (under the pass of Succi, *Iter Burdigal.*: reading vi *Kal. Jun.* for *Jan.* in *C. Th.* vii. 4, 12, and prefixing vi to *Kal. Jun.* in *C. Th.* xiv. 2, 1). June 2, 8, 11 Naissus. June 19 Mediana (so Ammianus xxvi. 5, 1). July 10 Naissus. July 29, Sirmium. Dec. 16 CP. Reject laws dated Apr. 22 Antioch, May 6 Nicomedia, June 26 CP. Sept. 27 Edessa. Oct. 31 Philippopolis. Dec. 9 Naissus. The two last are addressed to Mamertinus, and therefore belong to Valentinian.

365. Jan. 1 CP (Ammianus xxvi. 5, 6). Feb. 16, Mar. 19 CP, then *consumpta hieme* (Ammianus xxvi. 6, 11) hurries to Syria. July 4 Cæsarea. July 30 CP. Oct. Cæsarea (Ammianus xxvi. 7, 2). Transfer (*a*) the laws of Jan. 31, Mar. 9, Nov. 18 to 368, (*b*) those of June 10, 27, July 5, Dec. 12 to 370, (*c*) that of Aug. 4 to 373. Those of July 30 and Sept. 25 (to Aequitius) must also be rejected.

366. Removing *C. Th.* xi. 1, 14 *ad Modestum P. O.* to 371, no law of Valens can be assigned to this year.

367. May 10, 30 Martianopolis. Sept. 25, Dorostolum. Reject law dated Oct. 25 Nicomedia.

368. Jan. 31, Mar. 9 Martianopolis (both transferred from 365, though the latter breaks the order). In summer on the Danube, returning (Ammianus xxvii. 5, 5) from *Carporum vicus* to winter at Martianopolis, where we find him Nov. 9 (from 373), Nov. 12 (from 370), Nov. 18 (from 365), Dec. 13. *C. Th.* xi. 30, 35 *ad Modestum P. O.* dated Aug. 1, 365, from Martianopolis is best

removed (Tillemont *Emp.* v. 697) to Hierapolis in Syria, and dated in 373.

369. Mar. 11, May 3, Dec. 11 Martianopolis. Dec. 29 CP. In *C. Th.* x. 19, 5 and xv. 2, 2 (Antioch, Apr. 30 and Oct. 29) read *reddita* for data.

370. Some time at Nicomedia, then June 10, 27 Cyzicus. July 5 Heraclea. Dec. 8, 11 CP.

371. Jan. 16, Feb. 11, Mar. 1, Apr. 7 CP. July 13 Ancyra. Reject *C. Th.* viii. 7, 11 dated Dec. 23 from Emesa. Being addressed *Severo magistro militum*, it must be assigned to Valentinian.

372. Jan. 6 Cæsarea. Apr. 4 Seleucia. Apr. 13 Antioch. June 5 Berytus. Aug. 21 in Cilicia. Visit to Edessa perhaps this year, or in 375.

373. Jan. 1 Berytus. Aug. 4, 10, Sept. 18, Oct. 17 Hierapolis. Winter at Antioch (Zos. iv. 13).

374. Feb. 16, Mar. 11, May 21 Antioch.

375. June 2, Dec. 3 Antioch. Perhaps in Mesopotamia (Basil *Ep.* 213) during this year.

376. May 29, 30 Antioch.

377. Jan. 25, Apr. 4 Antioch. July 6, Aug. 9 Hierapolis. Reject law dated Oct. 17 CP.

378. May 30 reaches CP. Thence June 11 by Melanthias and Nicé to Aug. 9 Hadrianople.

THEODOSIUS.

379. Jan. 19 Sirmium. June 17 Thessalonica. July 6 Scopi. *C. Th.* vi. 30, 1, dated from Sirmium Feb. 24, seems Gratian's: see Hänel's note.

380. Jan. 15, 26, 30; Feb. 2, 27; Mar. 17, 27; Apr. 3; June 12, 16, 17, 18, 24; July 8, 24 Thessalonica. Aug. 17 Hadrianople. Aug. 31, Sept. 20, Nov. 16 Thessalonica. Nov. 24 enters CP (Socr. and *Chron. Pasch.*: the Idatian *Fasti* have Nov. 14). Dec. 30 CP. Reject laws dated Jan. 29 and July 27 CP, and refer Sept. 8 Sirmium to Gratian.

381. Jan. 10, Feb. 3, Mar. 31, May 2 CP.

INDEX OF NAMES.

*Names marked * are discussed in Appendix I; but names* ONLY *found in the Appendix are not included here.*

The semicolon separates references to distinct subjects.

*Ablavius, 112n, 114
Acacius, bp of Cæsarea, 26n; 64; attack on Marcellus, 84n; 114; 115n; 128; appoints Cyril at Jerusalem, 149; 160; 164; forms Homœan party, 167; at Seleucia, 177-9; character, 183; appointments Nicene, 186; evasive sermon, 187; on doctrine of Holy Spirit, 210, 236; joins Nicenes, 212, 230, 236
Achillas the Arian, perhaps exiled, 69n; perhaps elected bp of Alexandria, 70n
Achilleus rebel in Egypt, 37; 158
*Aequitius (*mag. mil.*), in Procopian war, 231n, 241
Aetius the Anomœan, 63; ordained by Leontius, 138; 139n; condemned at Ancyra, 166; exiled again, 183-4; connexion with Julian, 205; 212; narrow escape, 242
Aetius, archdeacon of Constantinople, 270n
Agapetus, bp of Synnada: legend of, 139n
Agathangelus, history of, 235n
*Agilo (*mag. mil.*), 197; betrays Procopius, 241
Alaric, 263
Alexander, bp of Alexandria, 18; 32; date of his death, 70n
Alexander, bp of Thessalonica at Tyre, 89, 90
Aligern, 272
Alphius, bp of Apamea, 19n
Ambrose, bp of Milan, 232; 239n; 248; holds Illyrian council, 257; 265
Ammianus Marcellinus, 60; sums up charges against Athanasius, 87; on Magnentius, 147; on Constantius, 198n; on Julian, 201n; on the barbarians, 213n; on Jovian, 230n; on Valentinian and Valens, 231
Amphilochius, bp of Iconium, 59n
Amphion, bp in Cilicia: no Arianizer, 34n
Anastasius (Emperor 491-518), 94; 159; 213; 216; 263
Anatolius, bp of Emesa, 19n
Anatolius, bp in Eubœa, 209n
*Anatolius, Pf. P., 113n
Anianus (bp) of Antioch, 179
Anthemius (Emperor 467-472), 265n
Anthimus, bp of Tyana, joins Basil, 248; quarrels with him, 249, 256
Antony. Legend discussed, *Note B.*
Apodemius, 115
Apollinarius of Laodicea; expulsion by Theodotus, 59n; by George, 149, 167n; 236; system, 250-254; 256
*Araxius, Pf. P., 241n
*Arbetio (*mag. mil.*), 113n; 197; in Procopian war, 241
Arbogast, 205; 263
*Arinthæus (*mag. mil.*) died a Christian, 58n; at election of Jovian, 229; and of Valentinian, 231n; in Procopian war, 241; in Gothic war, 244; 246n; 247n
Arius: Lucianist, 17; his system, 18-28; outbreak of the controversy, 32-34; personal disciples of, 32n; abandoned at Nicæa, 41; exiled, 52; recalled, 90; confession of, 91; sudden death, 93
Arsenius, bp of Hypsele at Tyre, 100; 118

INDEX.

Ascholius, bp of Thessalonica, 268
Asclepas, bp of Gaza, exiled, 79; at Sardica, 125
Asterius, bp of Amasea, 59n; 229n
Asterius, bp of Petra at Sardica, 126; exiled, 128; at Alexandria, 209
Asterius the Sophist, 24n; Arianizes, 34n; 44n; joins reaction, 65; doctrine, 72; at Jerusalem, 91; defends Lucianic creed, 120, 171; from Cappadocia, 245
Atarbius, bp of Neocæsarea, 256
Athanaric, the Visigoth: war with Valens, 243; flight from Huns, 258; death, 267
Athanasius, bp of Alexandria: *de Incarnatione*, 28, 29; and Alexander's encyclical, 32n; persistence at Nicene Council, 43; estimate of it, 54n; error concerning Zenobia, 61n; election and character, 70-74; date of election, 70n; of birth, 71n; ascetic leanings, 72n; quotations, 72n; *de titulis Psalmorum* spurious, 73; success against Meletians, 75; criticism of Marcellian controversy, 86; at the *comitatus*, 87; charges against him, 87; at Tyre, 88; condemned at Jerusalem, 91; exiled to Trier, 92; list of exiles, 95; the boy-baptism, 99; story of Arsenius, 100; never mentions Antony, 103; index to *Festal Letters Note* C; date of expulsion by Philagrius, 108, 116n; return from Trier, 113; expelled by Philagrius 116; defended by Julius of Rome, 117; at Sardica, 125-6; return to Alexandria, 131; use of Semiarian paraphrases, 133; on rebaptism, 134; 136n; 137; return (in 337) discussed, *Note* CC; on Constans, 146n; intrigue of Magnentius, 148; accused at Milan, 152; expulsion (in 356), 156; his *de Fuga* and *Hist. Ar.*, 157; results of his flight, 158-9; objects to persecution, 167n; on dated creed, 174; his *de Synodis*, 179-182; Julian's hatred of him, 206; reappears at Alexandria, 208; holds council, 208-211; exiled by Julian, 211; return (in 362) discussed, *Note* J; reception by Jovian, 230; letters to Serapion, 236; on reception of Arians, 237; attempts of Valens to expel him, 240-243; supports Basil, 248; and Apollinarius, 251; last years, 254; and Marcellus, 255; method contrasted with Arian, 274
Athanasius, bp of Anazarbus, 24n; Arianizes, 34n

Athanasius, bp of Ancyra, 186; 205; signs Nicene Creed, 231
Aurelian (Emperor 270-275): relation to Christians, 37, 268; to Goths, 258; 263
*Ausonius, 59n
Auxano Novatian presbyter, 264
Auxentius I., bishop of Milan, 151; 174n; 185; left by Valentinian, 232; from Cappadocia, 245
Auxentius, bp of Mopsuestia: legend of, 139n
*Auxonius, Pf. P., 243; 244; 258
Avidius Cassius, 158; 214; 233n

Babylas, legend, 138n
Bacurius the Iberian: a Christian, 59n; informant of Rufinus, 99; escapes from Hadrianople, 261
Balacius, *dux Ægypti*, 103
Barses, bp of Edessa, 248n
Basil II. (Emperor 963-1025), 94
Basil, bp of Amasea: no Arianizer, 34n
Basil, bp of Ancyra, 149; 150n; at Ancyra, 164-6; persecutes, 167n; at Sirmian conference,170n; minute of, 172-3; at Seleucia, 177; 181; deposed, 185; returns from exile, 208; 246
Basil, bp of Cæsarea Mazaca: correspondence with Libanius, 59n; on rebaptism, 135n; connexion with Julian, 205, 207; plan of, 246; pride of, 249; on restoration of Marcellians, 255; 256
Basilina, mother of Julian, 79n; 90n
Belisarius, 264; 272
Brasidas (notary) restores Athanasius, 243

Cæcilian, bp of Carthage, 37
Caius, bp in Illyricum, 151n
Calanus, 11
Candidus the Anomœan, quoted, 23n
Carpones the Arian, perhaps exiled, 69n; at Rome, 117
Castinus, 233n
Cecropius, bp of Nicomedia, 95
*Celsinus, P.U., 148
*Cerealis (Neratius), P.U., 158n
Charisius, creed of, 212n
Chrysanthius, philosopher, 200; 202
Claudius Gothicus (Emperor 268-270), 260
Claudius, bp in Picenum, 182
*Clearchus, proconsul of Asia, 241n
Clement of Alexandria, on tradition, 7n
Constans (Emperor 337-350), 112; demands a council, 124; presses decrees of Sardica, 130; reign and character, 146; baptism, 242n

Constantia, widow of Licinius, 50; 71
Constantine I. (Emperor 306-337):
view of Arianism, 34-37; legislation, 35n; letter to Alexander and
Arius, 37; summons council at
Nicæa, 38; explains ὁμοούσιον, 51;
action at Nicæa, 52; exiles Arius
and Eusebius, 53, 55; services to
the Empire, 87, 214, 259; summons
councils at Cæsarea and Tyre, 88;
Tricennalia, 89; exiles Athanasius
to Trier, 92; Asiatic influence on,
86-96; persecution, 93n; death of,
110; baptism, 242n; test of orthodoxy by subscription, 268
Constantine II. (Emperor 337-340):
receives Athanasius at Trier, 92;
112; releases Athanasius, 113, 140
Constantine Copronymus (Emperor
741-775): 208
Constantius II. (Emperor 337-361):
his court, 64; leans on Asia, 64,
94-96; 112; share in the massacre,
112n; character, 113; recalls Athanasius, 131; legislation discussed,
Note D; victory of Mursa, 148, 149n;
accuses Athanasius at Milan, 152;
attacked by Lucifer, 153; by Athanasius, 157; Sirmian manifesto,
161n; at Sirmian conference, 170-
171; evades Ariminian deputation,
175; not Anomœan, 183; exiles
Meletius, 187; death, 197; plunder
of temples, 206
Cymatius, bp of Paltus, 209n
Cyril, bp of Alexandria, 21n; 74; 159;
256
Cyril, bp of Jerusalem, 4; ascetic
leanings, 72n, 106; compared with
μακρόστιχος, 130; *Catecheses*, 135-7;
compared with dated creed, 136n;
bishop, 149; at Seleucia, 177n; deposed, 185; joins Nicenes, 212; 256;
265; at Constantinople 271n
Cyrion, bp of Philadelphia, joins reaction, 54

*Dagalaifus (*mag. mil.*), 58n; at elec-
tions of Jovian, 229, and of Valenti-
nian, 231n
Damasus, bp of Rome, 174n; 268
Danius, bp (=Dianius?), 117
Datianus, 146n; at election of Valen-
tinian, 231n
Demophilus, bp of Constantinople,
184n; 185; 232; 239n; succeeds
Eudoxius, 244; blunders, 256; gives
up churches, 268
Demosthenes the cook, 64n; 228
Dianius, bp of Cæsarea Mazaca, 4;
letter of Julius, 117; 119n; 128;

signs Creed of Nicé, 185; 199; 212;
patron of Asterius, 245; and Basil,
246-7
Diocletian (Emperor 284-305): con-
quest of Egypt, 158-9
Diodorus, bp of Tarsus, 29; 137-8
Diogenes (notary), 155n, 156
Dionysius, bp of Alexandria, 14; 48;
51n
Dionysius, bp of Milan, 151; exiled,
153
Dominica, empress: Arian, 238; de-
fends Constantinople, 262
*Domitian, Pf. P., 150n
Donatus, bp of Carthage, 127
Dorotheus, bp of Antioch: disciples of,
34n
Dracontius, bp of Pergamus, deposed,
187n

Edesius, 97
Eleusius, bp of Cyzicus, persecutes
Novatians, 139n, 167n, 206; at
Sirmium, 166; at Seleucia, 176-9;
deposed, 181; 212; and monks, 235;
at Lampsacus, 237; at Constantinople, 269
Elias, *præses Cappadociæ*, 246n
*Elpidius, renegade, 59n; 202; 228;
imprisoned, 242
Epictetus, bp of Centumcellæ, 151n;
185
Epiphanius, bp of Salamis: on re-
baptism, 134n, 135n
Eudoxius, bp of Constantinople:
Arianizes, 34n; confession of, 42n;
179n; refused ordination by Eu-
stathius, 79n; elevation of, 96;
119n; rebaptizes, 134; 157n; 164;
exiled, 166; scandalous profanity,
179; 185; translation to Constantinople, 186; 212; not zealous for
Aetius, 230; 232; influence over
Valens, 238, 242; death, 244; from
Cappadocia, 245
Eugenius, bp of Nicæa, 95; 164
Eugenius, deacon of Ancyra, 255
Euippius, bp; at Constantinople, 184n;
and Basil, 246n, 247
Eunomius the Anomœan, 63; 134;
139n; 171n; bp of Cyzicus, 186;
203; 236n; exiled by Auxonius and
Modestus, 243; from Cappadocia,
245; and Theodosius, 268
Euphrasius, bp of Nicomedia, 271n
Euphrates, bp of Cologne, at Antioch,
128; not an Arian, 157n
Euphronius, bp of Antioch, 77; from
Cappadocia, 245
Eusebius, bp of Cæsarea: Arianizes,
19n, 34; on Numenius, 21; con-

fessor, 39n; conservative creed at Nicæa, 41–45; 49n; letter to his diocese, 50; signs Nicene Creed, 52; caution after Nicæa, 69n; refuses see of Antioch, 77; attack on Marcellus, 84–87; at councils of Tyre and Jerusalem, 88–90; silence on Antony, 103; flattery of Constantine, 111; orthodoxy and good faith, 111n; 127n; 171

Eusebius, bp of Cæsarea Mazaca, 247

Eusebius, bp of Emesa: declines see of Alexandria, 116; not at Antioch, 119n; 136n; 139n

Eusebius, bp of Nicomedia: Arianizes, 34n; 35; Arianizing creed at Nicæa, 41; signs Nicene Creed, 50; 52; exiled, 53, 69n; spurious letter of, 53n, 90n; joins reaction, 54; translation from Berytus denounced, 55n; return from exile, 75; character and policy, 75–77; 139n; bp of Constantinople, 199

Eusebius, bp of Samosata: signs Nicene Creed, 231; joins Basil, 248n; murder of, 266

Eusebius, bp of Vercellæ, 127n; exiled, 153; returns, 208

Eusebius (chamberlain), 114; 228

Eustathius, bp of Antioch, 3n; 19; 24n; confessor, 39n; at Nicæa, 44n, 48, 68; exile, 77; date of death, 78n

Eustathius, bp of Epiphania, 119n

Eustathius, bp of Sebastia, 32n; at Ancyra, 164; at Sirmium, 166; deposed, 185; succeeded by Meletius, 187; deposition at Gangra, *Note* E; and monks, 235; undecided at Lampsacus, 237; exile, 238, 240; mission to Rome, 240; relations with Basil, 246, 250; conduct discussed, *Note* O

Eutherius, Armenian eunuch, 146n; 199n

Eutropius, bp of Hadrianople, exiled, 78n; 79; 90n

Euzoius the Arian exiled, 69n; confession of, 91; bp of Antioch, 187; 212; 230; decided Arian, 236

Felix, bp of Rome, 151n
Festus, proconsul of Asia, 241n
Firmus (Africa), 159n
Firmus (Egypt), 158
Flaccus, bp of Hierapolis, joins reaction, 54
Flacilla, empress, 268
Flacillus, bp of Antioch, 117; 119n
Flavian, bp of Antioch, 60; 137–8; 271n
Flavianus, Pf. of Egypt, 240
*Florentius, Pf. P., 114; 148; 150n; 198

Fortunatian, bp of Aquileia, at Sardica, 125; 163n
Fritigern the Visigoth, takes refuge in the Empire, 258; at Hadrianople, 261–2; death, 267
Fronto, bp of Nicopolis, 258
Frumentius, 97

Galerius: rescript of, 34; 111; 214
Galla, empress, Arian, 268n
Gallus (Emperor 351–354): 62; 150n; 198
George of Cappadocia, bp of Alexandria: 17; 19; 63n; arrival at Al., 156; expulsion, 157; not unlearned, 160; at Sirmian conference, 170n; at Seleucia, 179; letter of Homœans to, 184n; 199; 205; murder of, 208; 232
George, bp of Laodicea: Arianizes, 34n; refused ordination by Eustathius, 79n; 119n; not at Sardica, 128; 136; 139; 159n; mocks at Ath., 157; letter to Basil of Ancyra, 164; expels Apollinarii, 167n; if at Sirmian conference, 170n; minute of, 172–3; at Constantinople, 184n; not deposed, 185; Arian sermon, 187
Germinius, bp of Sirmium, 91; 95; 149; at Sirmian conference, 170n; controversy with Valens of Mursa, 243n
Gratian (Emperor, 375–383): 147n; 260–1; edict of toleration, 266; proclaims Theodosius, 266–7
Gratus, bp of Carthage, 125
Gregory of Cappadocia, 18; 63n; date of his death, 109; chosen bp of Alexandria, 116; not at Antioch, 119n; receives Philippopolis encyclical, 127; 156
Gregory, bp of Berytus: Arianizes, 19n, 34n
Gregory of Nazianzus (bp of Constantinople), 205; 207; 266; installed at Constantinople, 268
Gregory, bp of Neocæsarea, Creed of, 120, 122
Gregory, bp of Nyssa, 256; 271n
Gregory (Pope 590–604): 273
*Gumoarius (*mag. mil.*) deserts Procopius, 241

Harmatius, 246n
Hecebolius, renegade, 59n; 199; 202
Helladius, bp of Cæsarea, 271n
Heraclius (Emperor 610–641): 91; 159; 214; 216
Heraclius the Cynic, 241n
Hieracas, 22

308 INDEX.

Hilary, bp of Pictavium: comments on letter of Arius, 22n; 63; on re-baptism, 135n; character and exile, 154; his *de Synodis*, 168–170; at Seleucia, 176–7; 180; on bishops at Seleucia, *Note* G; on doctrine of Holy Spirit, 210

Honoratus, 150n

Hormisdas, 58n

Hosius, bp of Cordova: sent to Alexandria, 37; confessor, 39n; 48; 52; accused from Philippopolis, 78n; at Sardica, 125–6; 151; exiled, 154; 164

Hypatianus, bp of Heraclea: at Sirmian conference, 170n; at Lampsacus, 237

(Iamblichus), *de mysteriis*, 13

Ildibad, 272

Innocent, Pope, 61n

Isaac, bp of Armenia: signs Nicene Creed, 231; joins Basil, 248n

Joannes Lydus on Constantine's Gothic war, 87n

John Archaph, Miletian: exiled, 92

John the Persian, bp at Nicæa, 39n

John Zimisces (Emperor 969–976): 94n

Jordanis, 272

Jovian (Emperor 363–4): *primus domesticorum*, 58n; story of him, 100; reign and character, 229–231; restores the eunuchs, 238

*Jovinus (*mag. mil.*), 58n; 240n; consul, 241

*Jovius, *quæstor*, 204n

Julian (Emperor 361–363): his generals, 58n; 60; toleration, 148; Cæsar, 153; Alemannic war, 162, 185; reign of, 197–216; legislation, *Note* H; authorities for his persecution, *Note* I; arrival at Antioch, *Note* K; results of his reign, 228; 230; on the monks, 234n; found Cappadocia Christian, 245; 249

Julianus, *comes Orientis*, 207n

Julius, bp of Rome: his estimate of Nicene Council, 55n; 90n; and Marcellus, 92n; receives Athanasius and Marcellus, 115–6; letter to *Danius* &c., 117; gives up Photinus, 130; 155

Justina, Empress, 271

Justinian (Emperor 527–565): 159; 216

Karl the Great, 100; 273

Lactantius, 30

*Lampadius, P.U., 240n

Lauricius, *comes*, 176–7

Leo "the Isaurian" (Emperor 716–741): 216

Leonas, *comes*, 177–9

Leontius, bp of Antioch, 19; Arianizes 34n; scandal, 55n; refused ordination, 78n; 79n; bp of Antioch, 129; policy 137; legend of Babylas, 138n; mocks at Ath., 157; death of, 157n; 186

Leontius, bp of Tripolis, 139n

Leontius, 150n

Leovigild, 272

Libanius: his friends, 59n, 60; caution, 202; 246

Liberius, bp of Rome, 151–155; return, 163n, 166; his fall discussed, *Note* F; receives Semiarian mission, 240

Licinius (Emperor, 307–323): persecution of, 34n

Lucian of Antioch, no heretic, 17n; disciples of, 34n, 76; creed, 69, 120; legend of, 138n

Lucifer, bp of Calaris, 3; 63; puns, 129n; character and doctrine, 153; 163n; return from exile, 208; consecrates Paulinus, 211; on doctrine of Holy Spirit, 210n; schism of, 236, 248

*Lucillianus, *comes*, 197

Lucius, bp of Alexandria, 19; 63n; 254; 257

*Lupicinus (*mag. mil.*), 58n; vexation of Massalians, 107, 234n, 240; in Procopian war, 241

Lupicinus, *comes Thraciæ*, 259; 262n

Macarius, bp of Jerusalem, 19n; at Nicæa, 44n; influence with Constantine, 79n

Macarius the Arian, 115

Macedonius, bp of Constantinople, 138; 164; persecutes, 167n; at Seleucia, 177; deposed, 185; 212

Macedonius, bp of Mopsuestia, confessor, 39n; 49n; joins reaction, 54; 119n; 139n; deposed, 185

Magnentius (Emperor 350–353): his reign, 147–9; neutral on Arianism, 151

Magnus, bp of Damascus, 19n

*Mamertinus, Pf. P.: a heathen, 58n; 114

Manuel Comnenus (Emperor 1143–1180): 94

Marathonius, bp of Nicomedia, 167; and monks, 235

Marcella: Jerome's romance of, 104

Marcellus, bp of Ancyra, 22; 45; 46; caution after Nicæa, 69; his age,

INDEX. 309

character and system, 79–87; at Jerusalem, 92; not twice at Rome, 92n; 95; return from exile, 113; flees to Rome, 116; defended by Julius, 118; not at C. Antioch, 119n; attacks Lucianic creed, 122n; at Sardica, 125–6; condemned at Sirmium, 149; at Ancyra, 166; repudiated by Meletius, 187; returns from exile, 208; embassy to Athanasius, 254

*Marcellus (mag. mil.), 198n
Marcian (Emperor 450–458), 159
Mardonius, tutor of Julian, 199
Maris, bp of Chalcedon: Arianizes, 31n; joins reaction, 54n; 119n; at Constantinople, 184n; curses Julian, 207, 216
Mark, bp of Arethusa, 119n; 167n; draws up dated creed, 170; 185
Mavia, Saracen queen, 101
Maxentius (Emperor 306–312), 205
Maximin Daza (Emperor 305–313): policy of, 201
Maximin Arian, 174n
Maximus (Emperor 383–388), 263
Maximus, bp of Jerusalem at Tyre, 89, 90; 125n; succeeded by Cyril, 149
Maximus, præses Cappadociæ, 246n
Maximus, philosopher, 114; 200; imprisoned, 241
Maximus, Cynic, 247n; 270
Maximus, general in Thrace, 259
Meletius, bp of Antioch, 4; 19; 137; appointment and exile, 186–7; return, 211; signs Nicene Creed, 231; second exile, 240; recall, 243; disappointed in Homœans, 245; third exile, 240; joins Basil, 248n; 257; 265; presides at Constantinople, 269
Meletius, bp of Lycopolis: no Arianizer, 34n
Meletius, bp of Sebastopolis: no Arianizer, 34n
Menophantus, bp of Ephesus: Arianizes, 34n; joins reaction, 54
*Merobaudes (mag. mil.), 261; jealousy of Theodosius, 266n
Metrodorus, philosopher, 97, &c.
Michael III. (Emperor 840–867), 230n
Michael Palæologus (Emperor 1261–1282), 95
*Modestus (Domitius), renegade, 59n; at Edessa, 91; 202; 228; 234; influence on Valens, 238; a friend of Basil, 246; threats, 247
Mokaukas, 159
Montanus, notary, 155–6
*Montius, quæstor, 150n

Moses of Chorene, quoted, 34n
Moyses, bp of Saracens, 101
*Musonianus, comes, keeps order at Antioch, 78; 93n; 118n; at Sardica, 125

Narcissus, bp of Jerusalem, 234
Narcissus, bp of Neronias: Arianizes, 34n; 119n; mocks at Ath., 157
Nepotianus, 147
Nestorius of Gaza, Pf. of Egypt, 103, 171n
*Nevitta (mag. mil.), heathen, 58n; at election of Jovian, 229; not at Valentinian's, 231n
Numenius of Apamea, 21

*Olybrius P.U., 58
Olympius, bp of Aenos, 126n
Onkelos, Targum of, 12 and n
Optatus, P.U., 58
Origen: doctrine of eternal generation, 14, 28; contrast with Eusebius, 42; attacked by Marcellus, 81n; 85; 121; on use of ὑπόστασις, 211
Otreius, bp of Melitene, 248n

Palladius, Arian, 271n
Pancratius, bp of Pelusium: at Sirmian conference, 170n
Paphnutius, bp and confessor: at Nicæa, 39n; at Tyre, 90
Para, king of Armenia, 259
Paternus, bp of Petrocorii, 151n; 185
Patrophilus, bp of Scythopolis: Arianizes, 19n, 34n; joins reaction, 54; 119n; 149; among πνευματόμαχοι, 210n, 236n
Paul, bp of Constantinople, 125; 150
Paul, bp of Emesa, 248n
Paul, bp of Neocæsarea: confessor, 39n
Paul of Samosata, bp of Antioch, 14; 16; 22; use of ὁμοούσιον, 47, 181; condemned by Basil and George, 172
Paul Catena, 115; 232
Paulinus, bp of Antioch: Eustathian presbyter, 137; consecrated by Lucifer, 211; 257; ignored at Constantinople, 269
Paulinus, bp of Trier, 151; exiled, 152
Paulinus, bp of Tyre: Arianizes, 19n, 34n; attacked by Marcellus, 69n
Pegasius, bp of Ilium, renegade, 202
Pelagius, bp of Laodicea, 186; signs Nicene Creed, 231; joins Basil, 248n
Peter, bp of Alexandria, 255; 265; 267; and Maximus the Cynic, 270
Philagrius, dux Ægypti, expels Athanasius, 116; 156; from Cappadocia, 245
Philip (Emperor 244–249), legend of, 138n

310   INDEX.

Philippicus Bardanes (Emperor 711–713), 239
*Philippus, P.U., 150
Philo, 12
Phœbadius, bp of Agen: his pamphlet, 163–4; at Ariminum, 182; 210n
Photinus, bp of Sirmium, 91n; condemned, 130; 149; appeal, 149n
*Phronemius, P.U., 242
Pistus, Arian, bp of Alexandria, 115—117
Pœmenius, Arian, bp of Constantinople, 230
Pompeianus, P.U., 61n
Potamius, bp of Lisbon, 151n; 161
Potammon, bp and confessor, at Nicæa, 40n; at Tyre, 90
Potentius, son of Ursicinus, 261
Prætextatus, philosopher, 61n
*Prætextatus (Vettius), P.U., 58
Proæresius, 59n
Procopius (Emperor 365–366): 214; 216; 233n; rising of, 241
*Profuturus, 259

Rhodanius, bp of Toulouse, 151
Richomer, *comes domesticorum*, 61n; in Thrace, 261; escapes from Hadrianople, 261
Romanus, *comes*, 266n
Rufinus, historian, Note A.
*Rufinus (Vulcatius): supports Magnentius, 148; 150n

*Sabinian (*mag. mil.*), 214
Sabinus, bp of Heraclea, 39n
*Salia sent to Antioch, 129
*Sallustius Saturninius Secundus, Pf. P., 58; declines the Empire, 229; at election of Valentinian, 231; 241; 258
Saturninus, bp of Arles, 151; 154; at Constantinople, 184n; 185
Saturninus, general in Thrace, 260; escapes from Hadrianople, 261; finishes Gothic war, 267
"Scotinus," 129
*Sebastian (*mag. mil.*), a Manichee, 58n; *dux Ægypti*, 156; at Nisibis, 214; commands in Thrace, 261; killed at Hadrianople, 261; 266 *bis*
Secundianus, Arian, 270n
Secundus, bp of Ptolemais: Arianizes, 34n; exiled, 52; consecrates Pistus, 115, 117
Serapion, bp of Thmuis, 136n; 200n
*Severus (*mag. mil.*), 161n
Silvanus, bp of Tarsus, 122n; 137; at Seleucia, 176–7; deposed, 185; 240
Sisinnius, Novatian bp of Constantinople, 138n

Sopater, philosopher, 61n; 94; 114
*Sophronius, P.U., 246
Sophronius, bp of Pompeiopolis, 122n; 127n; 167n; at Seleucia, 176; deposed, 185
Soter, bp of Rome, 155n
Spyridon, bp in Cyprus, 97
Stephen, bp of Antioch: Arianizes, 79n; 128; plot and deposition, 128; 129n
*Symmachus (Q. Aurelius): P.U., 58; 240n
Syrianus, *dux Ægypti*, 156

Tarcondimantus, bp of Ægæ, 119n
Tatianus, Pf. of Egypt, 234n
*Taurus, Pf. P., 150n; 174
Teja, 272
Terentius, *comes*, 247n
Tertullian, on the divine Sonship, 14; 28; 42; 85; 235n
*Thalassius, 150n
*Themistius, P.U., 58
Theodahad, 272n
Theodora, 112
Theodore, confessor under Julian, 100
Theodore, bp of Heraclea, 119n; 184n
Theodore, bp of Mopsuestia, 19
Theodoric, 272
Theodorus, bp of Oxyrhynchus, 134n
Theodorus (ΘΕΟΔ.), 242n
*Theodosius (*mag. mil.*), 240n; his execution, 266n
Theodosius (Emperor 379–395): apotheosis of, 58; leans on Asia, 96; persecutor, 167n; 216; 239; baptism, 242n; 268; gives up Dacia, 263; associated by Gratian, 266; edicts against heresy, 268, 271; summons council of Constantinople, 269; last overtures to Arians, 271
Theodotus, bp of Laodicea: Arianizes, 19n, 34n; expels Apollinarii, 59n
Theodotus, bp of Nicopolis, 248n; suspects Basil, 250
Theognius, bp of Nicæa: Arianizes, 34n; signs, 50; δυνάμει error, 52n; exiled, 53; joins reaction, 54; return 75
Theonas, bp of Alexandria: elected by Meletians, 70n
Theonas, bp of Marmarica: Arianizes, 34n; exiled, 52
Theophilus, bp of Goths, at Nicæa, 39n
Theophilus, bp of Castabala, 240
Theophilus, Indian, 140n; 230
Theophilus of Libya, 184n
Theophronius, bp of Tyana, 119n; confession of, 122
Theudelinda, Lombard queen, 273

INDEX. 311

Tiranus, King of Armenia, 214
*Titianus, Pf. P., 148
Titus, bp of Bostra, 136n; 200n; 203; signs Nicene Creed, 231
Totila, 272
Trajan (Emperor 98-117): Theodosius compared to, 267
*Trajan (*mag. mil.*), in Thrace, 58n; 259; killed at Hadrianople, 261

Ulfilas, *Skeireins*, 27n; at Constantinople, 184n
Ursacius, bp of Singidunum. *See* Valens
*Ursicinus (*mag. mil.*), destroys Sepphoris, 62; 64; 114; at Sirmium, 161n; 261
*Ursulus, *comes S. L.*, 214

Valens (Emperor 364-378): inquisition for magic, 61n; 242; leans on Asia, 64, 94-96; edict against monks, 107, 234n; emperor, 231-2; Homœan policy, 238; expels exiles again, 240; and Procopius, 241; baptism 242; Gothic war, 243; meeting with Basil, 247; confusion in Asia, 256; work of his reign, 257; reception of the Goths, 258; killed at Hadrianople, 261; toleration of, 266; council of Lampsacus, *Note* M; the Eighty Clerics, *Note* N
Valens, bp of Mursa, 32n; court politician, 57, 64; disciple of Arius, 91n; confused doctrine, 127n; recants, 130; 151n; Sirmian manifesto, 161-2; 166; 167n; forms Homœan party, 167; at Sirmian conference, 170n; fraudulent signature, 171-2; at Ariminum, 172, 182-3; at Nicé, 173; at Constantinople, 184n; intercedes for Eunomius, 243
Valens, philosopher, 61n
Valentinian (Emperor 364-375): 58n; 148; emperor, 231-2; permits council of Lampsacus, 237; departure for Gaul, 240n; work of his reign, 255; edict against Manichees, 266n
Valerianus, bp of Aquileia, 248
Varronianus, infant consul, 231
*Vetranio (Emperor 350), 147
*Victor (*mag. mil.*): Christian, 58n; marries Mavia's daughter, 101; at election of Jovian, 229; in Egypt, 231; in Gothic war, 240; 246; at Hadrianople, 260-2
Victorinus (Marius), 59n
Vincent, bp of Capua: at Nicæa, 55n; at Sardica, 125; sent to Antioch, 128; yields at Arles, 152
*Volusianus, P.U., 240n

Zeno (Emperor 474-491): *Henoticon*, 239; reforms, 263
Zeno, bp of Tyre, 248n
Zeno, bp of Verona, 15
Zenobia, rabbis unfriendly to, 61n

www.ingramcontent.com/pod-product-compliance
Lightning Source LLC
Chambersburg PA
CBHW070230230426
43664CB00014B/2256